Jannie van Schu

# Let's Fold ...

# and be happy

## Origami is an adventure that never ends...

Published by JvSDesign
The Netherlands

presents:

# Let's Fold ...

and be happy

Origami is an adventure that never ends...



How to find Jannie van Schuylenburg:

e-mail: jannievanschuylenburg@gmail.com
Instagram: @jannievanschuylenburg
Facebook: jannie.vanschuylenburg.1
YouTube: @jannievanschuylenburgdesig2990

YouTube

Designs, diagrams, layout, text, cover: Jannie van Schuylenburg
Photographer: Jannie van Schuylenburg; page 7 Duo color Dragon Basket: Tricia Tait; page 61 flower Truussia: Monique Kolvers; cover author photo: Milis Fotografie
Test folders: Annette Bussmann, Yvonne Hulsman, Monique Kolvers, Annelies Visee
Proofreader: Tricia Tait

ISBN: 978 90 834695 0 8

# Thank You

*To all those who are so dear to me.*
*But... especially to my one Love,*
*who always supports me.*

Writing a beautiful book is not possible without the help of a beautiful team. What a privilege to have such a team around me.

Thank you, **Annelies** Visee, **Monique** Kolvers, and **Yvonne** Hulsman, for folding everything, meticulously checking the diagrams and detecting even the smallest errors. Also for the instructions to make the models even more accessible to fold with extra diagrams. Not always nice at that moment, but perfect for a better result.

**Annette** Bussmann, my dear friend, thank you also for your good advice for the photos and the layout, and for always giving me a pat on the back when I didn't know what to do.

Thank you, **Tricia** Tait and **Monique**, for proofreading the texts and giving good suggestions to make beautiful sentences from them. English is not my native language so your help is indispensable.

It is difficult and takes time to make a beautiful cover that suits the book and myself. Thank you, **Gabi** Ferraro, **Mirjam** de Vries, **Elina** Gor and **Annette** for your comments and instructions so that it has become a beautiful result.

Thanks to **Ilan** Garibi who gave me an encouraging pep talk and a list of tips 3 years ago, with which I could write a beautiful book myself. Great that I always could ask you something when needed. Also that you asked every year when the book will be finished.

Also thanks to the many orgami **friends**, other friends, and **family** , who gave me advice and encouraged me to make this book and had confidence in me.

Finally many thanks to my dear husband, **Hans**, who supports me, gives me advice, and cooks, so that I can still eat when I forget the time again.
It was a great journey to go on with you all.

Jannie

# Table of Contents


Introduction 6
Tips & Tricks, Materials 7
Symbols & Techniques 9
Calculation table Ori-Paper-Saver 11
How to make... 12
Callenge... 127
Origami associations 128
Other books of Jannie 129

**Containers** 13

Magic Duo Color Box 14
Susanna's Box 16
Treasure Box 22
Sycee Basket 26

Surprising Heart Bowl 29
Duo Color Dragon Basket 32
Pyramidal Etagiere Box 37

**Flowers** 42

Single Sunflower 43
Double Sunflower 46
Sunflower Henny 49
Duo Pansies 52


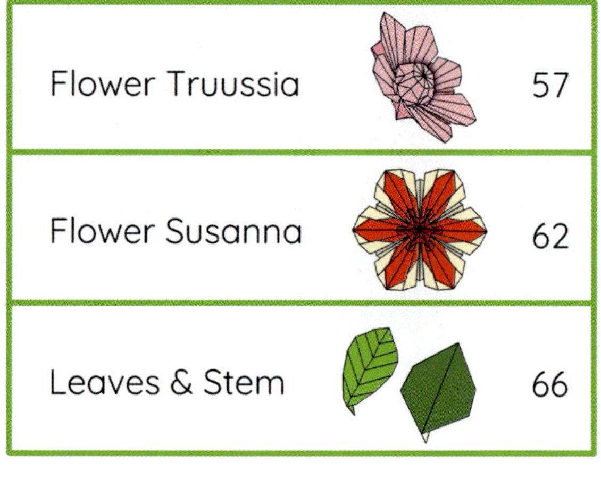


Flower Truussia 57
Flower Susanna 62
Leaves & Stem 66

My Specials 68

Rosa-fant 69

Butterfly Kisses 72

Cradle of Love 74

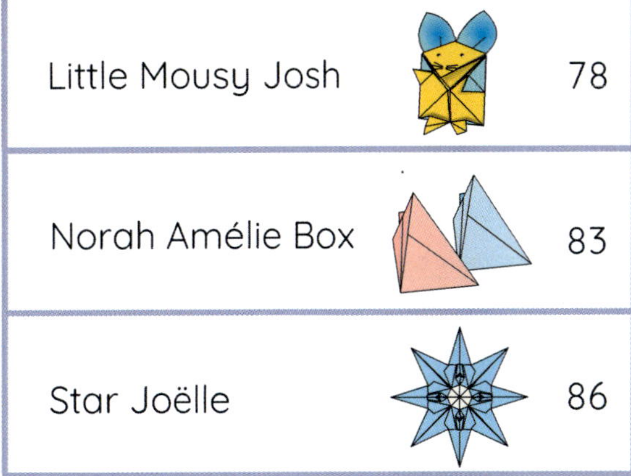

Little Mousy Josh 78

Norah Amélie Box 83

Star Joëlle 86

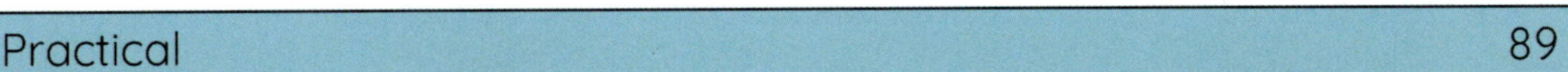

Practical 89

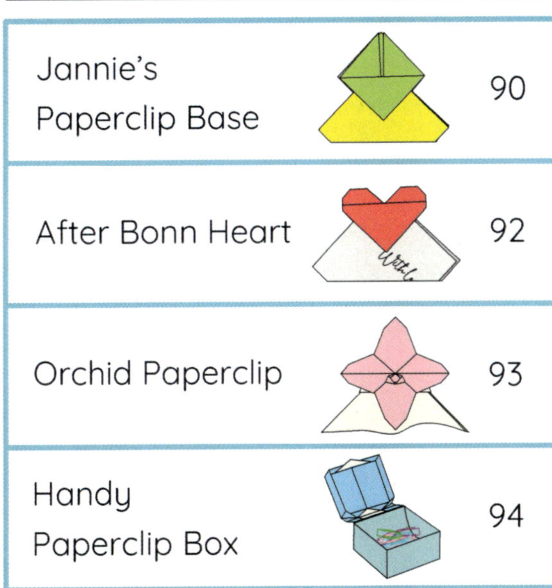

Jannie's Paperclip Base 90

After Bonn Heart 92

Orchid Paperclip 93

Handy Paperclip Box 94

Ori-Paper-Saver 98

Rosalina's Envelope 104

Heart Envelope 106

Willem's Vaart Envelope 108

Christmas 110

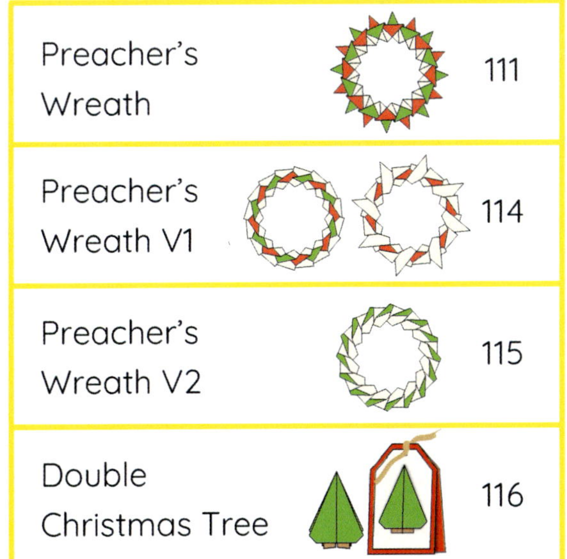

Preacher's Wreath 111

Preacher's Wreath V1 114

Preacher's Wreath V2 115

Double Christmas Tree 116

Angel Emma 118

Snowy Christmas Tree 120

Star Paperclip 122

Swimming Swan 124

# Introduction

Origami is my 'first love'. It has been a passion of mine since childhood, sparked by folding sessions with my aunt at the age of 6. This love for paper art led me to become a certified origami teacher in The Netherlands in 1995.

I love discovering models, and when playing with paper or having an assignment to make something specific, it's then I'm in my "Origami Bubble" and I can truly unwind. It also amazes me how paper can be transformed and how the logic of the folds work.

Online possibilities offer a great opportunity to teach origami, as well. I love this teaching. In addition to various origami books, published in The Netherlands, Germany and England, I now post videos of my models on YouTube that you can fold along with me.

For a few years, I've contemplated creating a new book, inspired by the encouragement of new friends made during the pandemic. An invitation to be a special guest at the CDO origami convention in Italy, motivated me to finally complete this project.

I couldn't choose from all my lovely designs, so maybe this book will be the first of a "Let's fold..." series. This book has a yellow border which stands for "happy" and "smile". Also the models make me happy. Hence the title, "Let's fold... and be happy".

The support and feedback from skilled individuals around me, spending their valuable time on this, has been instrumental in bringing this book to fruition.
The result is a book that makes me very happy and I hope you too!

Feel free to share your creations on social media. Please, remember to tag @jannievanschuylenburg and #jannievanschuylenburg, so I can see them.
Your feedback and ideas are always welcome.
Let's fold... and be happy.

Love from Jannie van Schuylenburg

Ter Aar, The Netherlands,
September 2024

# Tips & Tricks

## Imagine...

We always seek those models which make us happy, either for their wisdom, elegance, or cleverness. Imagine meeting a person who is exactly like that - smart, elegant, and sharp as a needle. Now, imagine that this person designs origami models, and puts them in a book. Well, there is no need to imagine anymore, you are holding this book in your hands!

- Ilan Garibi

### Tips & Tricks

| | |
|---|---|
| Work accurately & relax | This is the basis of origami. Place all edges, corners and/or points exactly on top of each other. First a soft fold, correct where necessary and, when everything is in place, flatten the fold. |
| Don't start too difficult | There are easy and more difficult models in this book. If you are just starting out, it is good to begin with simple models. |
| Look ahead | With the diagrams, it is good to always look at a subsequent drawing so that you can see how the model should look after the fold. Then follow the line and arrows on the step you are working on. |
| Keep practicing | When you fold a model for the first time, it will definitely not look perfect. It is also really an exercise. The next time it will be better. |
| Take a rest | If a model does not turn out well, put it away for a while and continue later. Then you will look at it again with a fresh mind. |
| Enjoy folding! | This is the most important tip. Enjoy folding... and be happy! |

# Materials

Origami is such fun to do. You only need your hands and paper.

- There are various beautiful **papers** for sale. When you start, I advise to use just kami. That is plain paper with a white back. There you see the folds well and how to fold. Choose a good quality paper. Paper is easily available online, such as at Amazon, OrigamiUSA, and plenty of other paper shops. The Tuttle brand also has beautiful double-sided paper. The Origami Shop (France) and Miyabi (Germany) sell special paper in addition to kami. It also comes in very large sizes.

- A **bone folder** or an old **credit card** is a good idea in case of thick paper. Just try it out. Work on a smooth surface, e.g. a **cutting mat**, and ensure sufficient contrast. If the surface and the paper are dark, place a light sheet between them. There are also **light gray** mats for sale that work with all colors. (see photo)

- Use only little drops of **glue**, if needed, so that it does not come out. Less glue sticks better and does not 'punch' through your paper.

- A small **cutting device** to cut the paper to the right size is great to use. You can also use a sharp **knife** and **cutting ruler**. An **envelope opener** is very useful to cut off an already folded straight edge. It is important that the fold is not too sharp, because then the paper will run next to the knife of the opener. Fold, in that case, the paper to the other side but don't accentuate the line. Then run the envelope opener along it.

# Symbols & Techniques

|  |  |
|---|---|
|  | Start with the white / colored side up. |
|  | Turn over / flip over the model like a book page. |
|  | Unfold. Pull out the paper part as far as the next step indicates. |
|  | Open the model as far as the next step indicates. |
|  | Rotate the model (the next step shows how far). |
|  | Repeat the step here again. The cross lines indicate how many times. |
|  | Zoom in: the next step is enlarged. |
|  | Zoom out: the next step is reduced. |
|  | Push in (and fold flat). |
|  | Roll-up. |
|  | Divide the paper into equal parts, as much as indicated. |
|  | Hidden line: insert paper below. |
|  | Hidden crease. |
|  | Hold the model at this point. |
| 3D | The model becomes 3-dimensional. |
| ① ② | Start with folding 1. Continue with folding 2. |
|  | Change point of view in the next step. |
| glue * | Use a drop of glue at this point. |
| 2x | Fold the unit as many times as indicated. |

# Symbols & Techniques

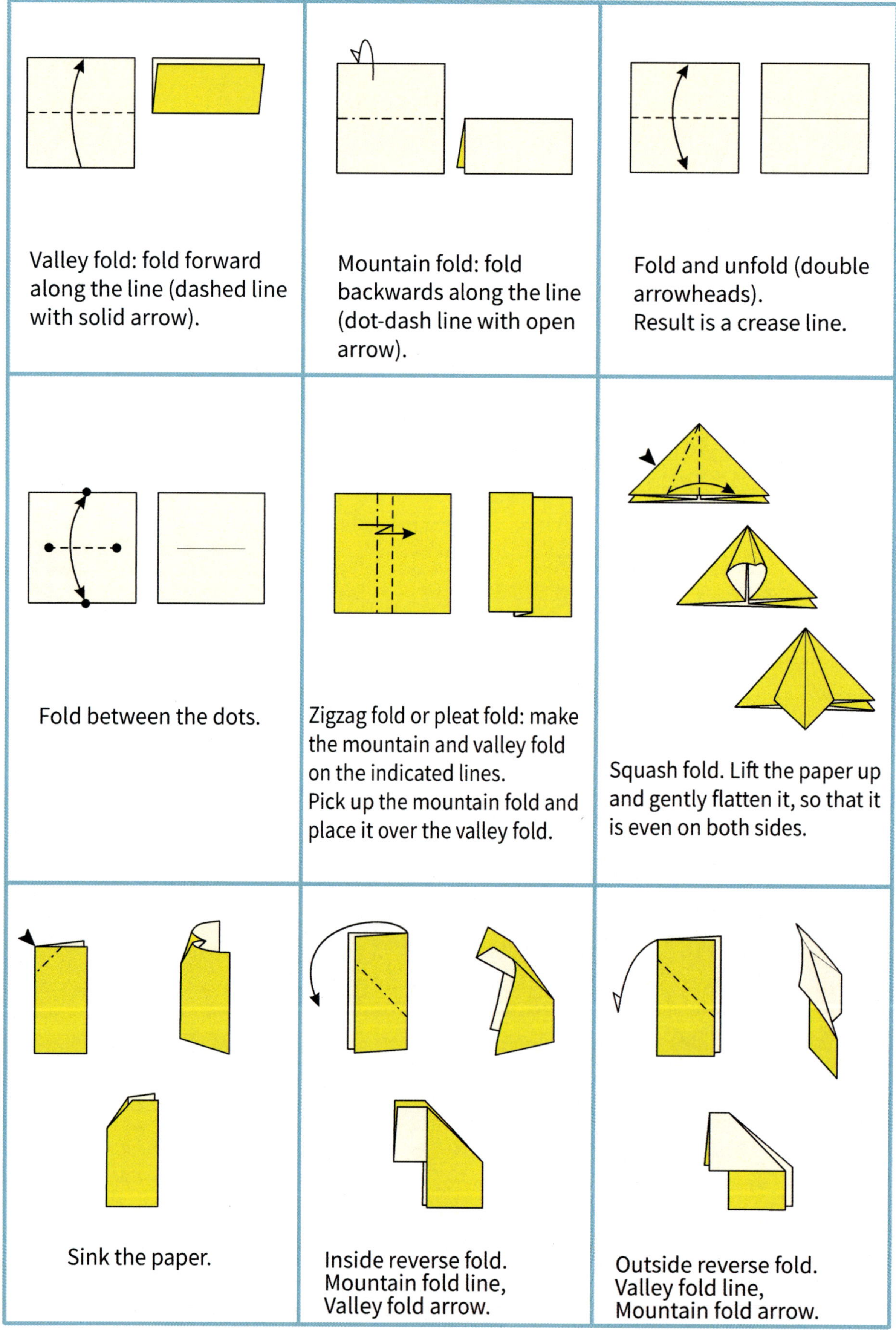

# Calculation table Ori-Paper-Saver

To fold this handy and sturdy paper container you need a large piece of paper. Below is a table for various paper sizes. How to use is described below.

## How to read this calculation table

For example: You make a box for a 7,5 cm square paper pack.

Length of the paper

- The size of a square paper + 0,5 cm is the **BASE**. (for 7,5 cm square paper the **base** is 7,5 + 0,5 = 8 cm) You need **6** times the **BASE**. (in this case that's 6 x 8 cm = 48 cm)
- You need extra paper for the **lock** (for the box in the table that's 4 cm). You also need extra paper for **reinforcement** (for the box in the table that's 1 cm)
- Calculation for the length: (6 x base =) **48 cm +** (lock =) **4 cm +** (reinforcement =) **1 cm = 53 cm**. This is the length of your paper.

Width of the paper

- For the width you need **2** times the **BASE**. (in this case that's 2 x 8 cm = 16 cm)
- You also need extra width for the **depth** of the box. (that's 2 cm for this box)
- Calculation for the width: (2x base =) **16 cm +** (depth box =) **2 cm = 18 cm**. This is the width of your paper.

So you need for a **7,5 cm square paper pack box: 53 cm length and 18 cm width**.

Calculation table (in centimeters):

| Paper + 0,5 cm=**Base** | | length = 6 x B | + lock + reinforcement: | width = 2 x B | + depth box: | Total paper in cm |
|---|---|---|---|---|---|---|
| 2x2 | **= 2,5** | 15 | 1,5+1 | 5 | 1,5 | 17,5 x 6,5 |
| 3x3 | **= 3,5** | 21 | 2+1 | 7 | 1,5 | 24 x 8,5 |
| 4x4 | **= 4,5** | 27 | 2+1 | 9 | 1,5 | 30 x 10,5 |
| 5x5 | **= 5,5** | 33 | 3+1 | 11 | 1,5 of 2 | 37 x 12,5 / 13 |
| 7,5x7,5 | **= 8** | 48 | 4+1 | 16 | 2 | 53 x 18 |
| 9x9 | **= 9,5** | 57 | 4+1 | 19 | 2 | 62 x 21 |
| 10x10 | **= 10,5** | 63 | 4+1 | 21 | 2 of 4 | 68 x 23 / 25 |
| 12x12 | **= 12,5** | 75 | 4+1 | 25 | 2 | 80 x 27 |
| 15x15 | **= 15,5** | 93 | 5+2 | 31 | 2 of 2,5 | 100 x 33 / 33,5 |

# How to make...

## Hexagon from a square

I saw this hexagon by Hyo Ahn. I simplified it. It is very accurate.

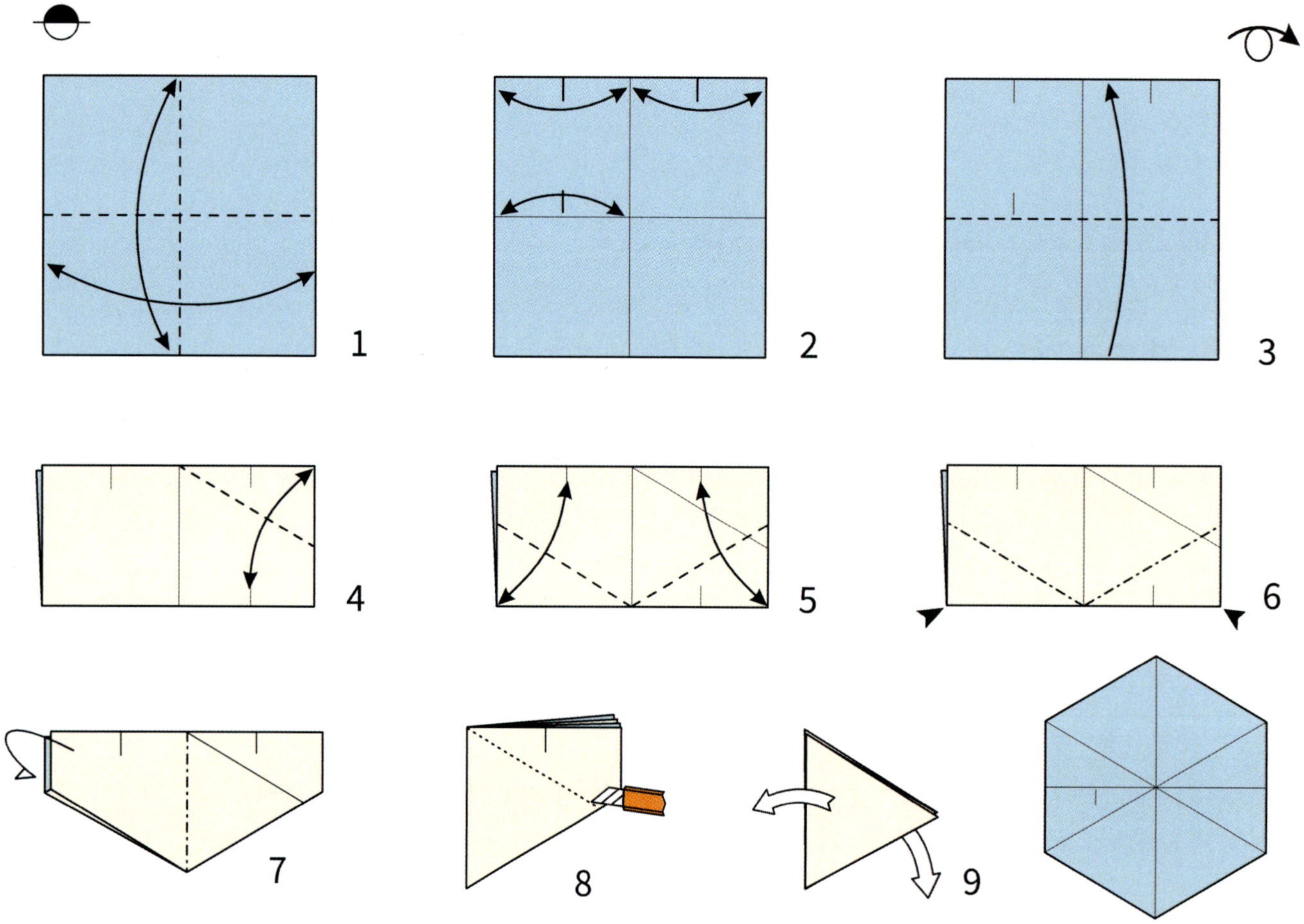

1 2 3

4 5 6

7 8 9

## A-size from a square

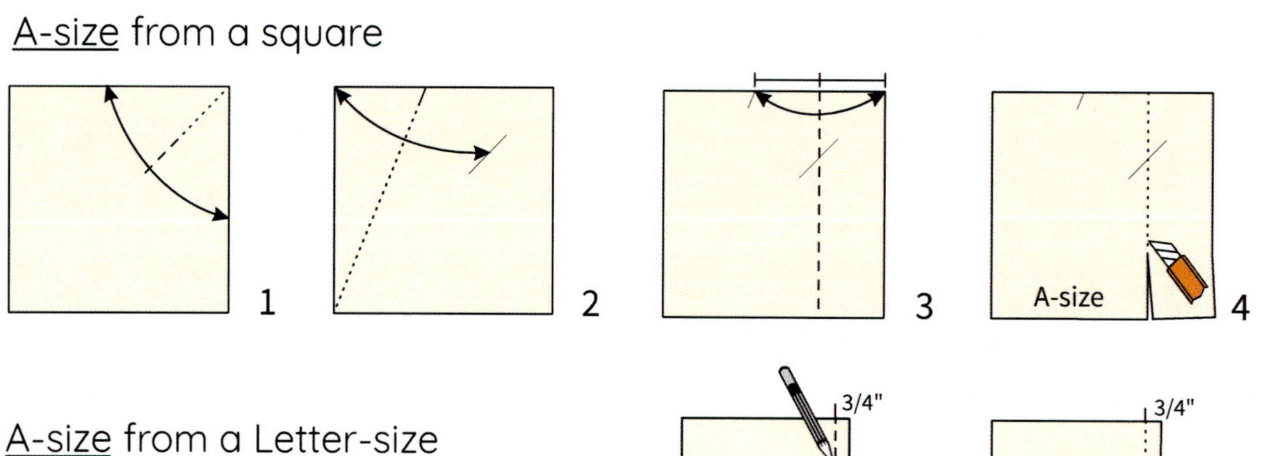


1 2 3 4

## A-size from a Letter-size

To make an A-size from Letter-size you have to cut off about 3/4" of an inch off the long side.

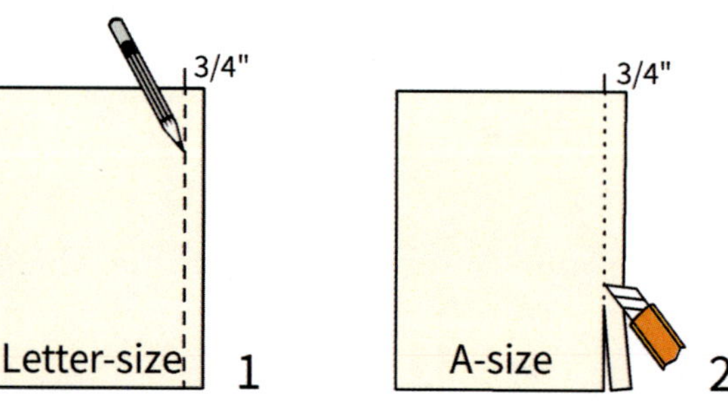


1 2

# Containers

You will not have missed that I like folding boxes. That is why we start this book with a chapter on containers. You will find all kinds of boxes, bowls, and dishes here. It is so much fun to give things away in them or to put them on a festively decorated table as a present.

# Magic Duo Color Box

13-04-2014

The Magic Duo Color Box is a beauty and one of my favorites. In the last step it gets it's shape, color change, sturdiness, and lock. The lock is surprising and invisible.
I love this practical model which is especially beautiful folded from double-sided paper or other special paper, like braille- or embossed paper. And, of course, there are several variations possible.

Paper:
- 15x15 cm duo color

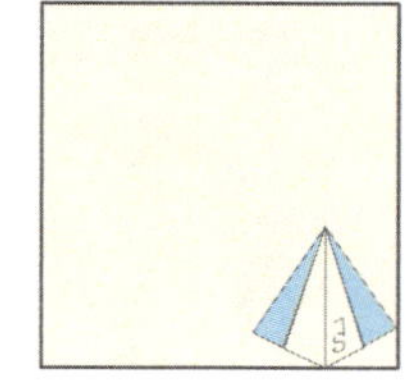

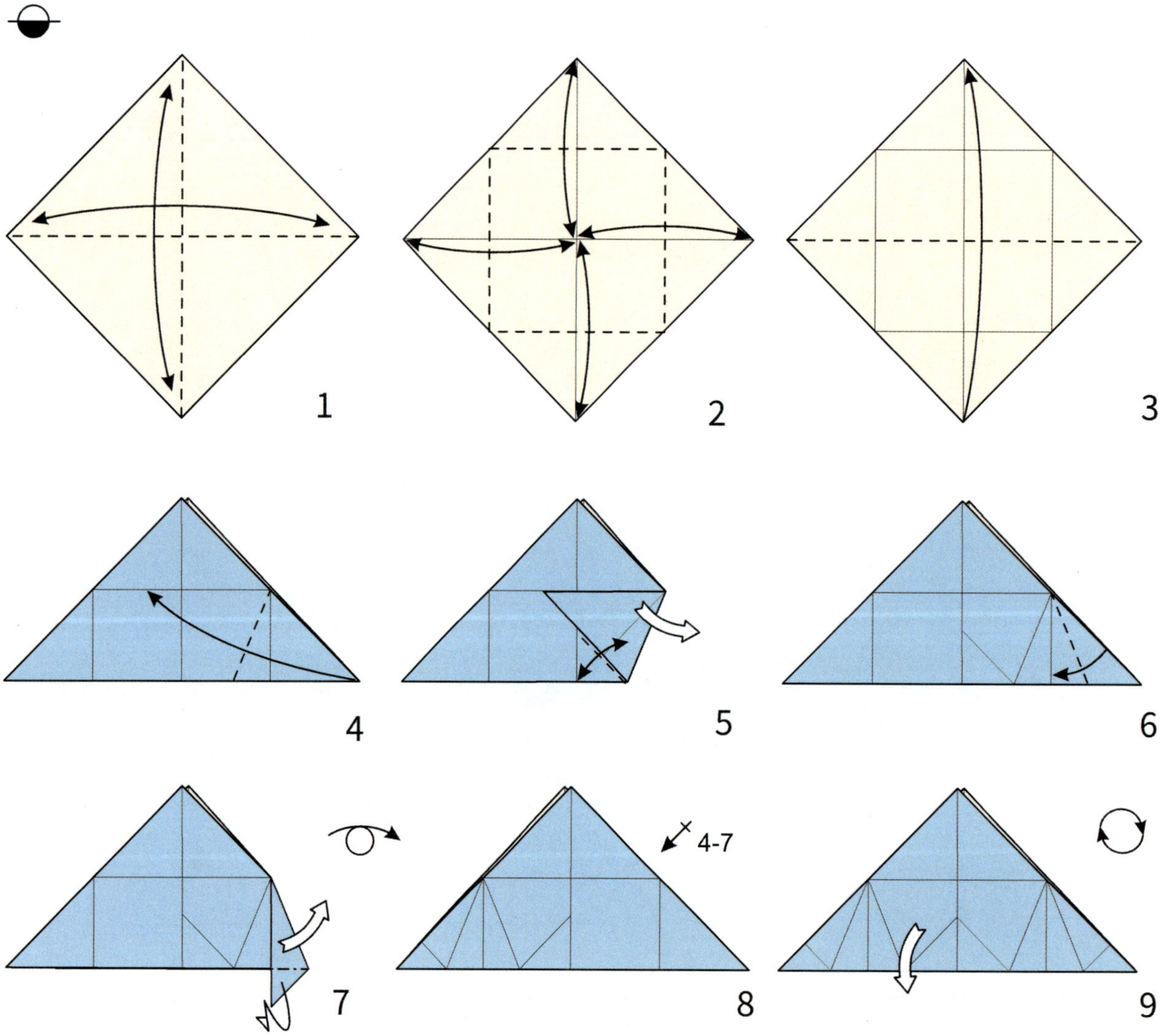

1

2

3

4

5

6

7

8 4-7

9

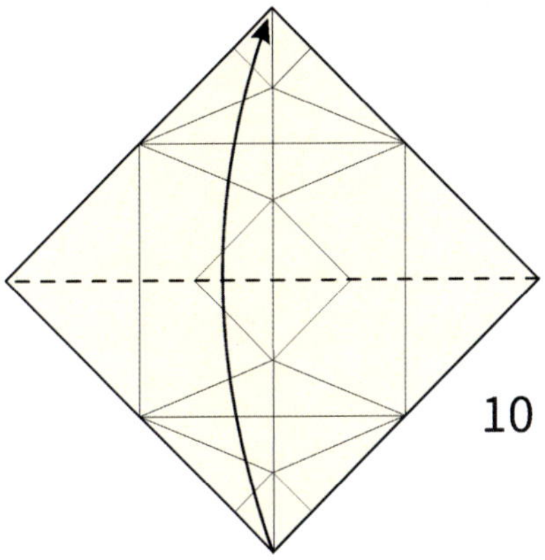

10

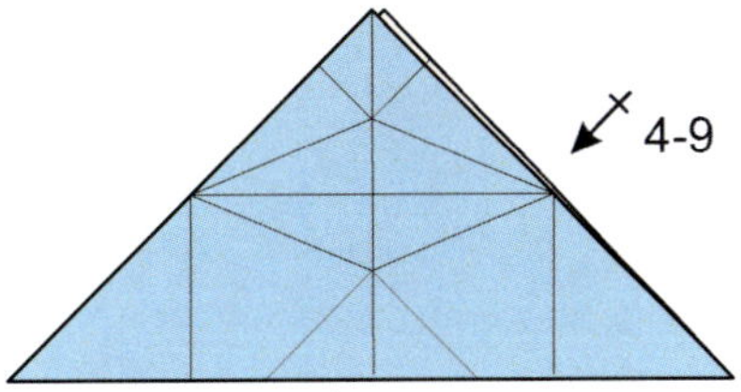

11

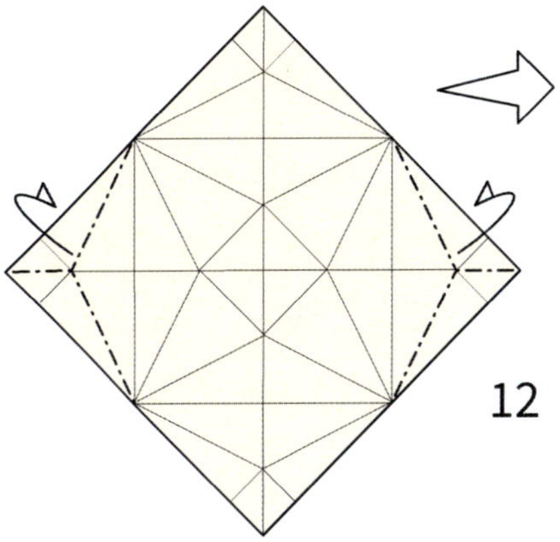

4-9

12

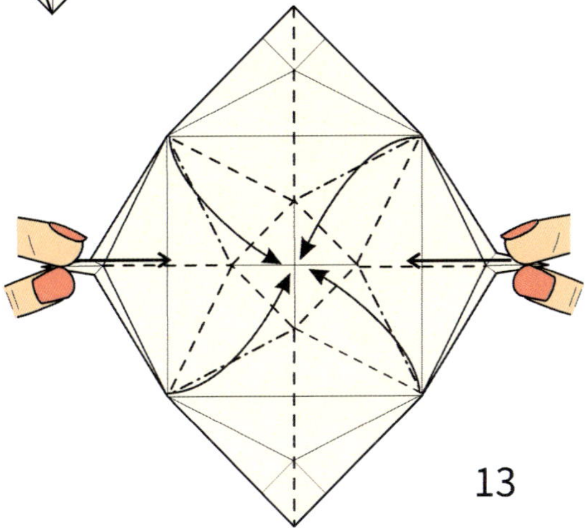

13

Hold the opposite corners and push them inwards together.

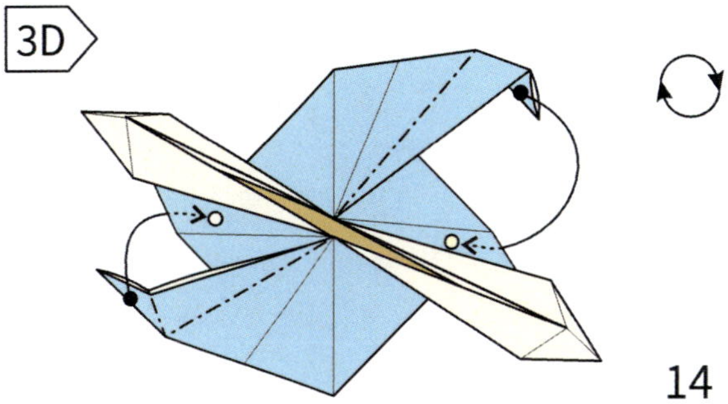

3D

14

Wrap the small corners behind the paper flaps with the colored corners.

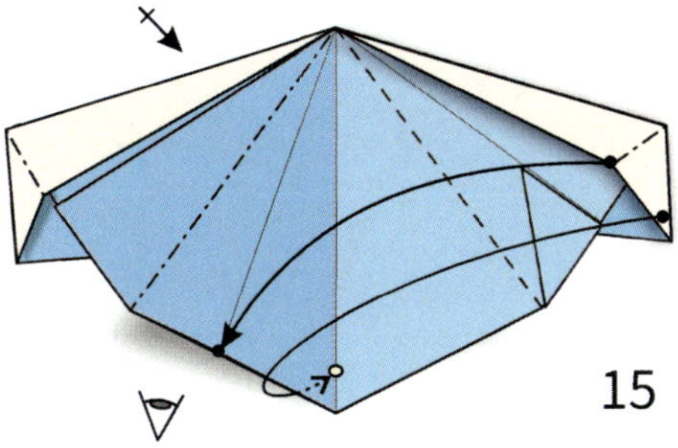

15

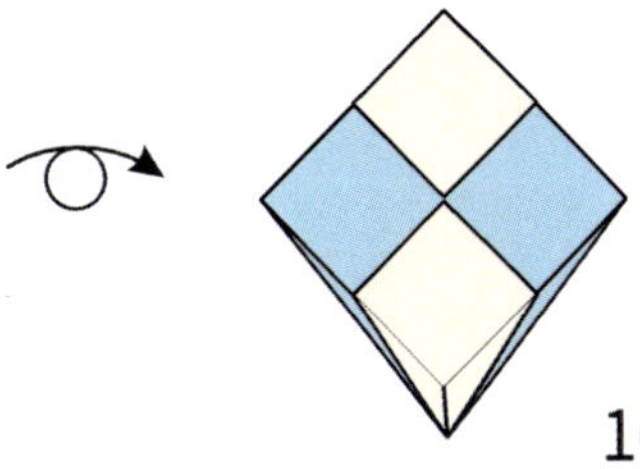

16

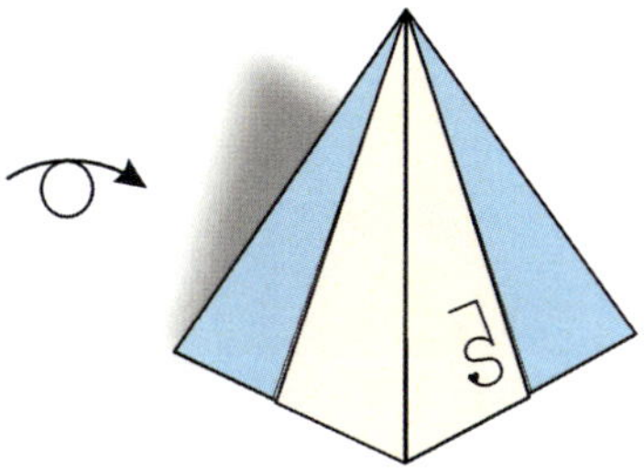

Wrap the remaining flaps around the pyramid like a windmill and slide the corners over the bottom corners.

*Variations*
*at step 12*

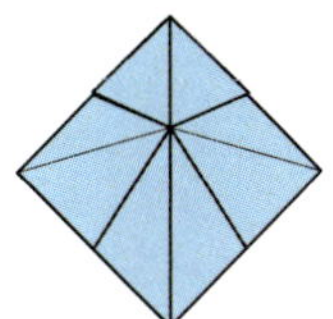

0 corners turned over

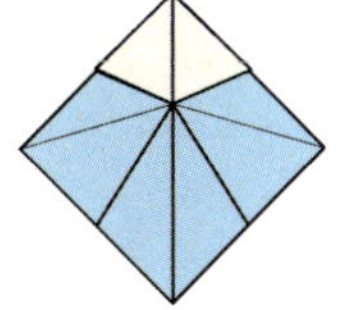

1 corner turned over

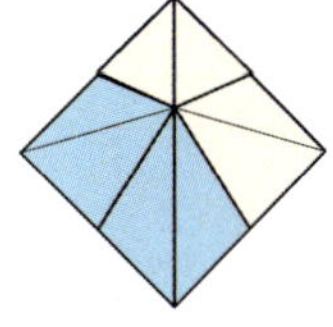

2 corners turned over side by side

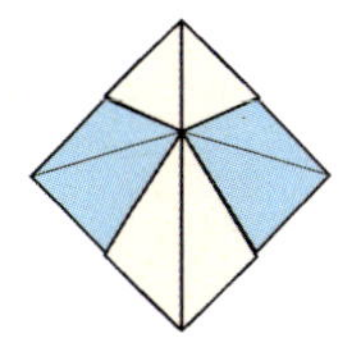

2 opposite corners turned over

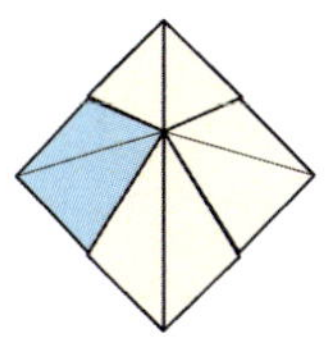

3 corners turned over

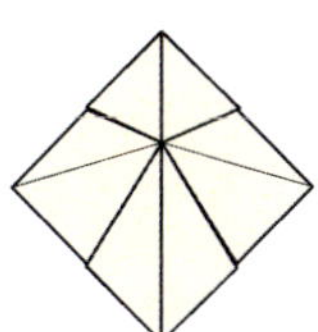

4 corners turned over

# Susanna's Box

15-08-2019

This model is based on an earlier design. I have adapted the container, 'Tulip Rosalina,' designed 01-06-2012, and developed a lid for it. I love the simple, yet stable structure of this container.

This model is dedicated to my dearest mother, Susanna.

Paper:
- box: 15x15 cm duo color
- lid: 15x15 cm duo color

## Box

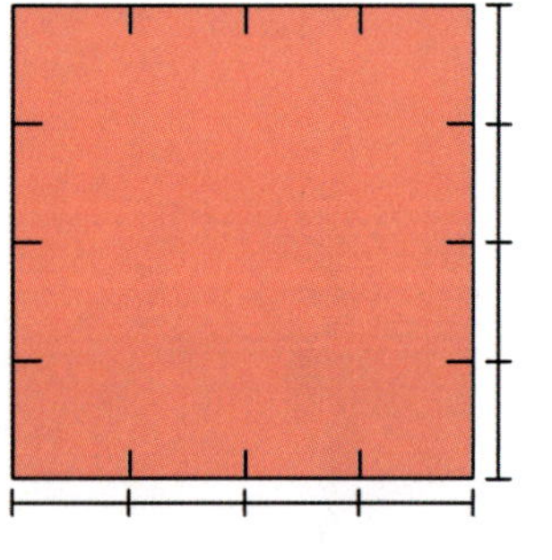

1

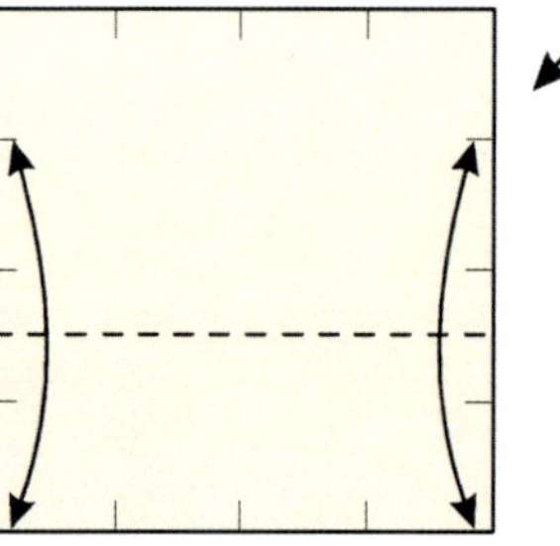

2

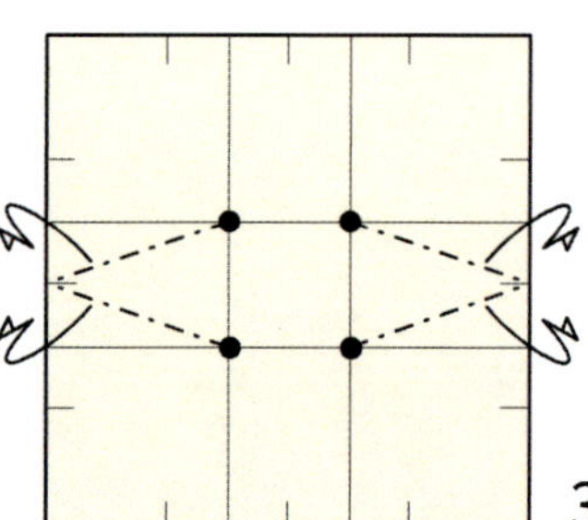

3

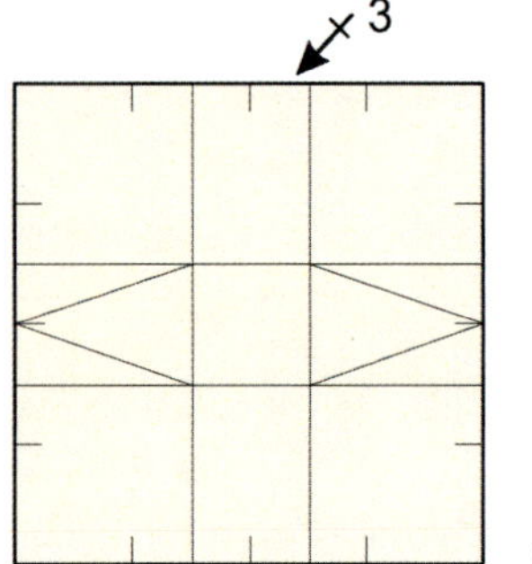



4

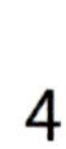

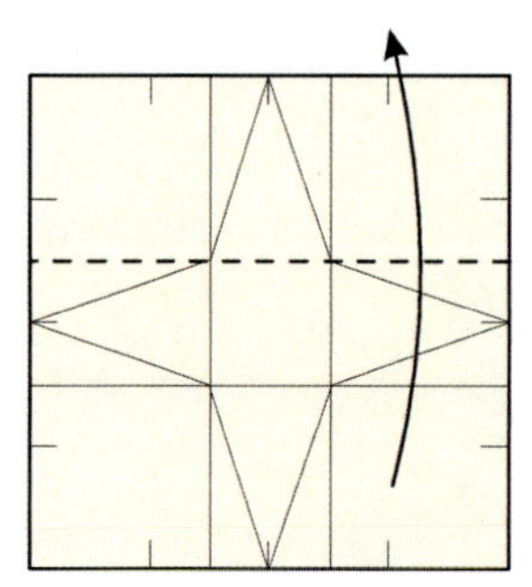

5

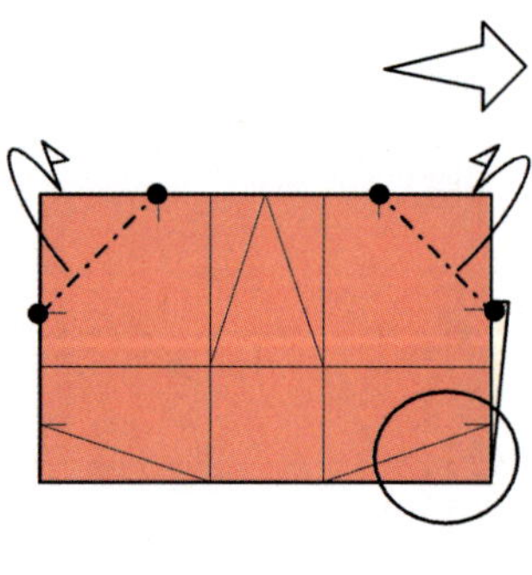

6

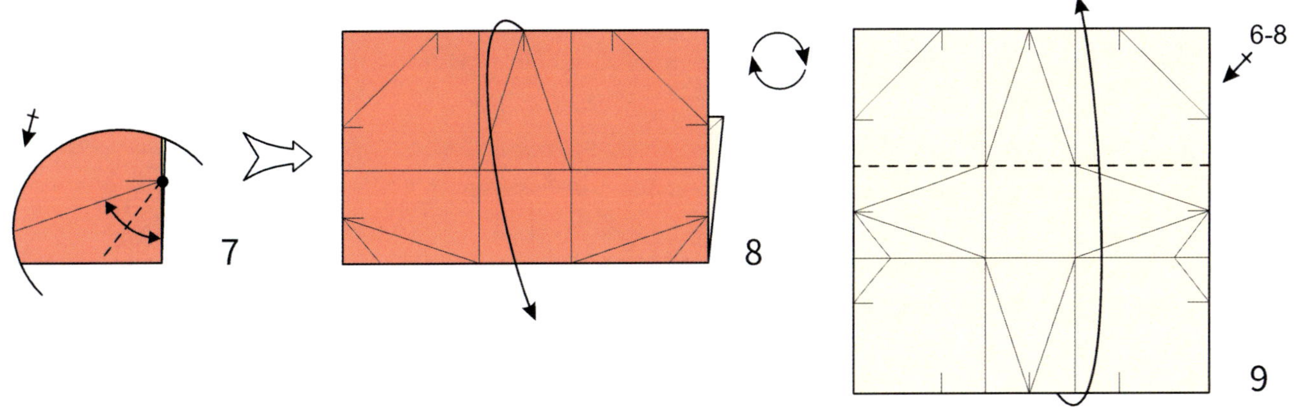
7
8
6-8
9

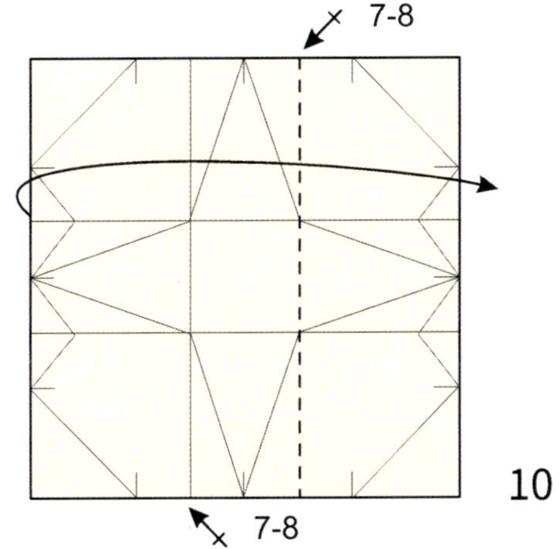
7-8
7-8
10

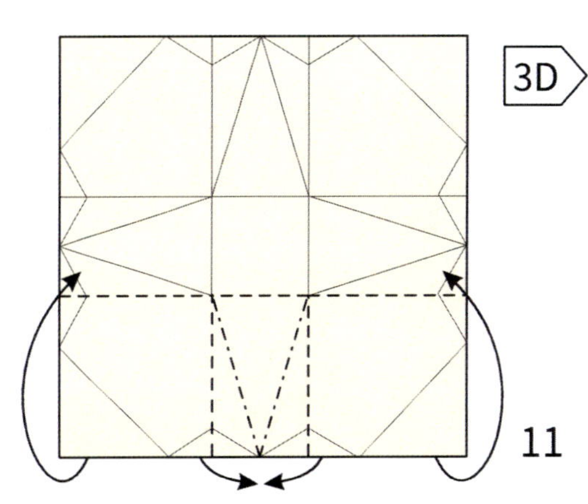
3D
11

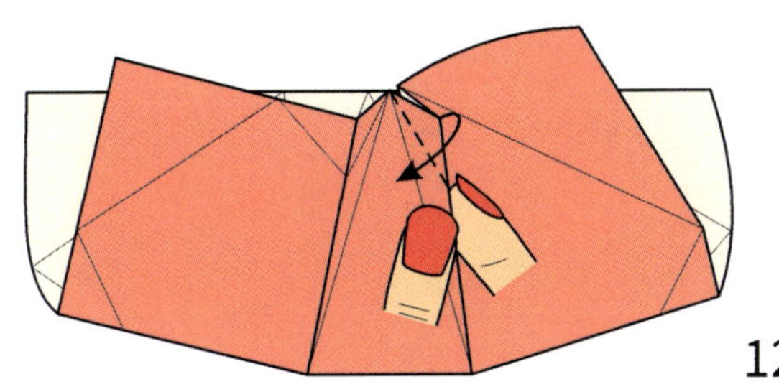
12

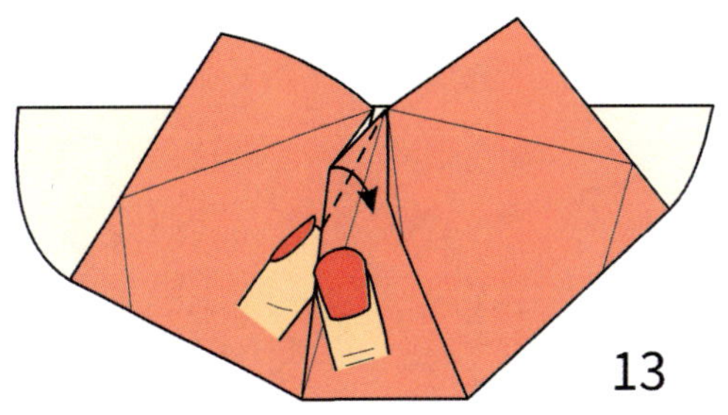
13

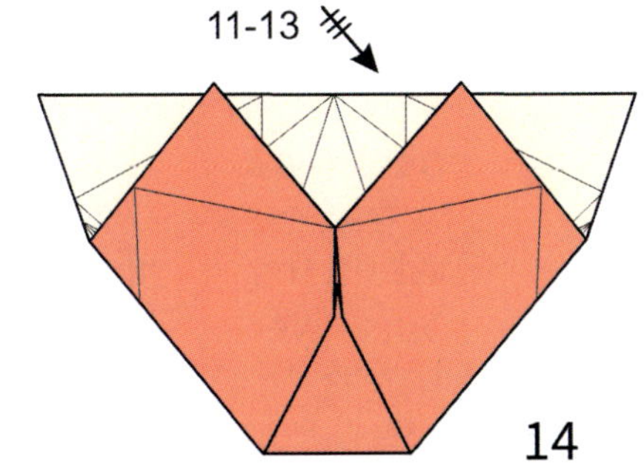
11-13
14

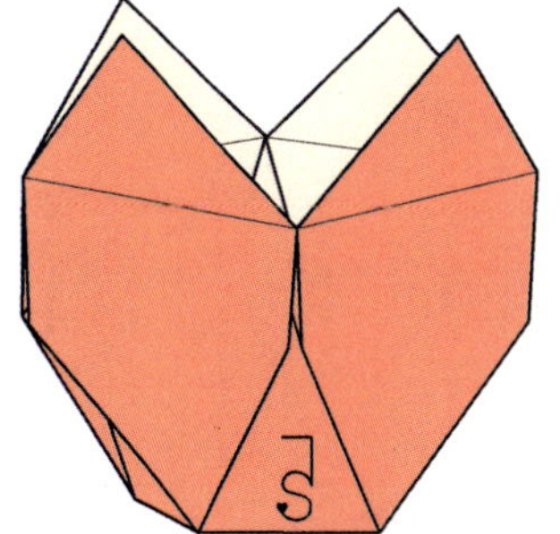

# Square-flower closure 1

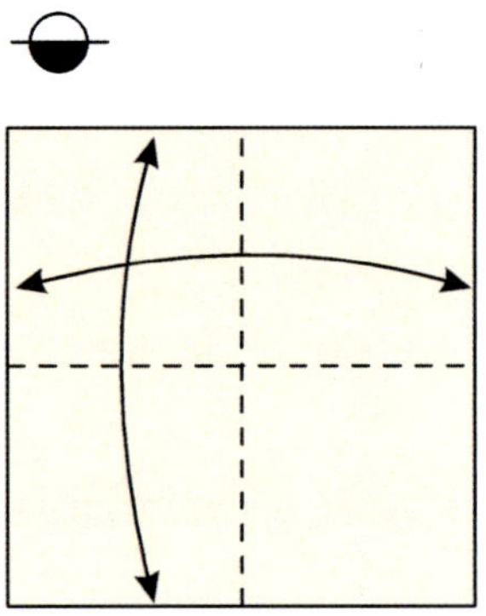

1

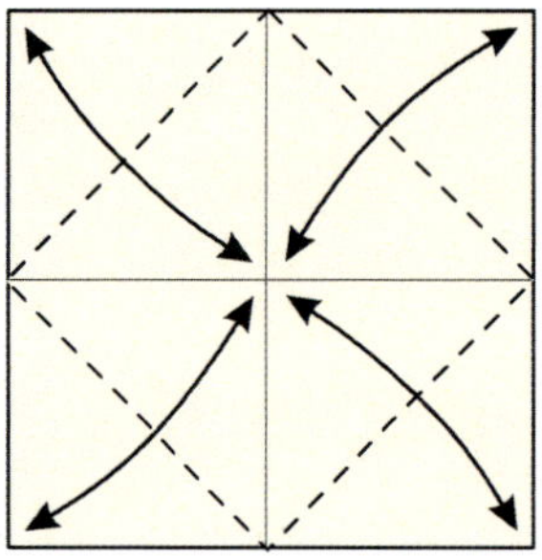

2

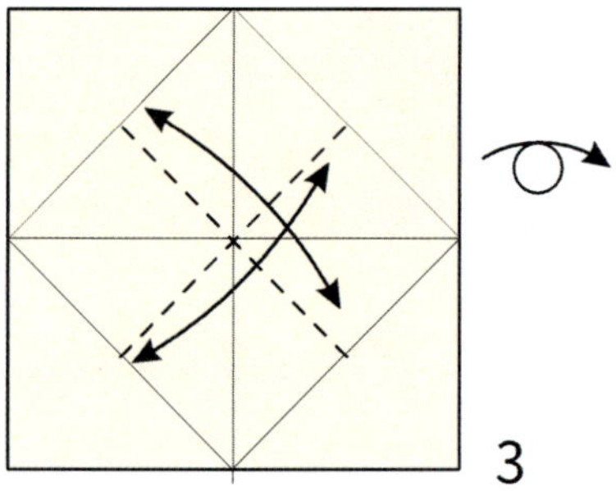

3

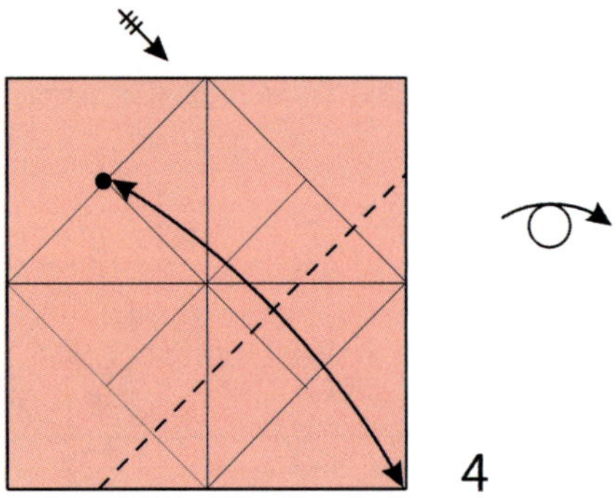

4

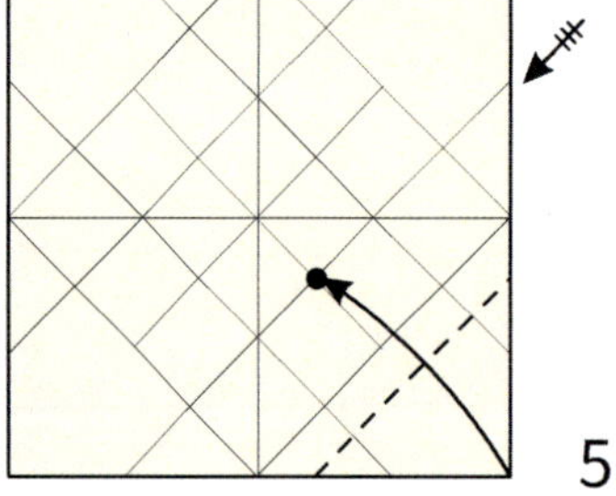

5

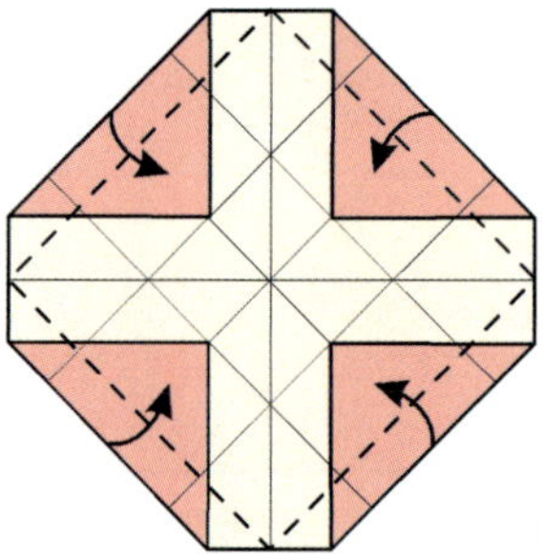

6

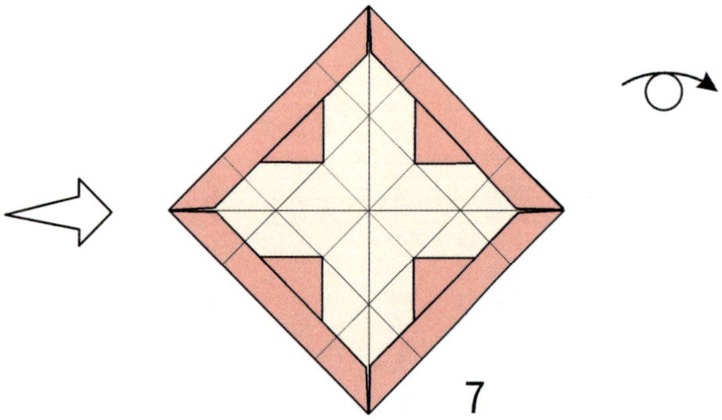

7

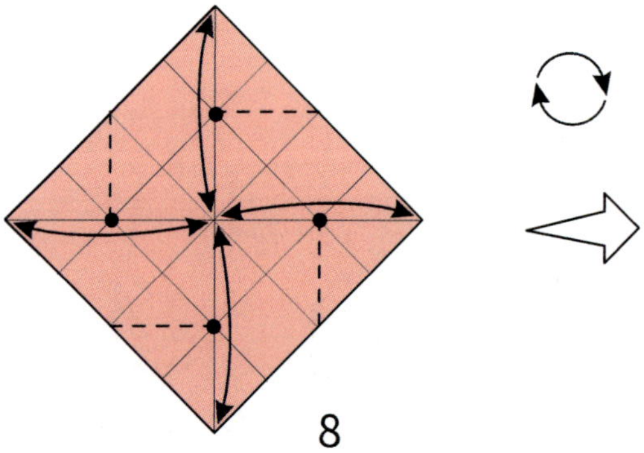

8

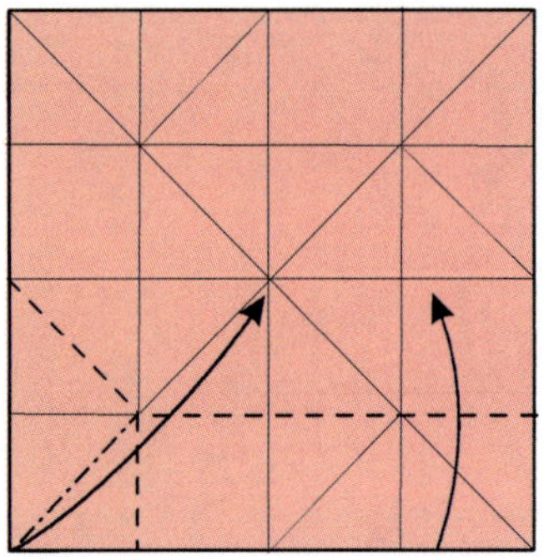

9

Rotate counterclockwise.

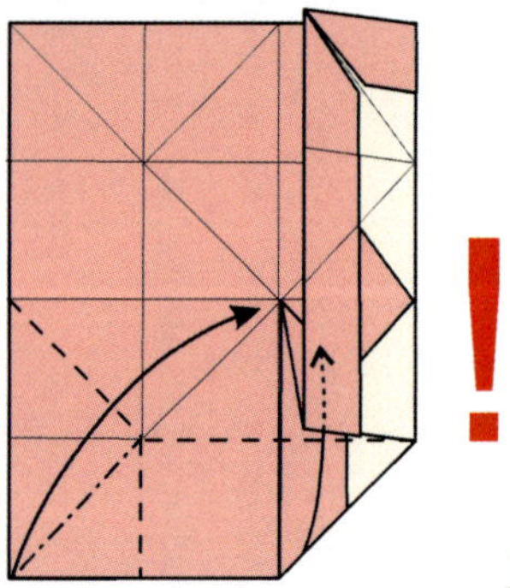

10

! Pay attention: on the right the flap goes **UNDER** the paper layer.

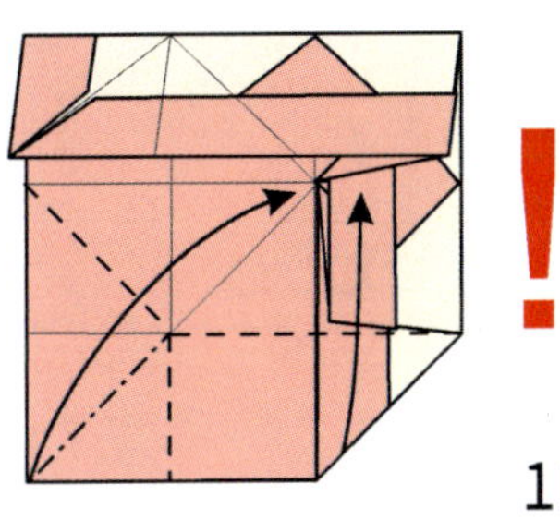


Pay attention: on the right the flap goes now **OVER** the paper layer.

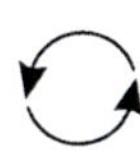

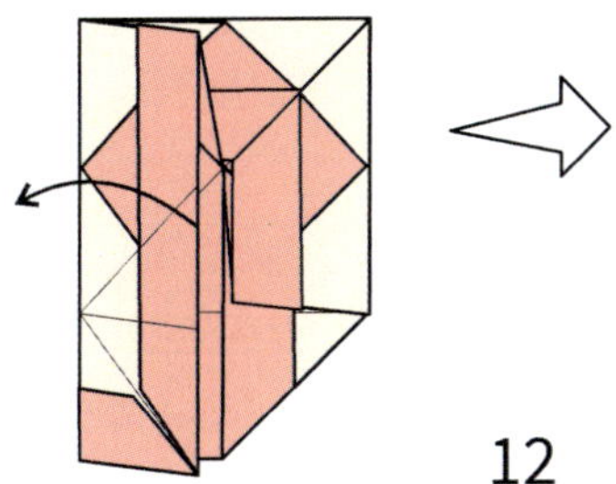


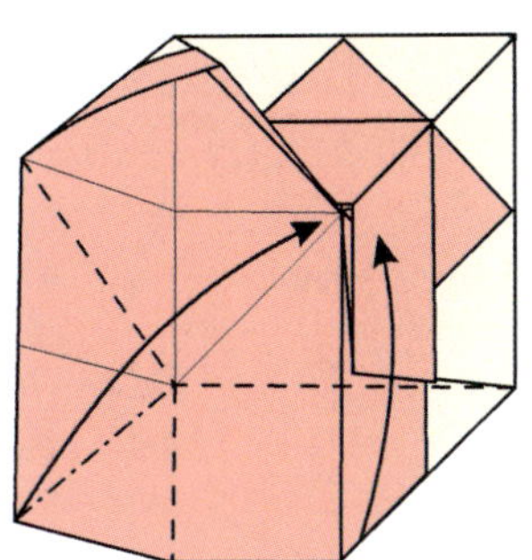


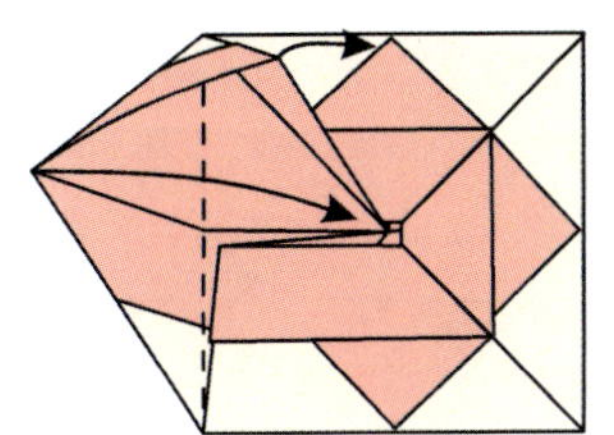


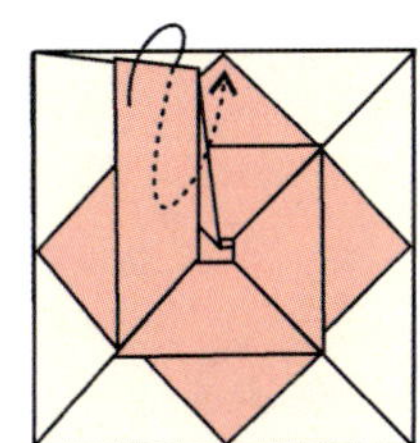

*Two ways to attach the lid in the box*

*Flower square closure*

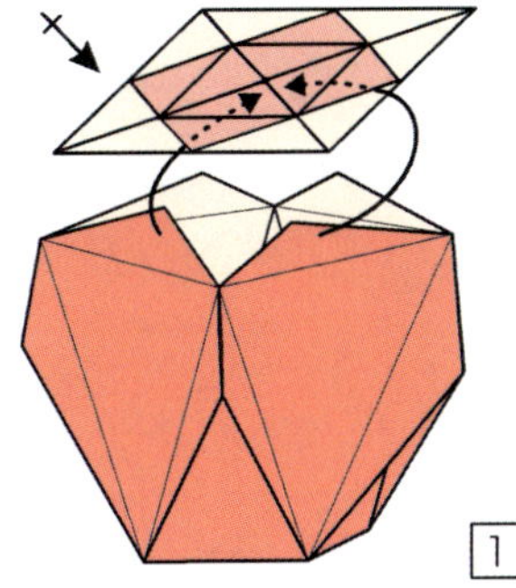


Slide the points of the box under both colored layers of the lid. The lose flap of the lid resemble a flower.

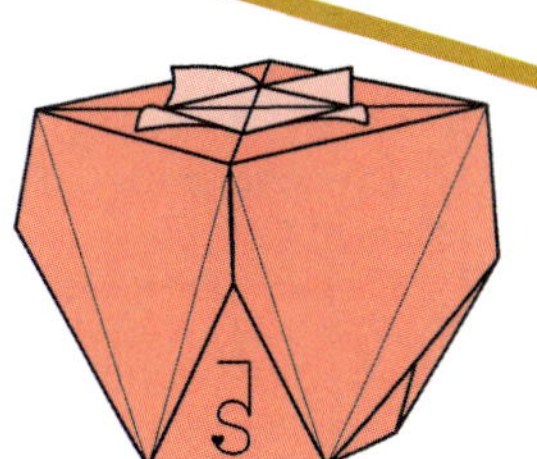

With a skewer you can shape the flower petals.

*Square closure*

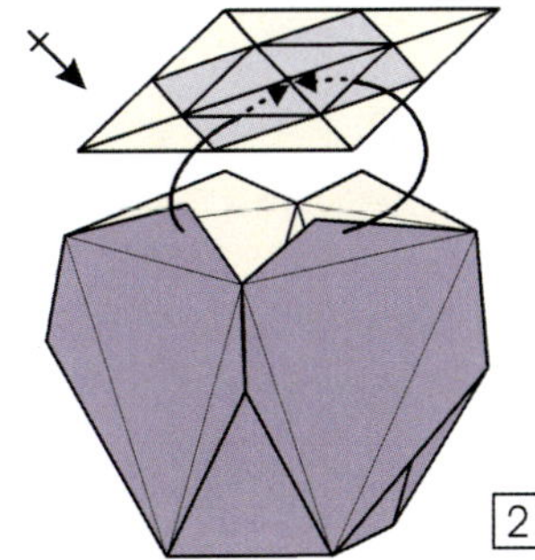


Slide the points of the box over the lose flaps and then under the triangles.

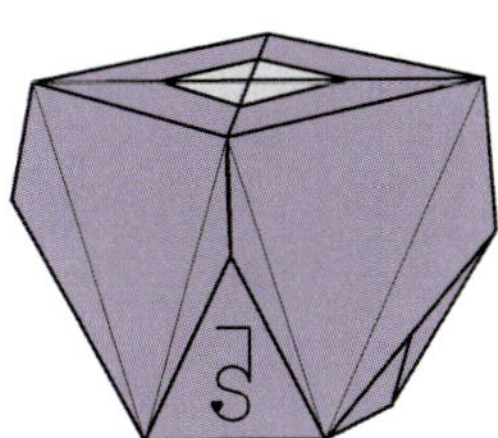

# Flower closure 2

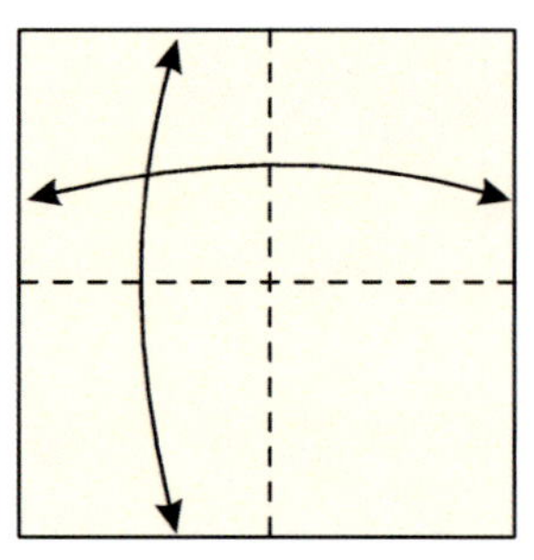

1

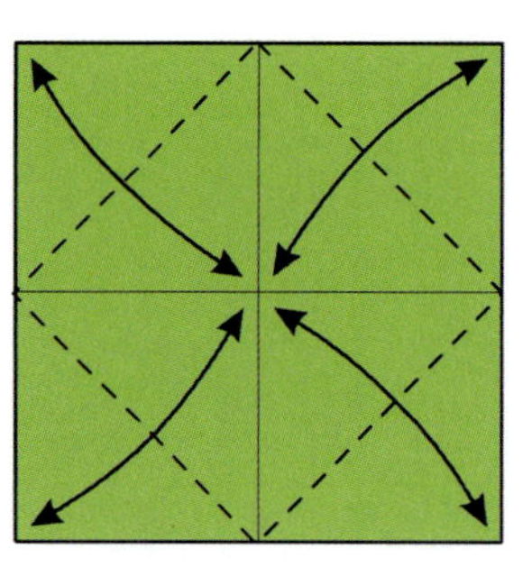

2

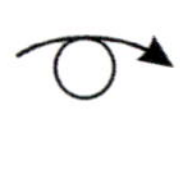

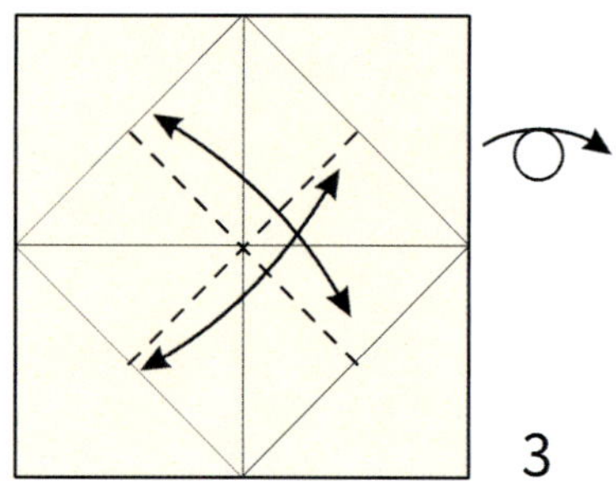

3

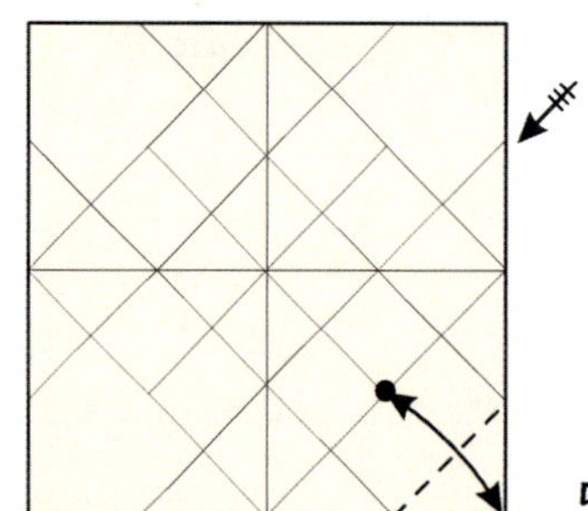

4

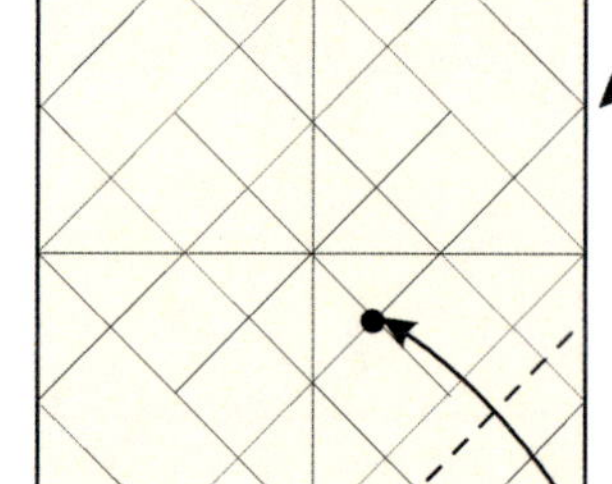

5

6

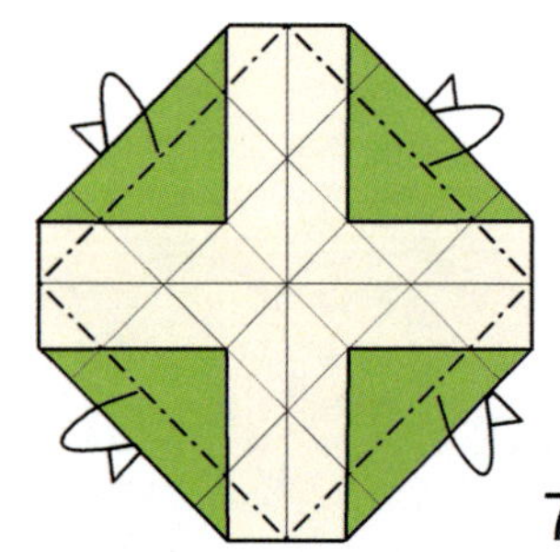

7

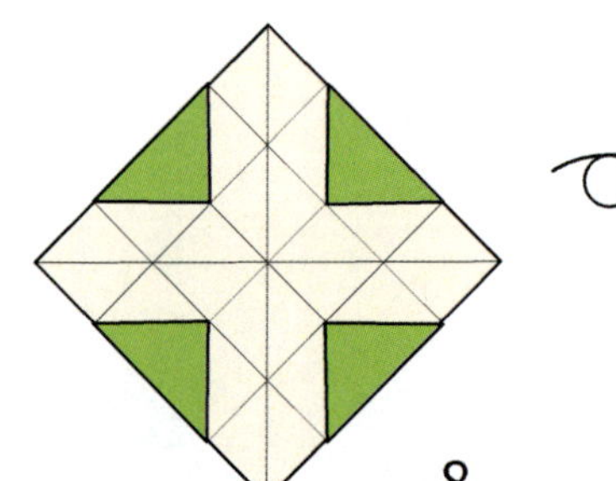

8

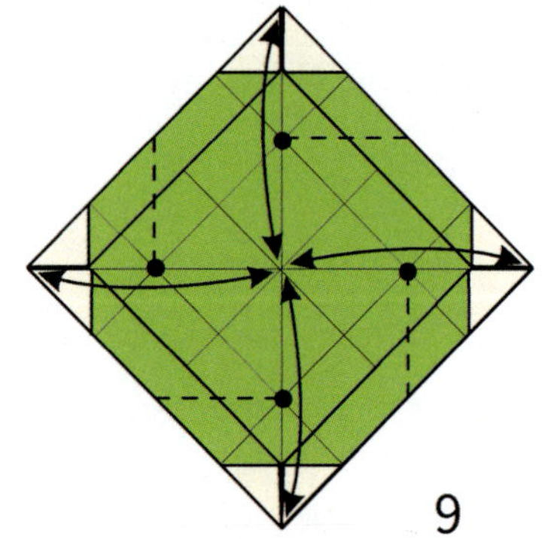

9

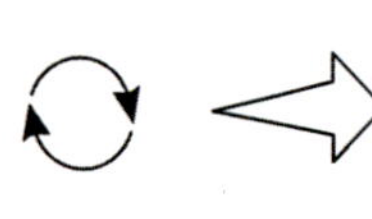

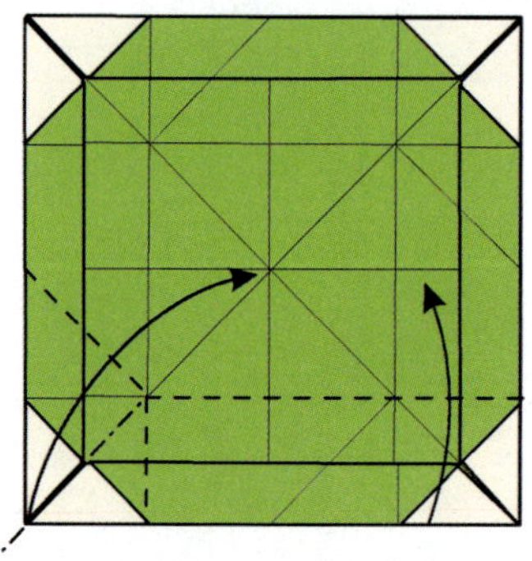

10

Rotate counterclockwise.

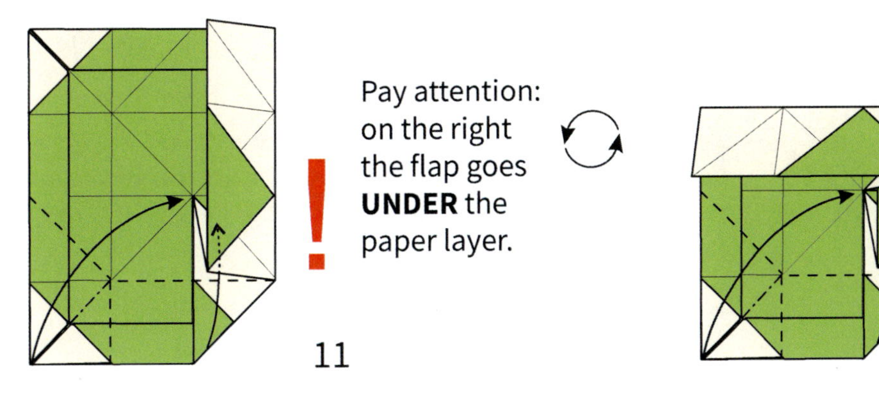


Pay attention: on the right the flap goes **UNDER** the paper layer.

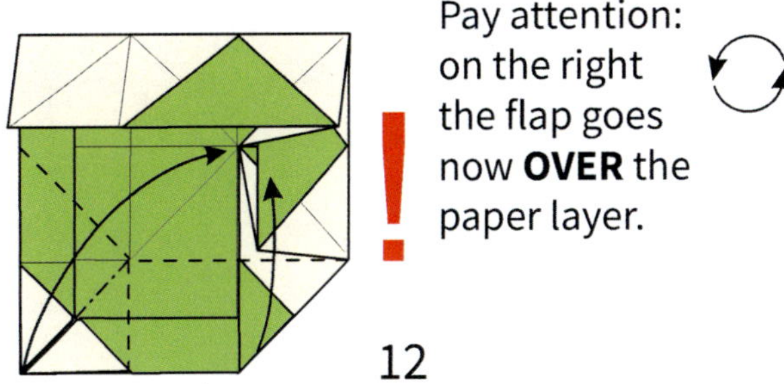


Pay attention: on the right the flap goes now **OVER** the paper layer.

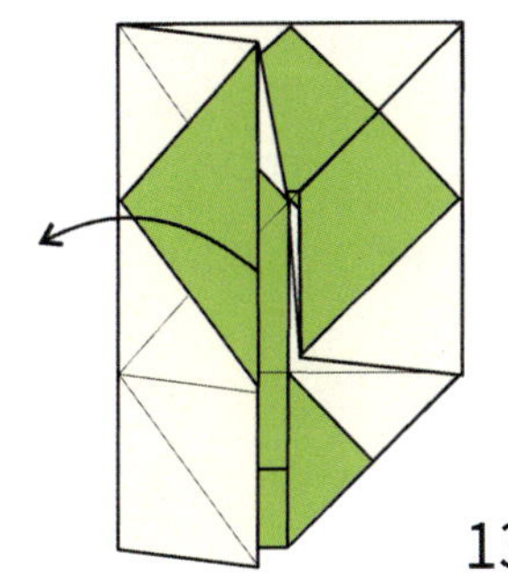


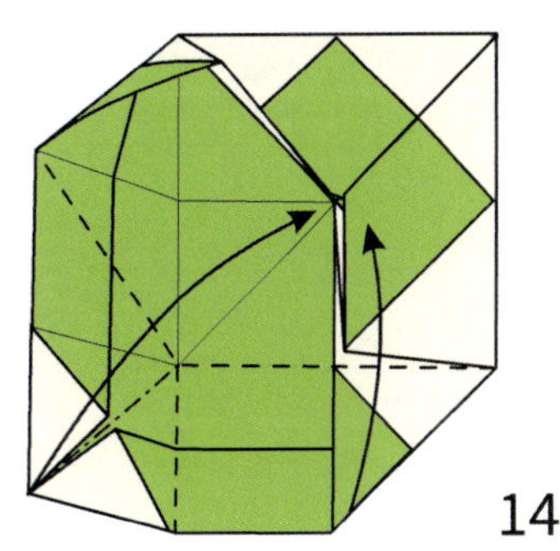


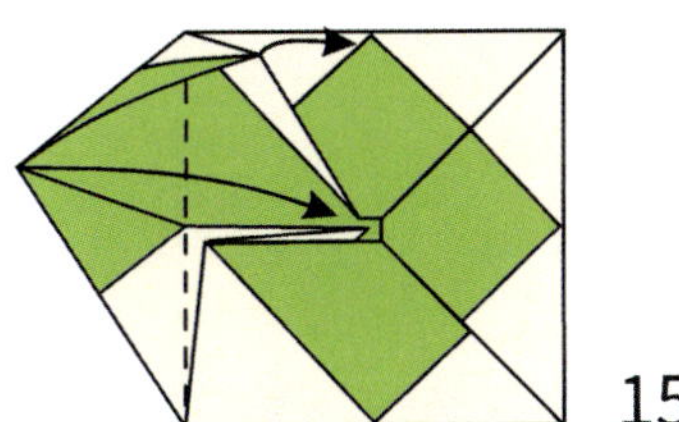


16

*Attaching the lid in the box*

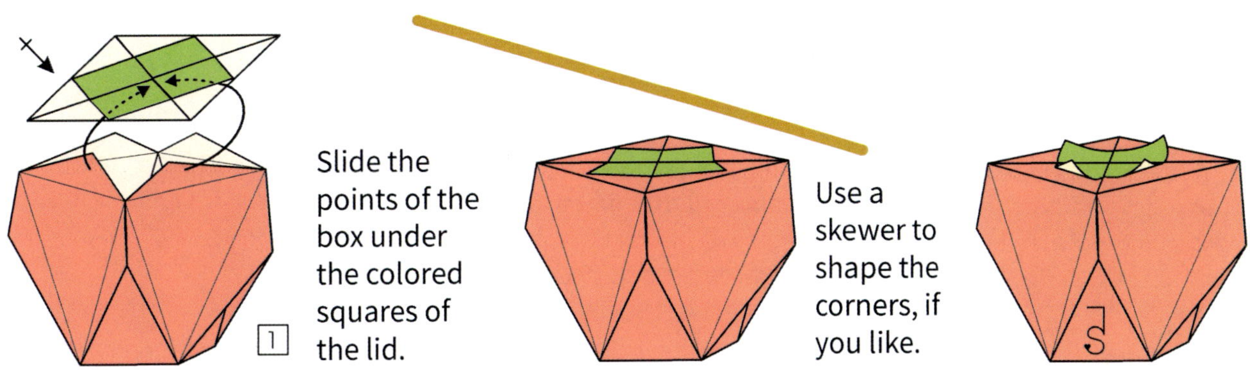

Slide the points of the box under the colored squares of the lid.

Use a skewer to shape the corners, if you like.

# Treasure Box

10-05-2014

This model has waited for over 10 years to be shown to the public. It's a lovely box with a woven closure. Sometimes, when playing with origami paper, something very special appears. Because you see so much of the paper, it's great to use beautiful paper. Enjoy folding this model!

Paper:
- 15x15 cm duo color 80 gr

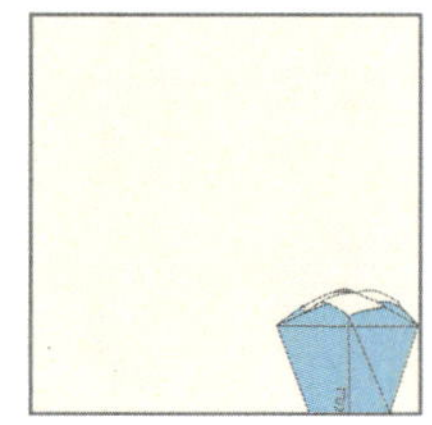

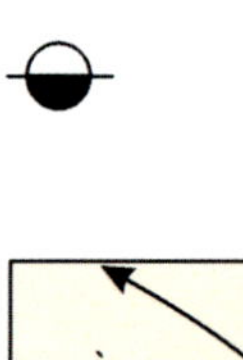

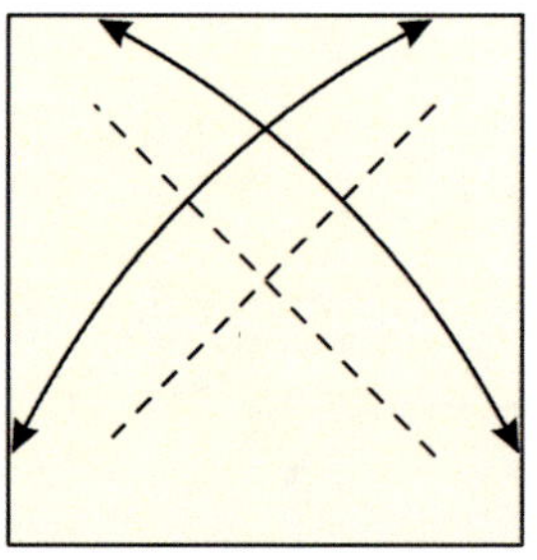

1

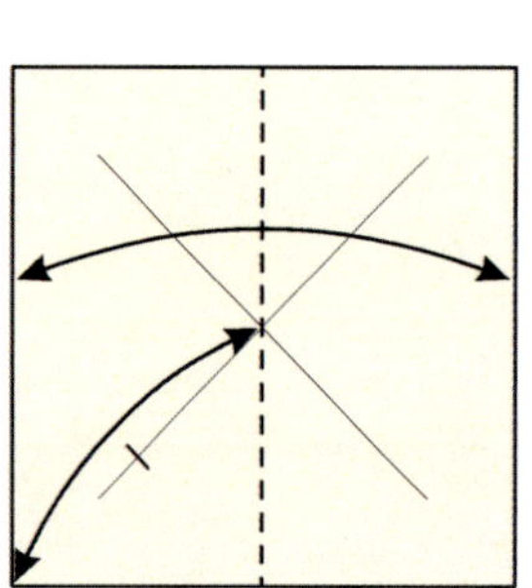

2

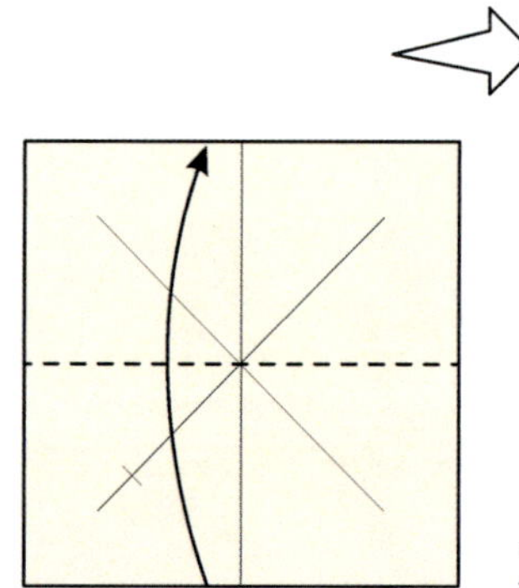

3

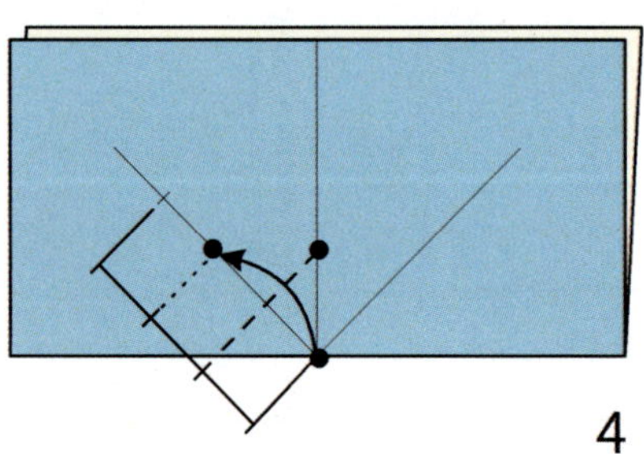

4

3D

Fold the left part, from the bottom center till the pinch, in 3.
You will notice that the distance between the folded part and the leftover to the pinch, by eye, is the same.

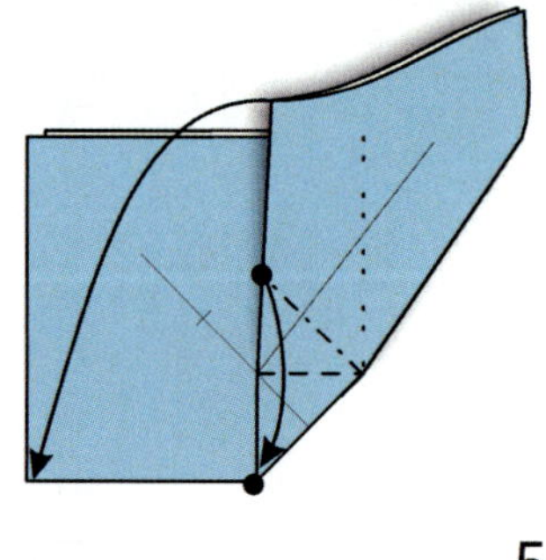

5

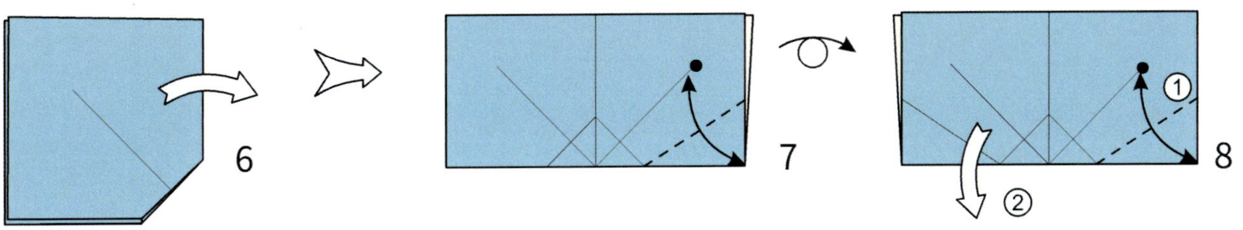

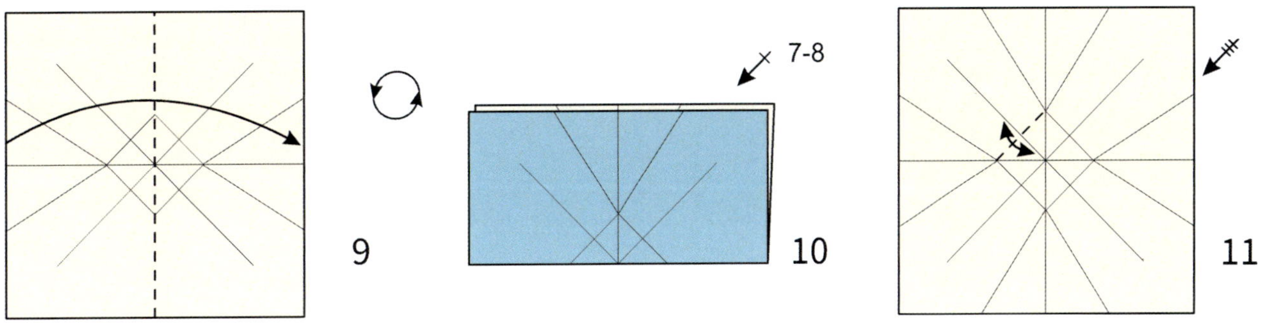

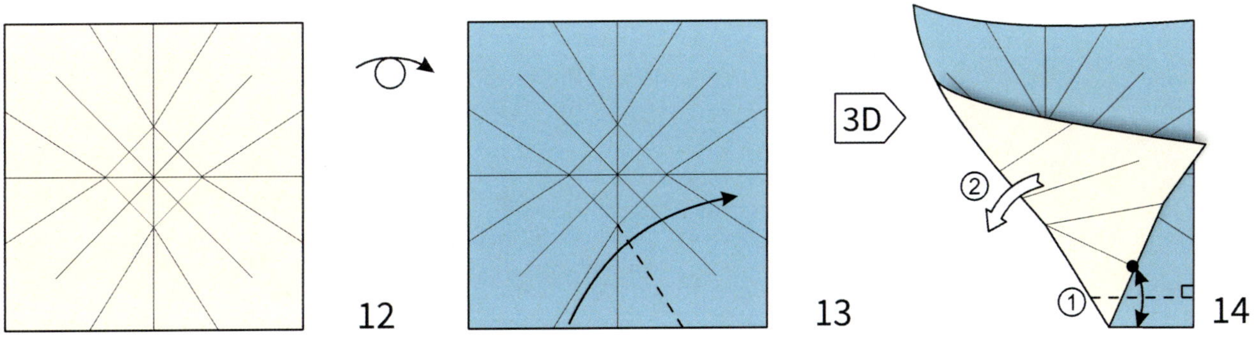

6

7

①

②

8

9

7-8

10

11

12

13

Be sure that you have here the colored side up.

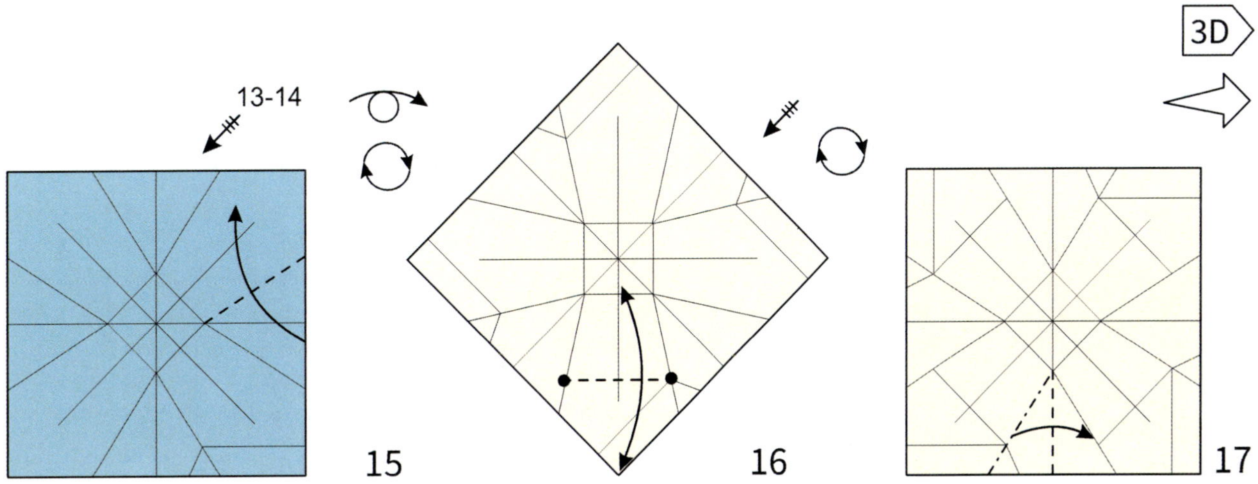

3D

②

①

14

13-14

15

16

3D

17

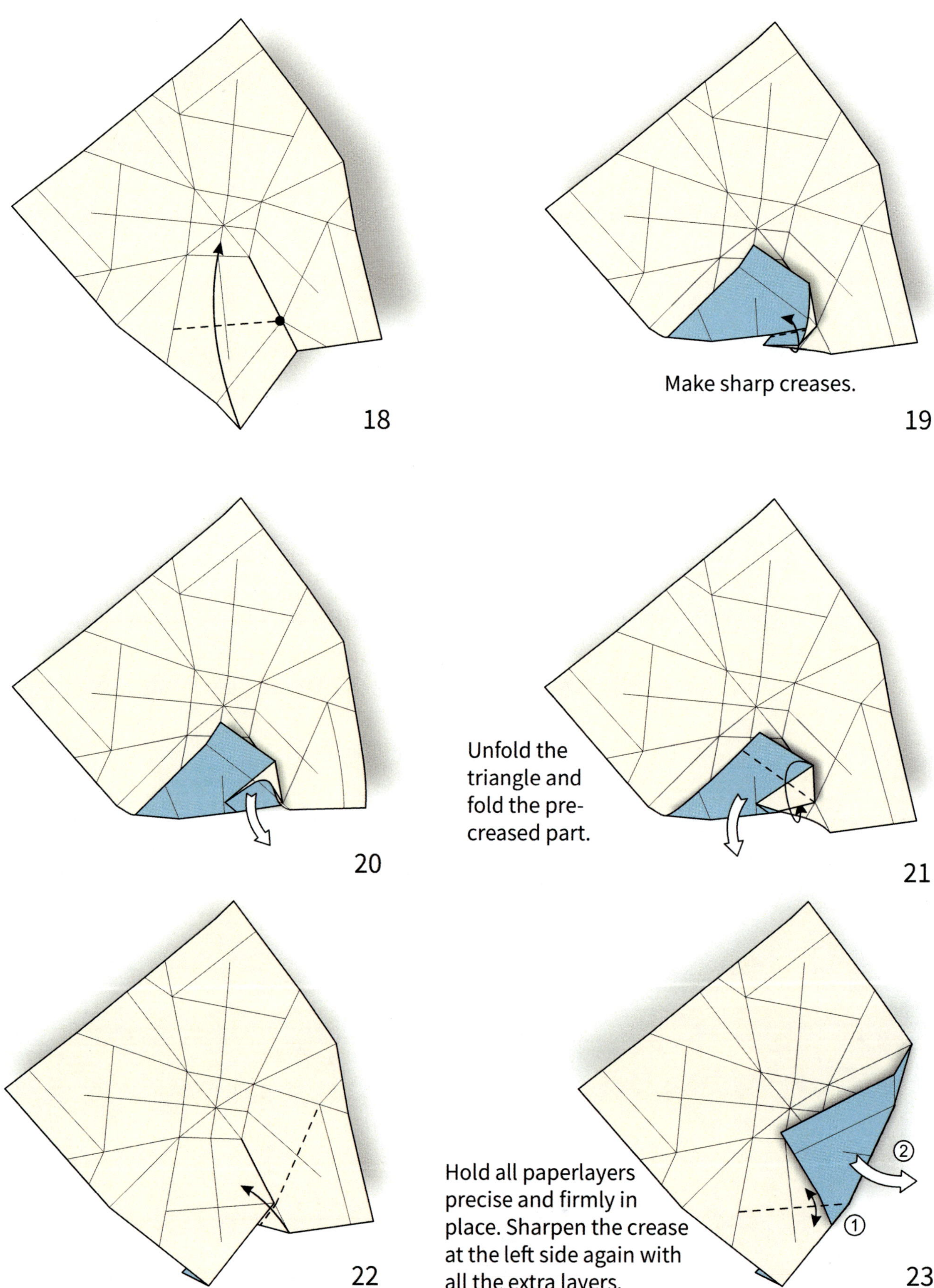
18
Make sharp creases.
19
20
Unfold the triangle and fold the pre-creased part.
21
22
Hold all paperlayers precise and firmly in place. Sharpen the crease at the left side again with all the extra layers.
①
②
23

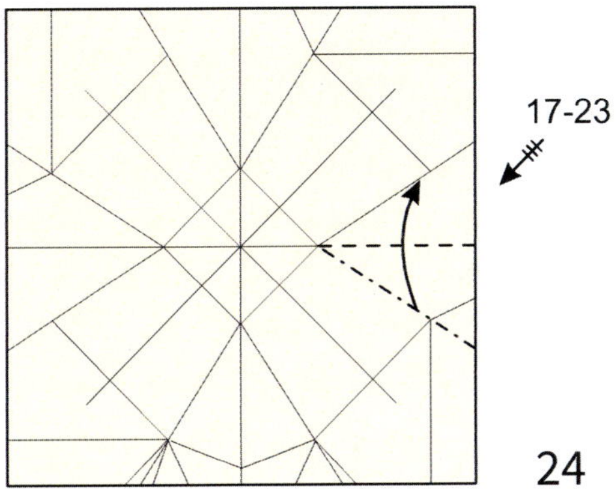

17-23

24

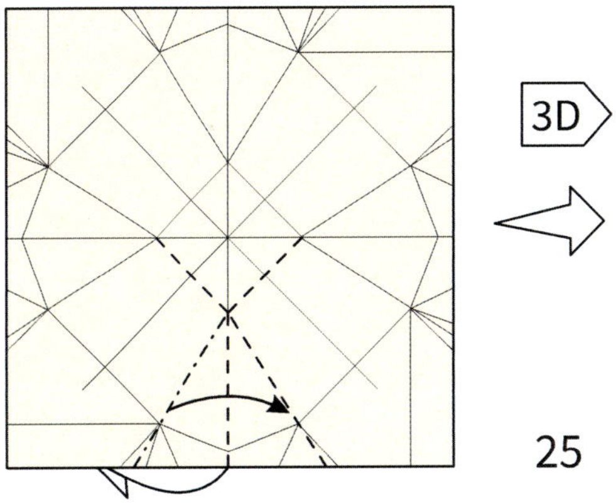

3D

25

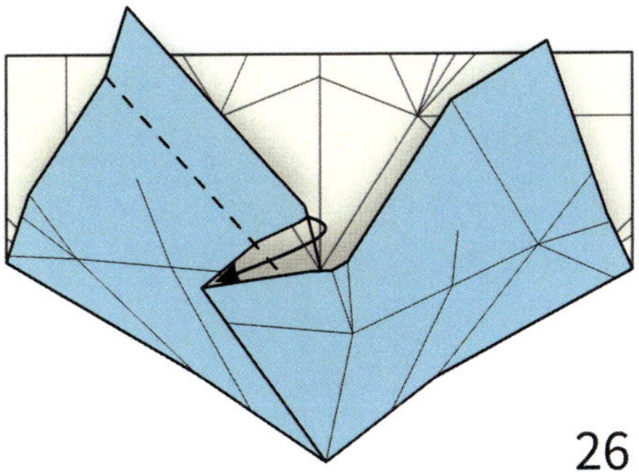

25-26

26

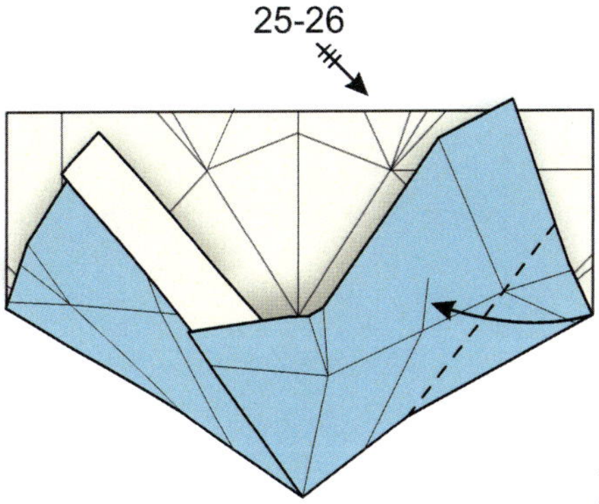

27

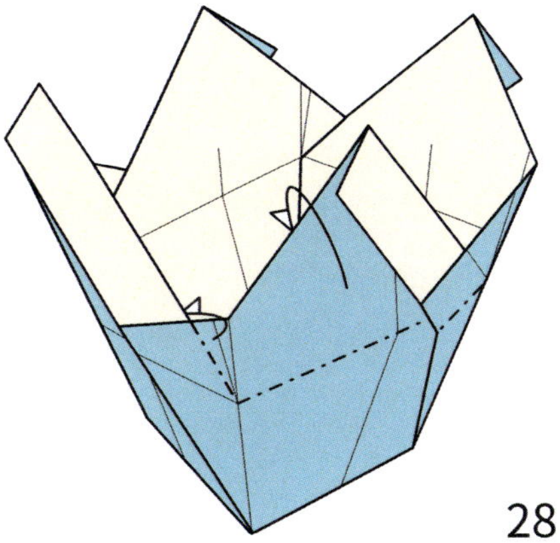

28

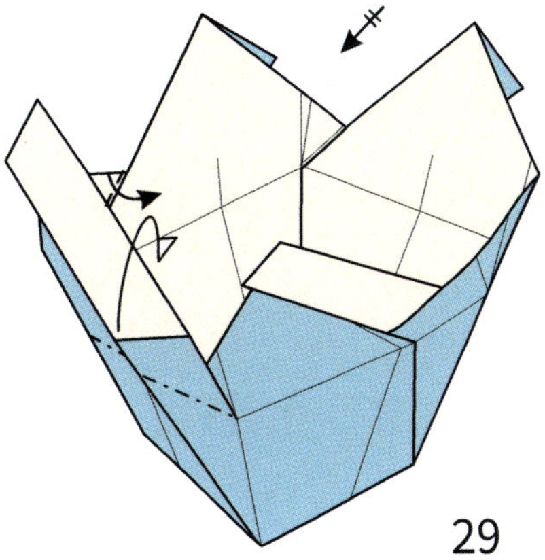

29

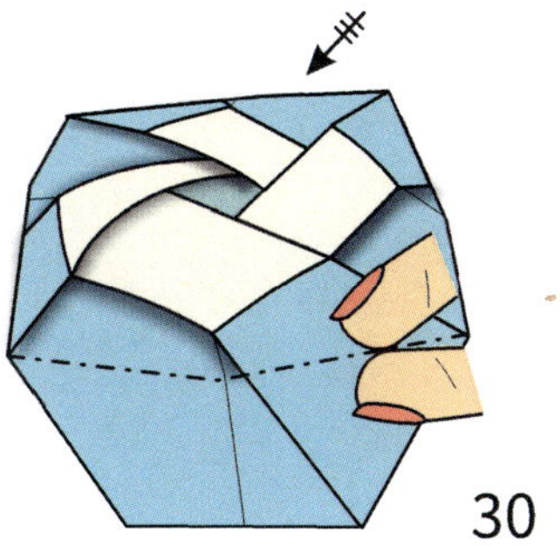

30

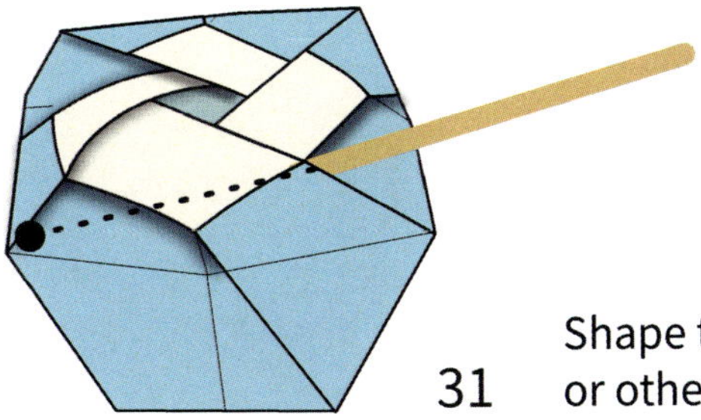

31

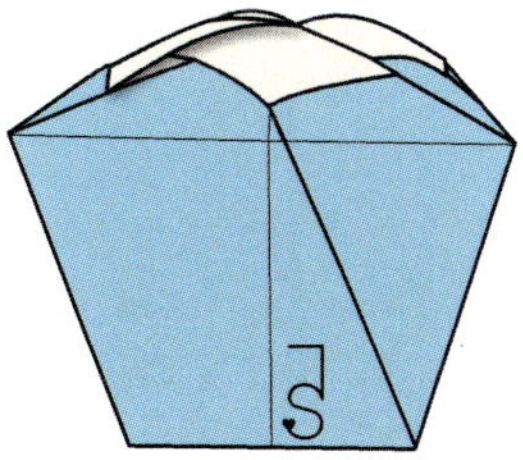

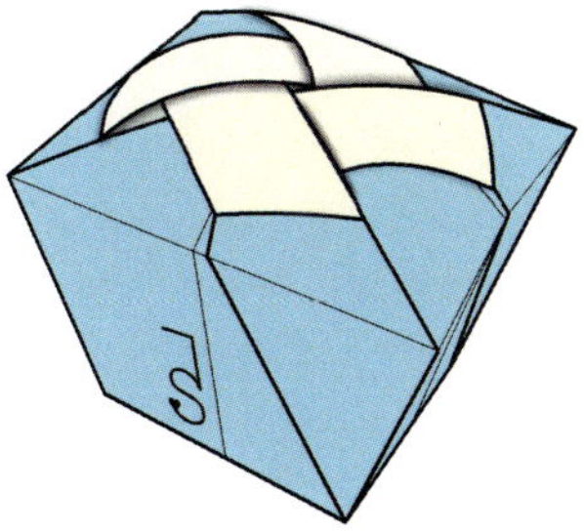

Shape the inner corners with a skewer or other tool. The top becomes a dome.

# Sycee Basket

08-04-2023

The Sycee or Yuanbao is a medium of exchange that was used in China until the beginning of the 20th century. These were made of gold or silver and usually in the shape of a boat. When I came up with this basket (it is a variation of my Easter Candy Basket which you can find on my YouTube channel) several people thought of the Sycee. Hence, the name.

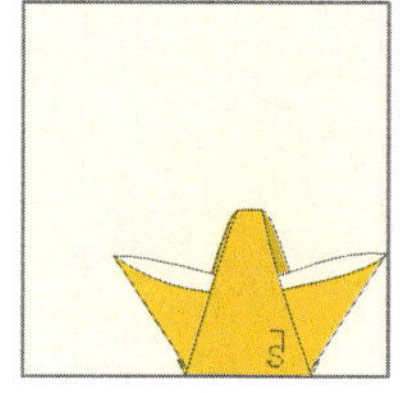

**Paper:**
**- 15x15 cm duo color**

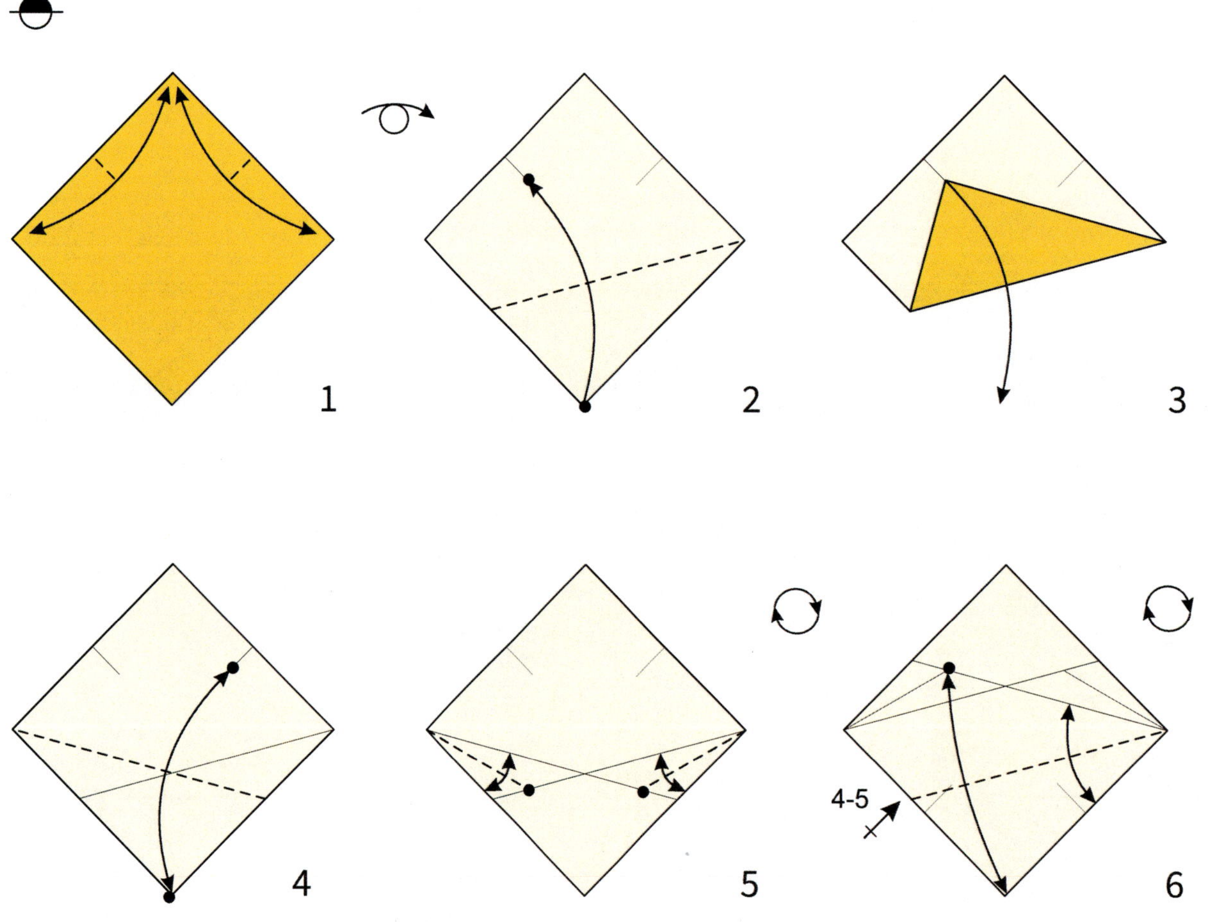

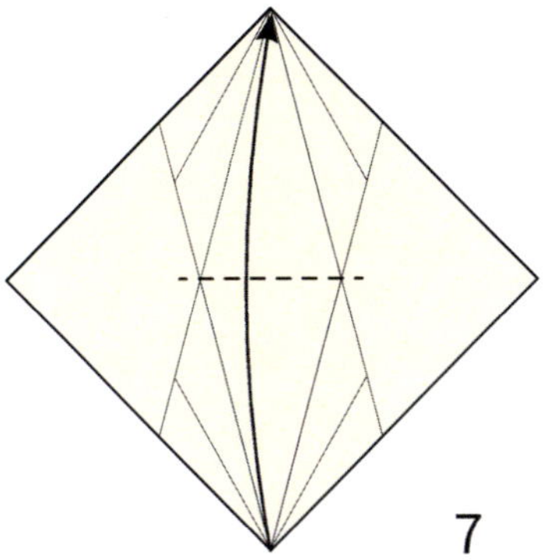

3D

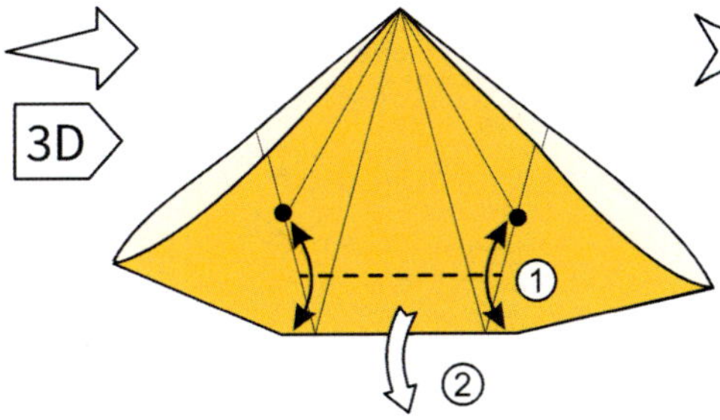

Fold to the marks. For a smaller bottom fold the crease lower. 8

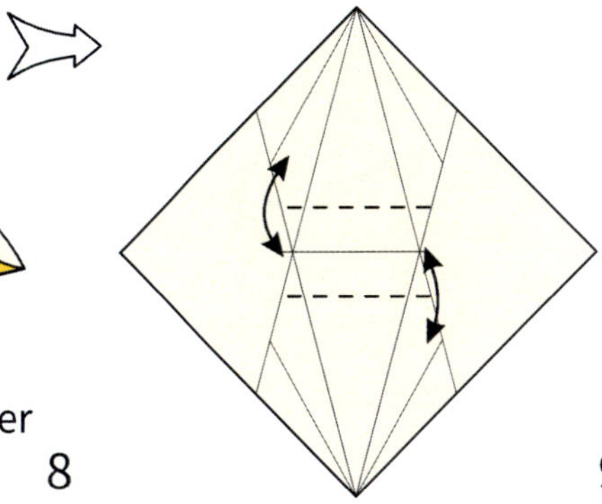

7

9

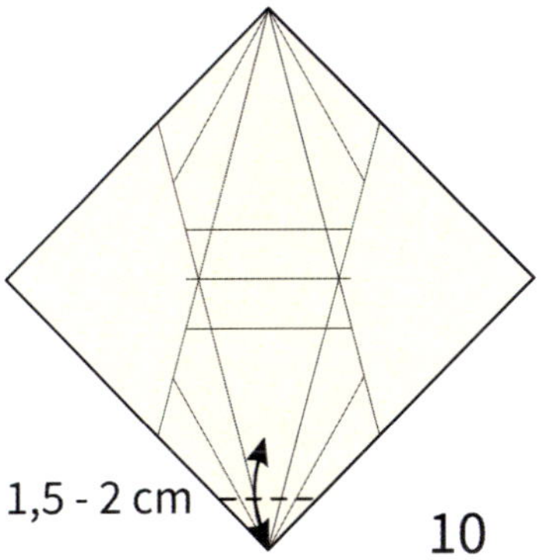

1,5 - 2 cm

10

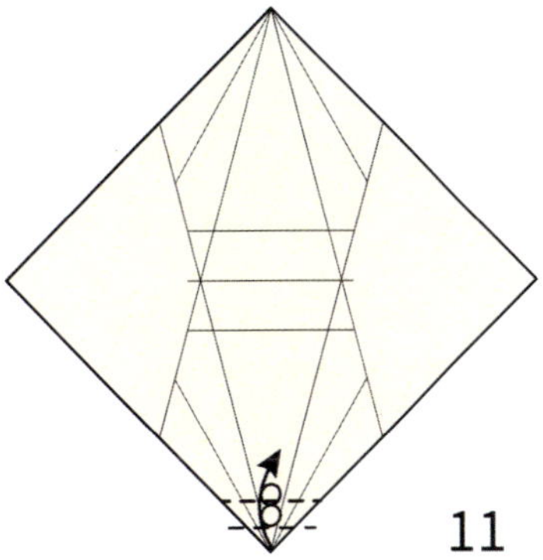

11

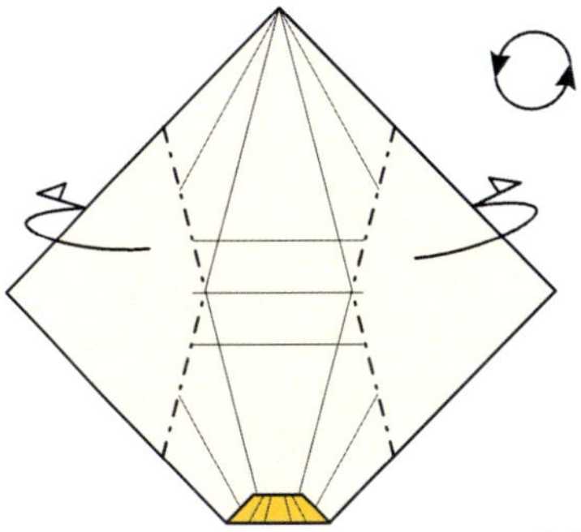

12

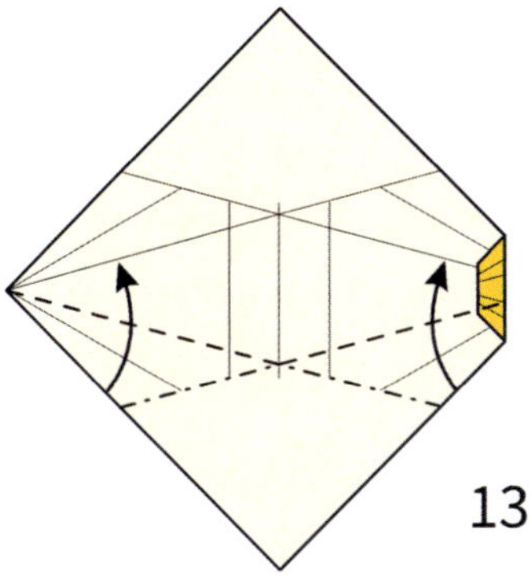

13

3D

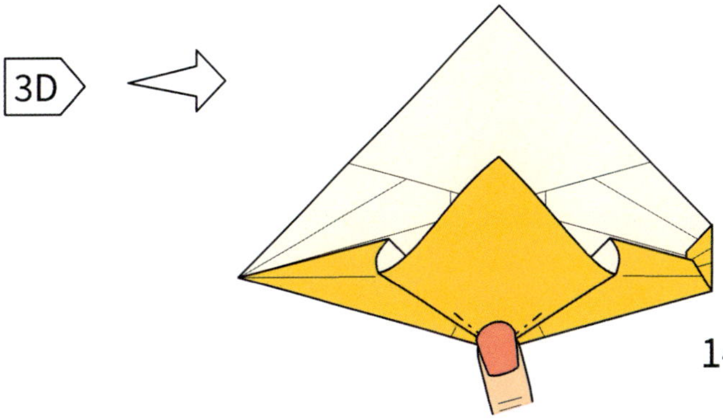

14

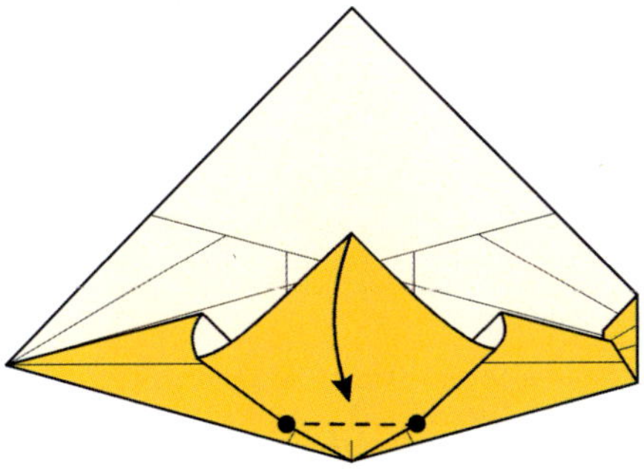

15

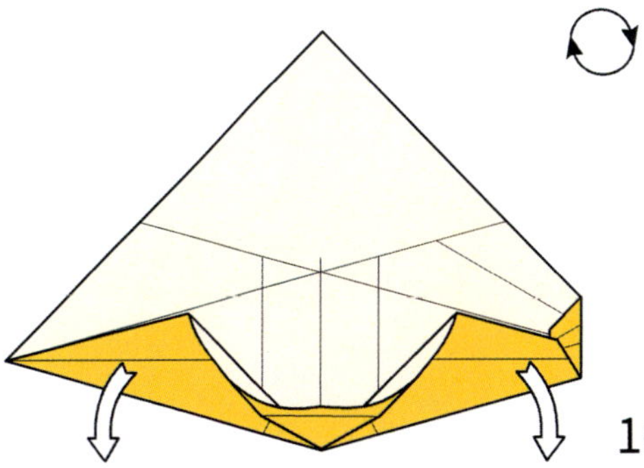

16

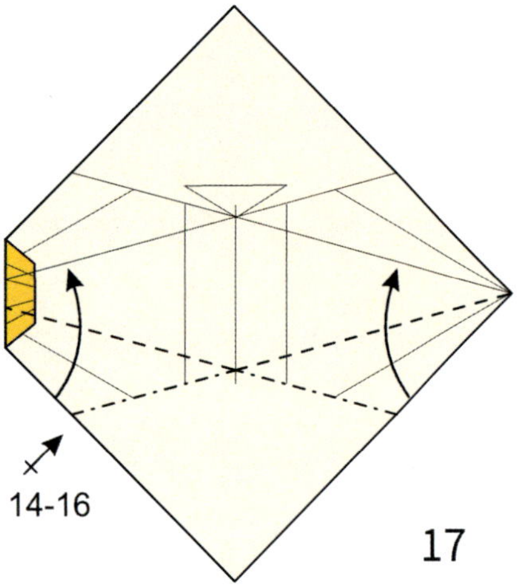

14-16
17 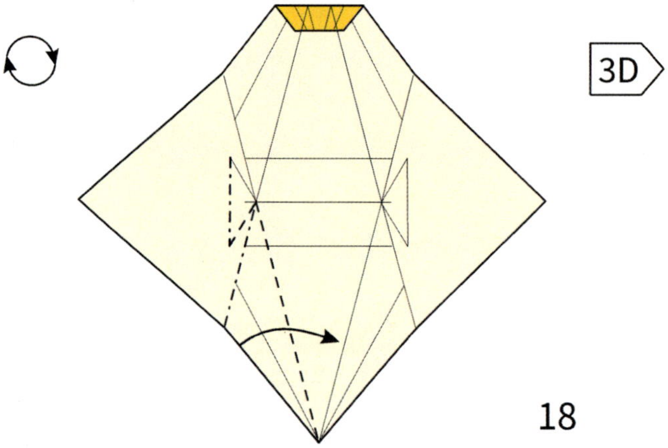
3D
18
19
18-19 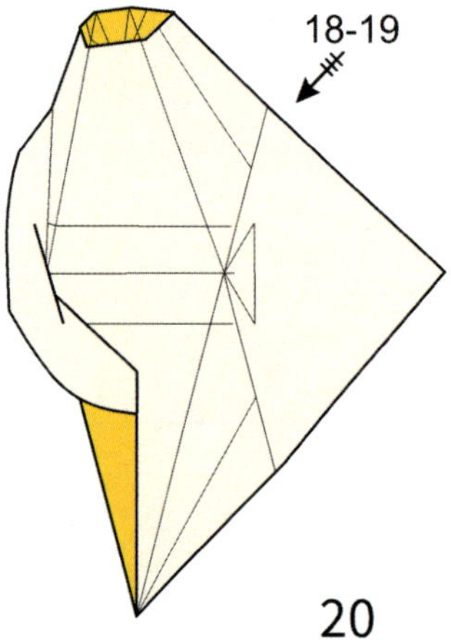
20 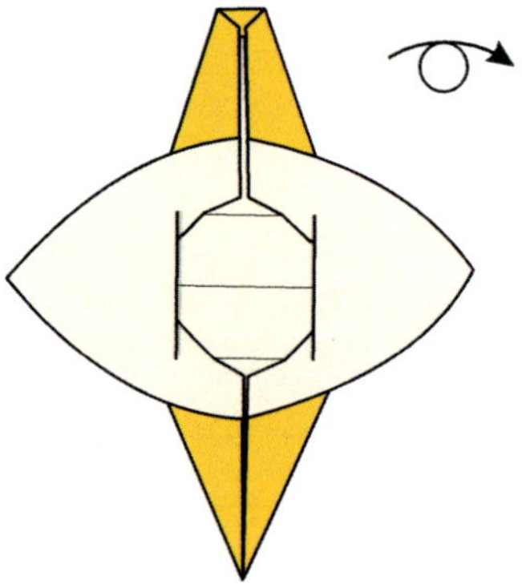
21 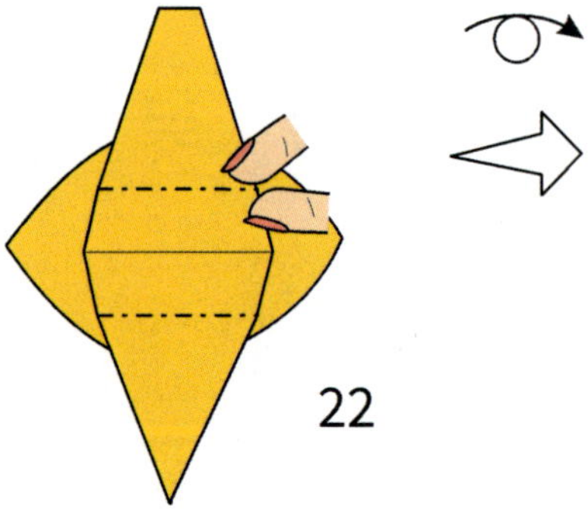
22 
23 
24 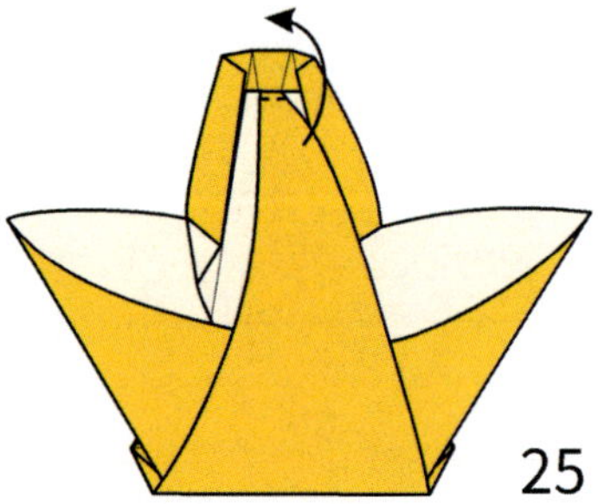
25 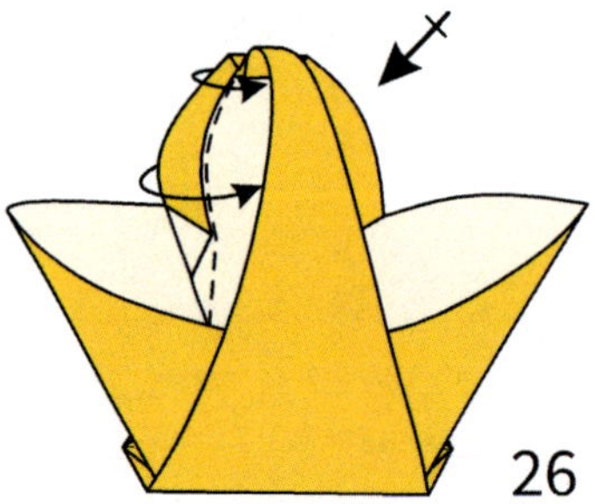
26

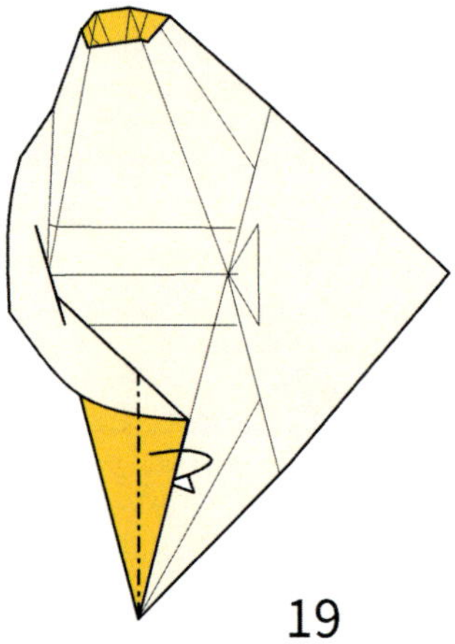

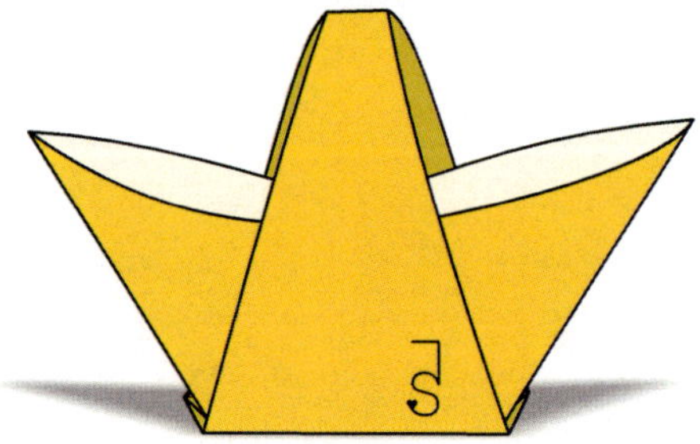

# Surprising Heart Bowl

25-06-2015

This heart bowl is a model I love so much because of it's shape. It's an 'oldie'. It looks very easy to fold but there are a few uncommon steps. It's the last step that gives the bowl and the hearts their shape. I remember how surprised I was! It's great for a battery light or for some sweeties inside.

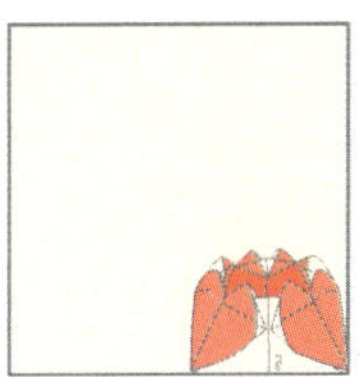

Paper:
- 15x15 cm duo color

Colored side is the heart color

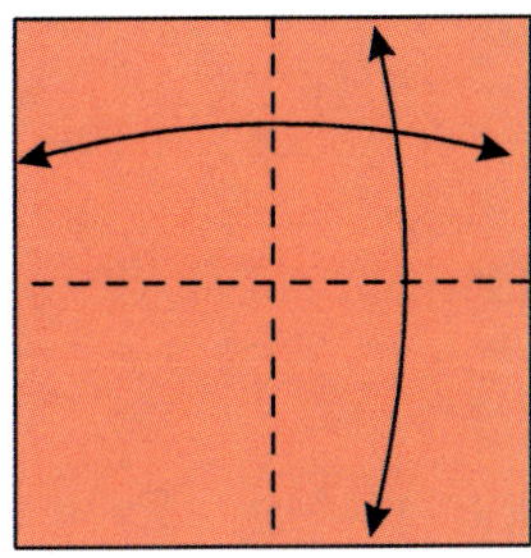

1

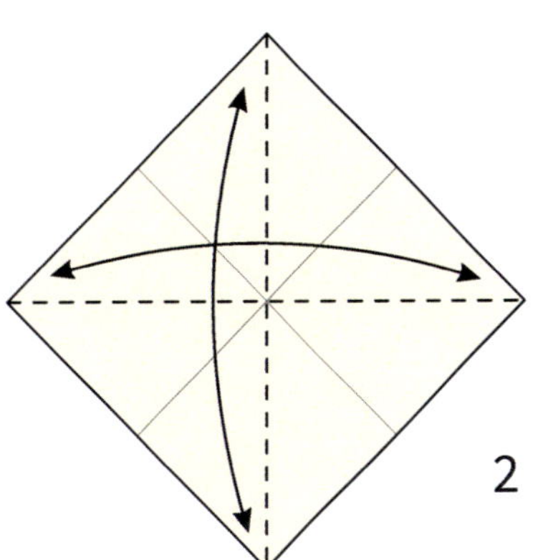

2

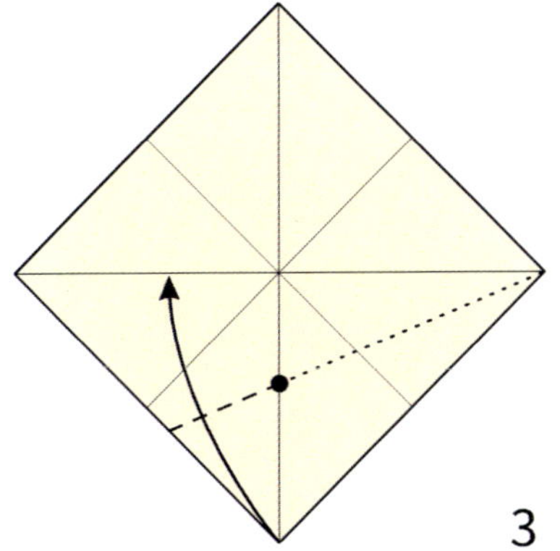

3

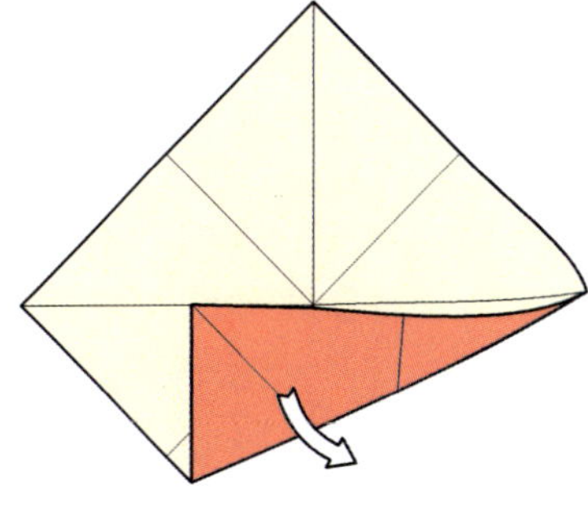

4

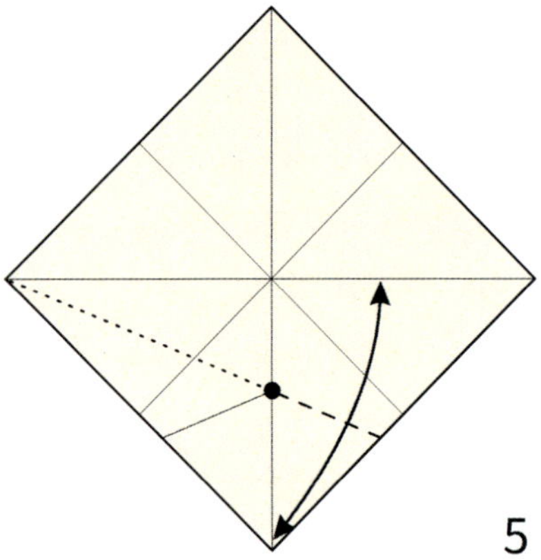

3-5

5

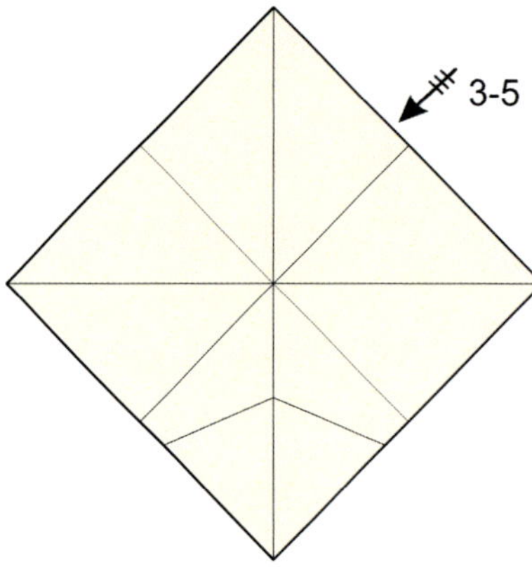

6

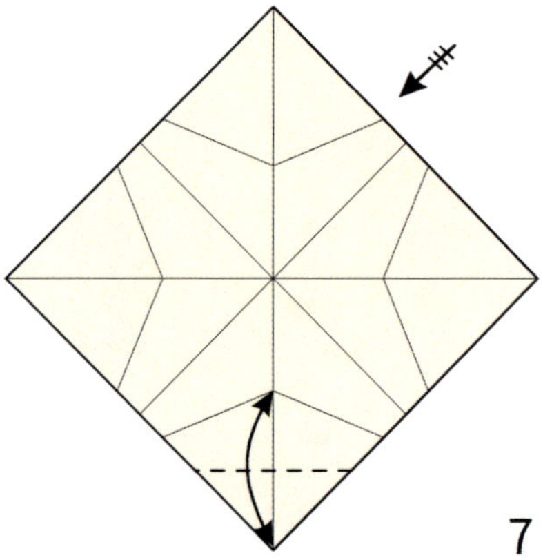

7

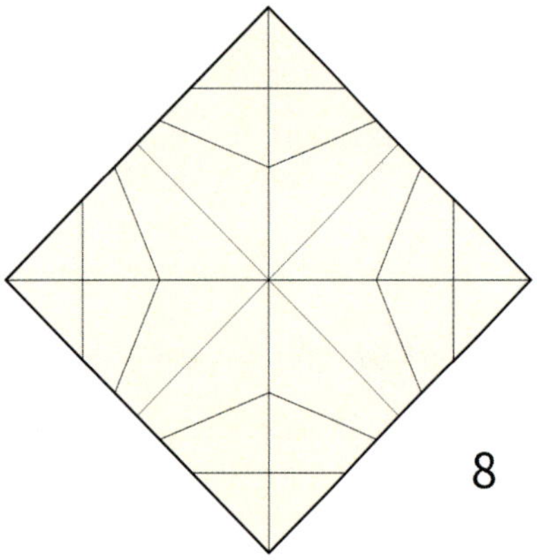

8

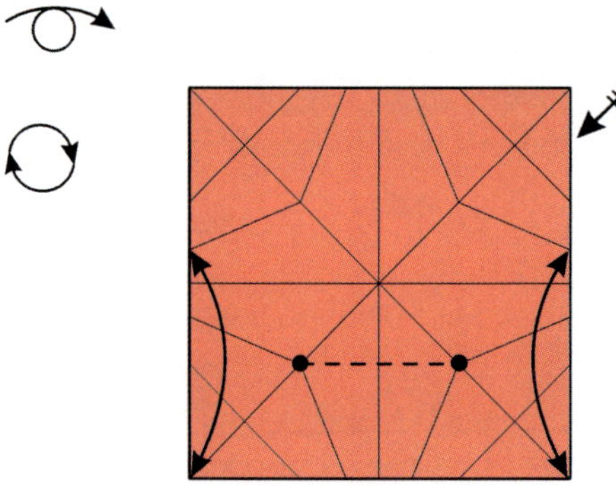

9

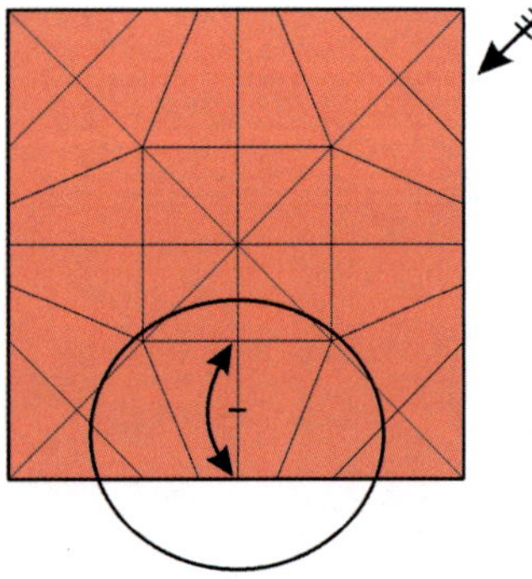

10

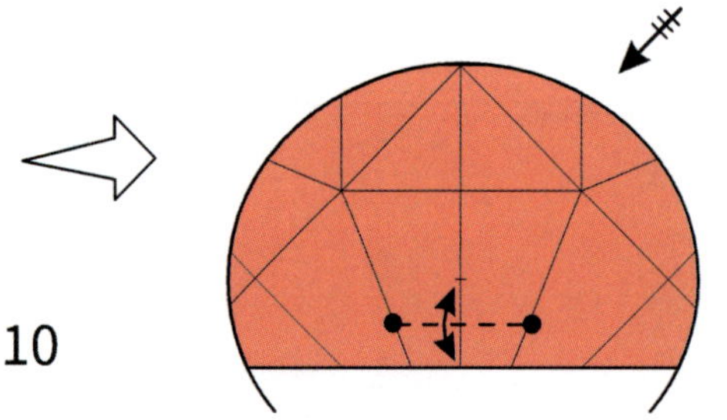

11

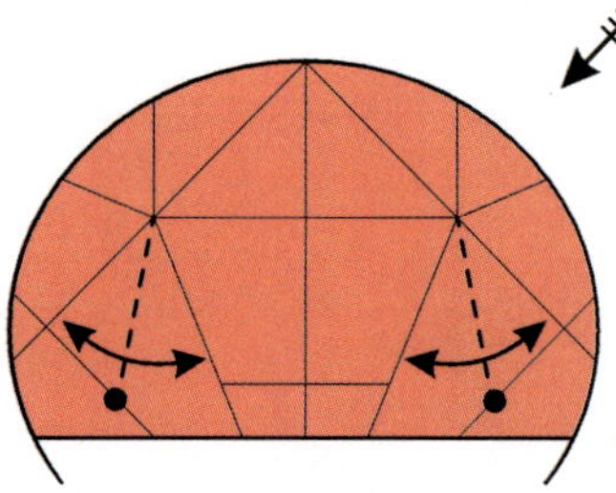

12

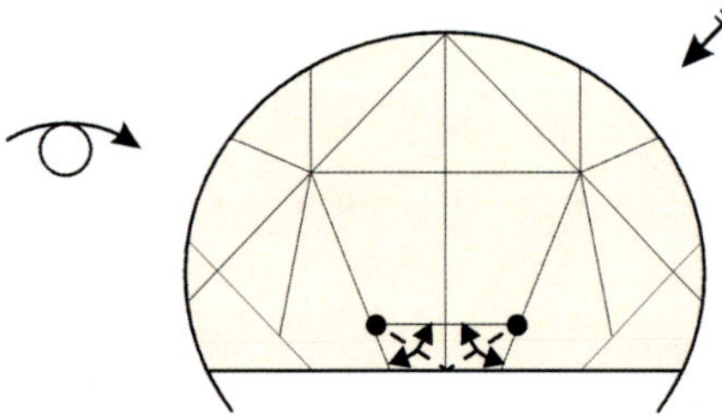

3D

13

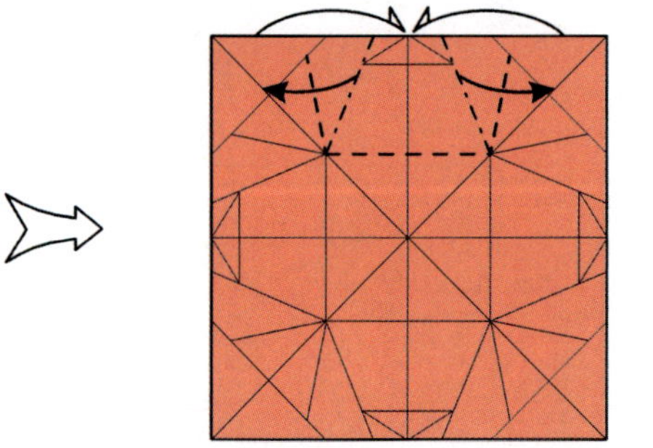

14

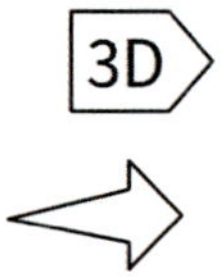

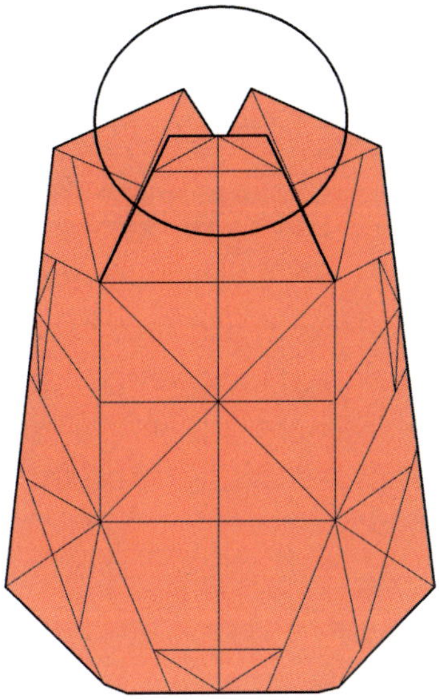

15

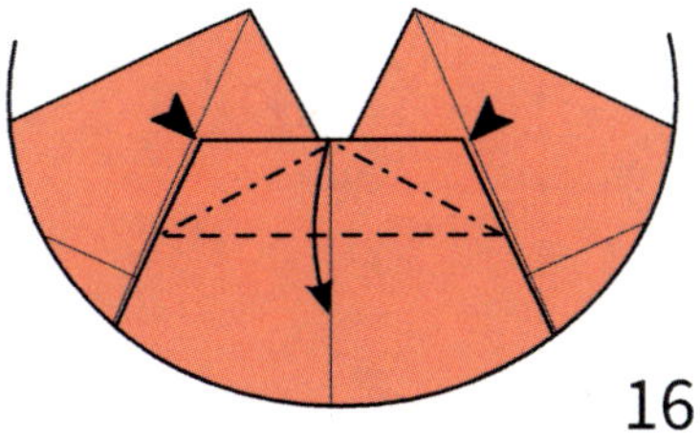

16

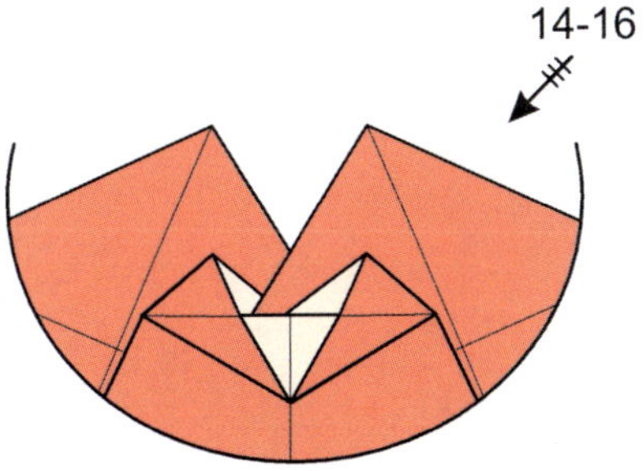

14-16

17

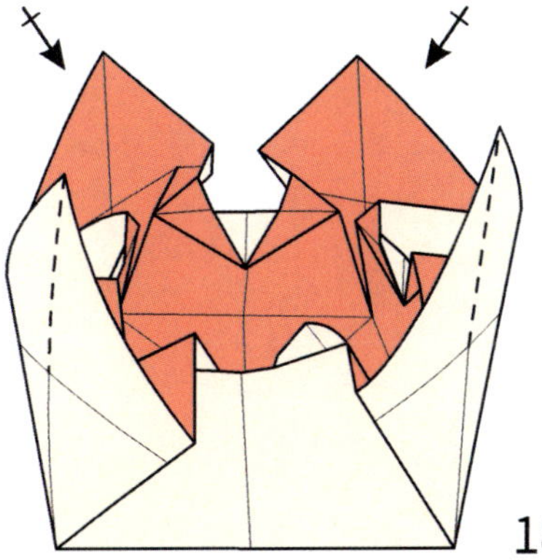

18

Sharp the valleys extra at this place.

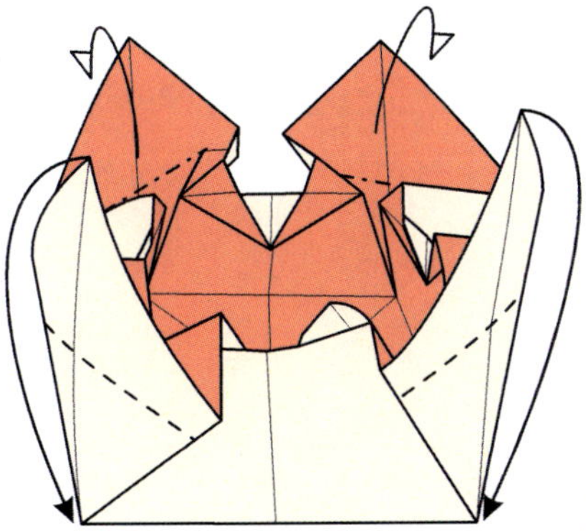

19

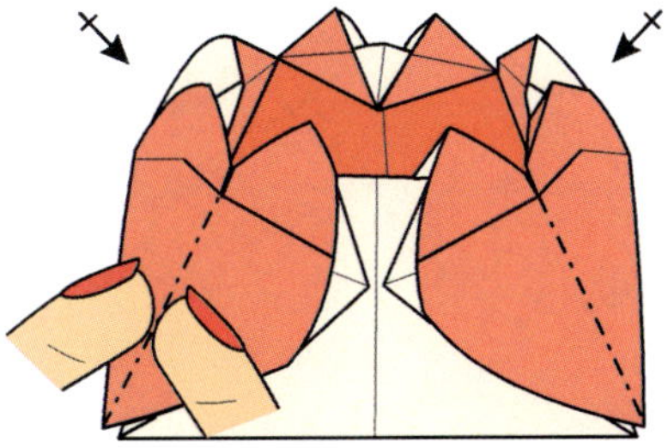

20

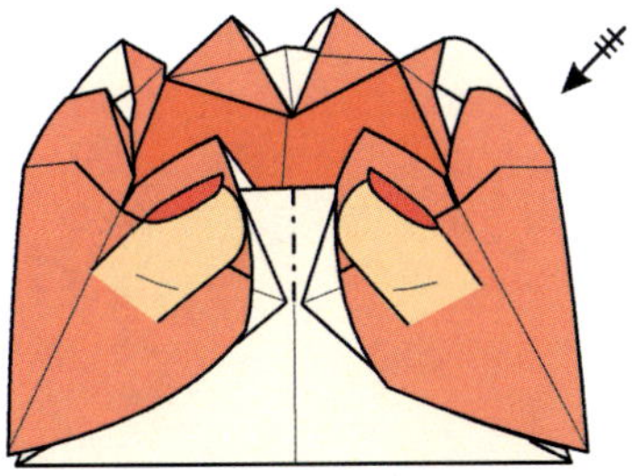

21

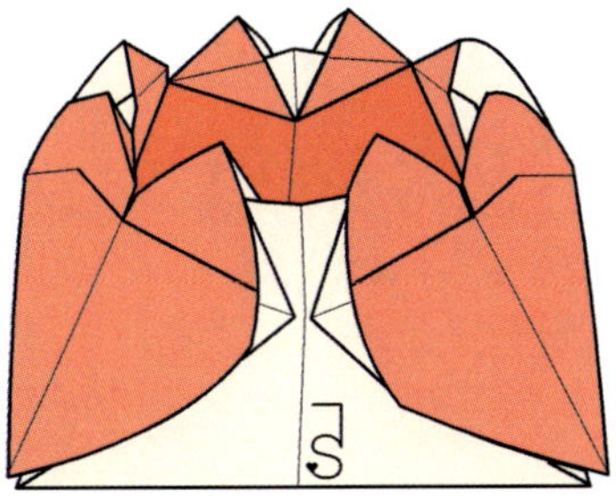

# Duo Color Dragon Basket

08-01-2024

2024 is the year of the dragon. So then publishing an origami book asks for a dragon model in it. I chose this box that I designed January the first, 2024. You can find it on my YouTube channel. I developed the color change for the head and tail a few days after. I added the earlier developed lock without glue for the handle. So here is a sturdy box for a Happy Year of the Dragon and the years to come.

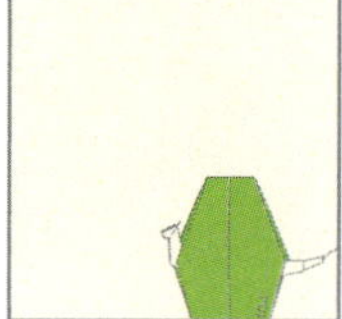

Paper:
- 15x15 cm or larger duo color or kraft paper, not too thick.

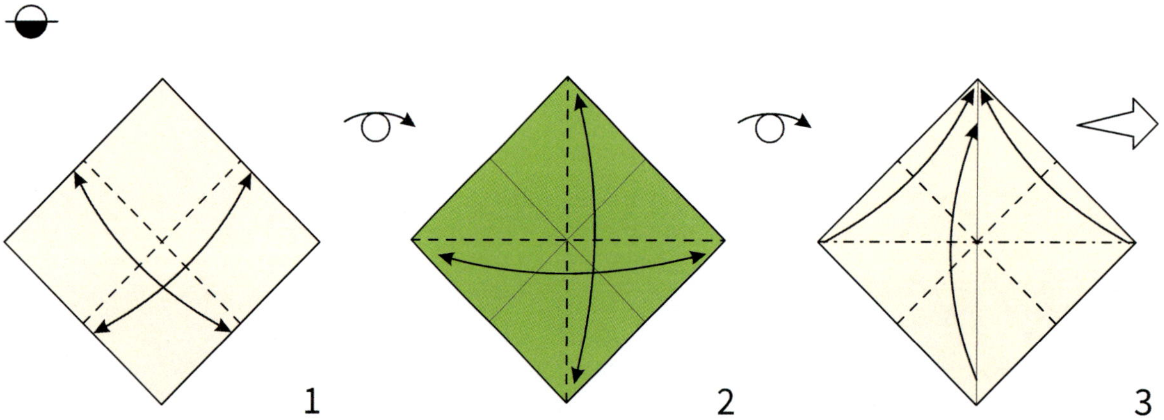

1

2

3

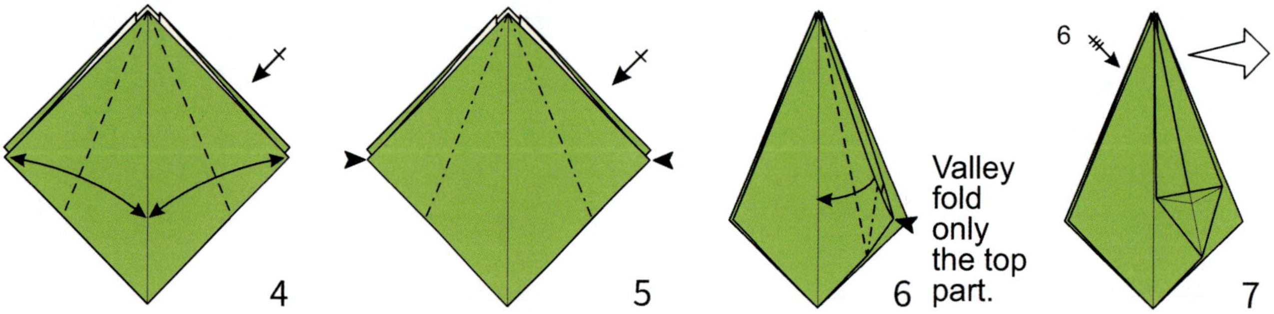

4

5

6 Valley fold only the top part.

6

7

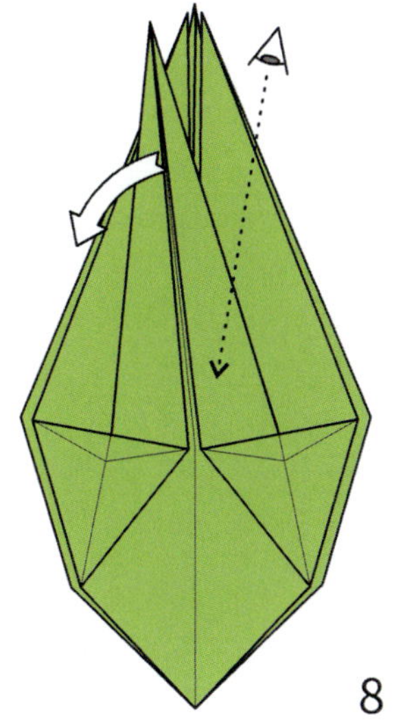

8

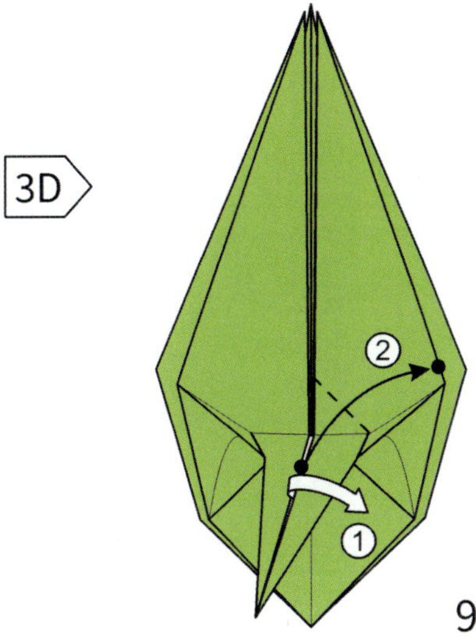


9

Pull out the paper layer from the top point from the center to the side.

10

When closing, the crease ends on the paper fold. See the marks.

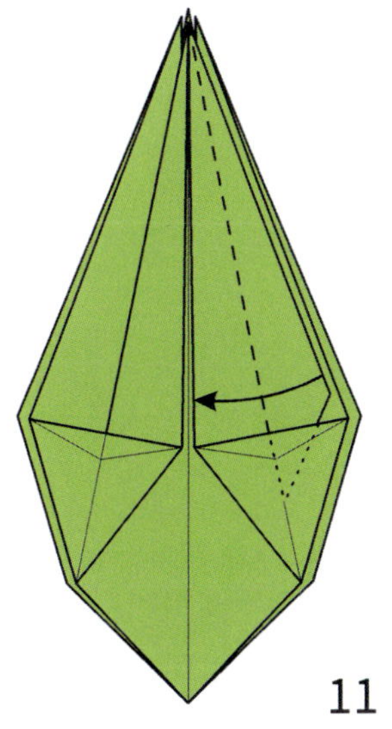

11

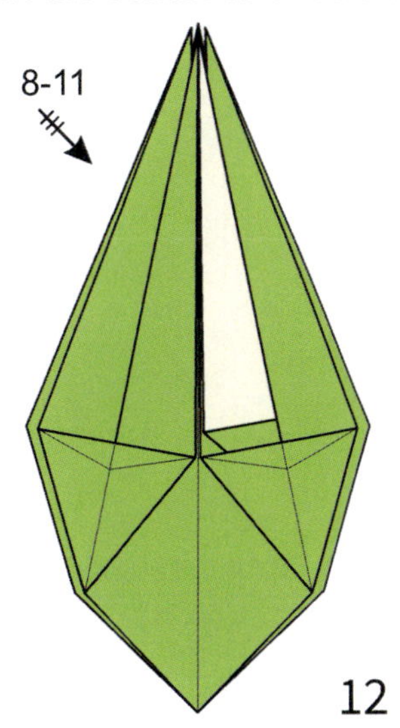


12

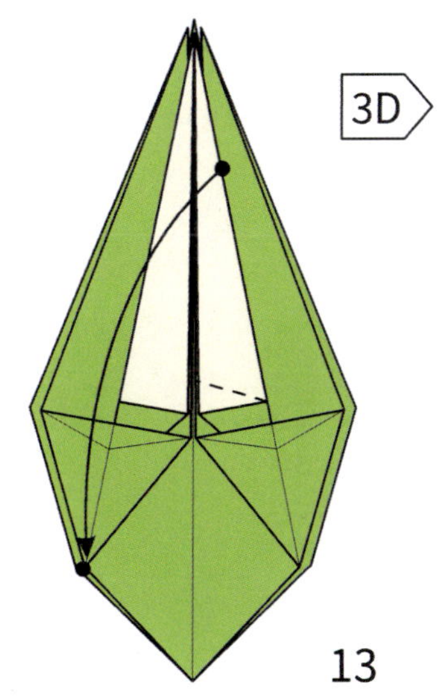


13

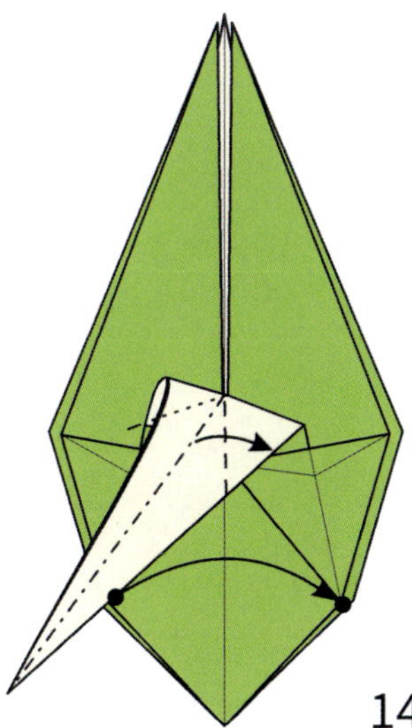

14

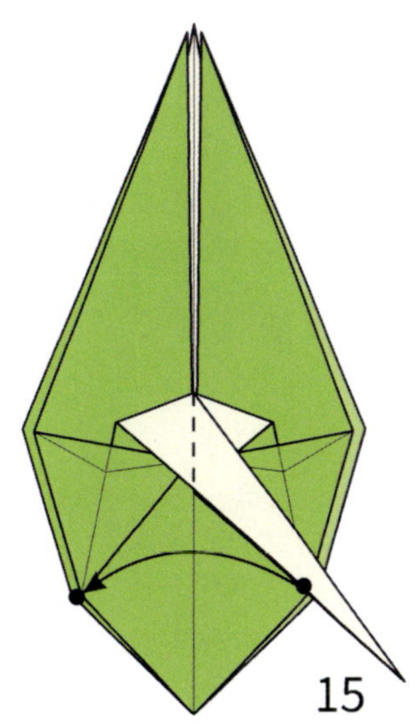

15

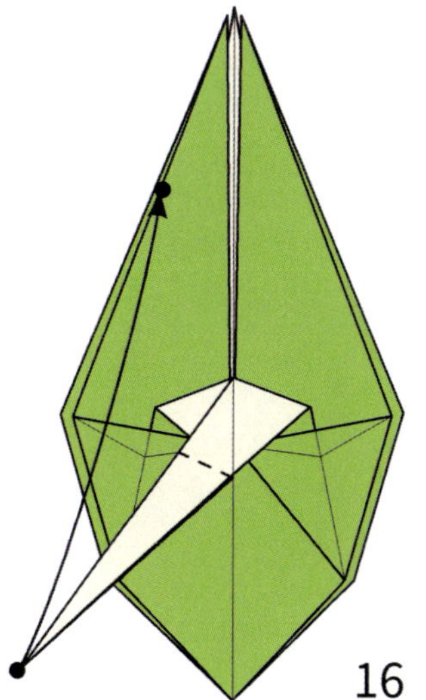

16

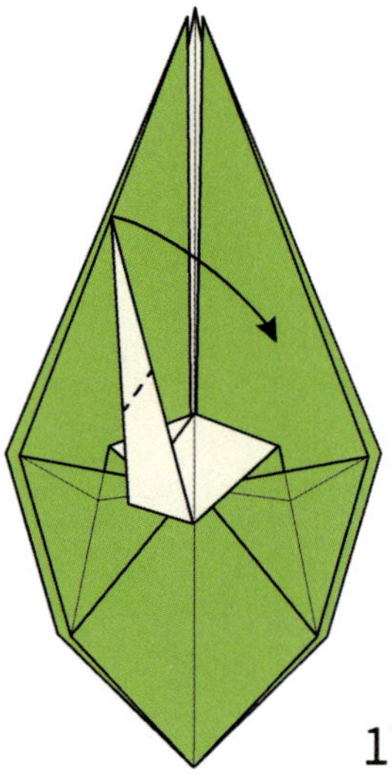

17

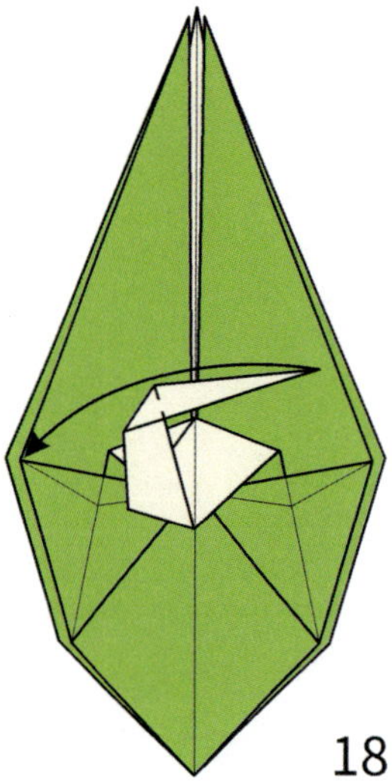

18

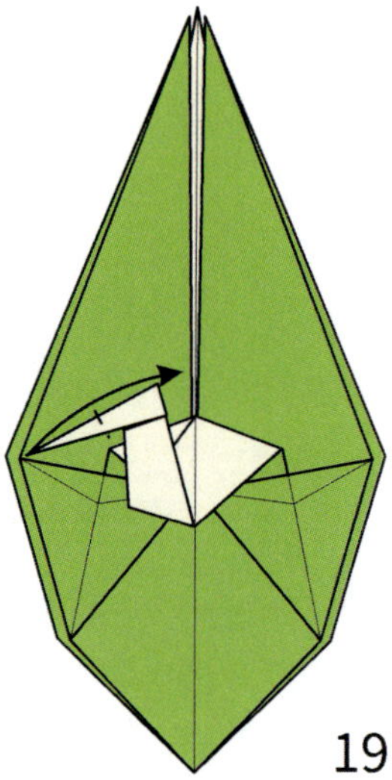

19

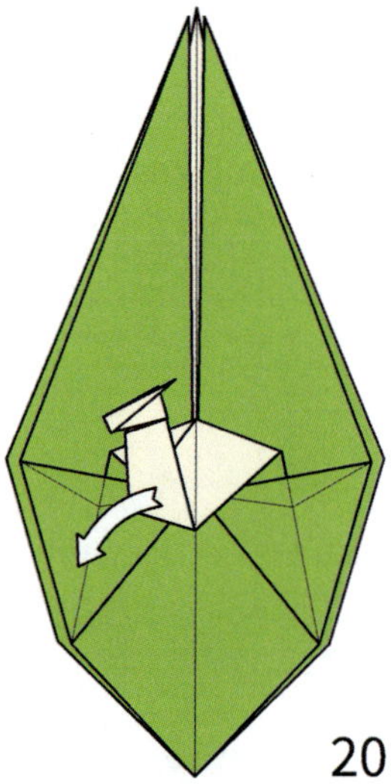

20

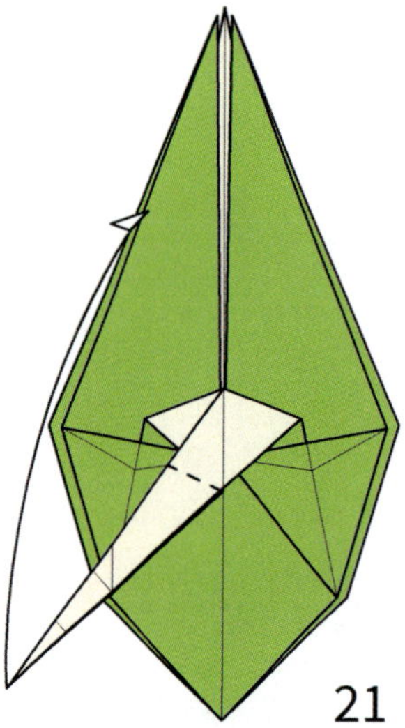

21

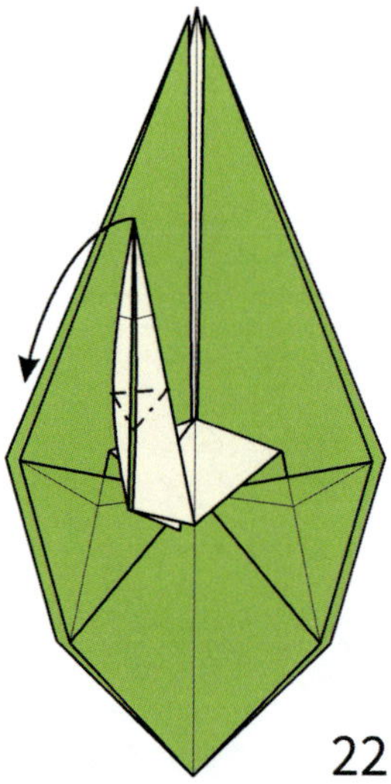

22

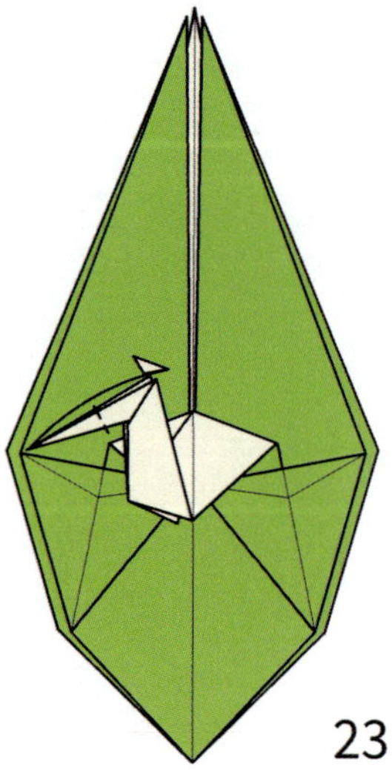

23

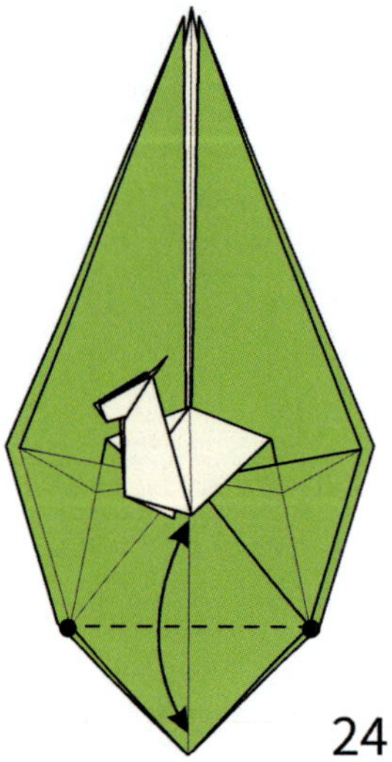

24

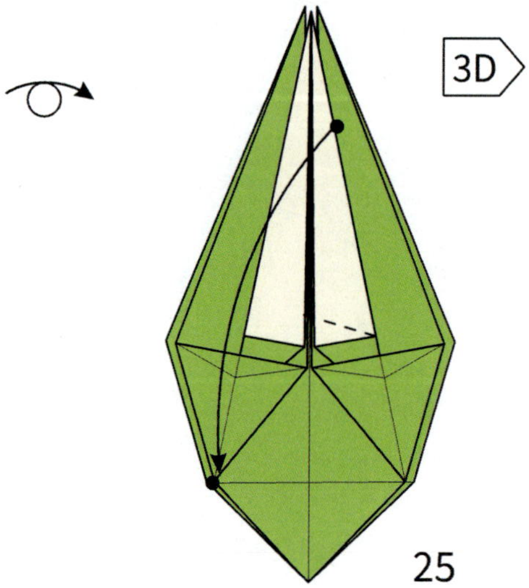

25

3D

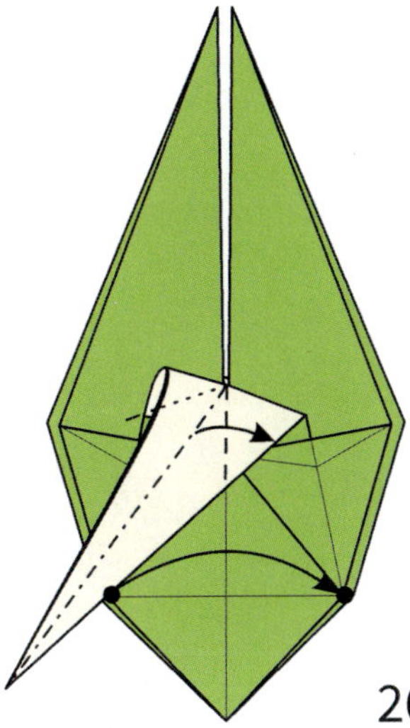

26

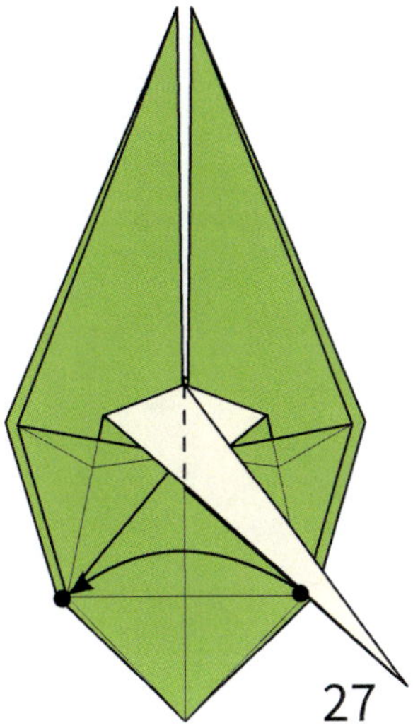

27

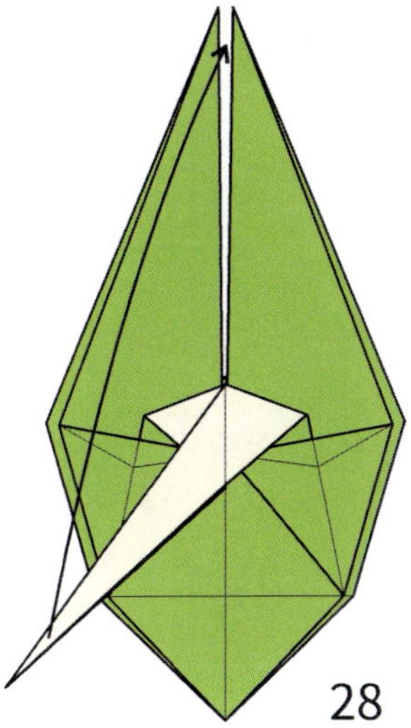

28

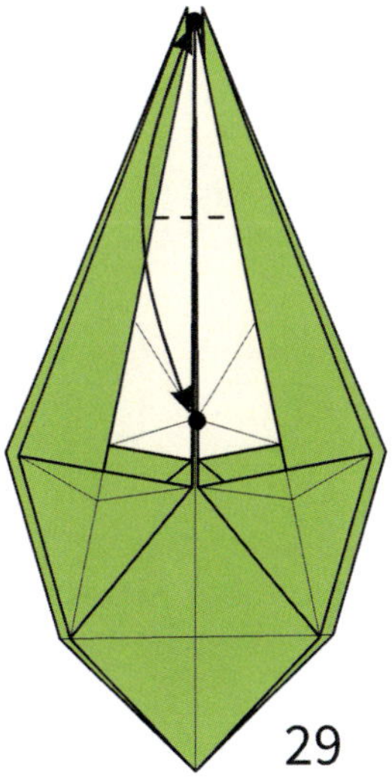

29

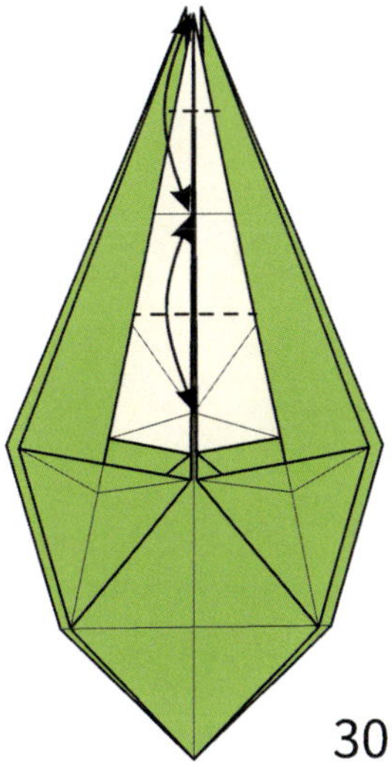

30

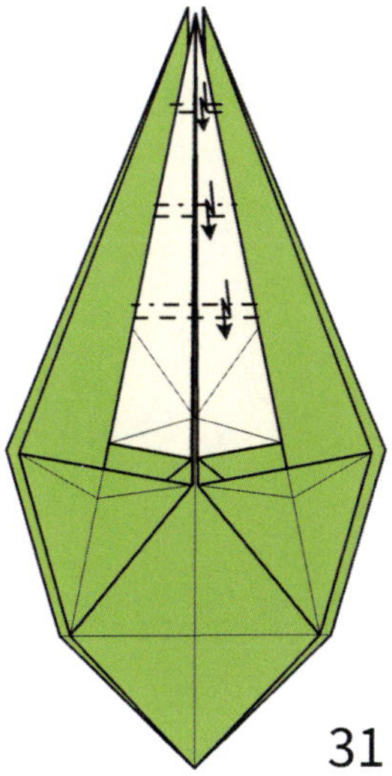

31

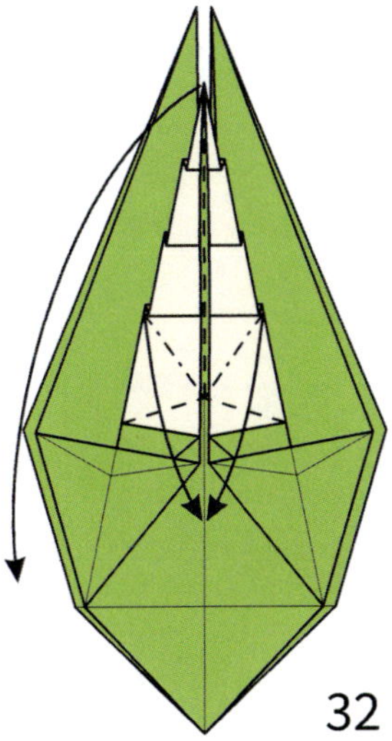

32

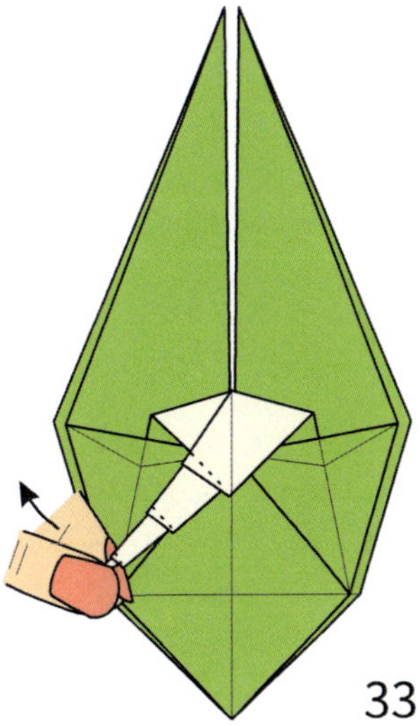

33

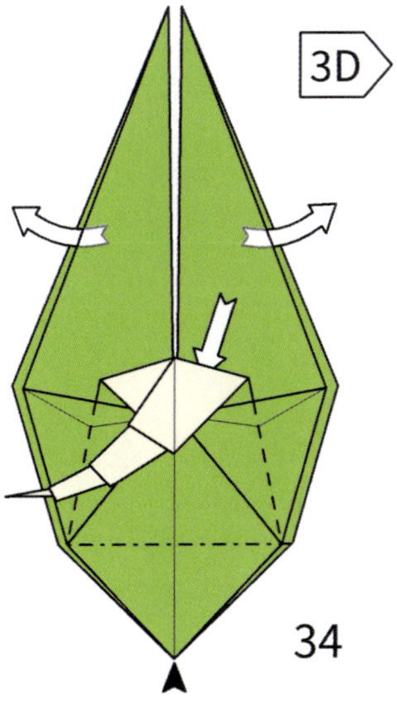

3D

34

①
②
②

35

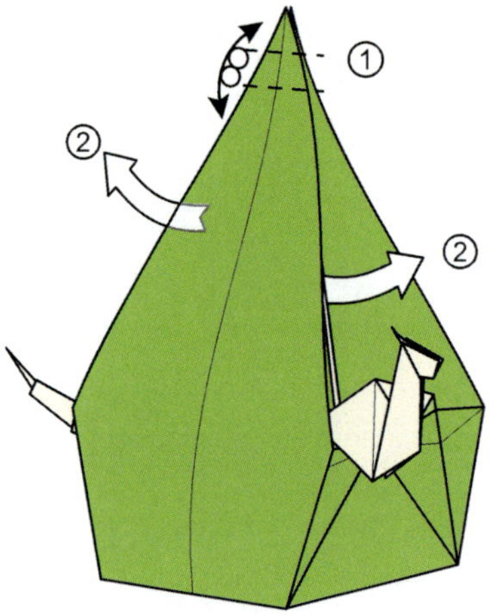

36

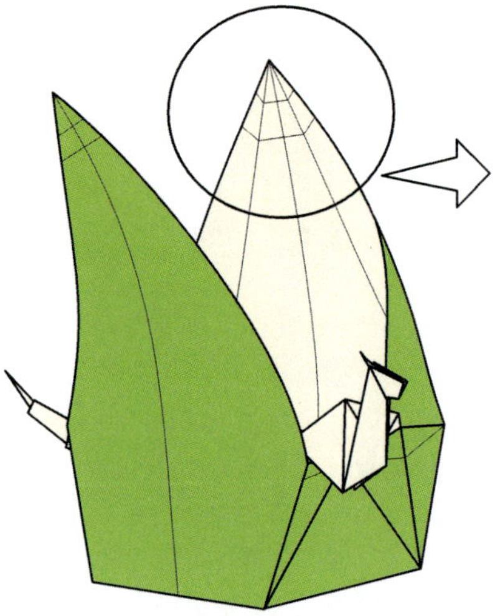

37

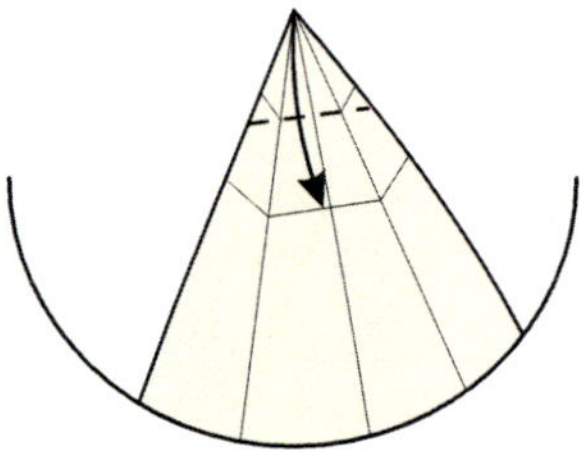

38

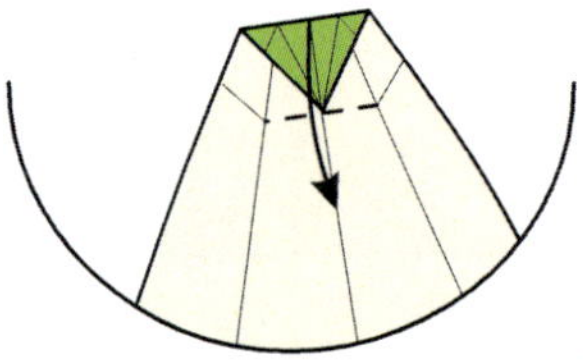

39

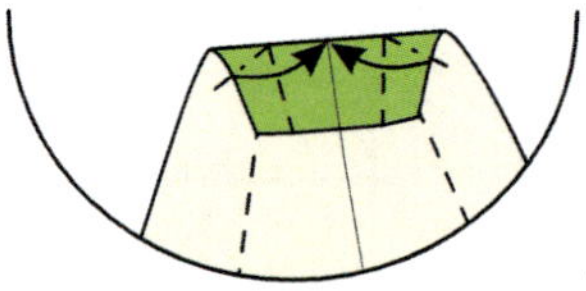

40

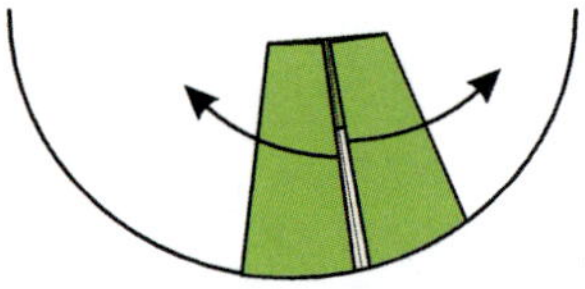

41

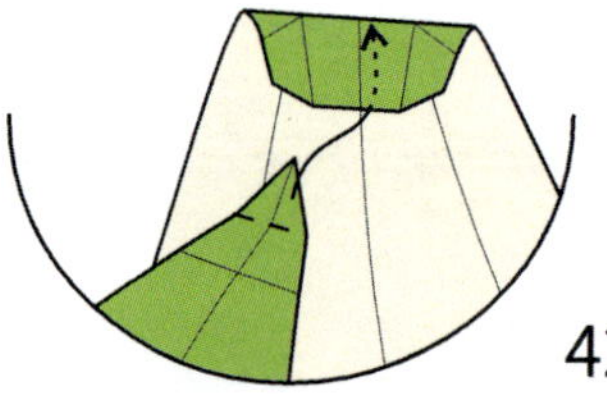

42

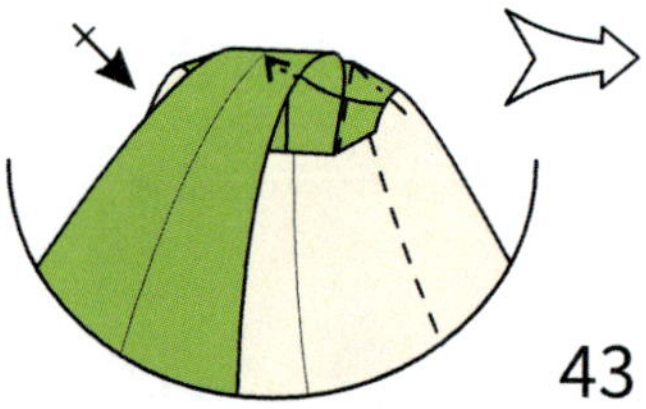

43

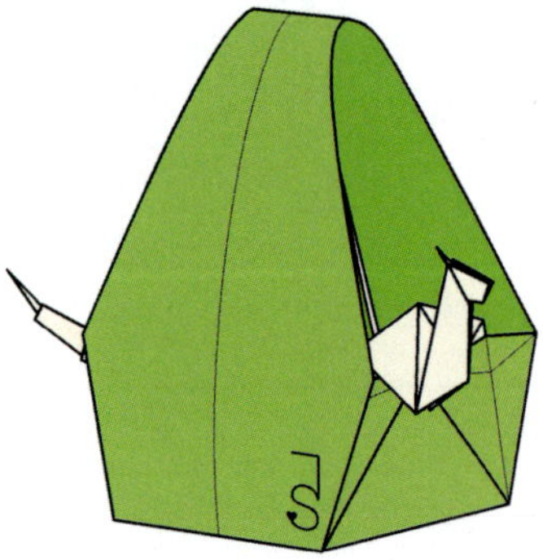

44

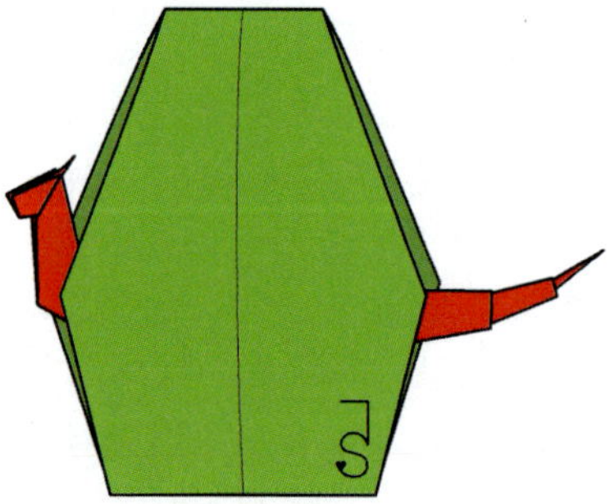

# Pyramidal Etagere Box

28-02-2020

The first 6 steps of this model were the result of just playing with A4 paper. Then I got curious if it would hold together. Well...it did and that's where the idea of an etagere box came to my mind. When I had to quickly tidy up my folds, the down part was on the box and it turned out that it could also function as a lid. In the end all that was needed was a lock to keep the candies inside during transport. Once secured you can slide the lock to open and close the box.

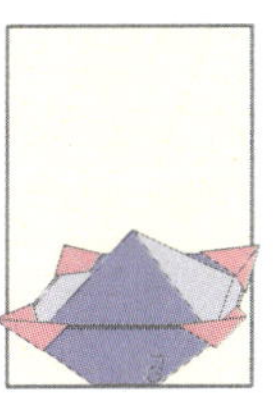

Paper:
- dish: 1 x A4/Letter-size or 4 x A6
- lid: 1 x A4/Letter-size or 4 x A6
- closure: 4 times 5 x 5 cm

You can use two separate colors for the box and lid, or use all one color.
A-size or Letter-size will both work well.
The size of the box is the width of your A-size/Letter-size paper.
I recommend for this box A6 or 1/4 of the A4/Letter-size. See the diagram beside.
For the lock, use 4 times half the width of your A-size/Letter-size. See the diagram beside.
That is now a 5,3 cm square. Also 5 cm can still be used.

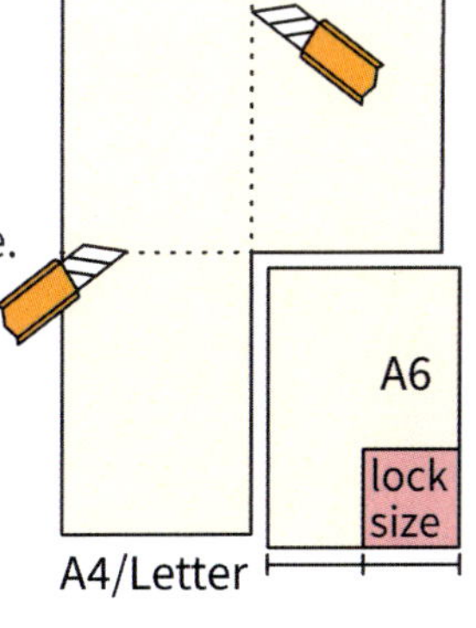


## Dish

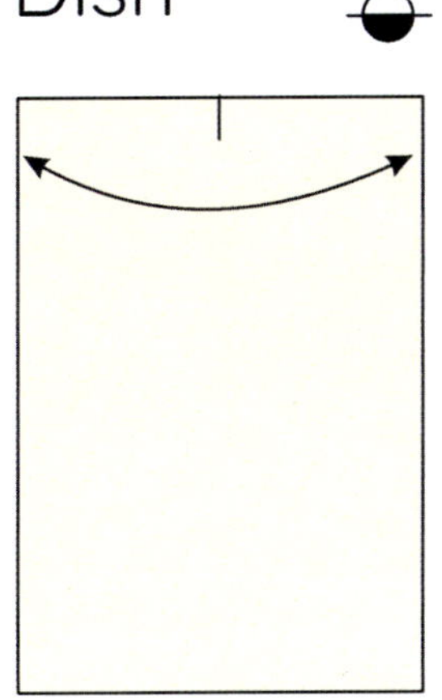

1

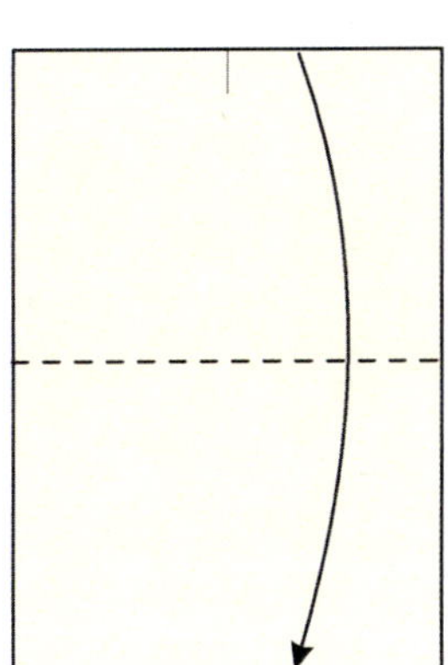

2

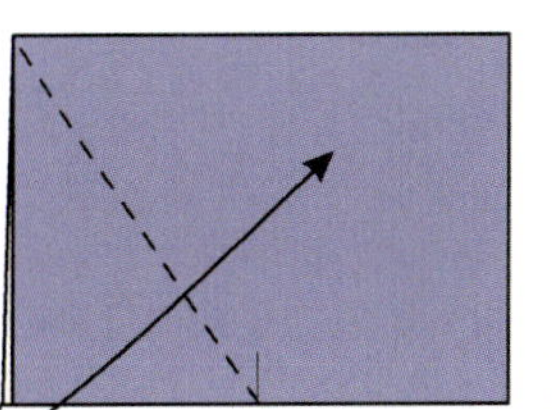

3

4

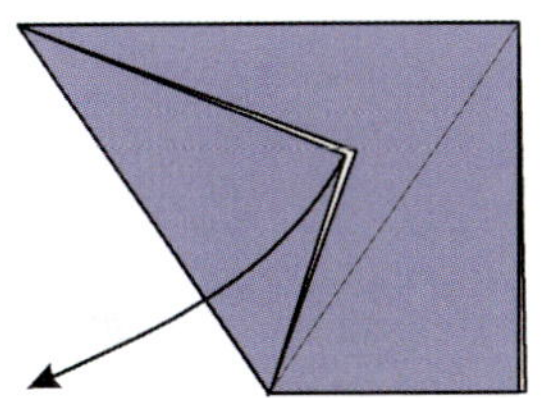

5

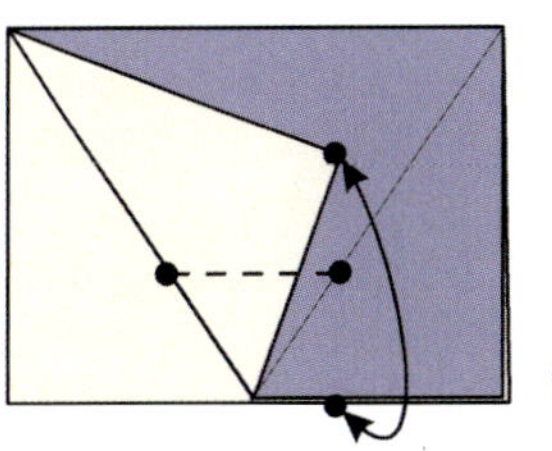

6

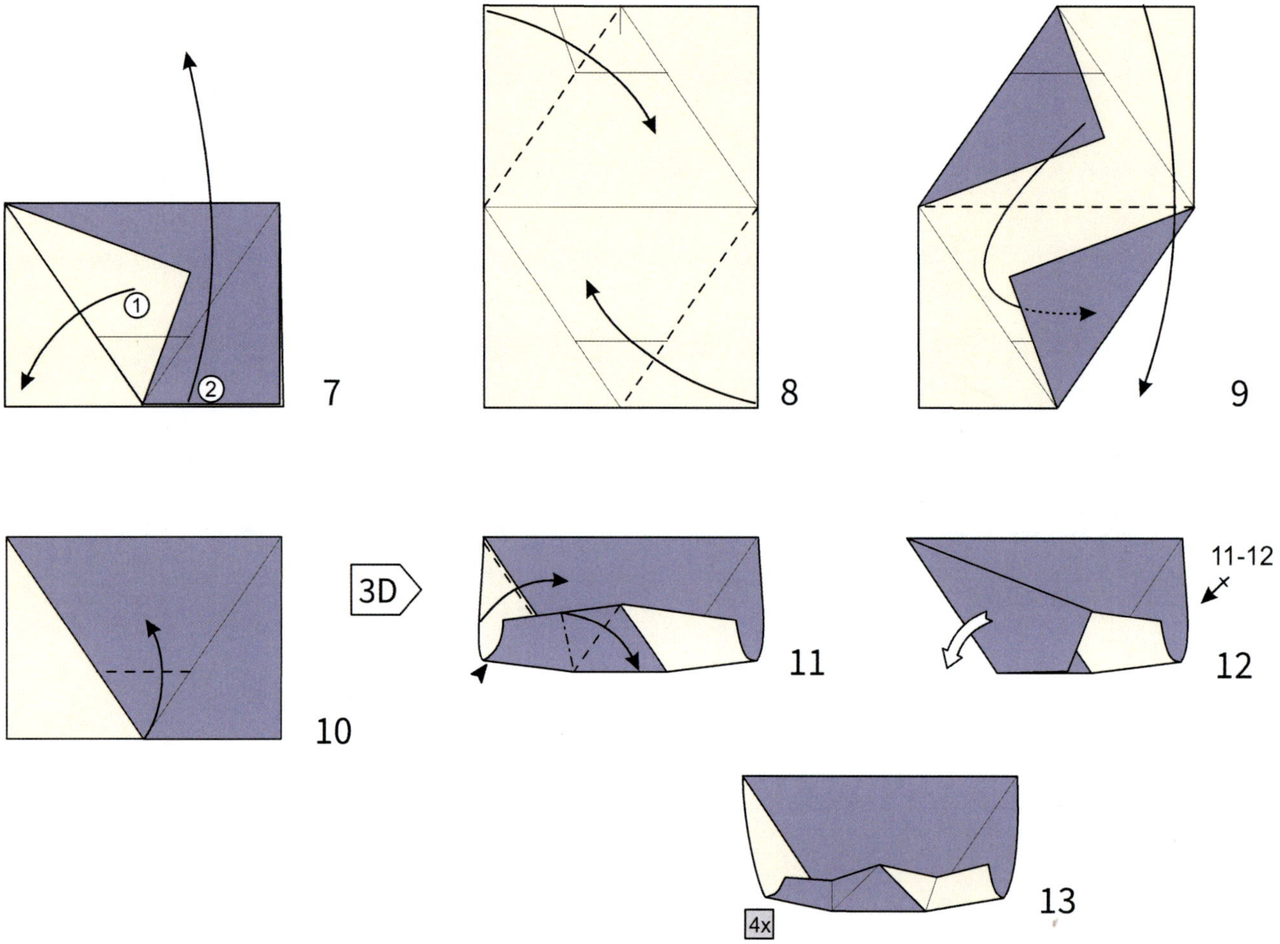

7

8

9

10

3D

11

11-12

12

13

4x

*Assembly*

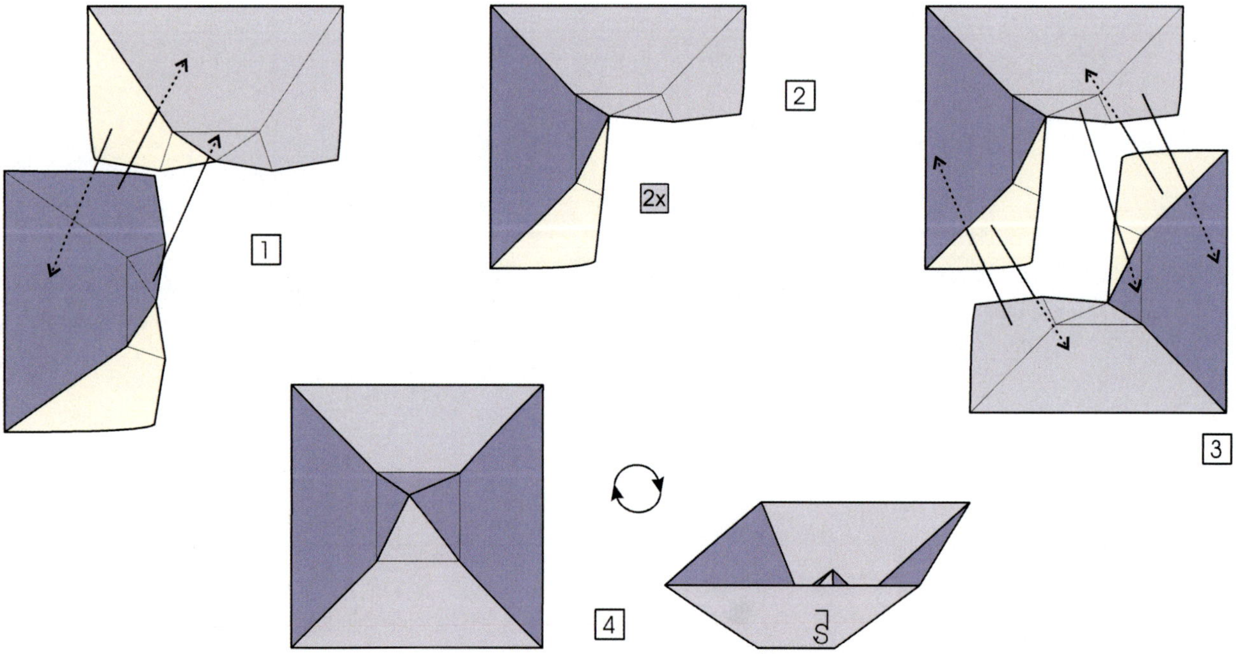

1

2

2x

3

4

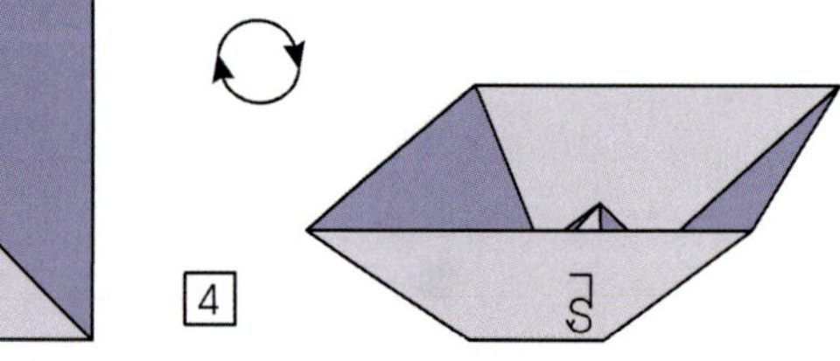

## Lid

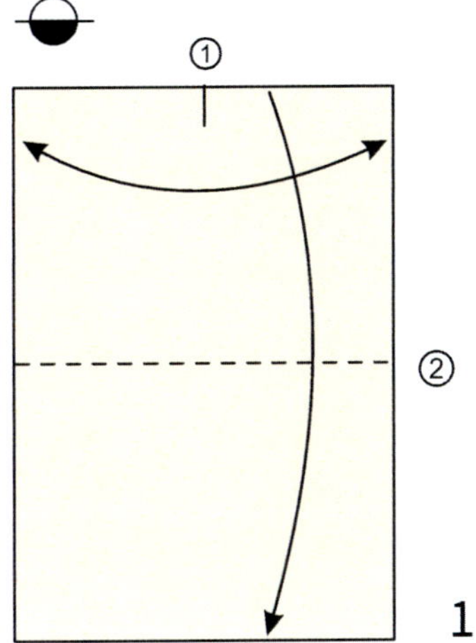


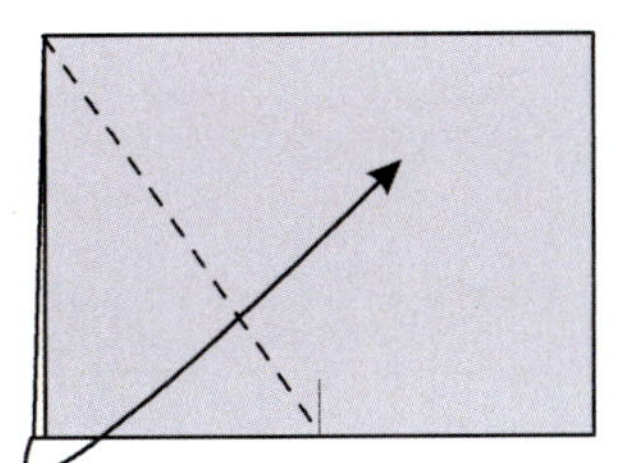


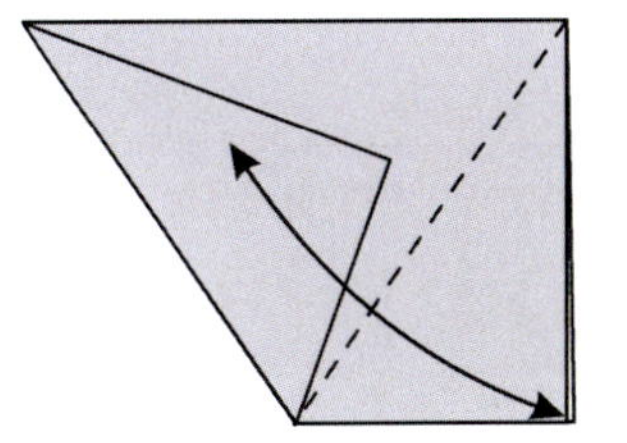


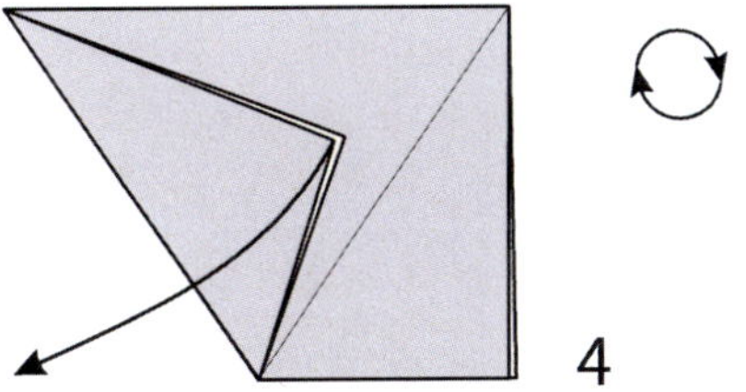


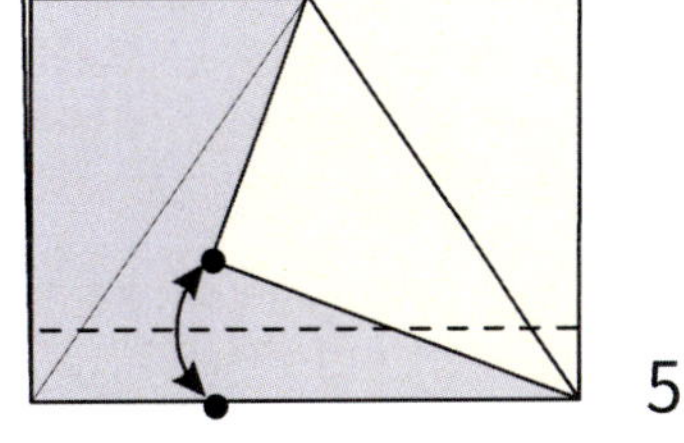


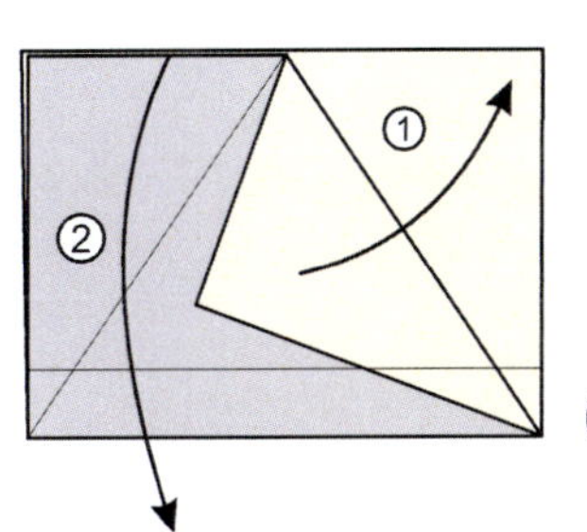


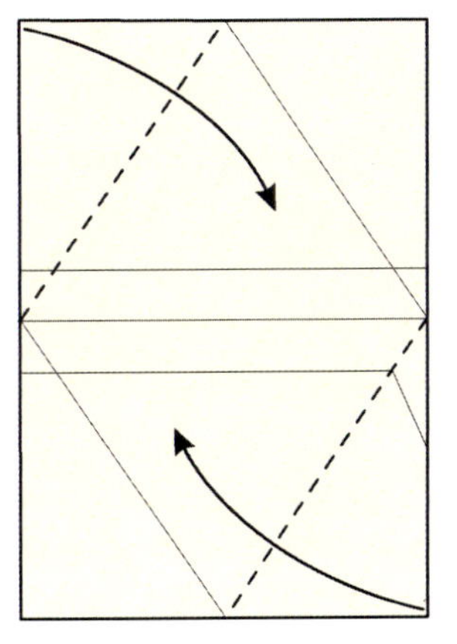


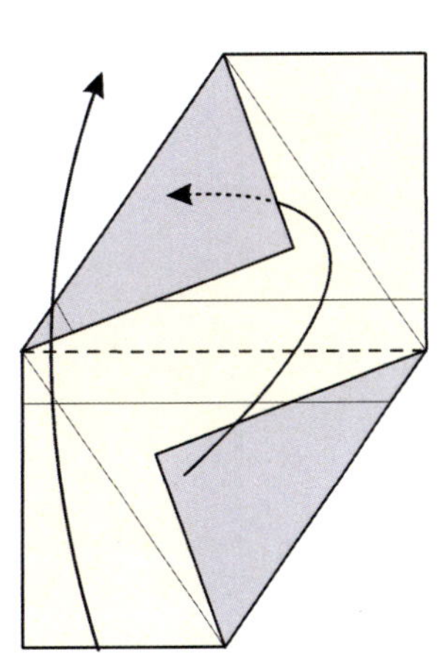


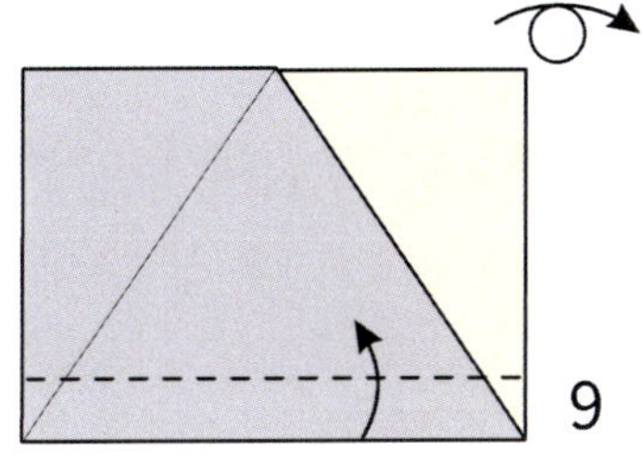


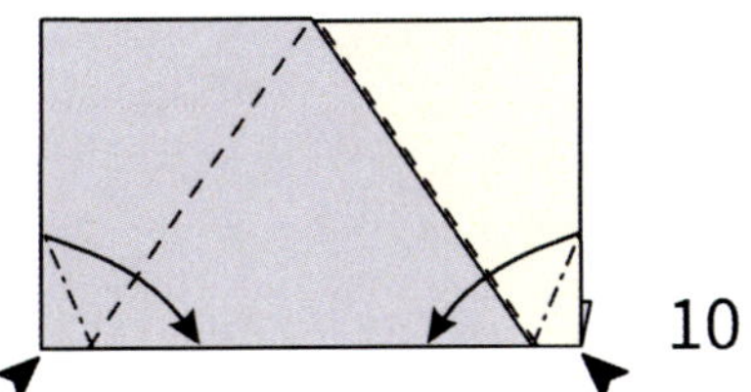


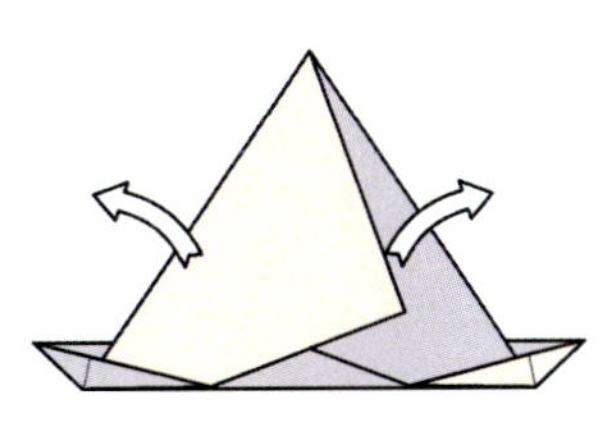


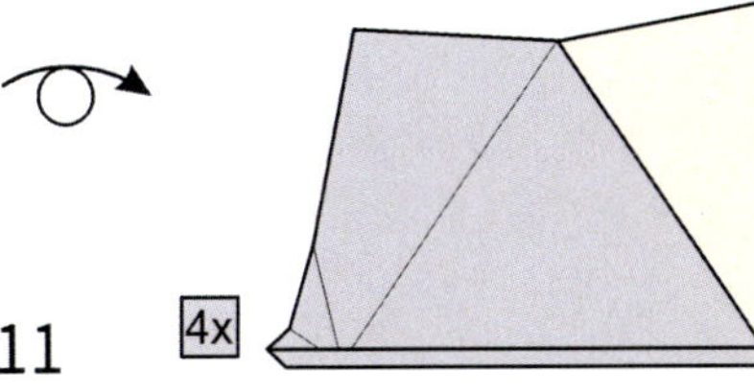

## Assembly

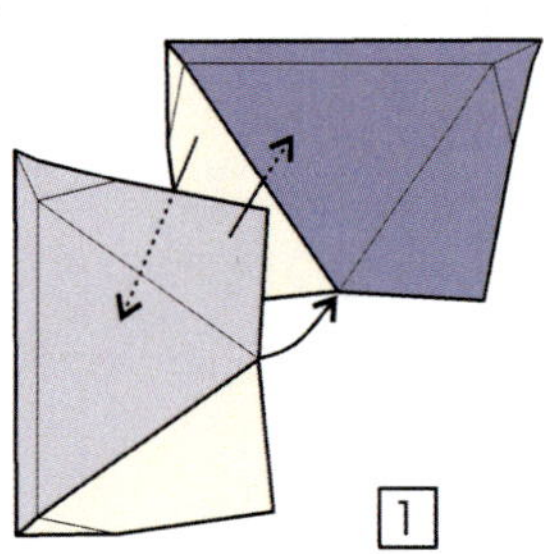


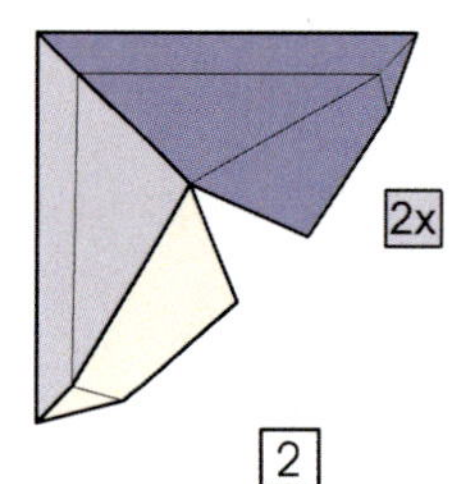


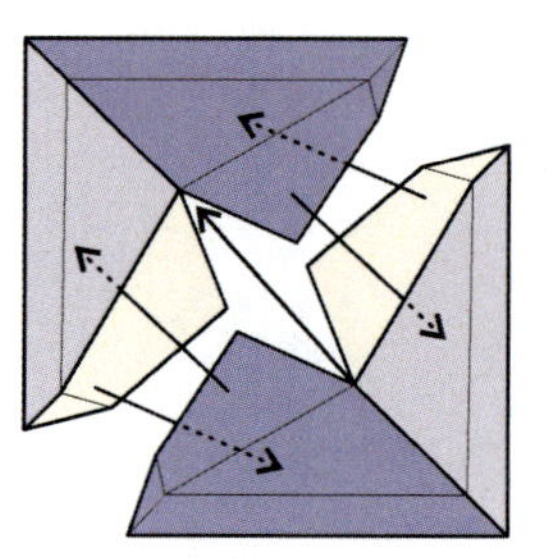


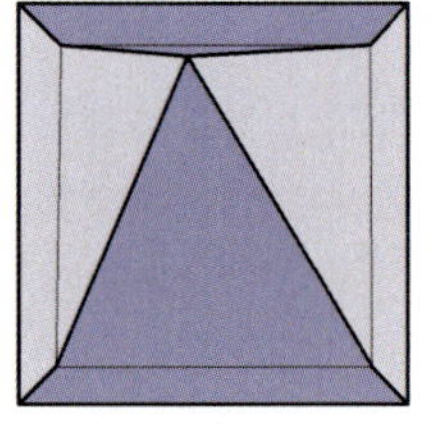


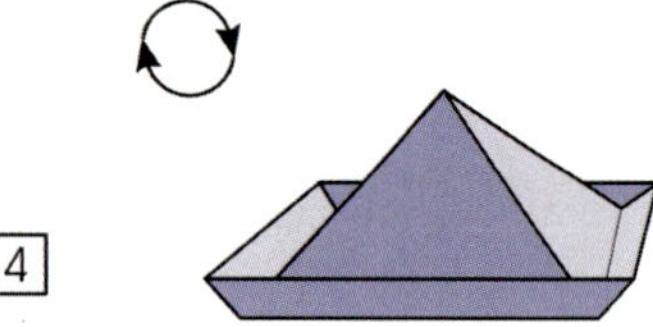

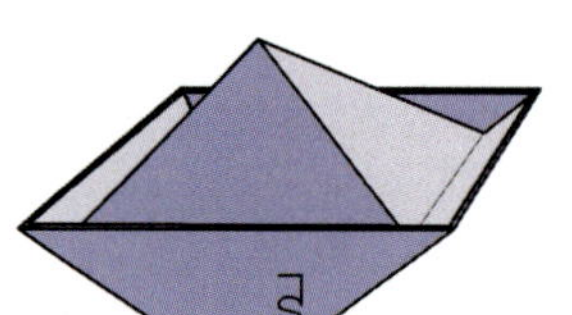

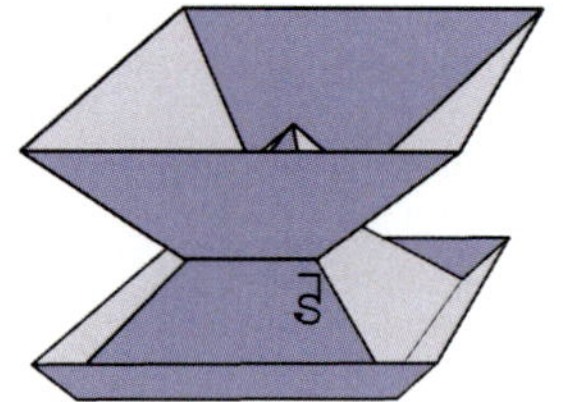

## Variation height of the lid

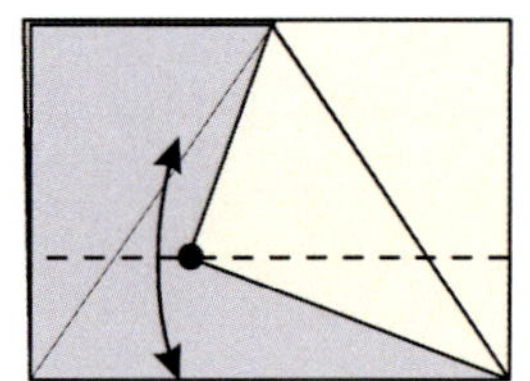

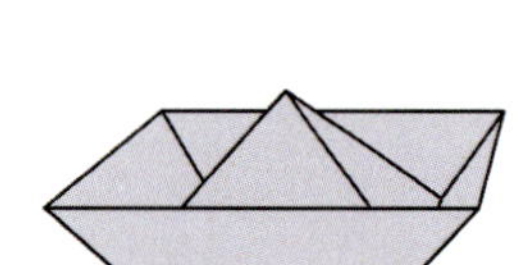

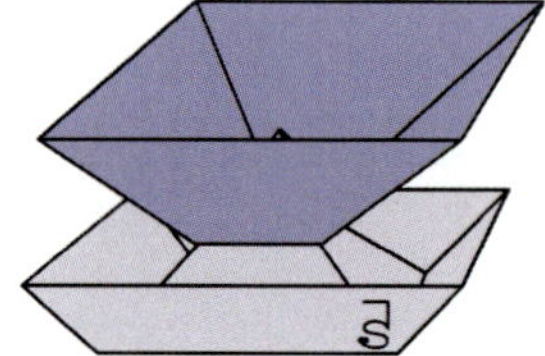

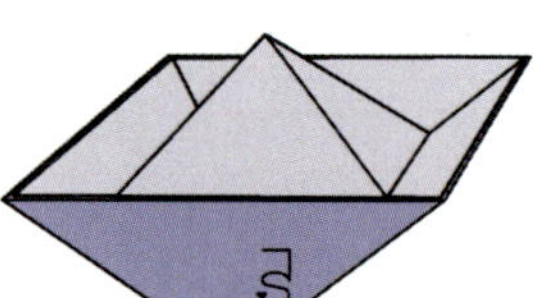

## Closure

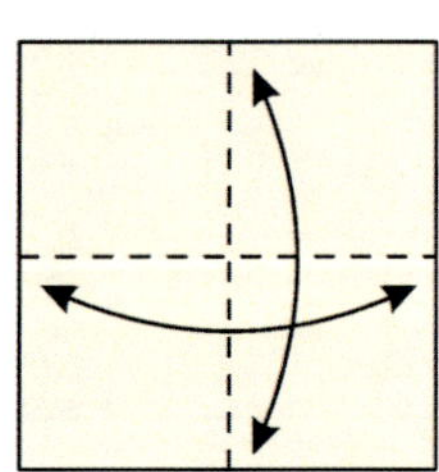


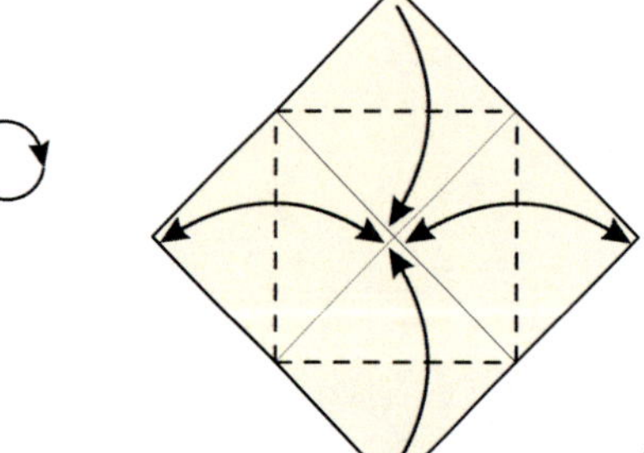

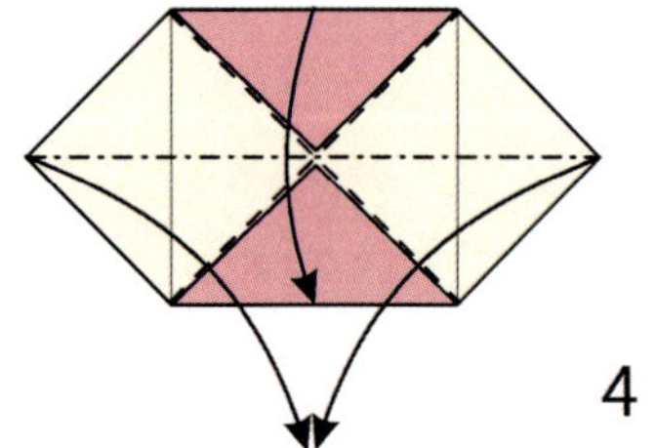

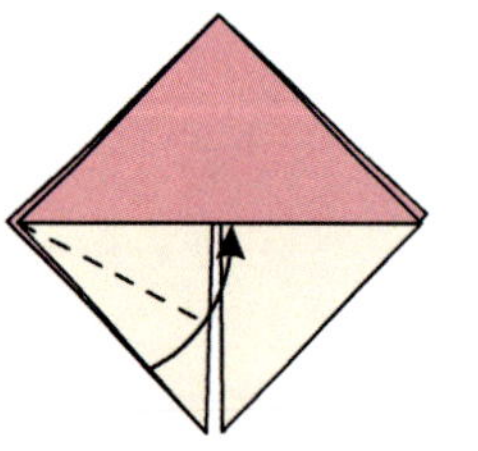


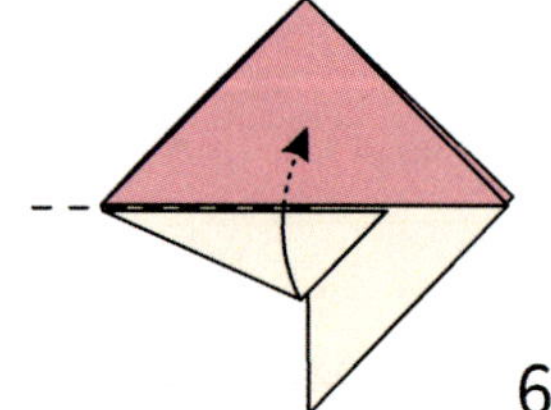

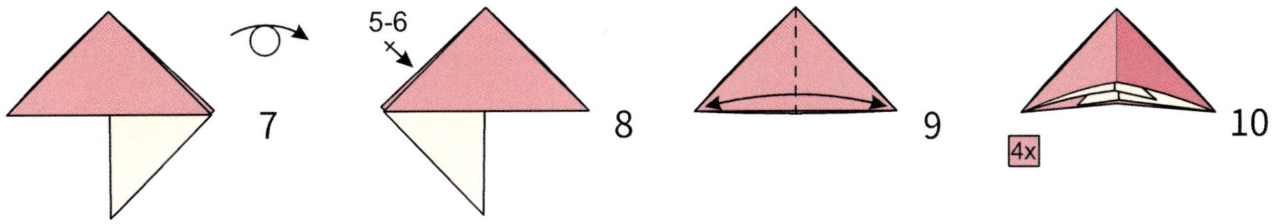

*Assembling closure*

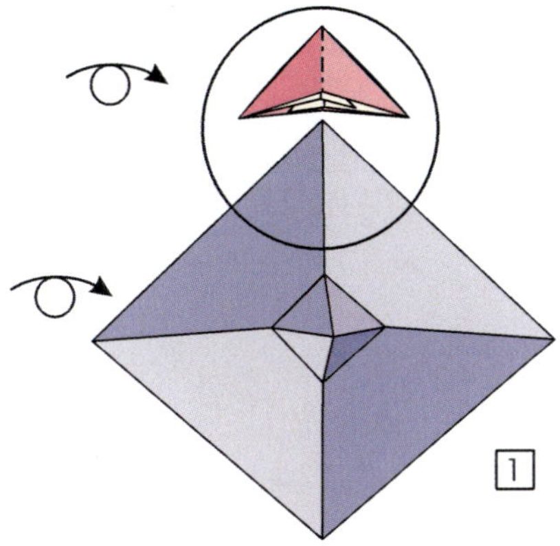

Outside of the dish and closure.

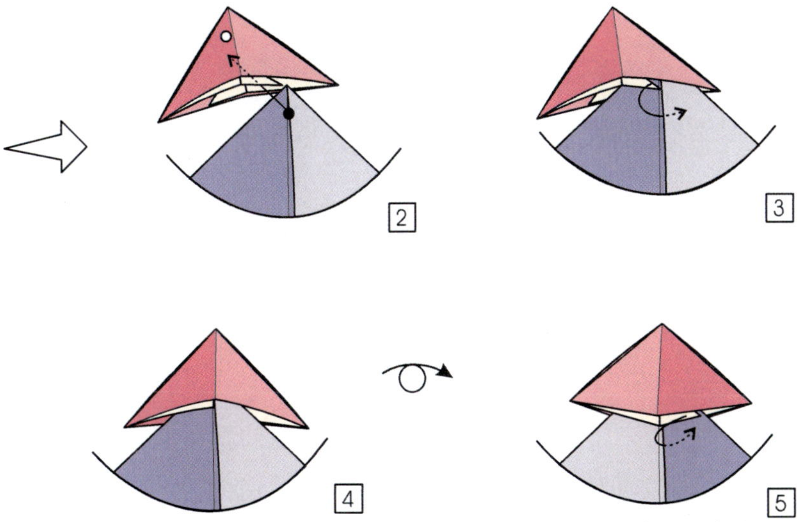

Inside of the dish.

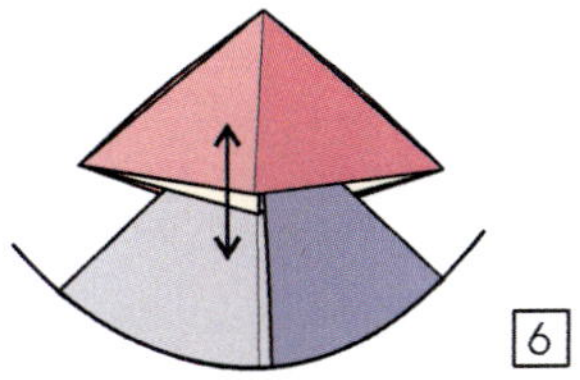

The closure can move freely.

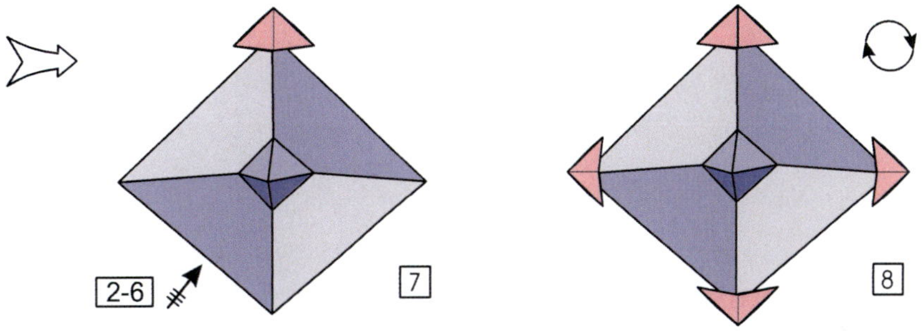

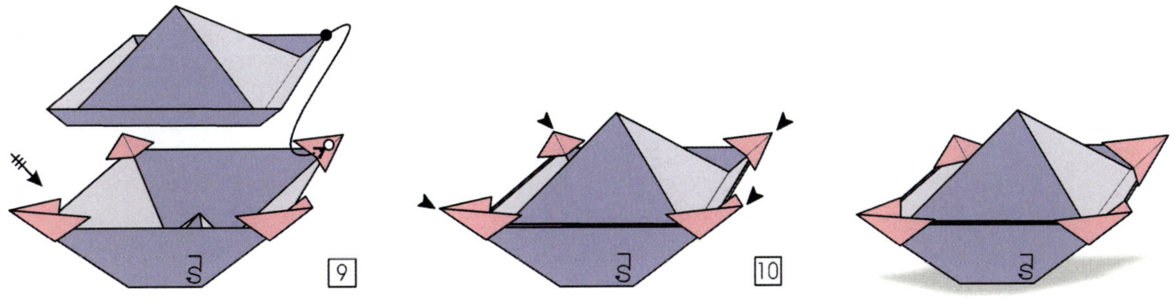

# Flowers

In this chapter you will find three sunflowers. They are great to fold and give as a present. Fold a few flowers, Truussia or Susanna, of beautiful colors and you have a beautiful bouquet. The stem and the leaves complete this chapter. With the Duo Pansies on a card you can convey a warm greeting. All flowers from this chapter can be arranged on a card to make a greeting card.

# Single Sunflower

07-06-2010

These 3 sunflowers are designed in two phases. The 'single' was the first. It was an order in 2010 for the Dutch hobby magazine, 'Hobby Handig'. During that time I had chemotherapy and had the feeling that I had to learn again how to fold.
The other two were designed just before my birthday, when it's 'sunflower time'.
Sunflower Henny is dedicated to a special and lovely woman, 'Tante Henny', who loved sunflowers very much. I've shared these models in the first Origami Zoom that I organized so I could celebrate my birthday in Covid time. (2020)

Paper:
- heart: 15x15 cm
- petals: 8 times 5x5 cm
- leaf: 3 times 10x10 cm
- stem: 30x10 cm
- For the card: halve all sizes

## Flower Heart

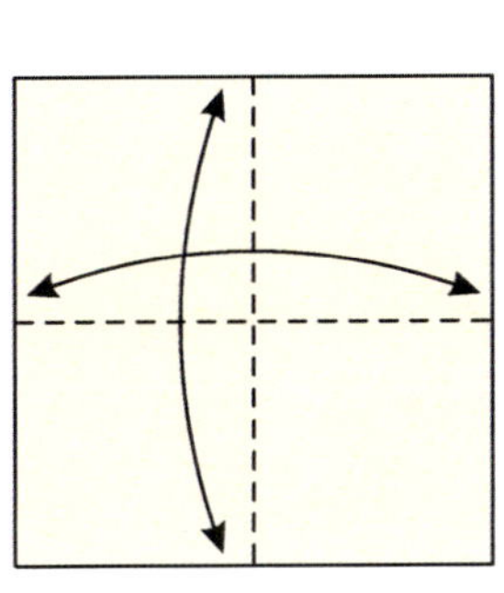

1

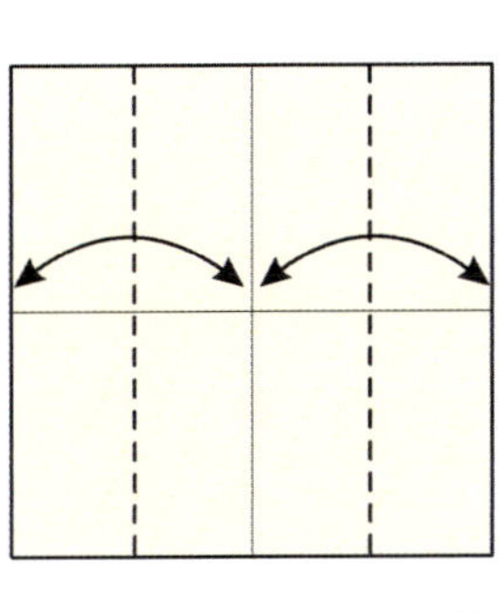

2

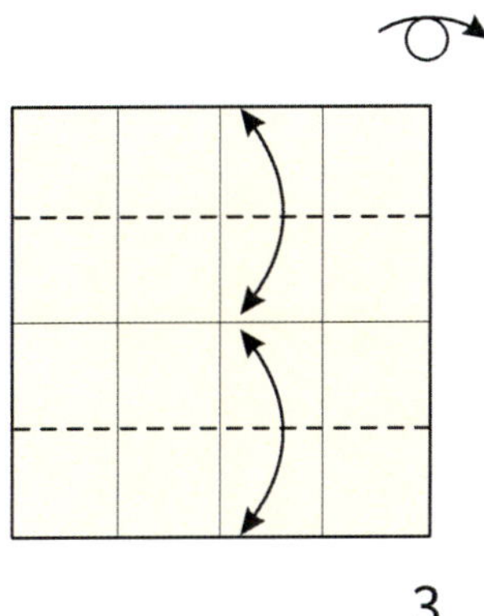

3

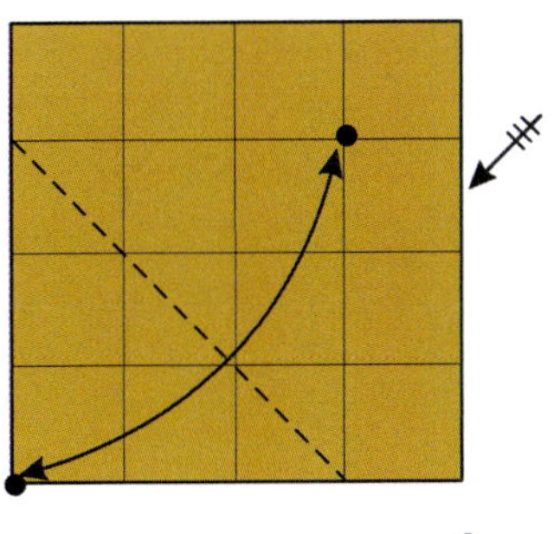

4

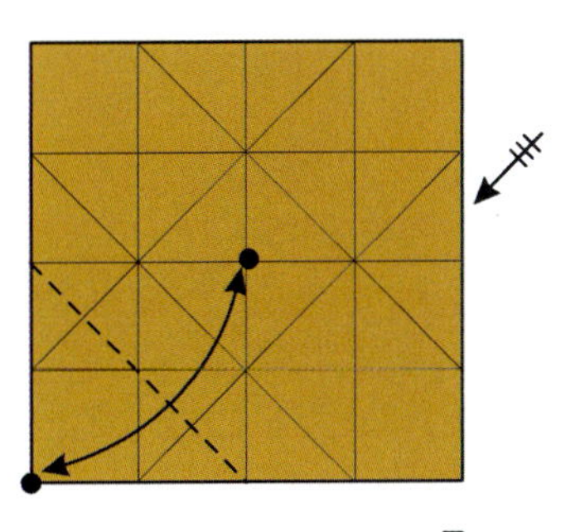

5

6

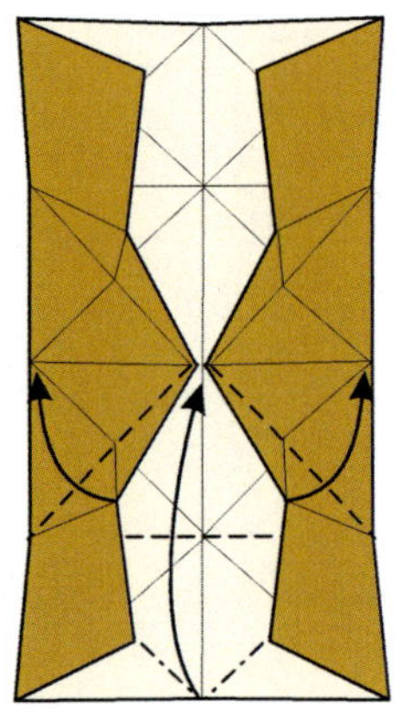
7

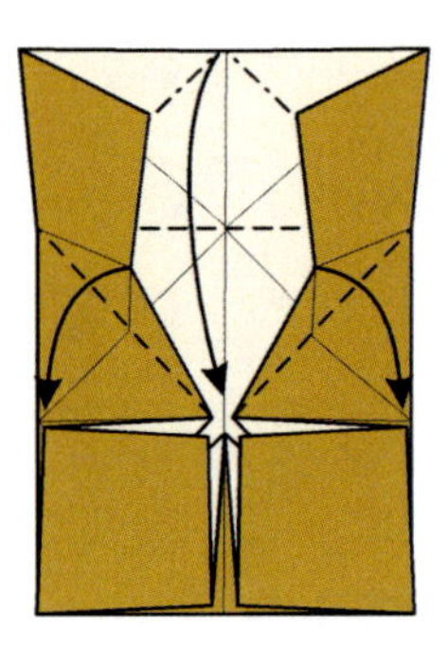
8

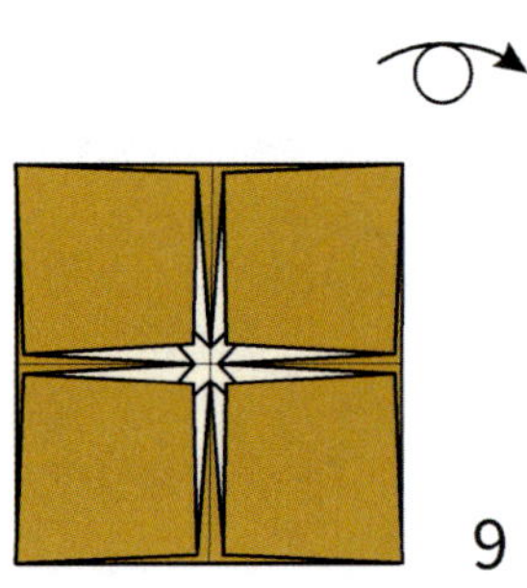
9

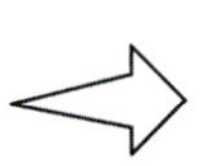

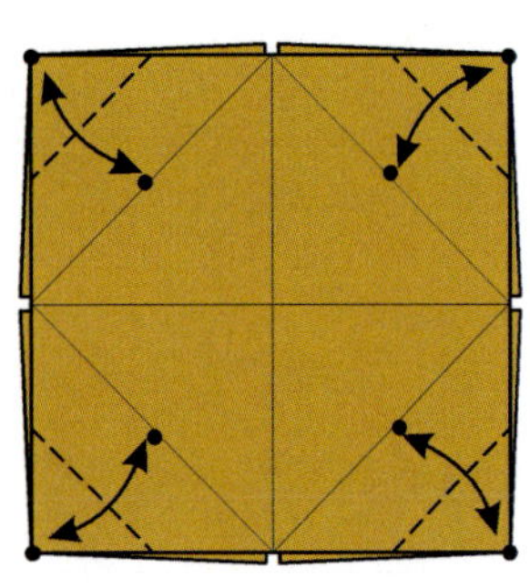
10

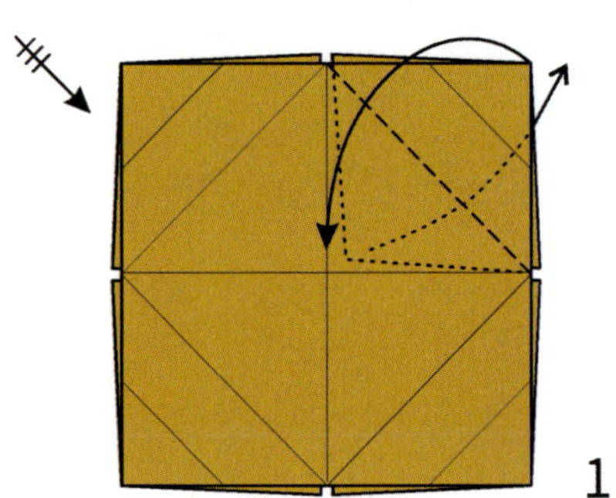
11

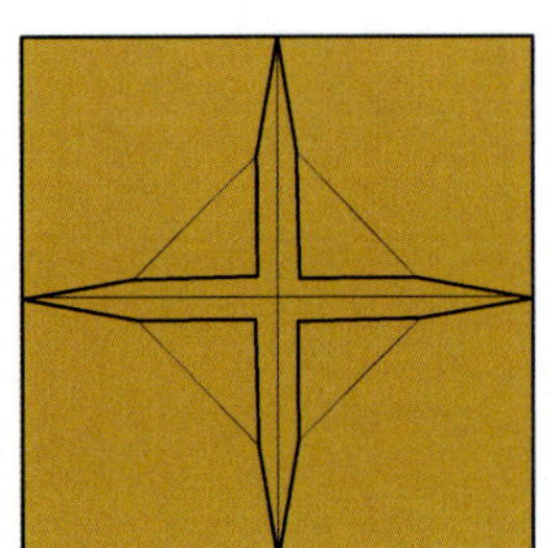
12

13

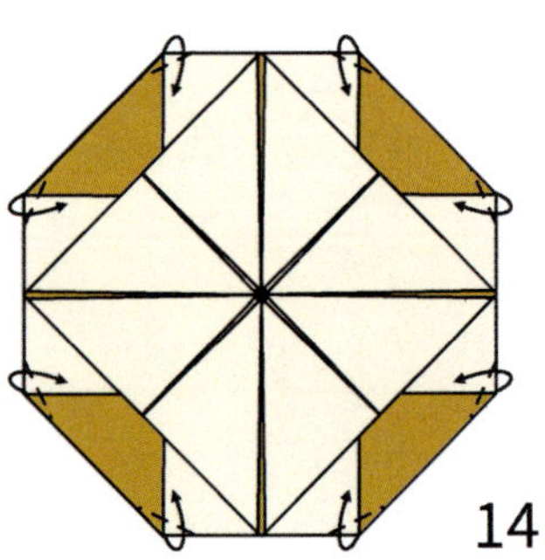
14

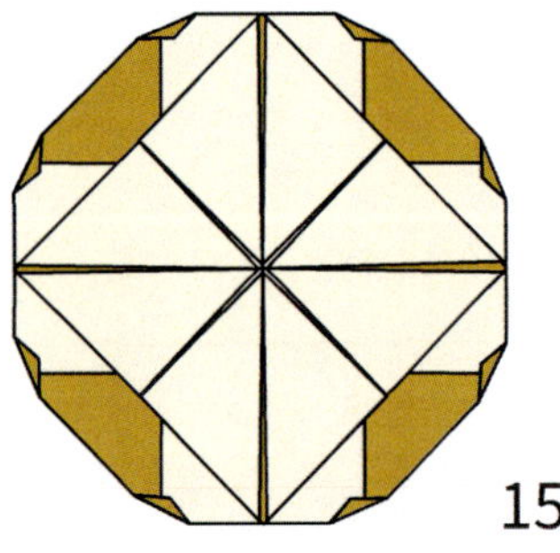
15

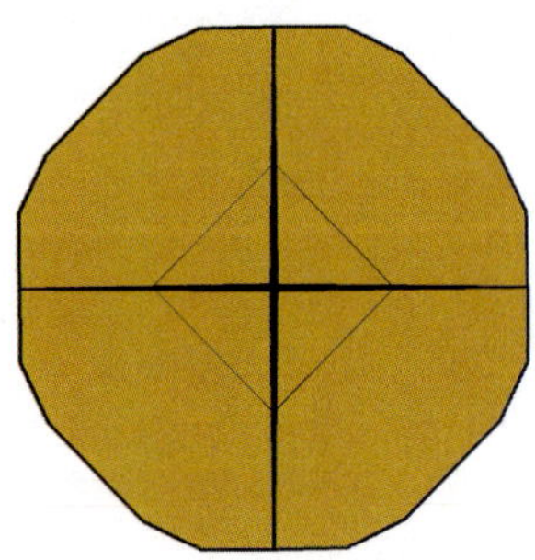

## Petal 1

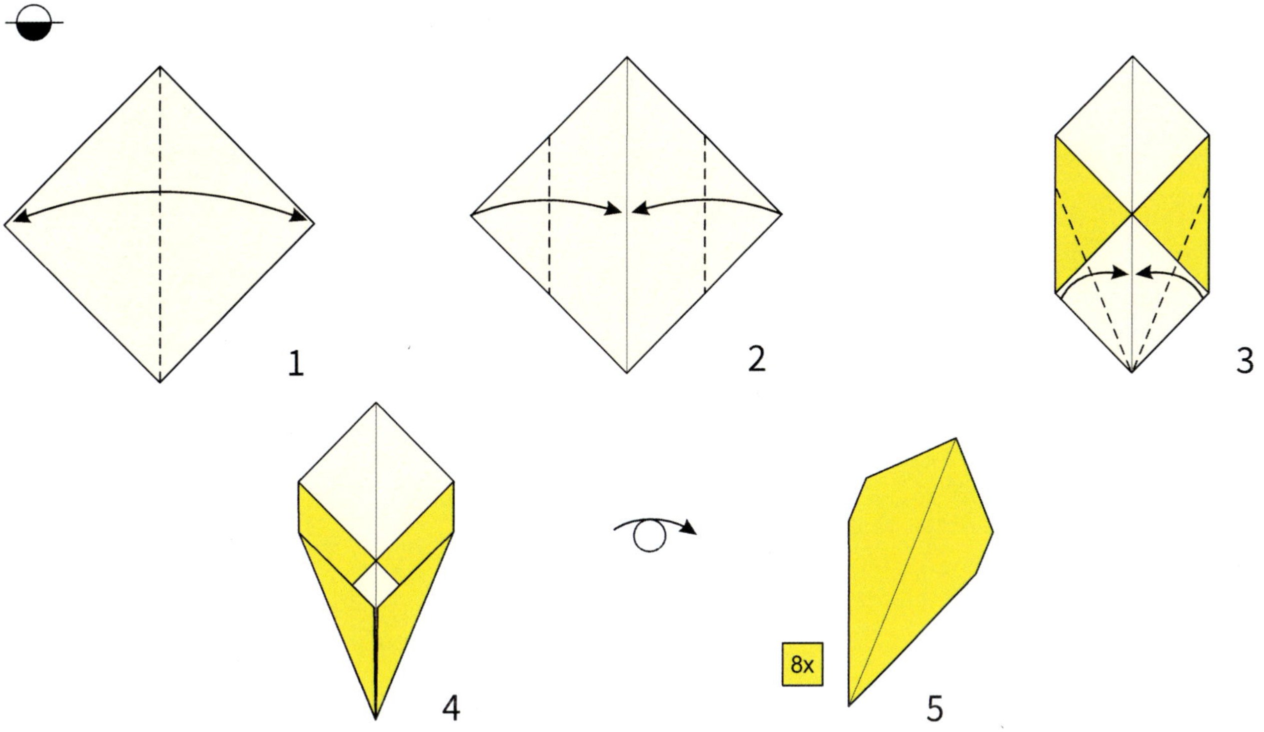

1

2

3

4

8x

5

*Assembly*

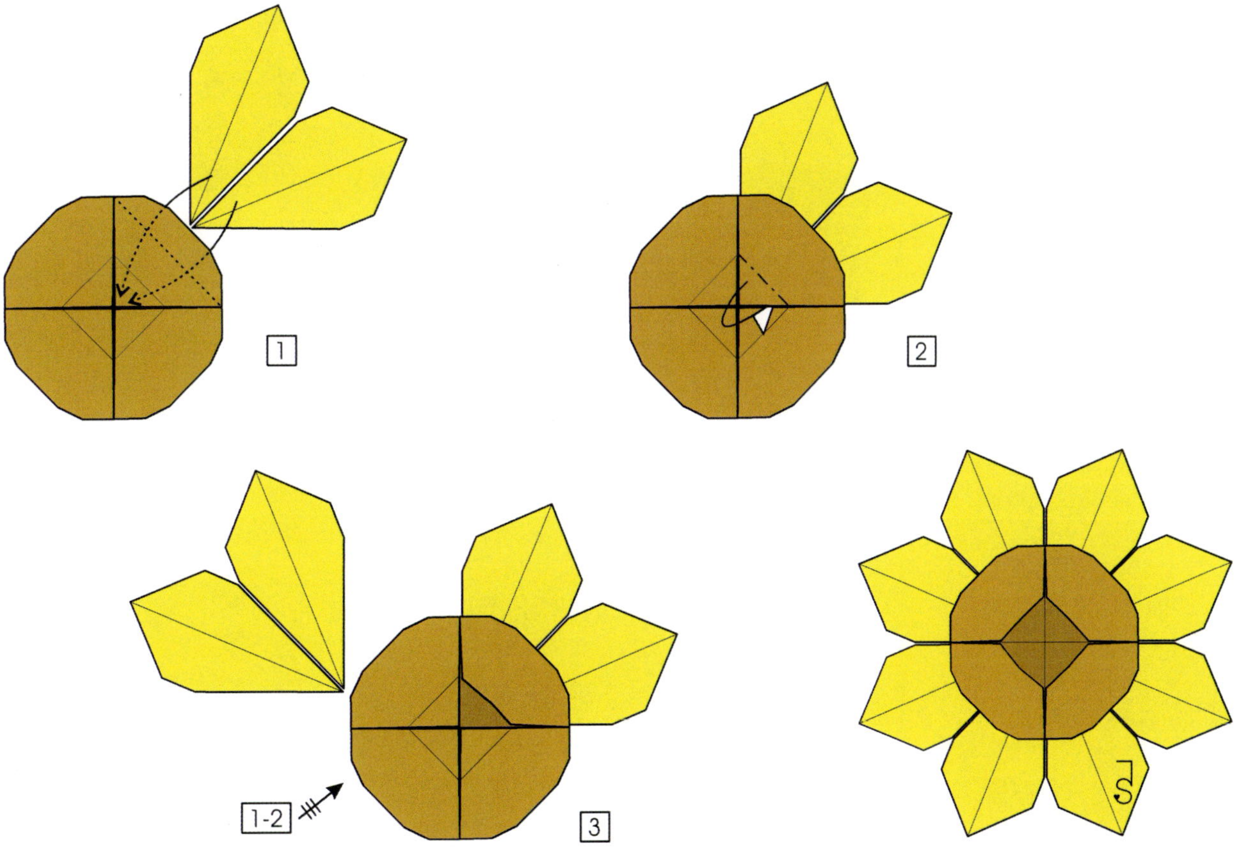

1

2

1-2

3

# Double Sunflower

14-07-2021

Paper:
- heart: 15x15 cm
- petals: 16 sheets 5x5 cm
- leaf: 3 sheets 10x10 cm
- stem: 30x10 cm

## Flower Heart

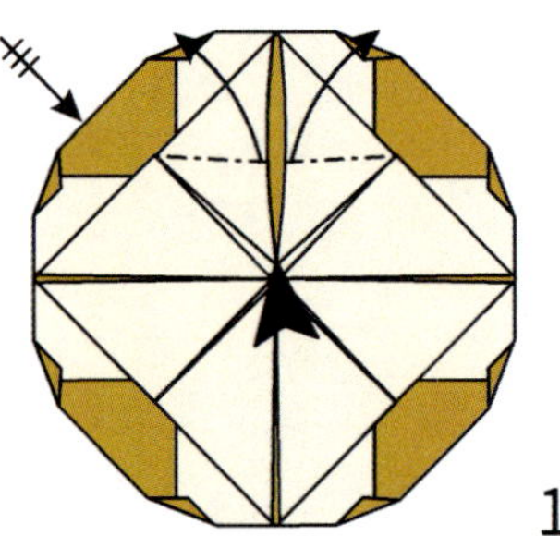

1

Fold steps 1-15 of Single Sunflower heart page 43

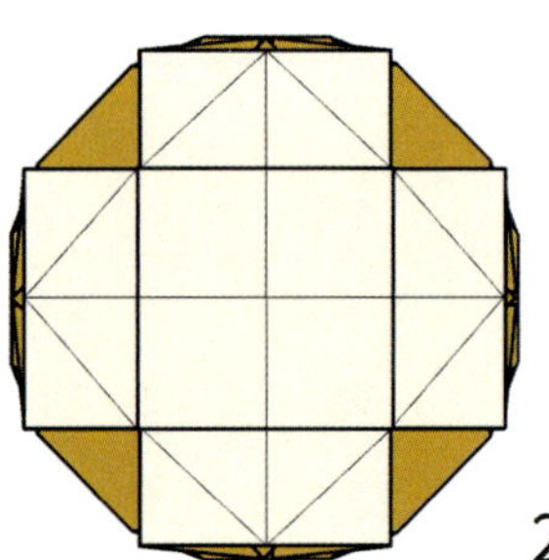

2

3

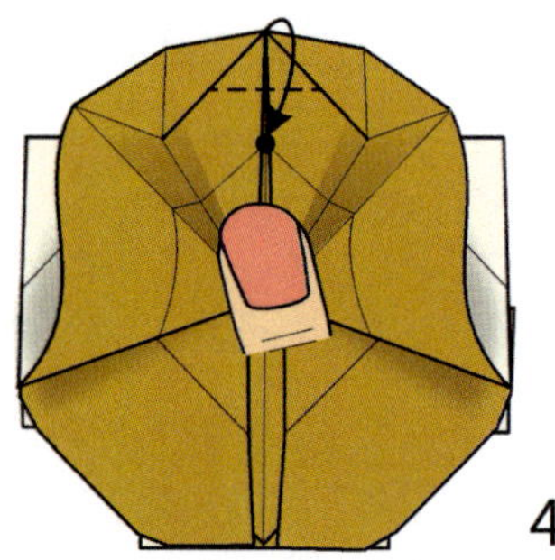


4

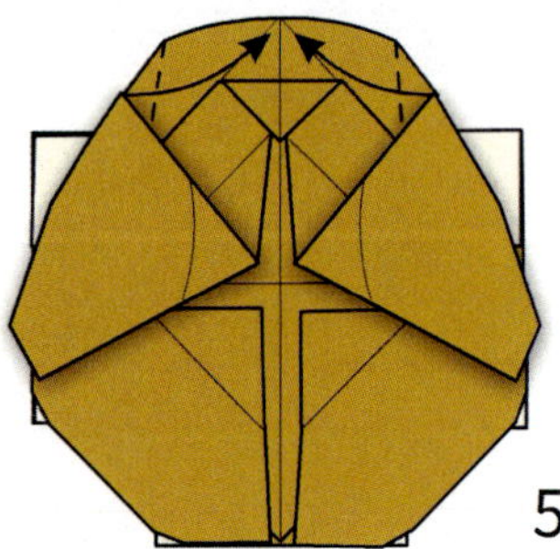

5

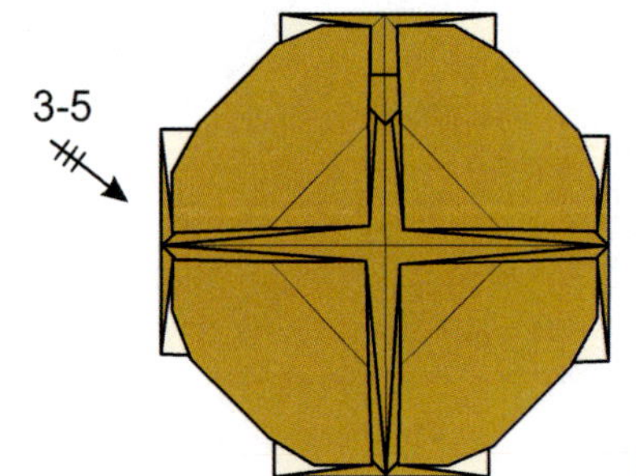


6

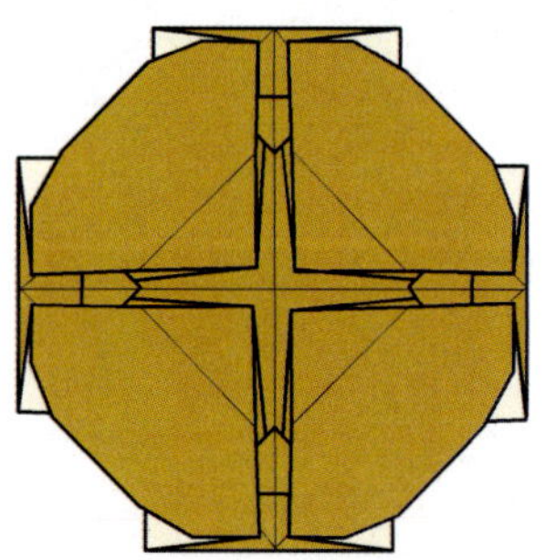

## Petal 1

Fold 8 times petal 1
of Single Sunflower

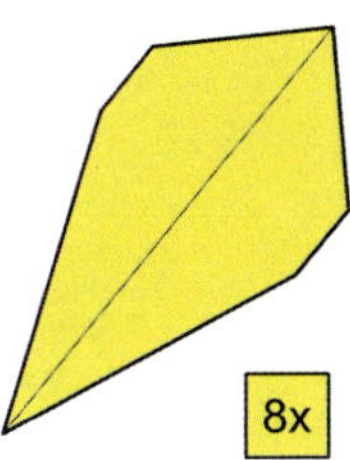


## Petal 2

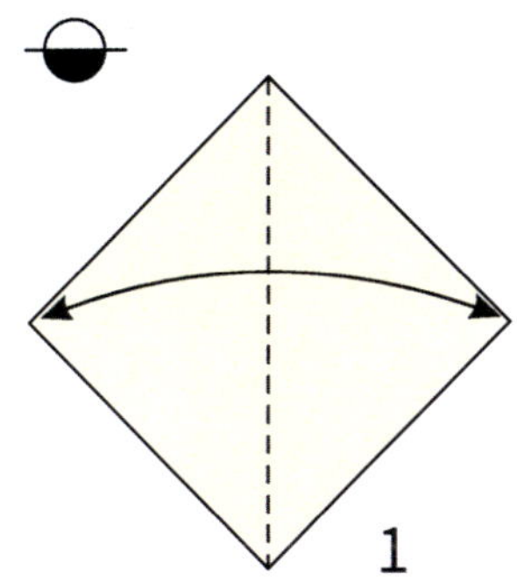


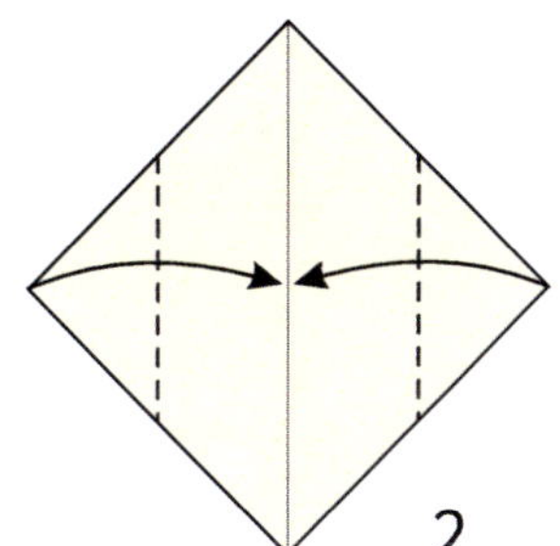


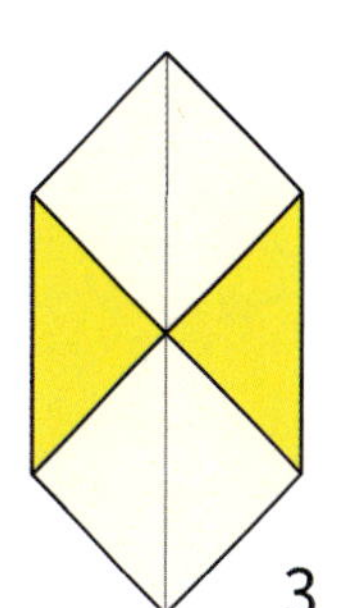


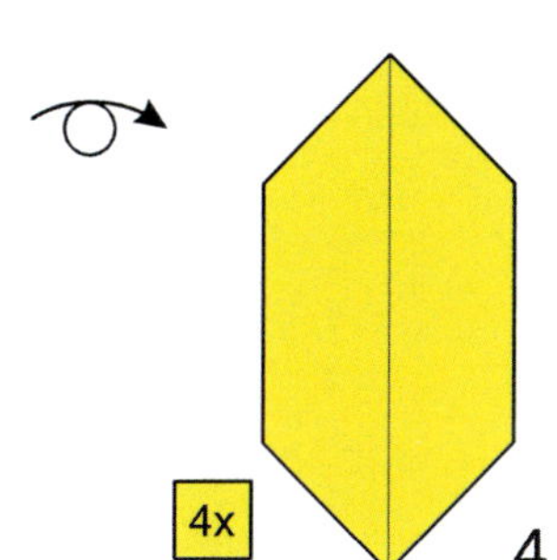


## Petal 3

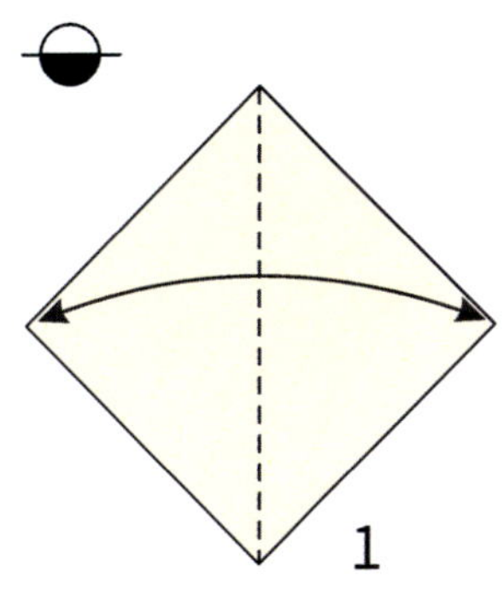


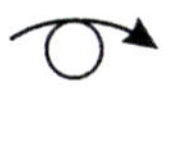

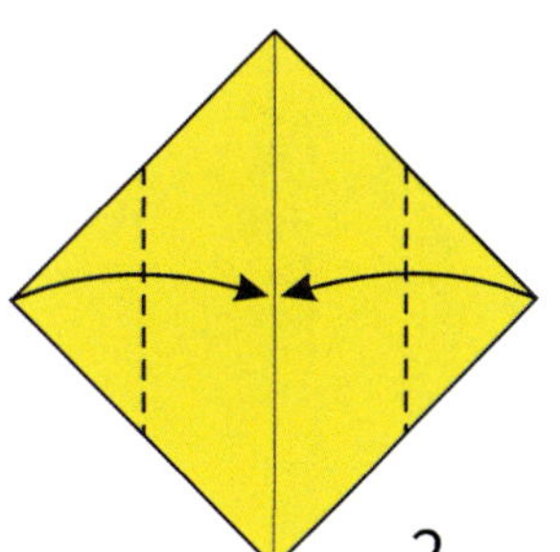

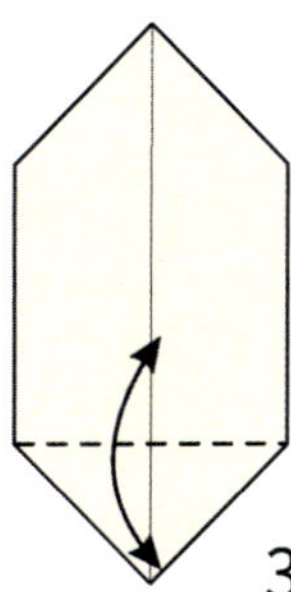


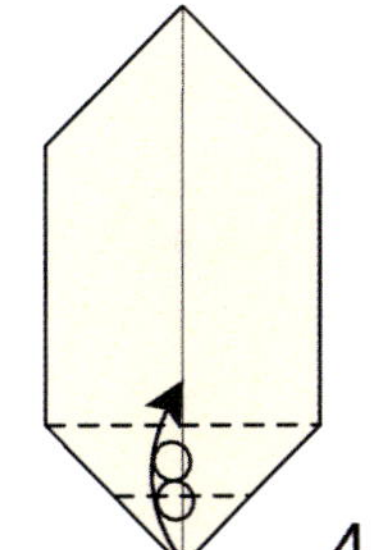


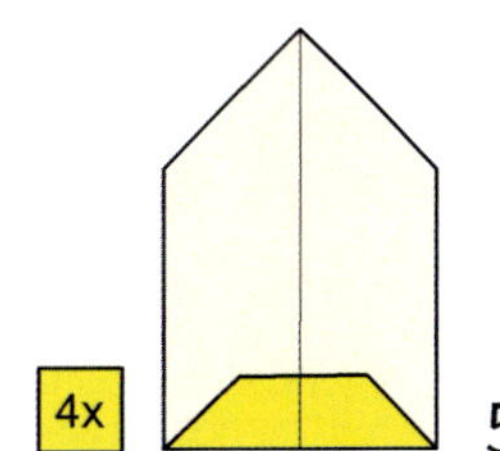

## *Assembly*

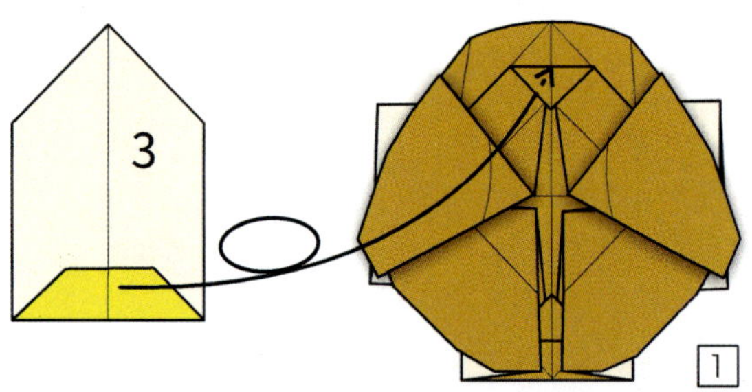


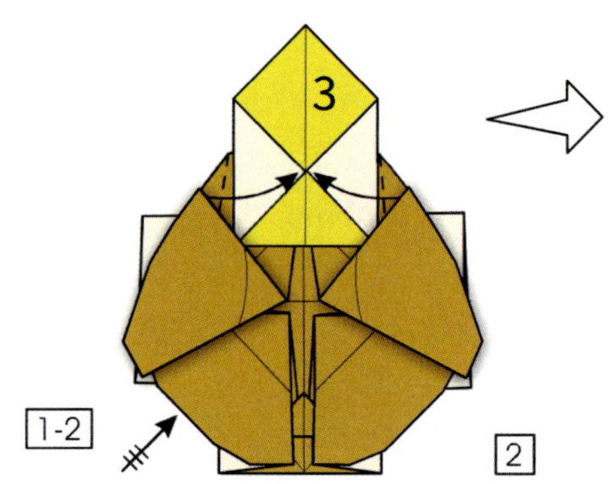


Unfold the sides as shown in step 3-4 of the flower heart. Slide the folded part of petal 3 under the folded triangle, both parts hook behind each other.

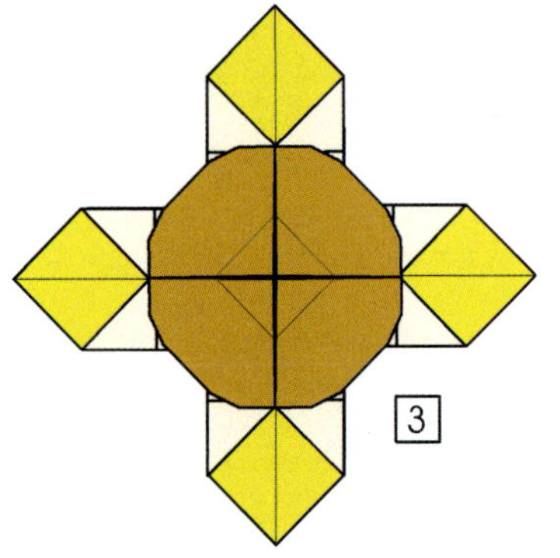


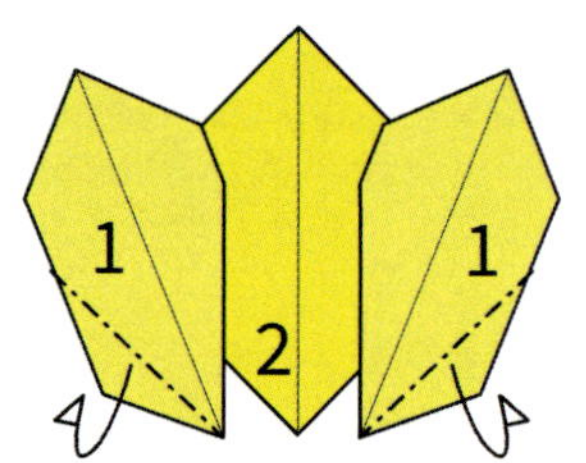


Place petal 2 under two petals 1. Fold the sides of Petal 1 around petal 2.

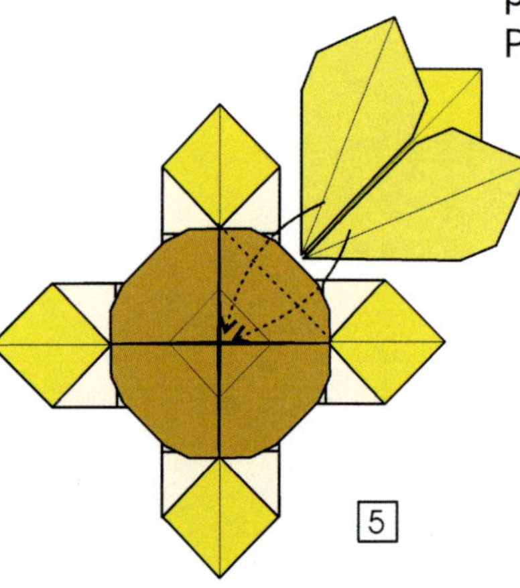


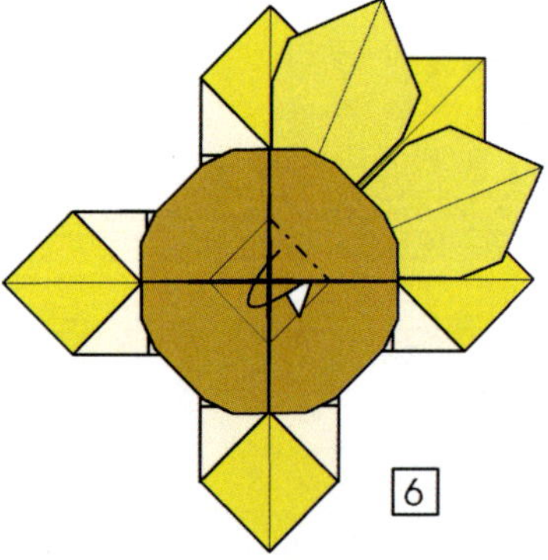


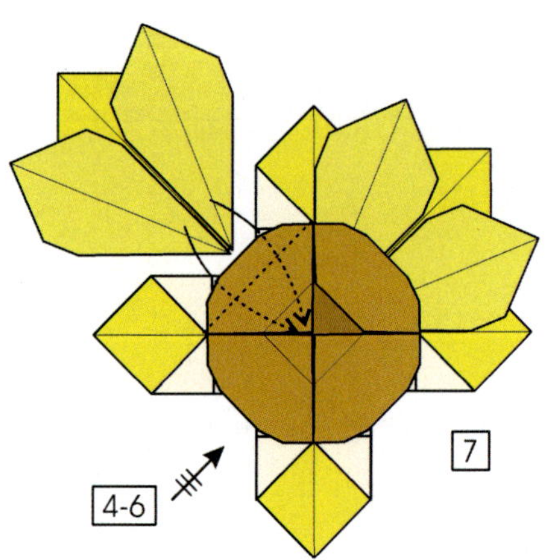

# Sunflower Henny

13-07-2021



## Flower Heart

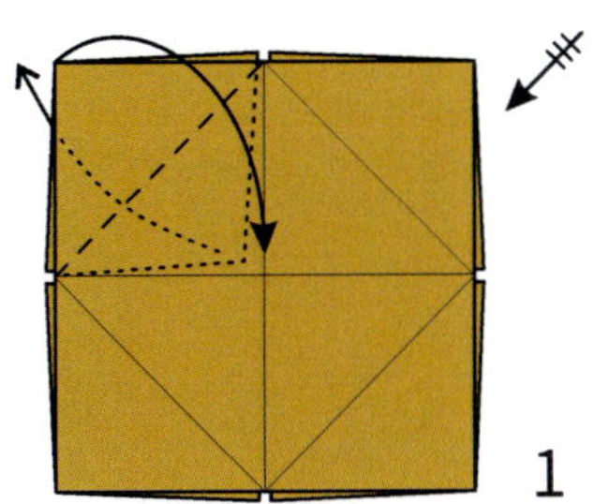

1

Fold steps 1-9 of Single Sunflower heart page 43

Paper:
- heart: 15x15 cm
- petals: 4 sheets 5x10 cm
- leaf: 3 sheets 10x10 cm
- stem: 30x10 cm

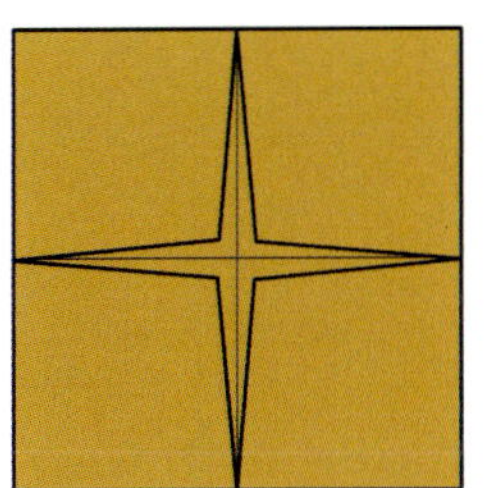

2

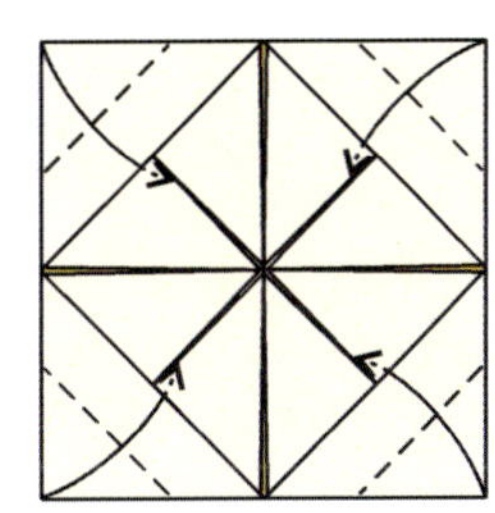

3

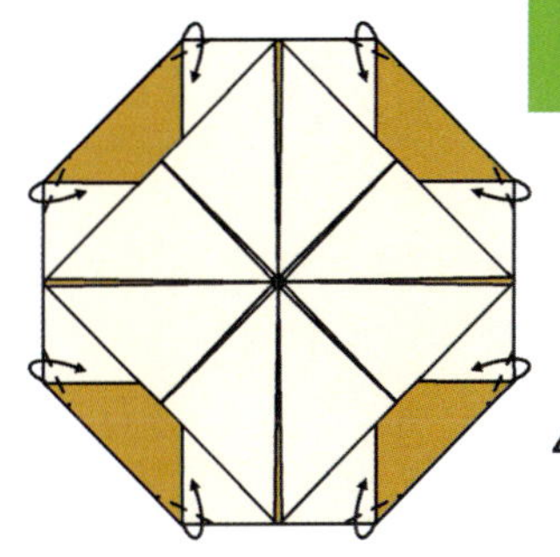

4

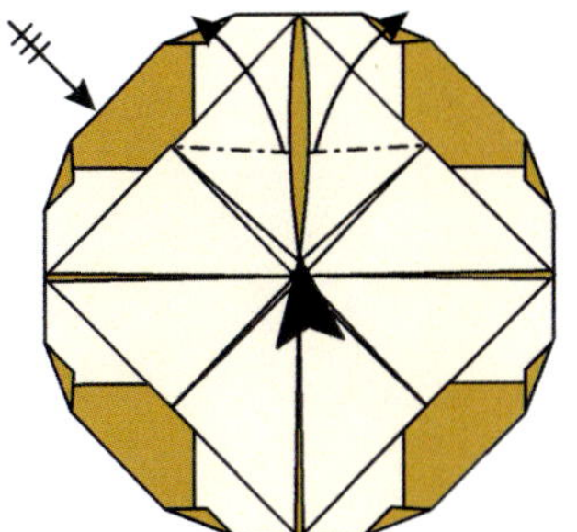

5

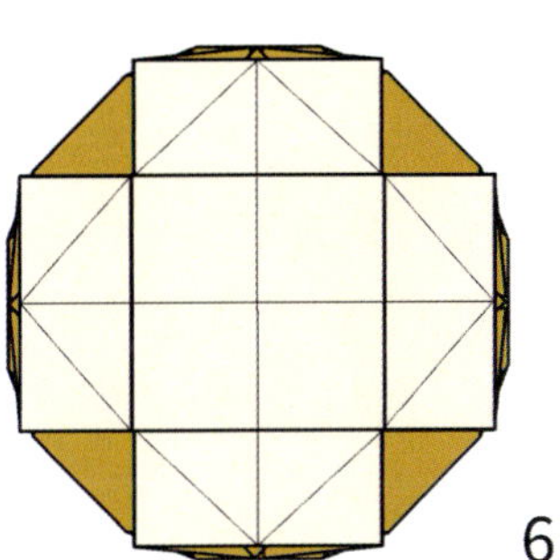

6

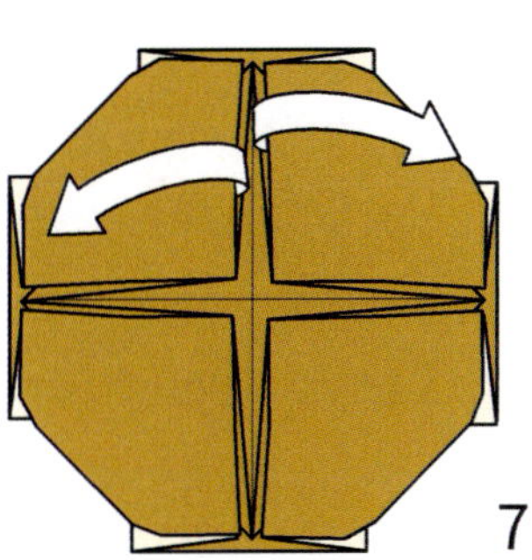

7

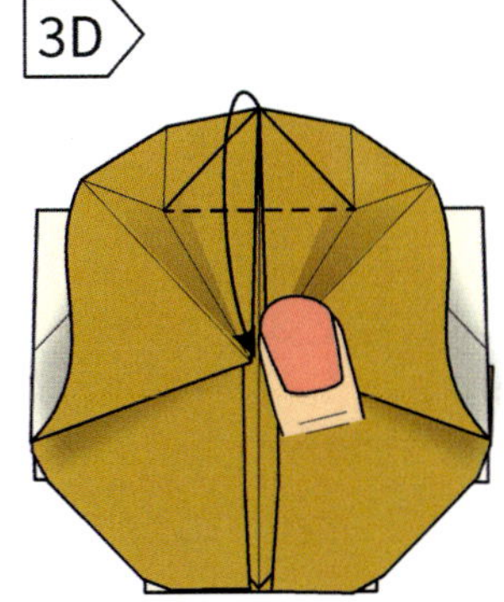


8

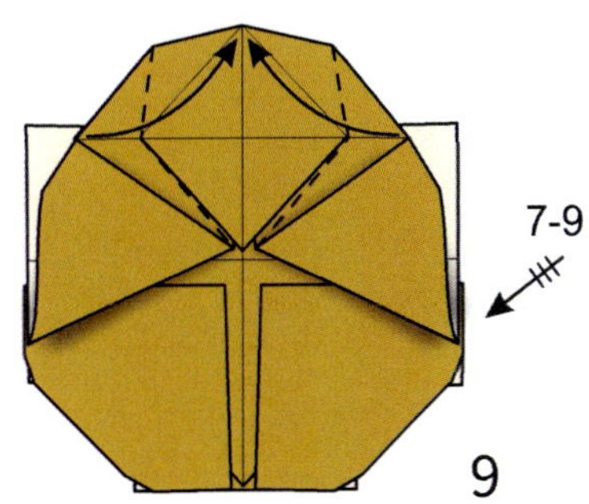


9

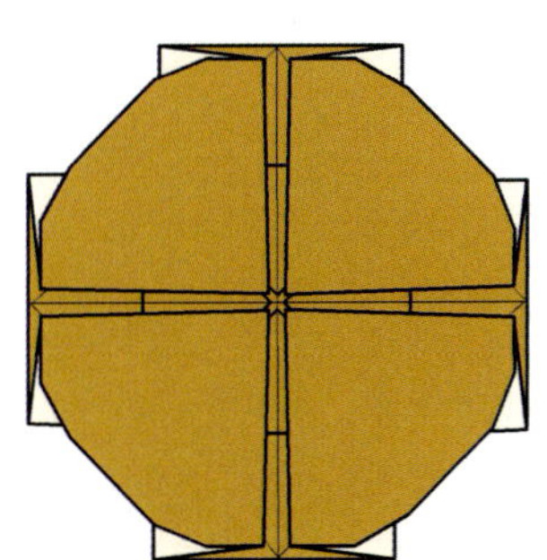

## Petal 4

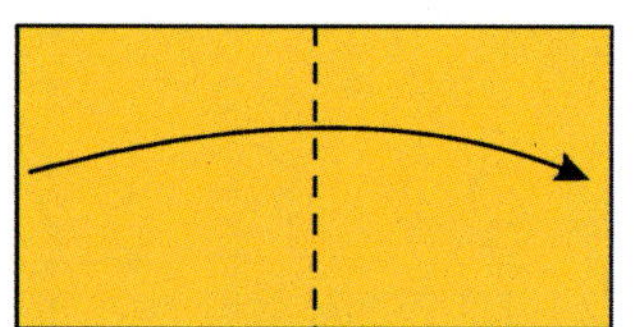

1

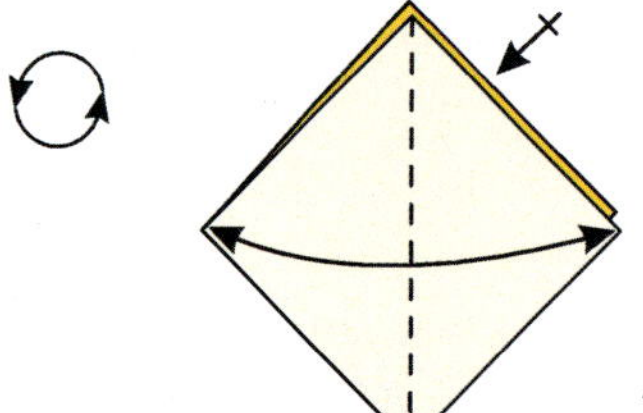

2

3

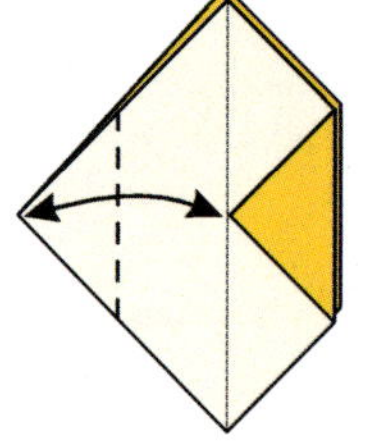

4

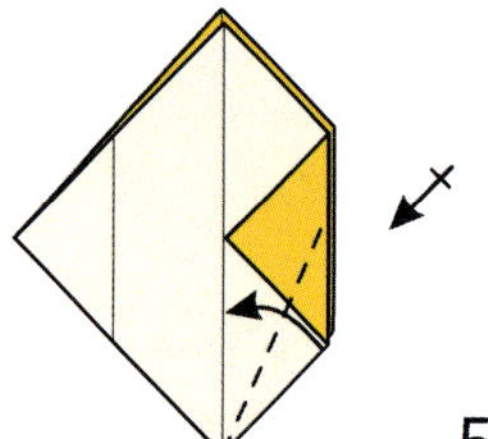

5

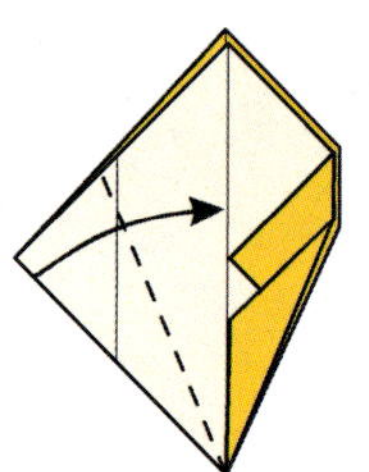

6

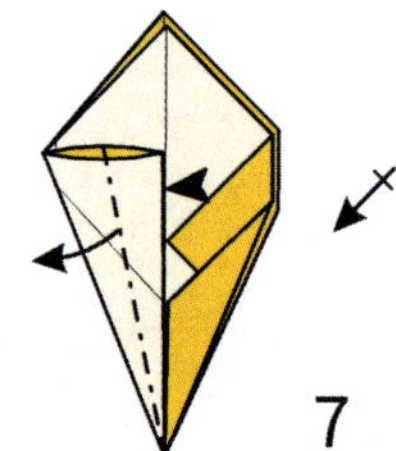

7

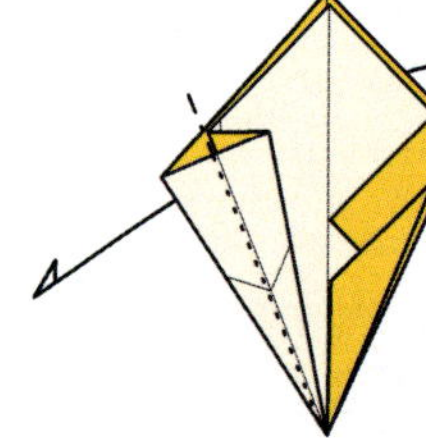

8

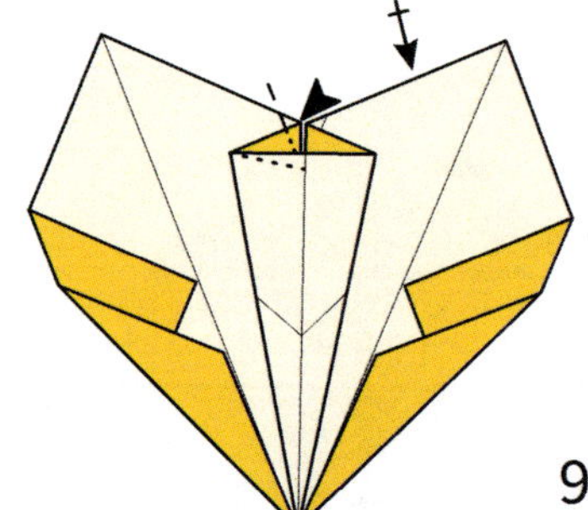

9

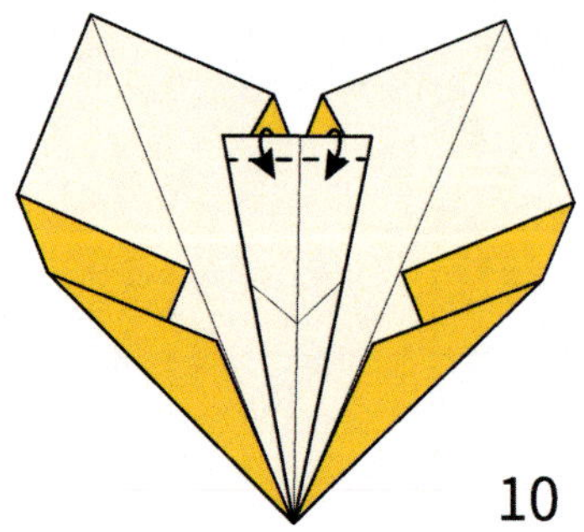

10

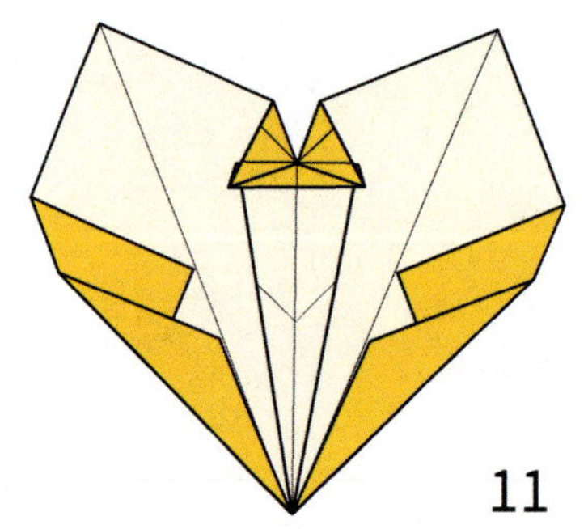

11

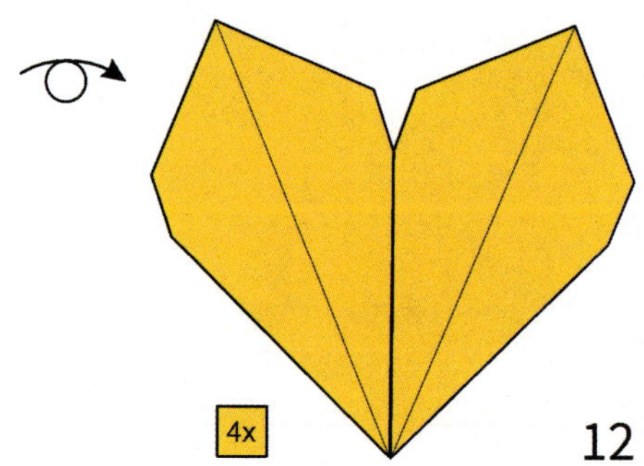


12

## *Assembly*

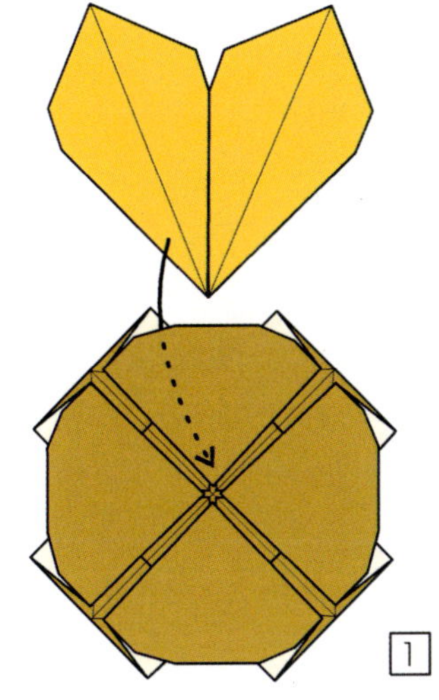


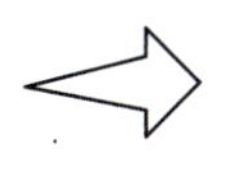

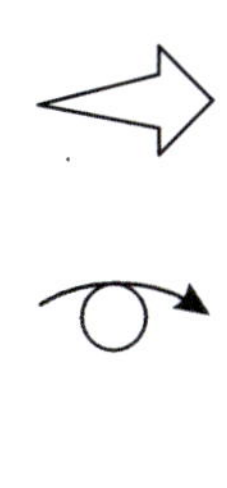

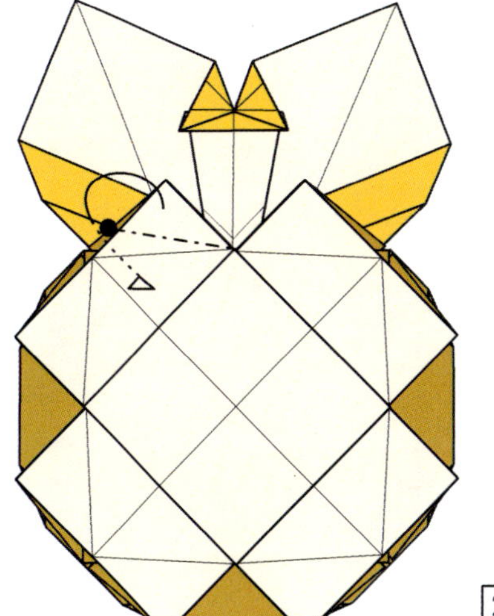


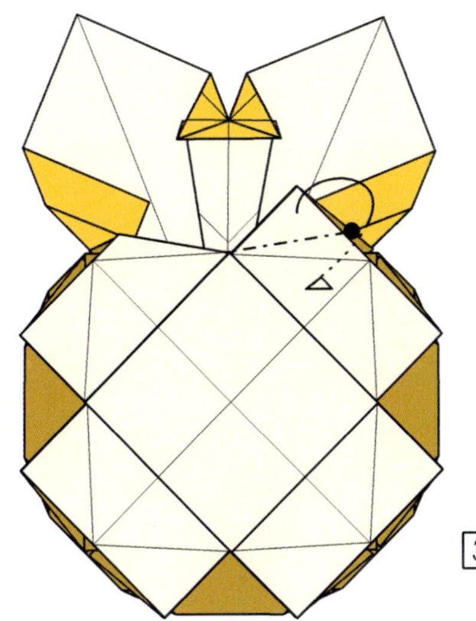


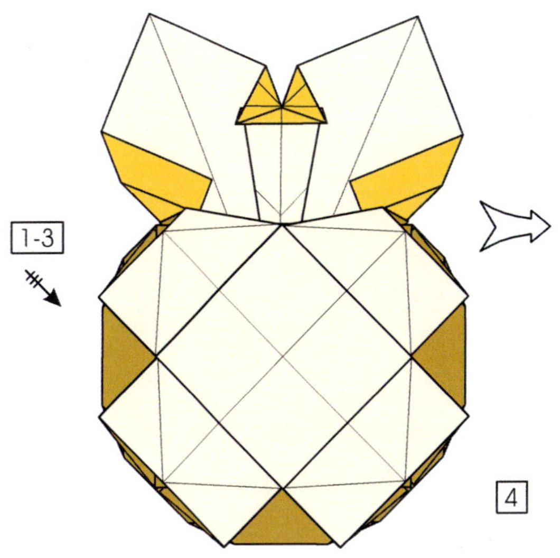

Let's fold... and be happy Flowers

# Duo Pansy

15-05-2023

The pansy is one of my favorite flowers. How I love all these beautiful colors. I always buy them in spring. The little ones smell so lovely. These duo pansies are made from one piece of paper. You can slide them through a card so they are visible on both sides. Try them.

Paper:
Duo color green/gradient paper 10x10cm or smaller

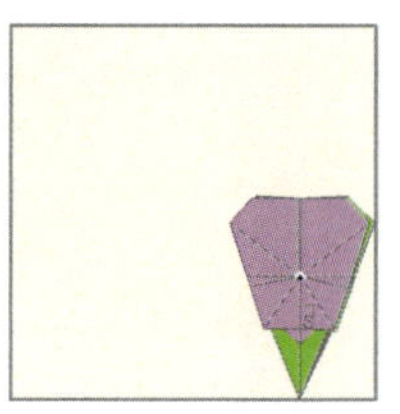

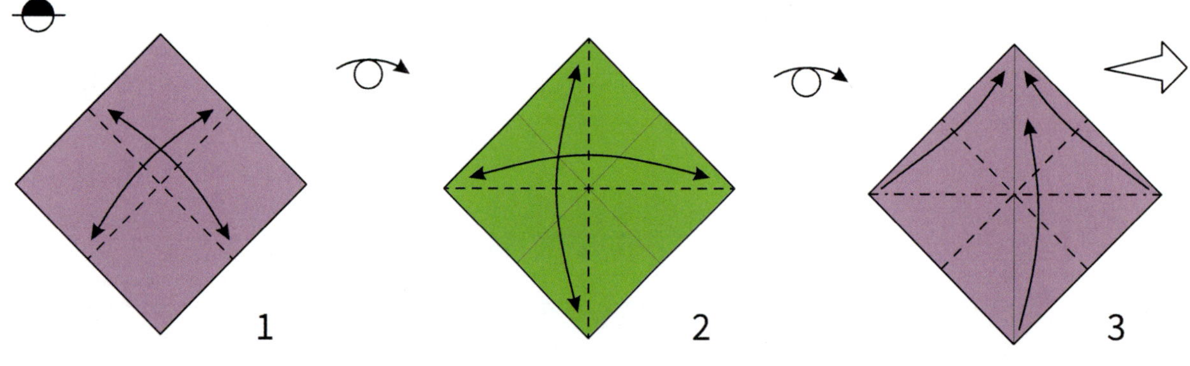


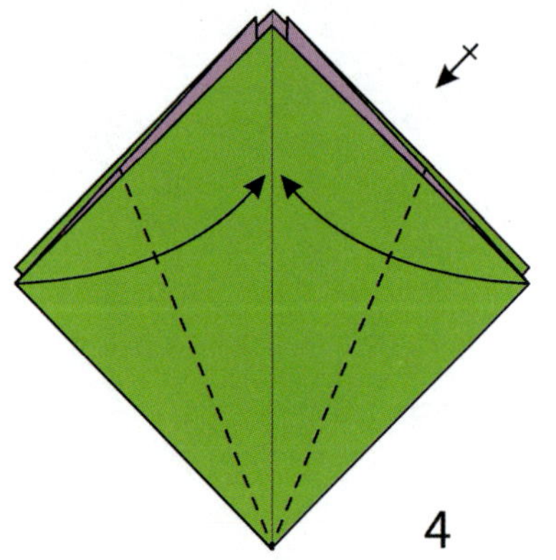


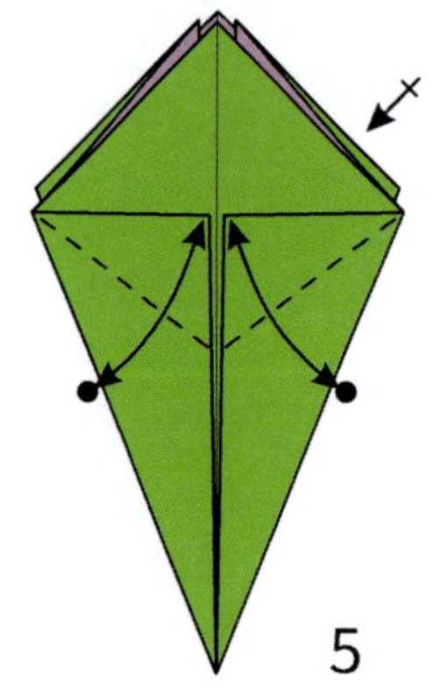


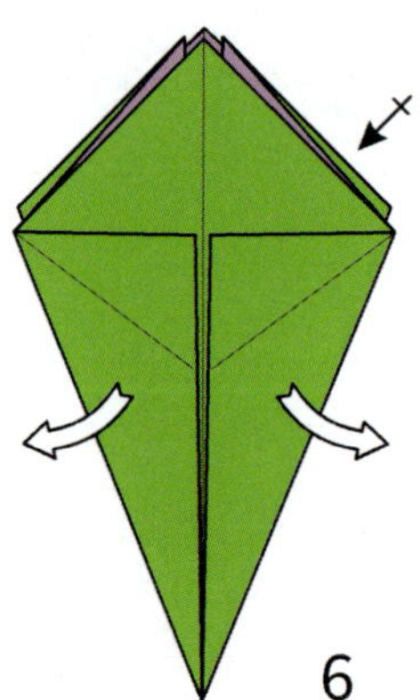

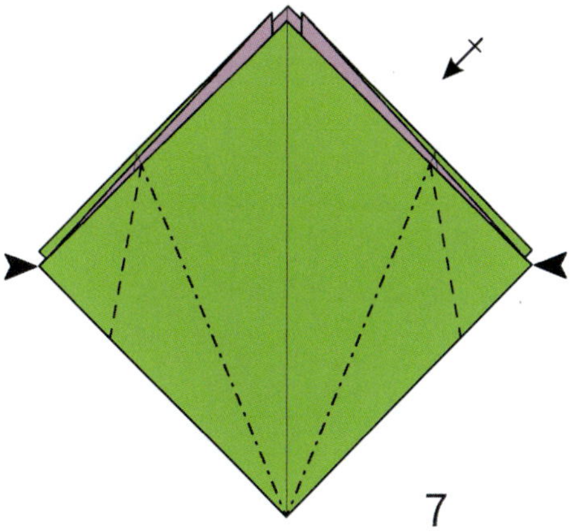

3D

7

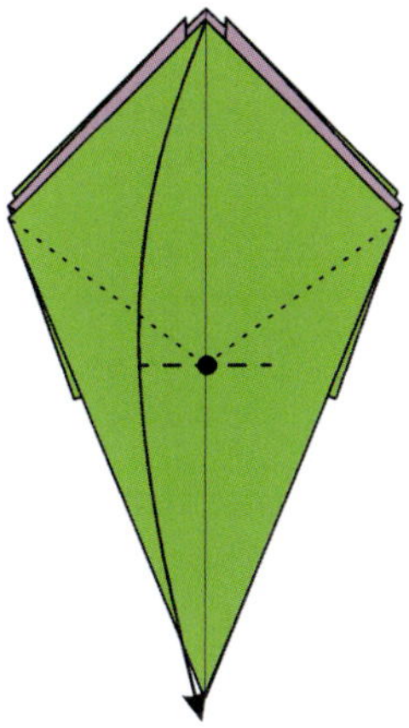

8

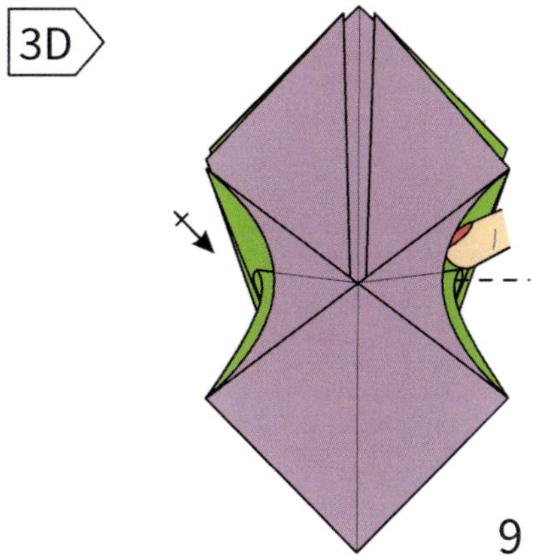

9

8-10

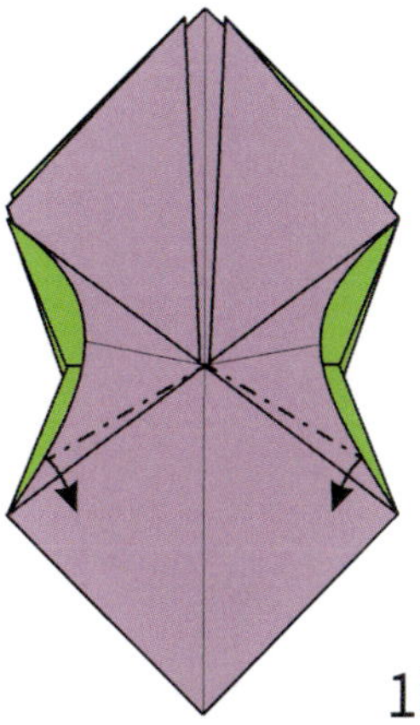

10

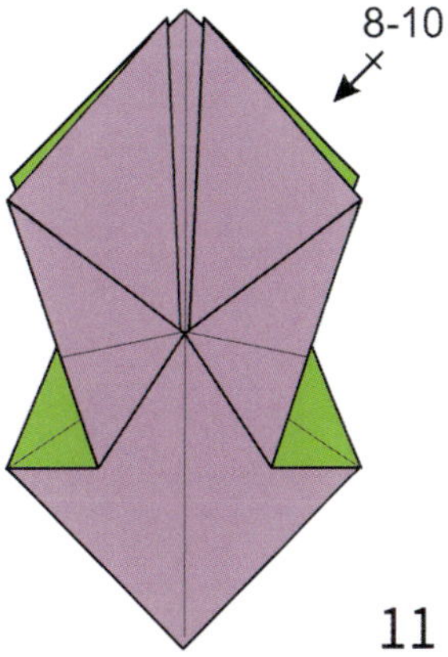

11

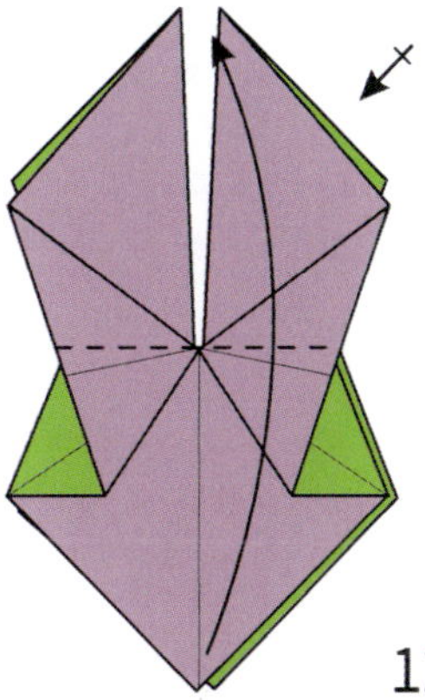

12

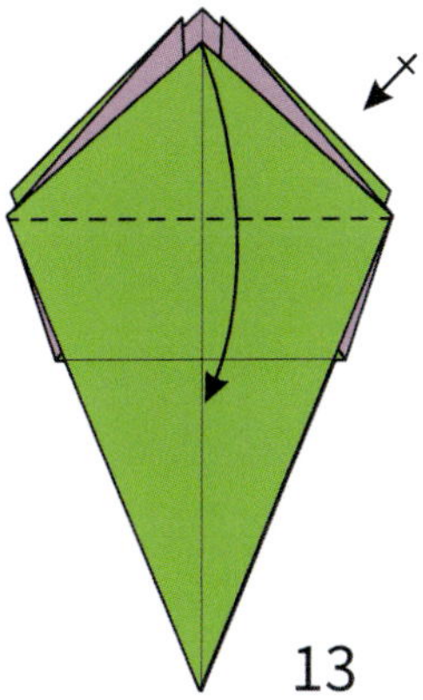

13

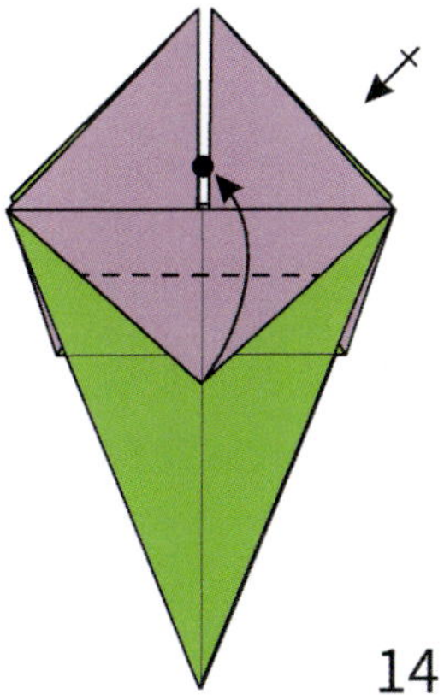

14

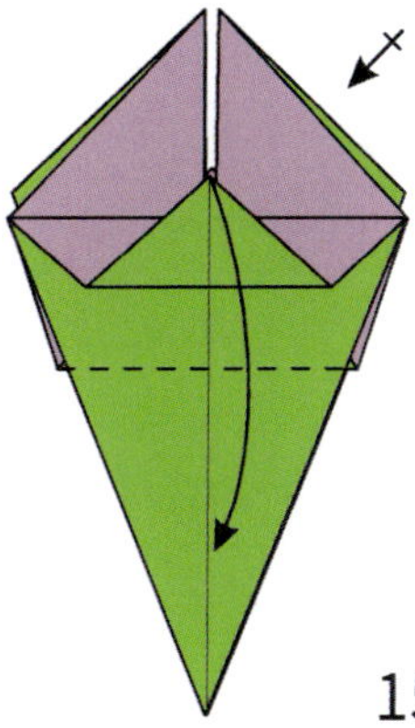

15

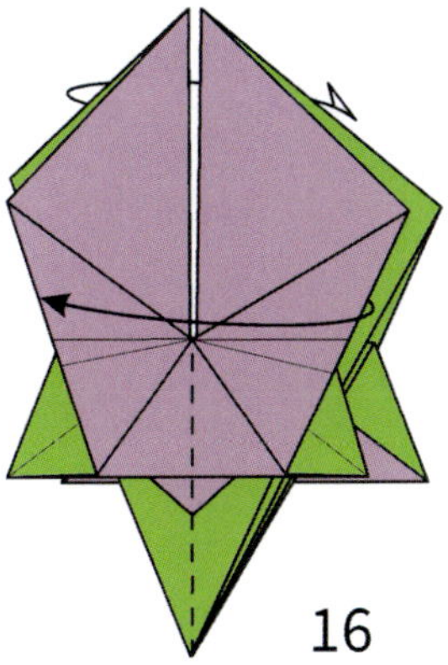

16

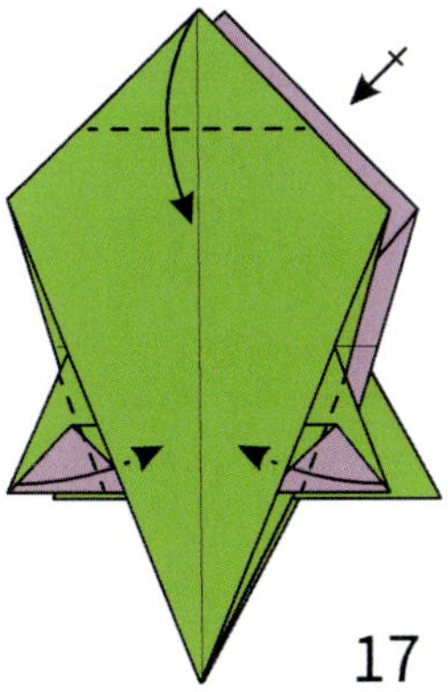

17

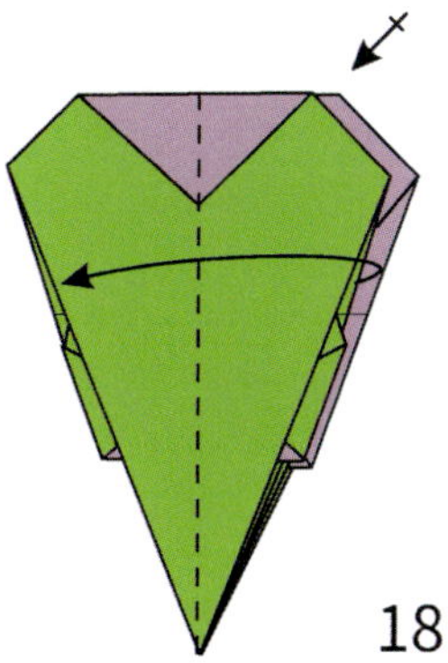

18

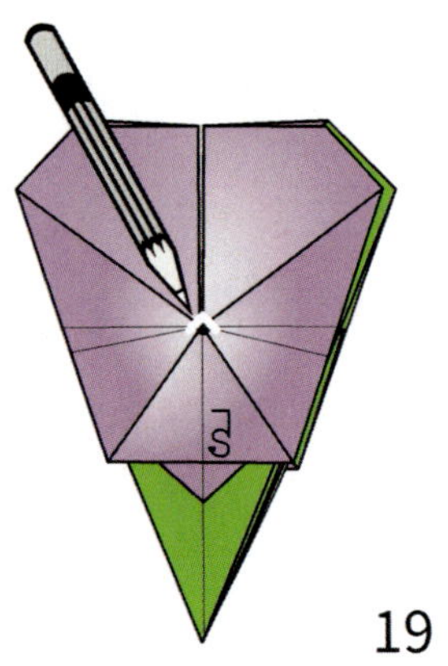
19

## *Variation*

You can also shape the pansy differently in step 17.
But in that case it can't be put through a card.

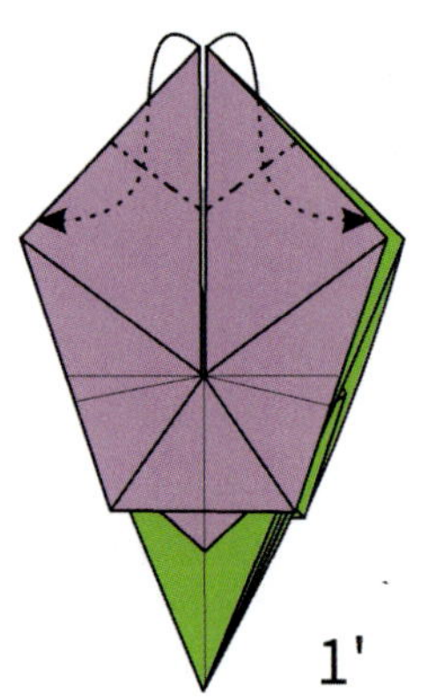
1'

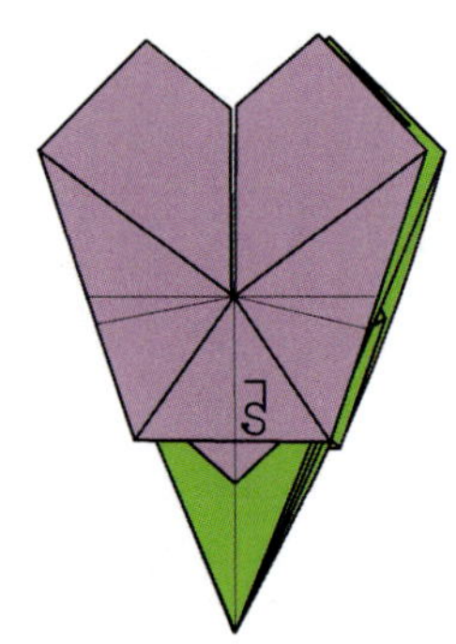

## *Attach to a card*

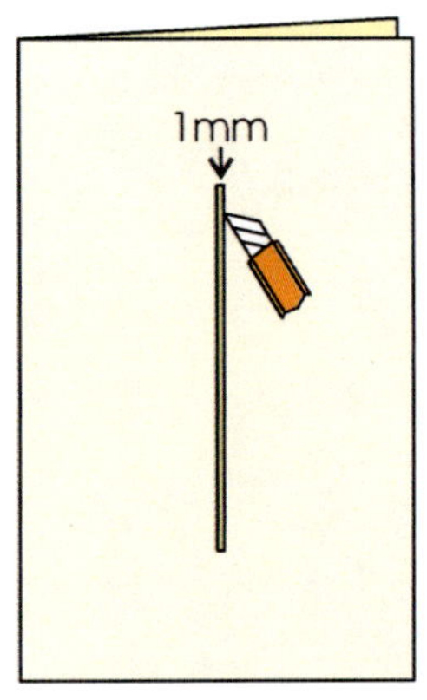

20

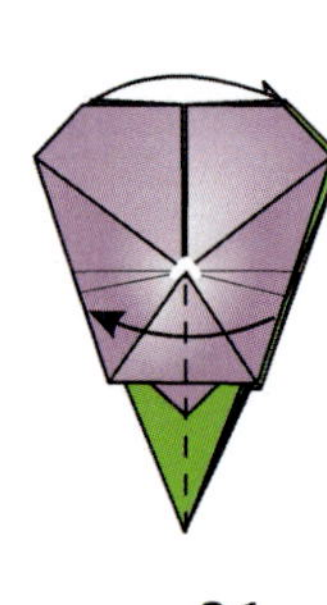
21

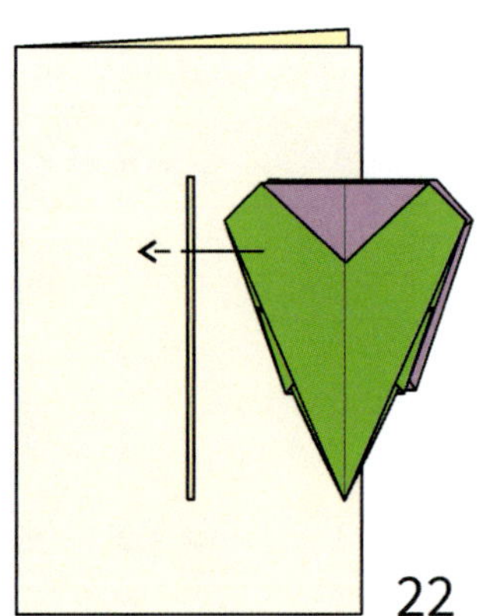
22

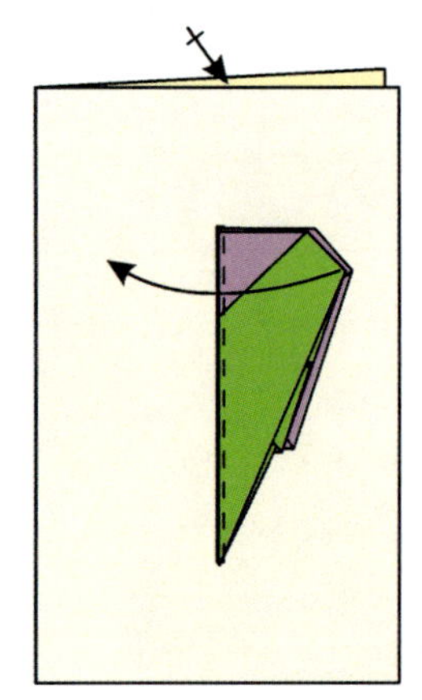
23

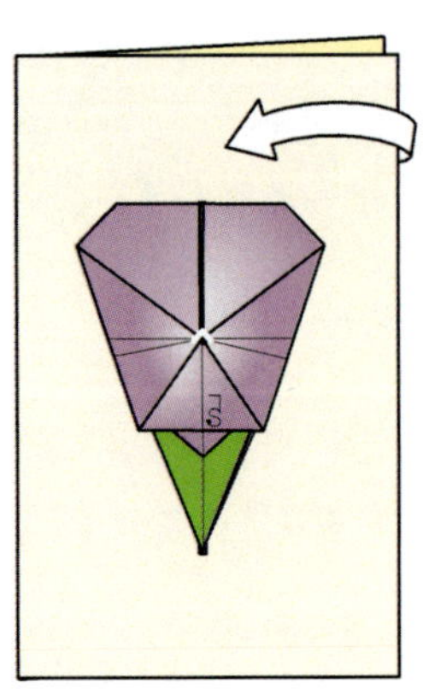
24

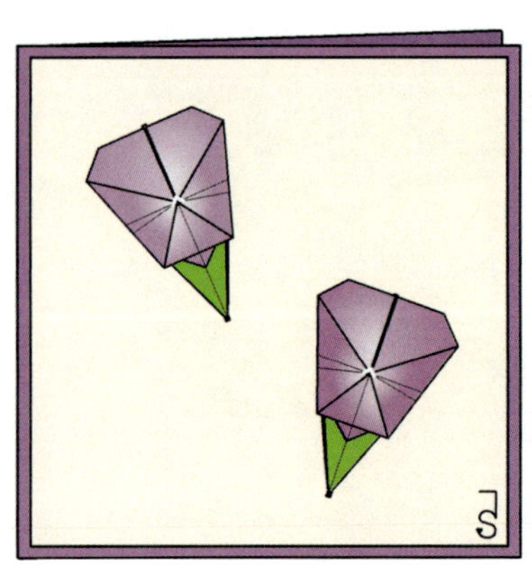

# Duo Pansy-Variation 1

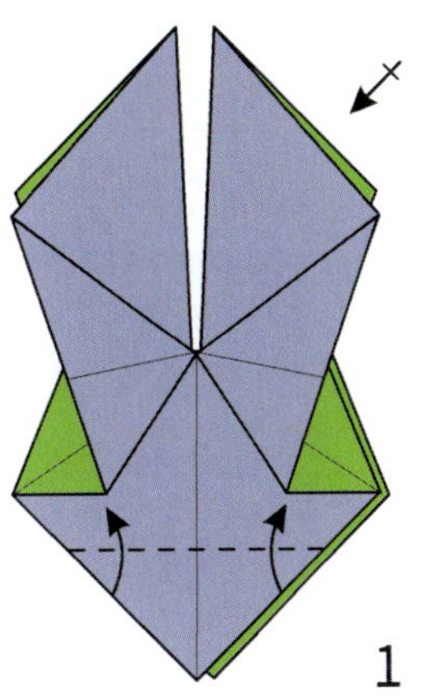

1

Fold steps 1-11 of Duo Pansy page 52

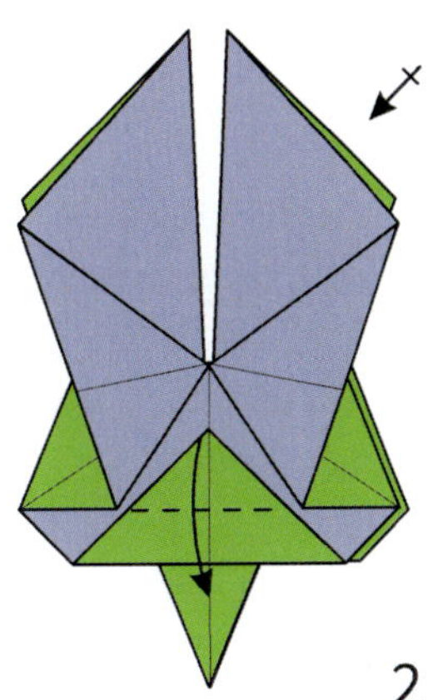

2

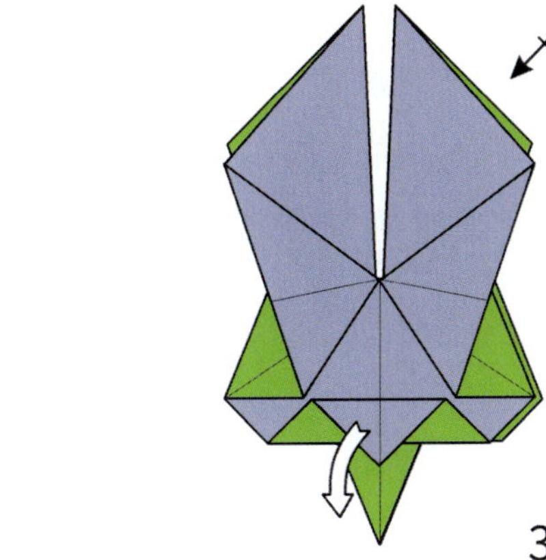

3

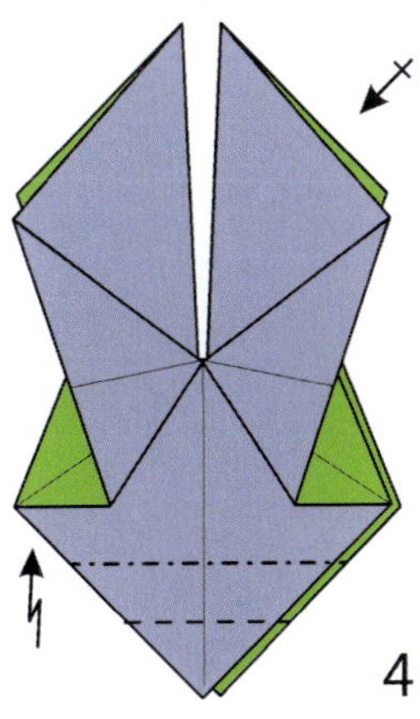

4

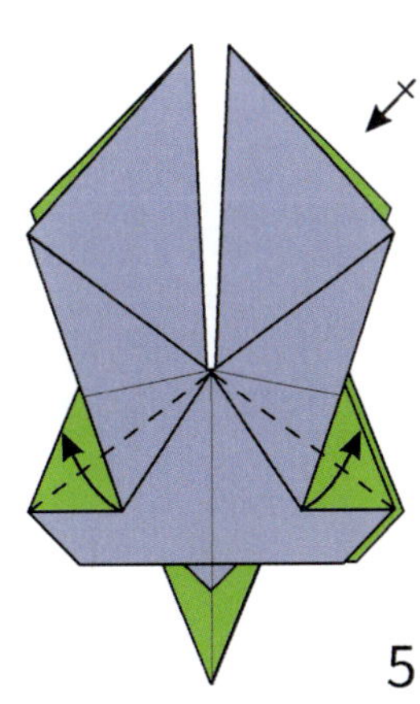

5

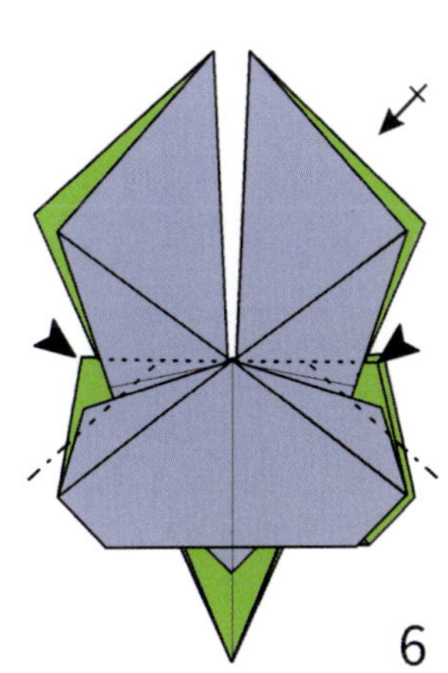

6

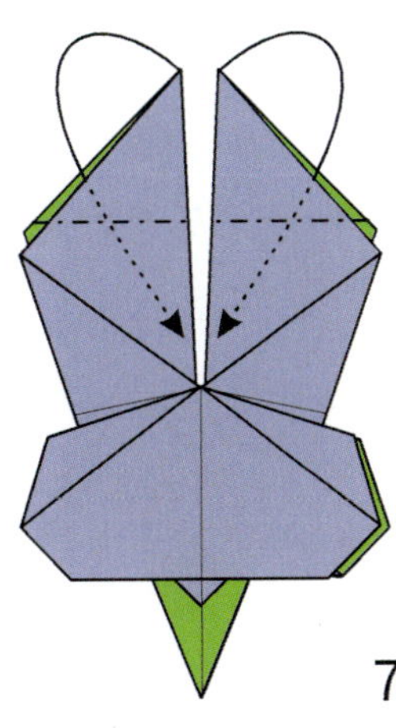

7

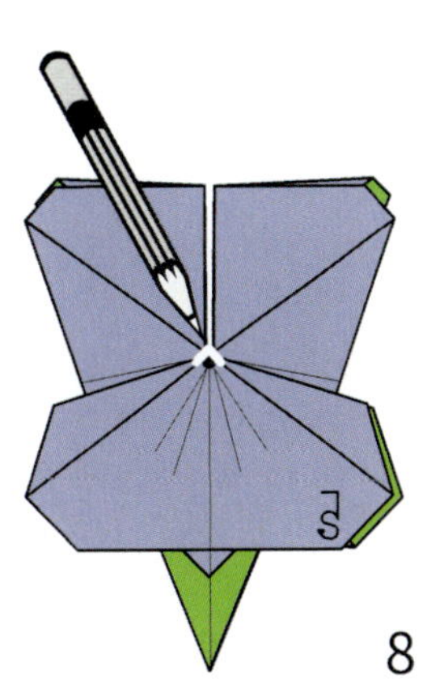

8

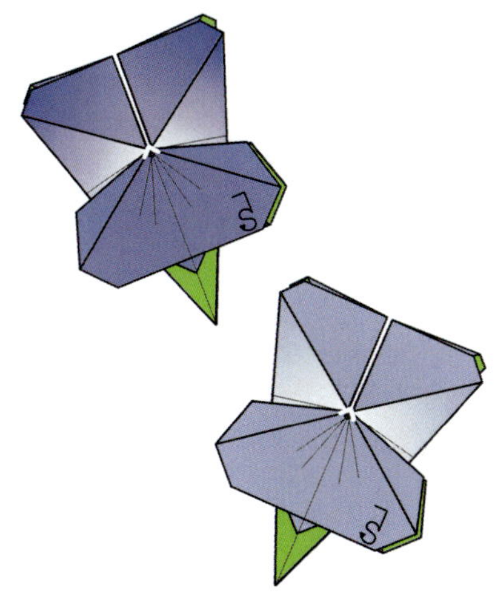

# Duo Pansy-Variation 2

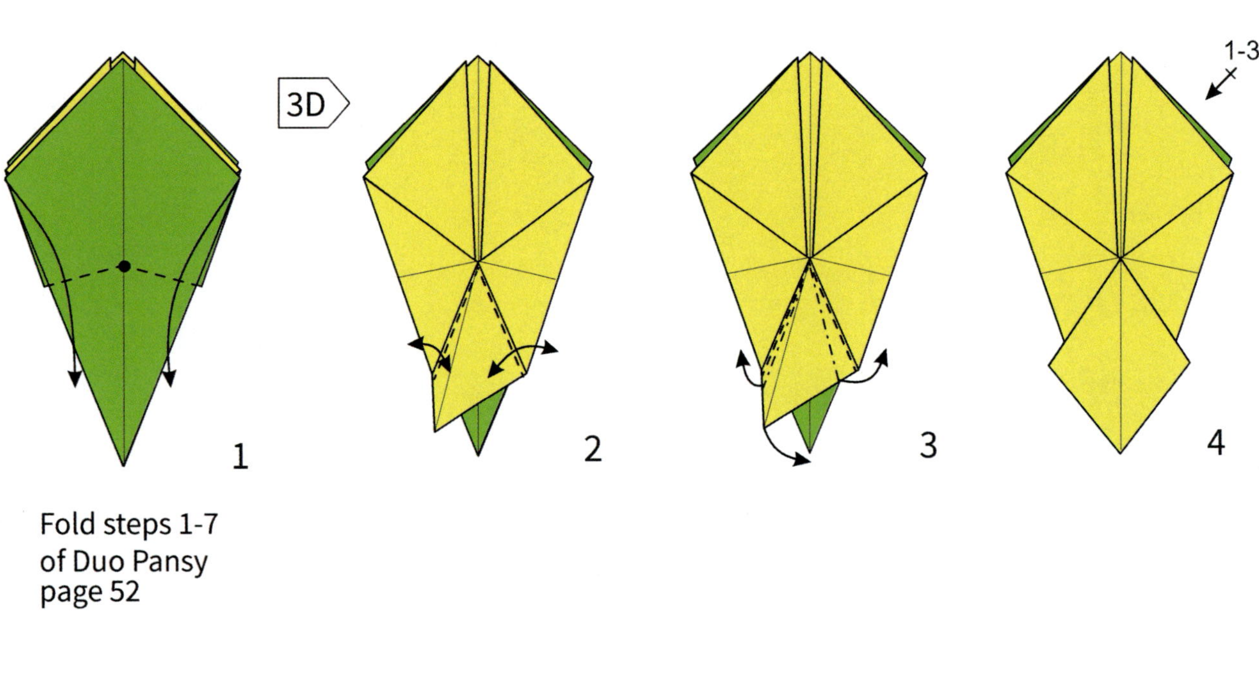


Fold steps 1-7 of Duo Pansy page 52

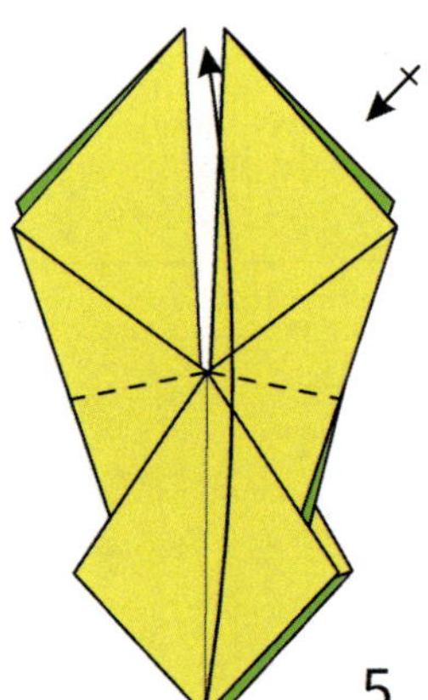


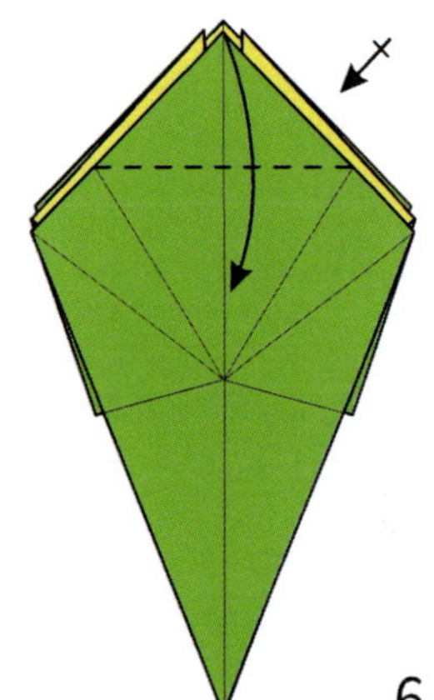


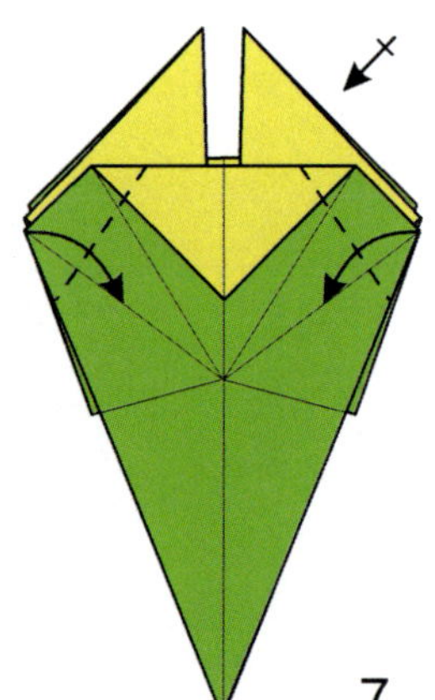


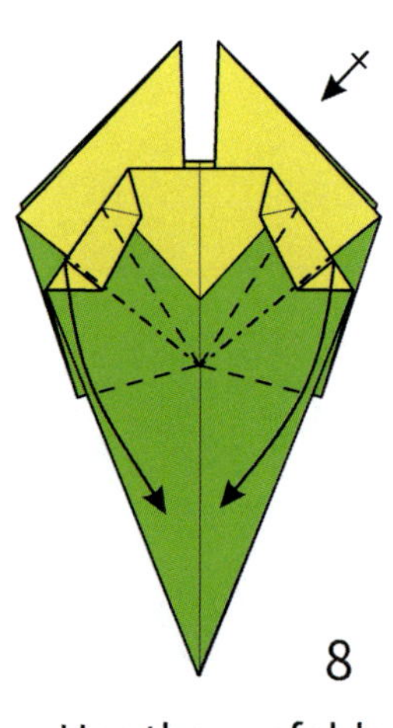


Use the prefolds made in steps 2-3

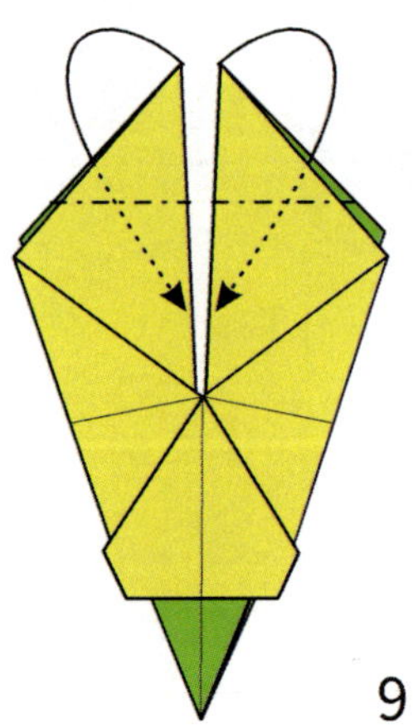


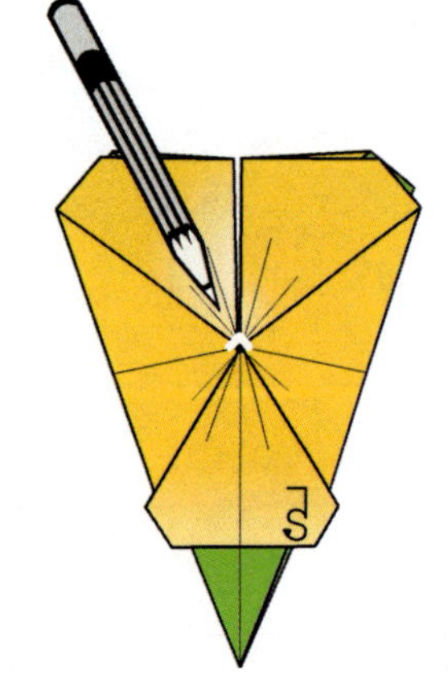

# Flower Truussia

18-08-2019

I designed several variations of these flowers and I have named this one after my mother-in-law. We lost her February 2020, a few weeks before Covid. She loved flowers and had lots of them on her balcony. Also, she loved people and they would often find her on her balcony. A special flower for a special woman.

Paper:

Flower: 1 hexagon 15x15 cm gradient or plain paper

Stem: 1 square 15x15 cm green kami

## Flower

Start with the hexagon on page 12

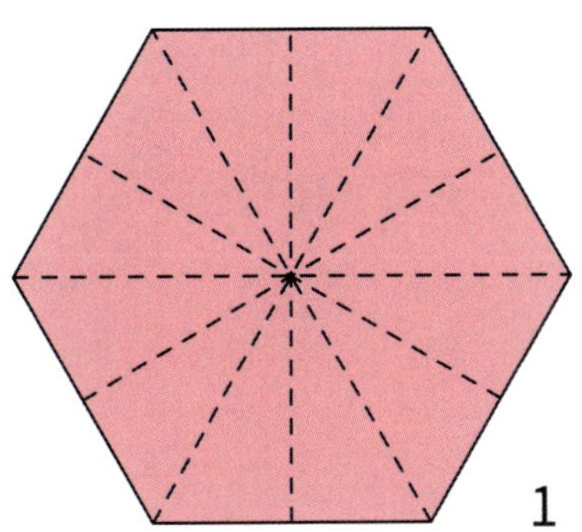

1

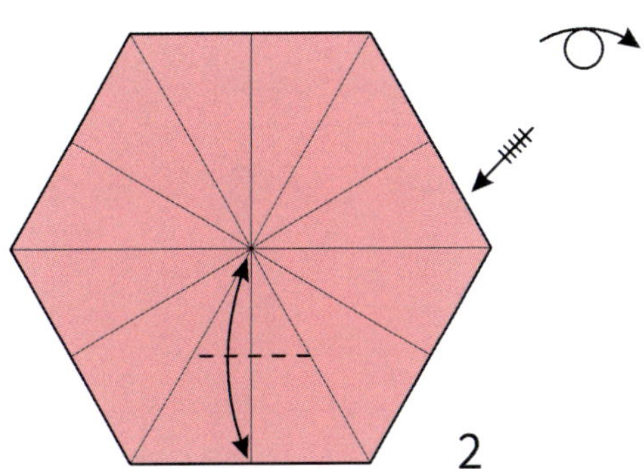

2

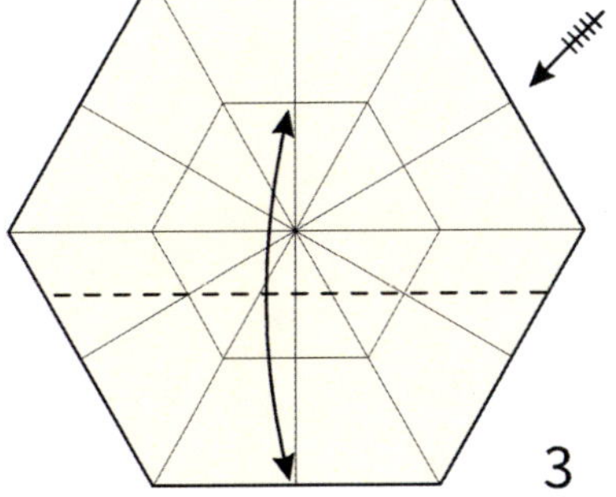

3

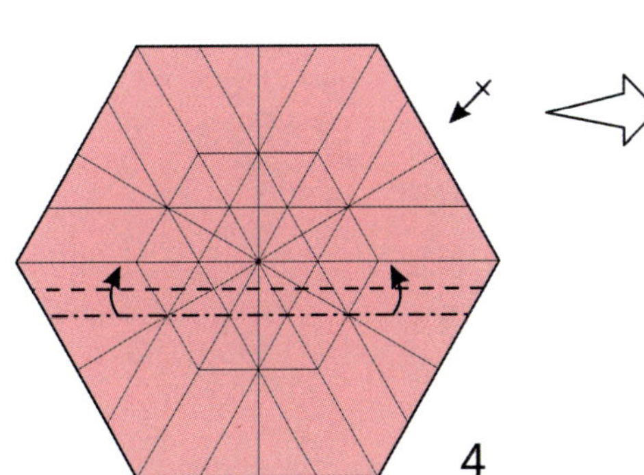

4

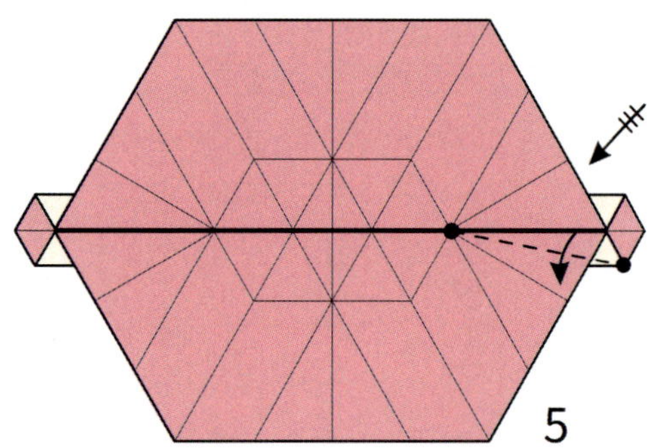
5

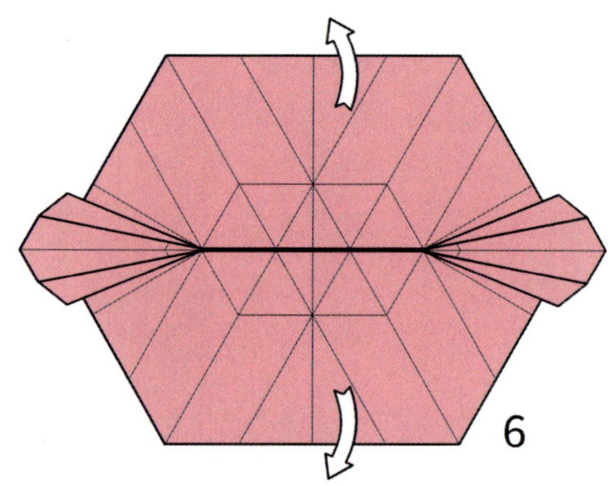
6

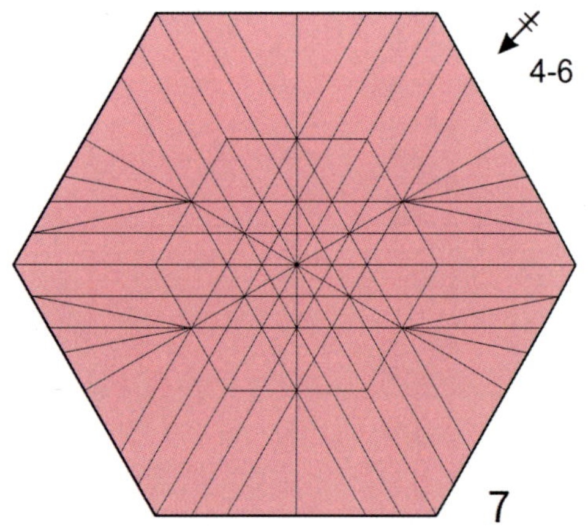
4-6
7

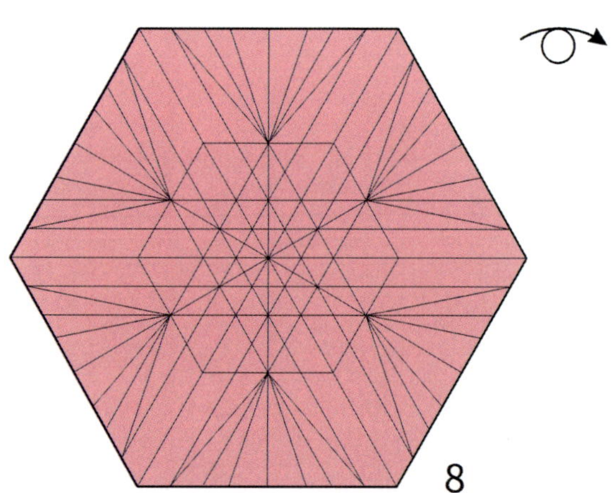
8

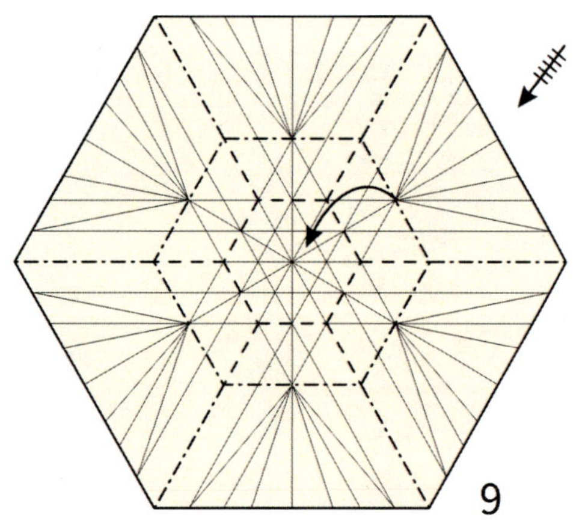
9

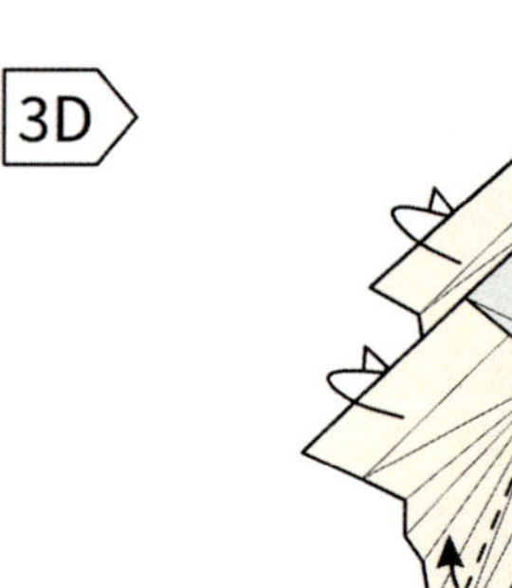
3D
10

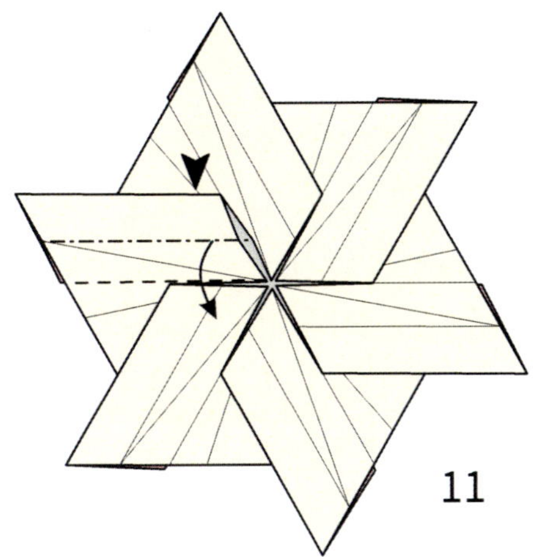


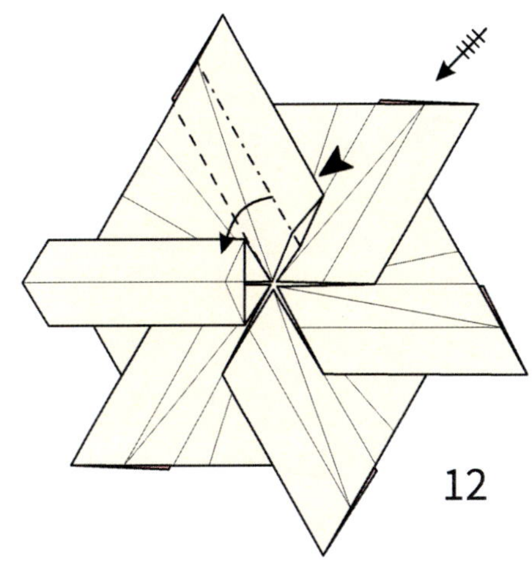


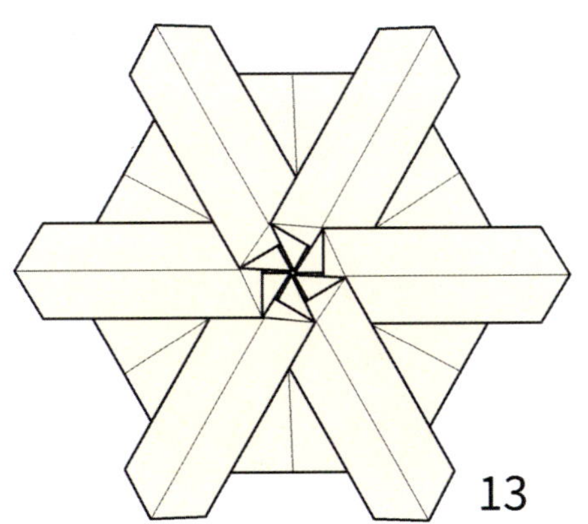

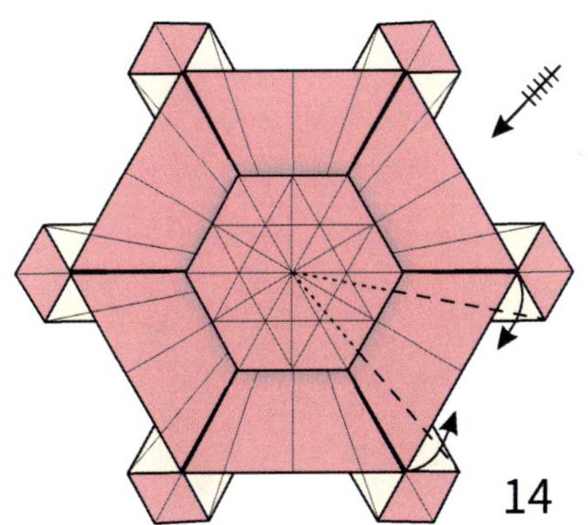


2D model finished

# 3D model

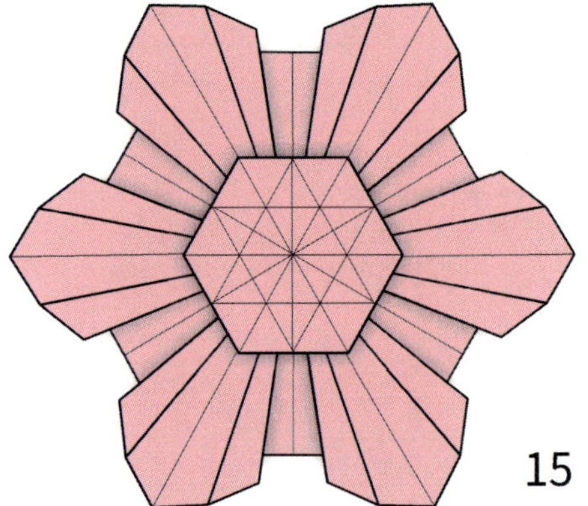
15

Fold steps 1-14
of the 2D flower
page 57

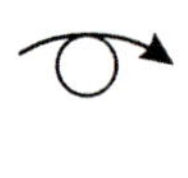

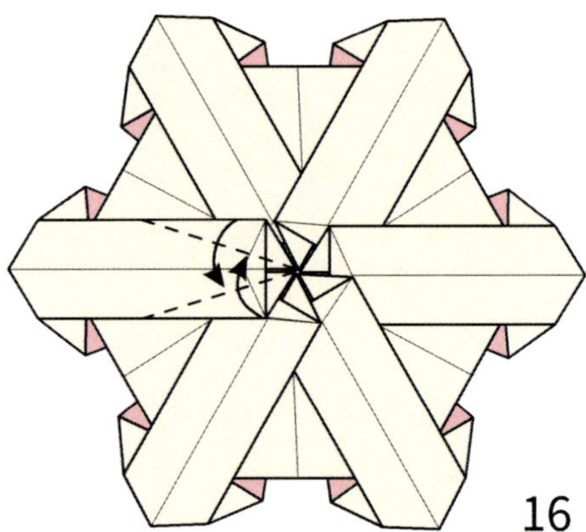
16

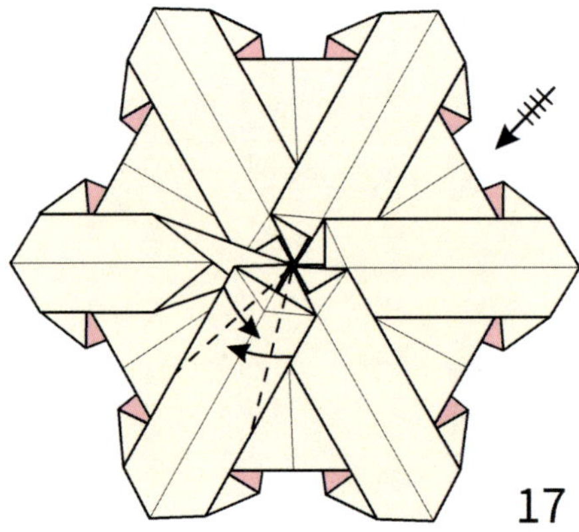
17

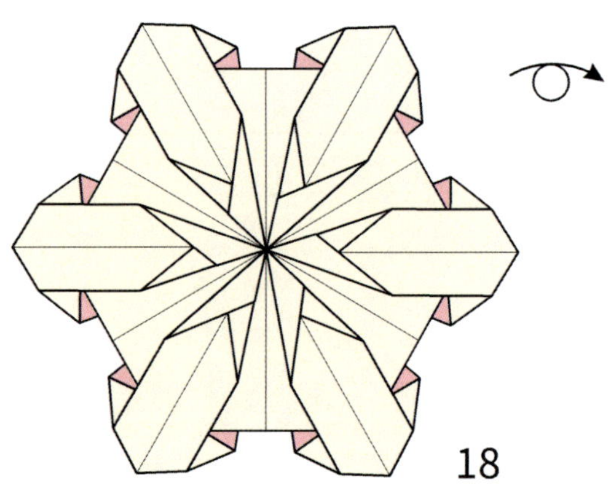
18

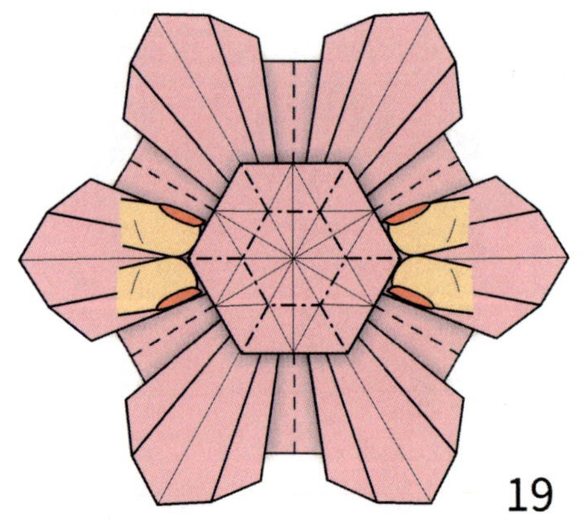
19

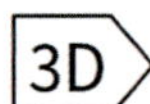

## Stem

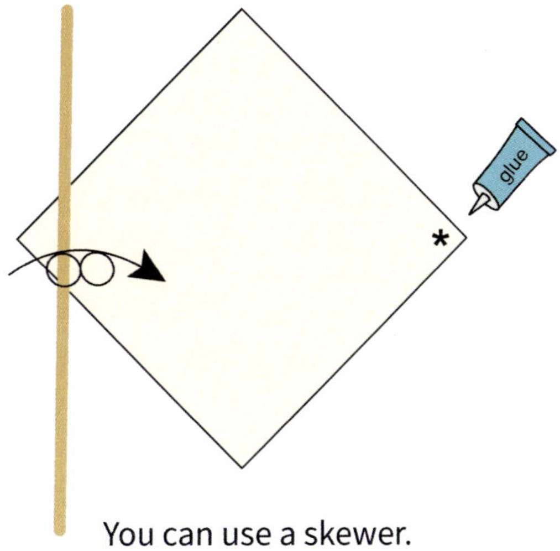

You can use a skewer.

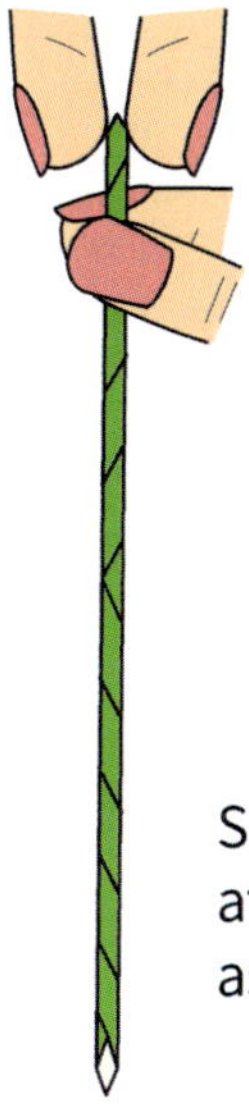

Squash the top at both sides, as showed.

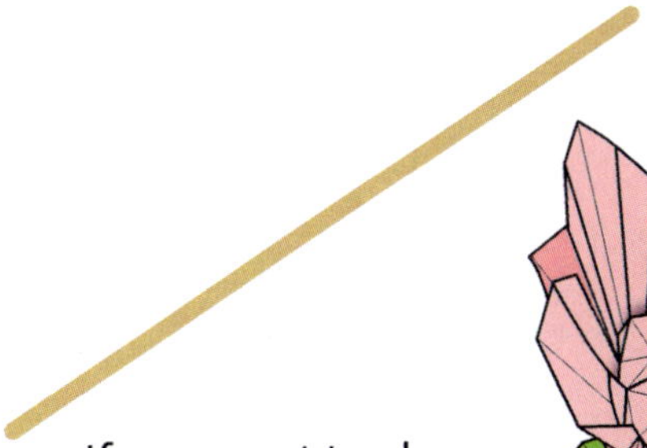

If you want to shape the flower tips, you can use a skewer.

# Flower Susanna

18-08-2019

The year 2019 I will not quickly forget because of all the worst things that happened. I lost my sister, my mother and almost my husband. But still then my faith and origami was a way for me to survive. This flower is named after my beloved mother, Susanna. She was a versatile woman with numerous talents, many of which I came to inherit.

Paper:
Flower: 1 hexagon 15x15cm
plane duo color paper
Stem: 1 square 15x15cm
green kami

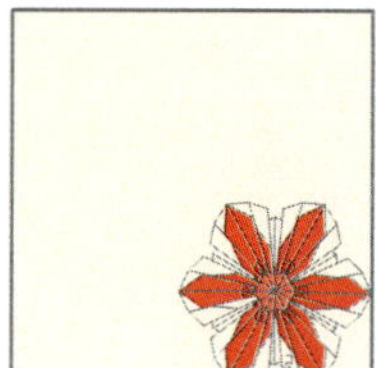

## Flower

Start with the hexagon on page 12

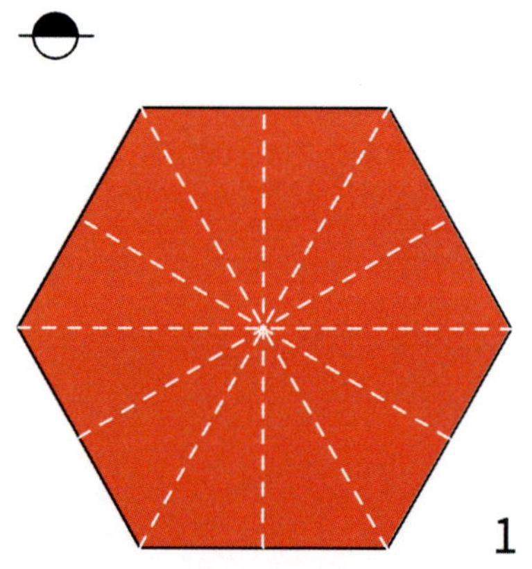

1

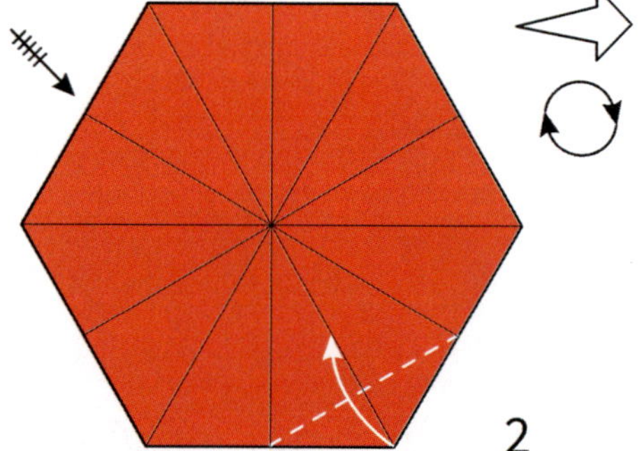

2

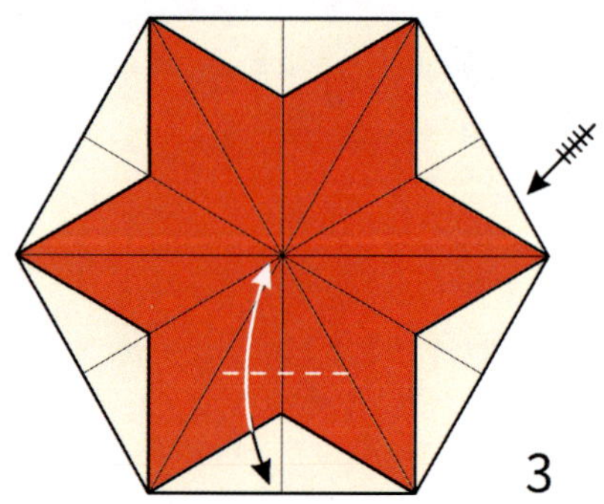

3

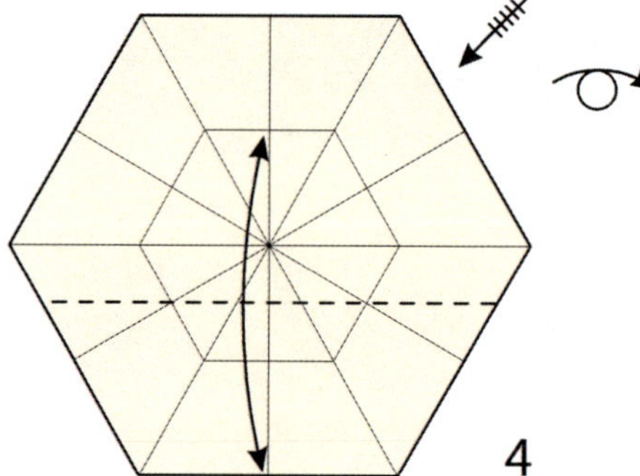

4

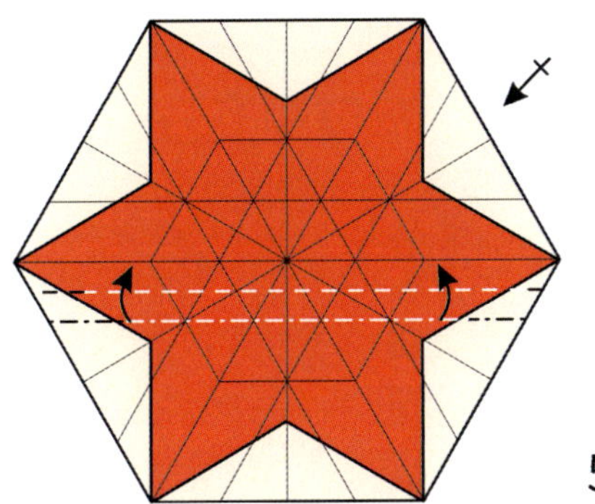

5

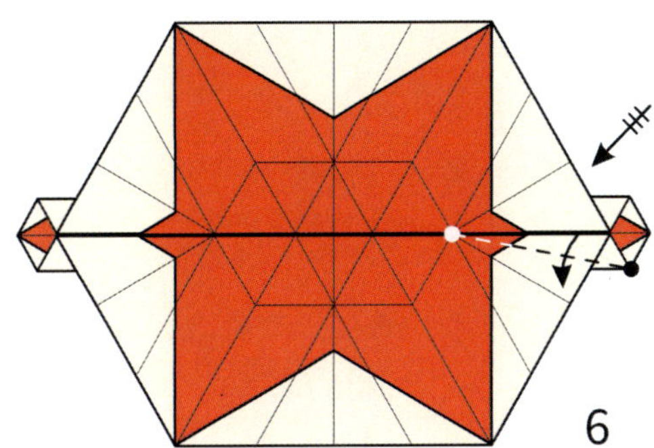

6

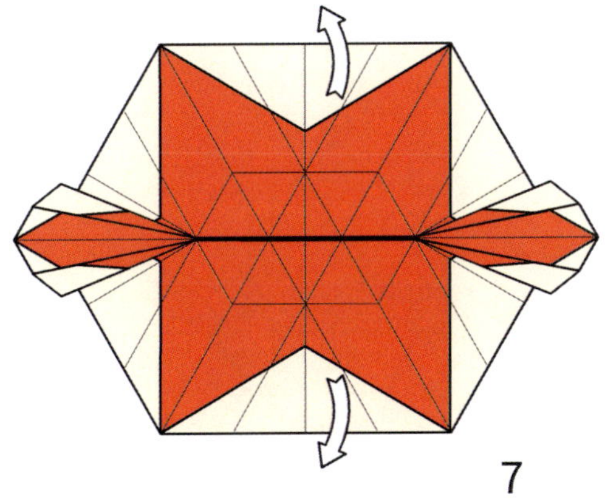

7

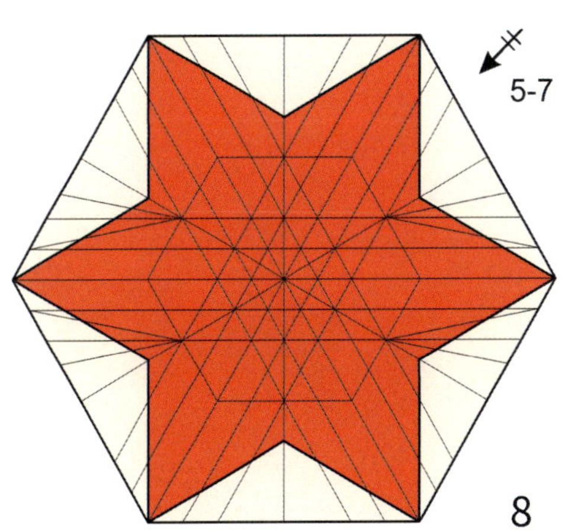


8

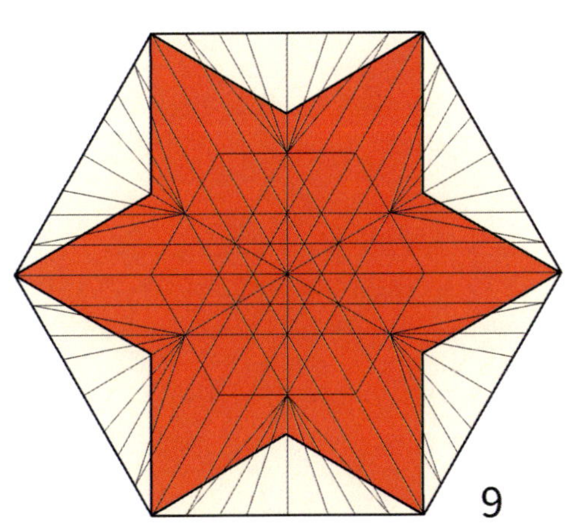

9

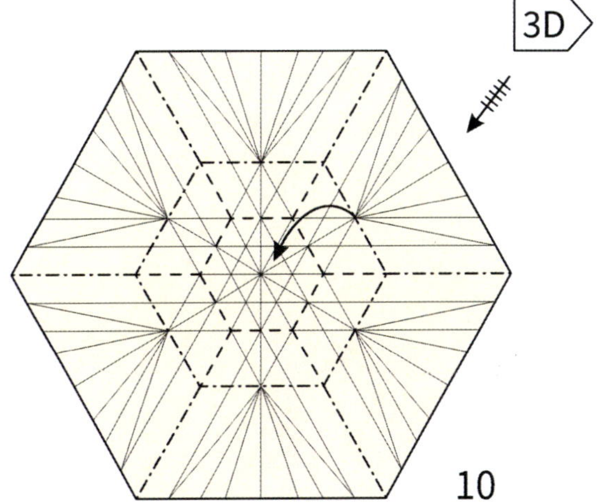


10

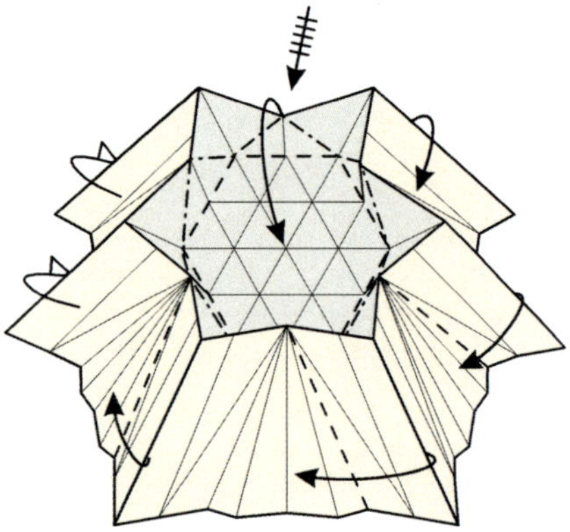

11

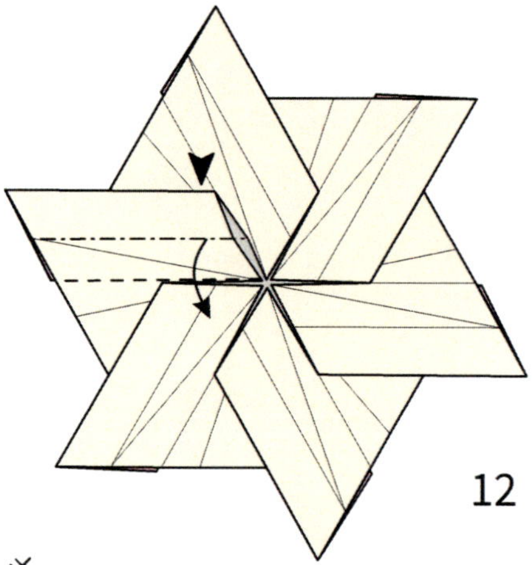

12

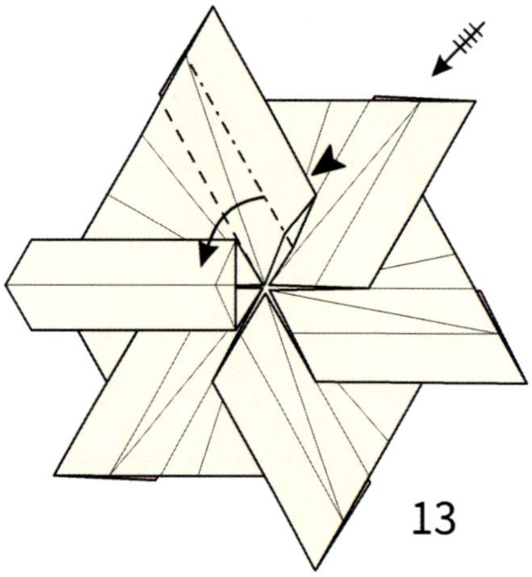

13

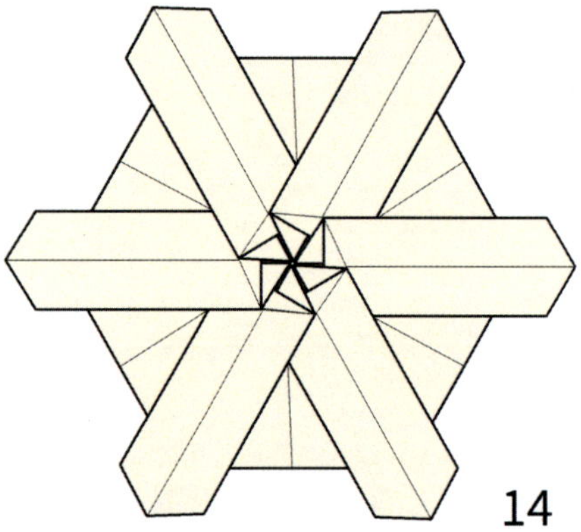

14

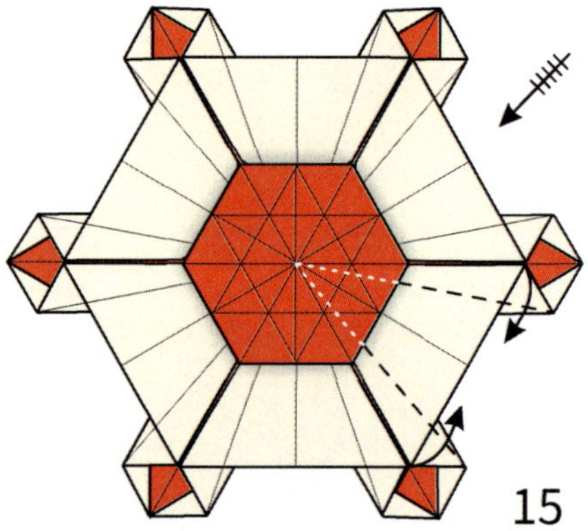

15

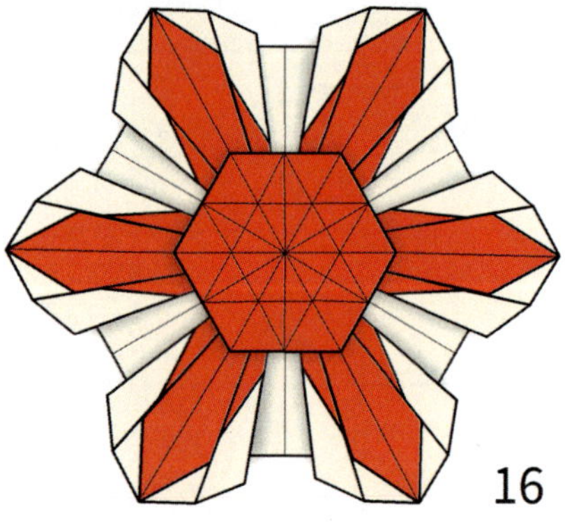

16

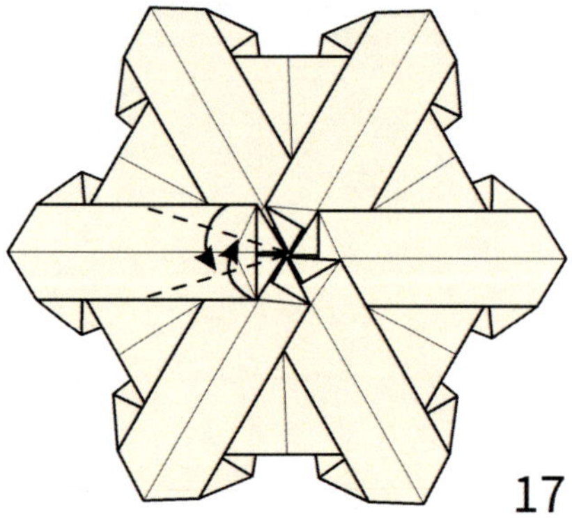

17

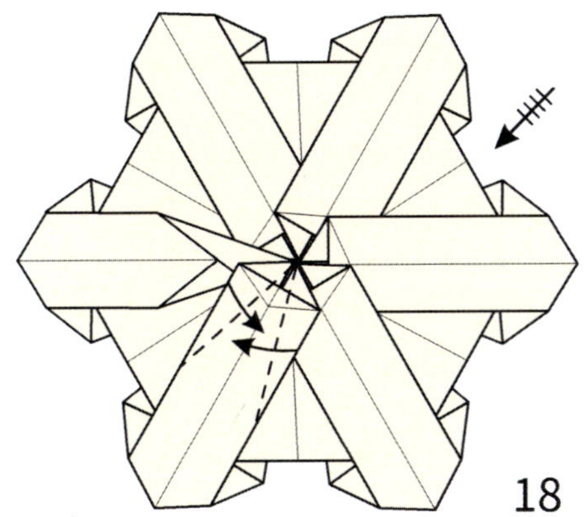
18

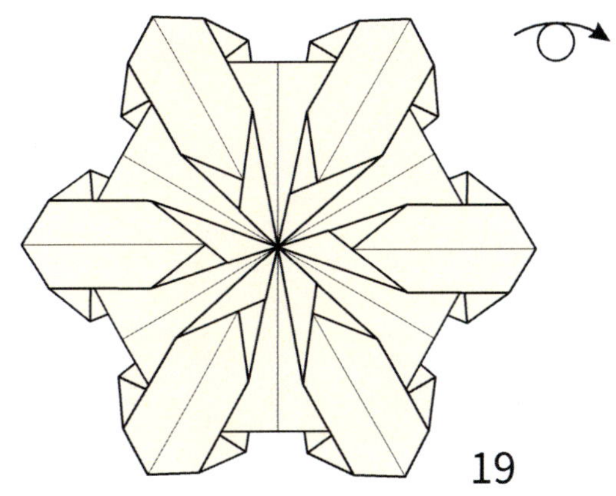
19

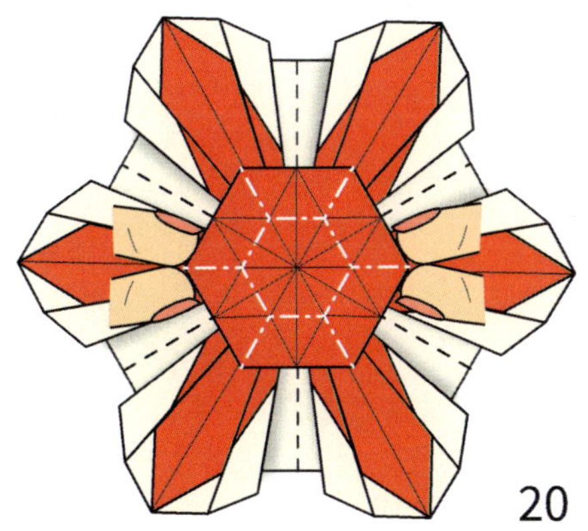
20

*Variation*

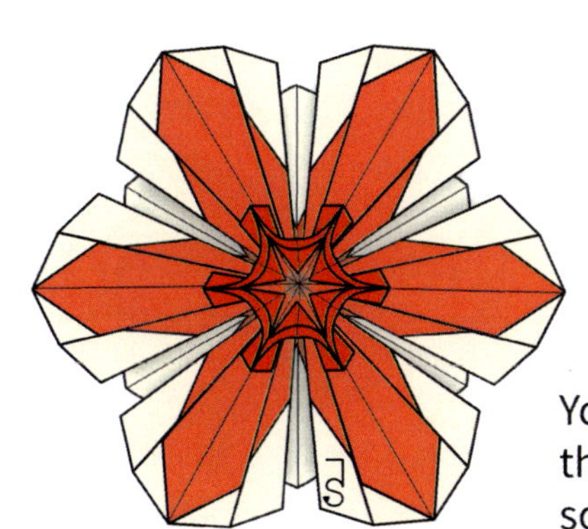

You can push the center down, so a star will appear.

Make the stem as shown on page 61 Flower Truussia.

# Leaves

07-06-2010

## Leaf 1

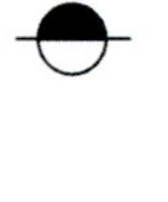

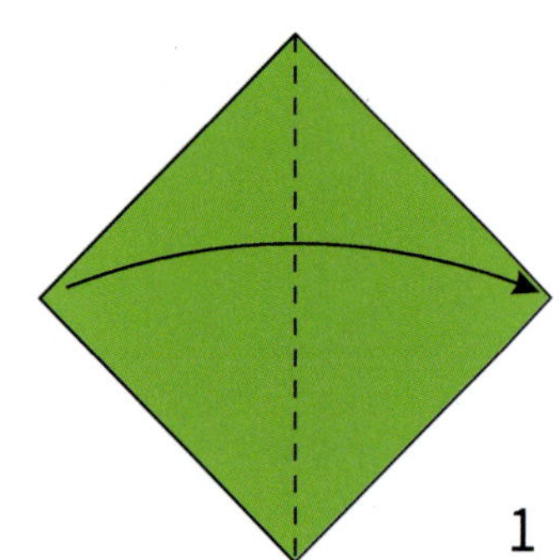

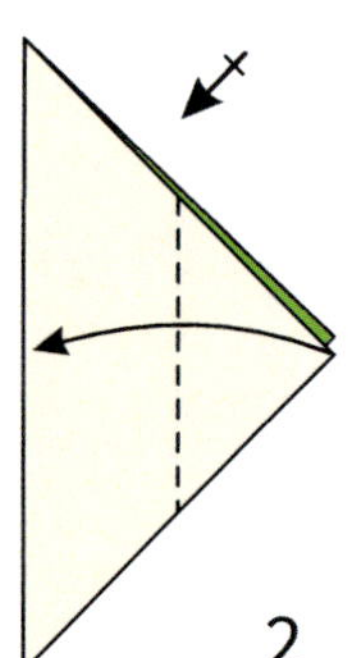


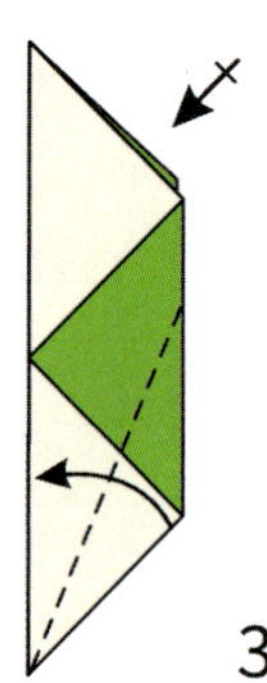

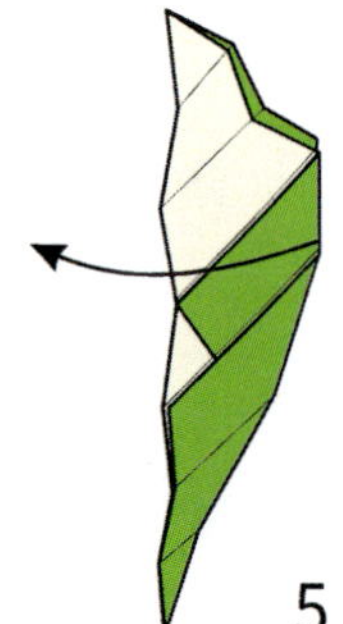

## Leaf 2

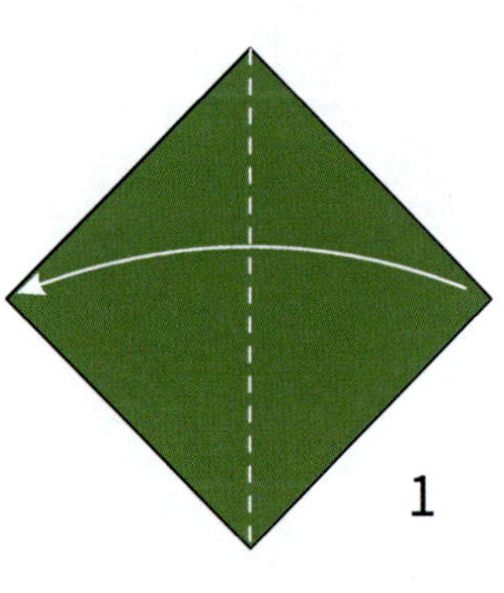


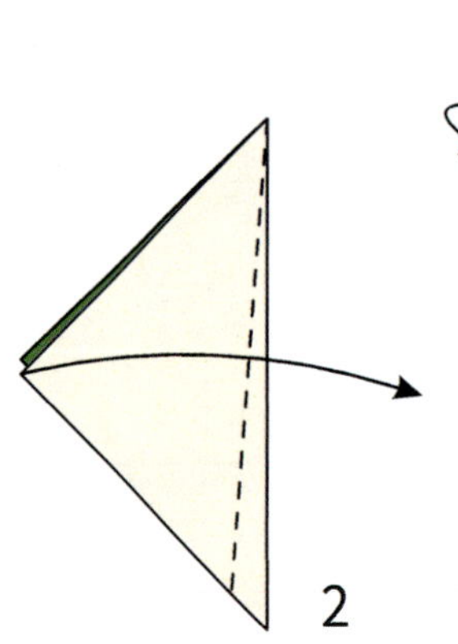


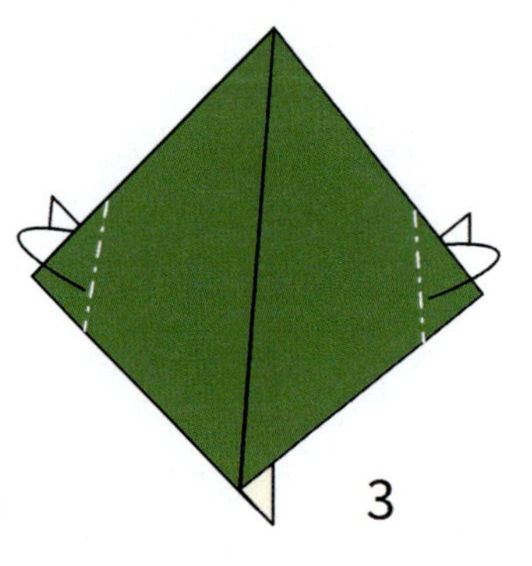


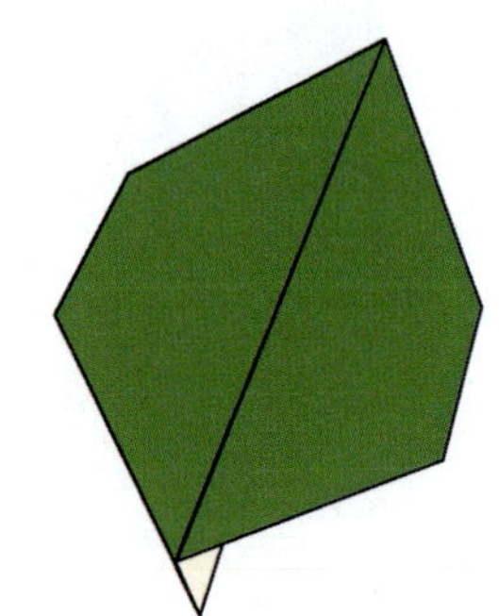

## Stem

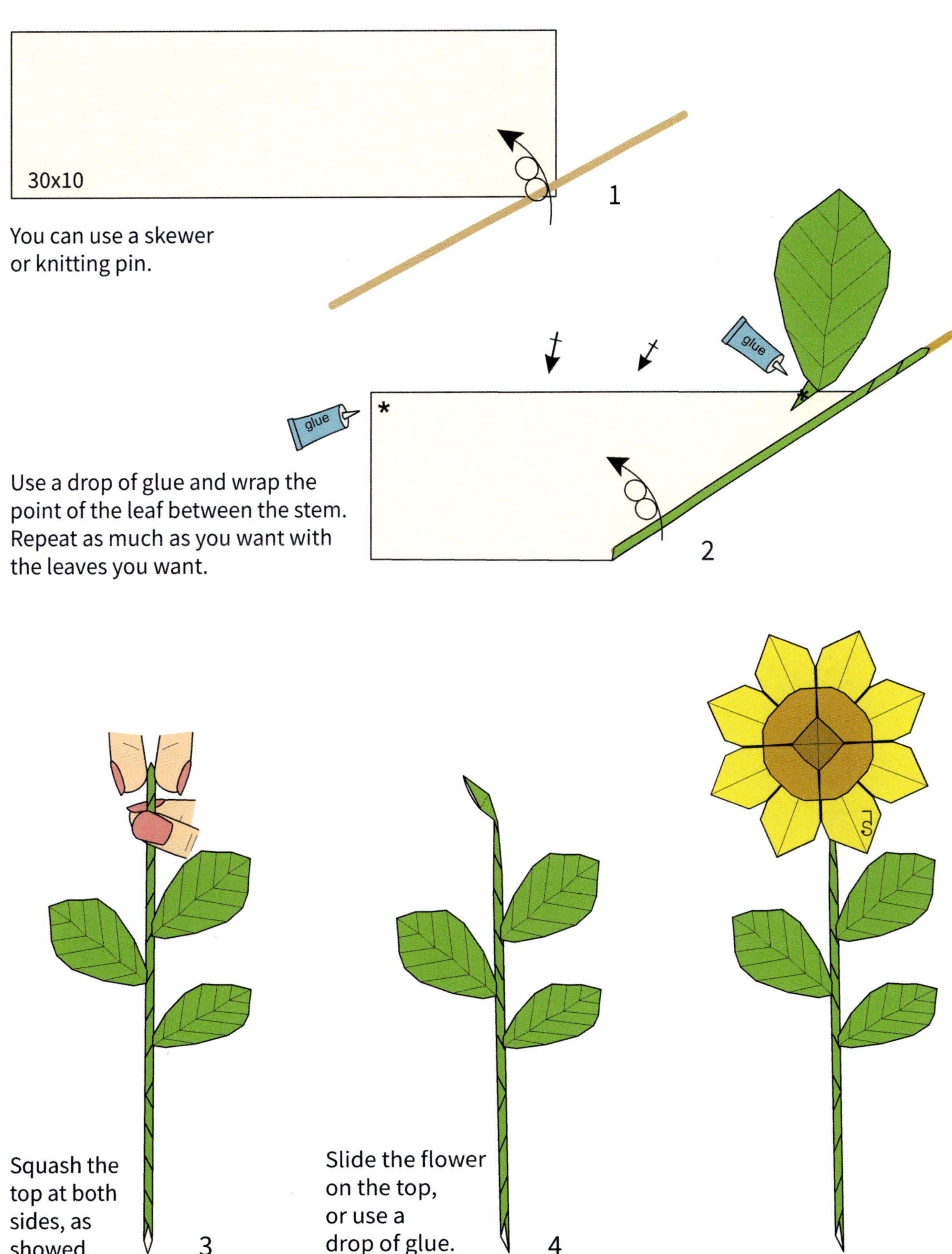


You can use a skewer or knitting pin.

Use a drop of glue and wrap the point of the leaf between the stem. Repeat as much as you want with the leaves you want.

Squash the top at both sides, as showed.

Slide the flower on the top, or use a drop of glue.

# My Specials

In this chapter I have collected the models for my grandchildren. So the chapter could actually be called “My Specials for my grandchildren“. Each model is named after one of them. Three of the models are specially made for their birth as a maternity gift. Enjoy these special models.

# Rosa-fant

27-01-2015

"Grandma, can you fold an elephant for me?", my 4 year old granddaughter, Rosalina, asked. I do have a lot of books books finding at once an elephant that can be folded quickly is not so easy. So in order not to let the little girl wait too long I took a piece of paper and made one up myself. It took me 15 minutes, surprisingly fast. That's how some models are created.

Paper:
- 15x15 cm all kinds of paper

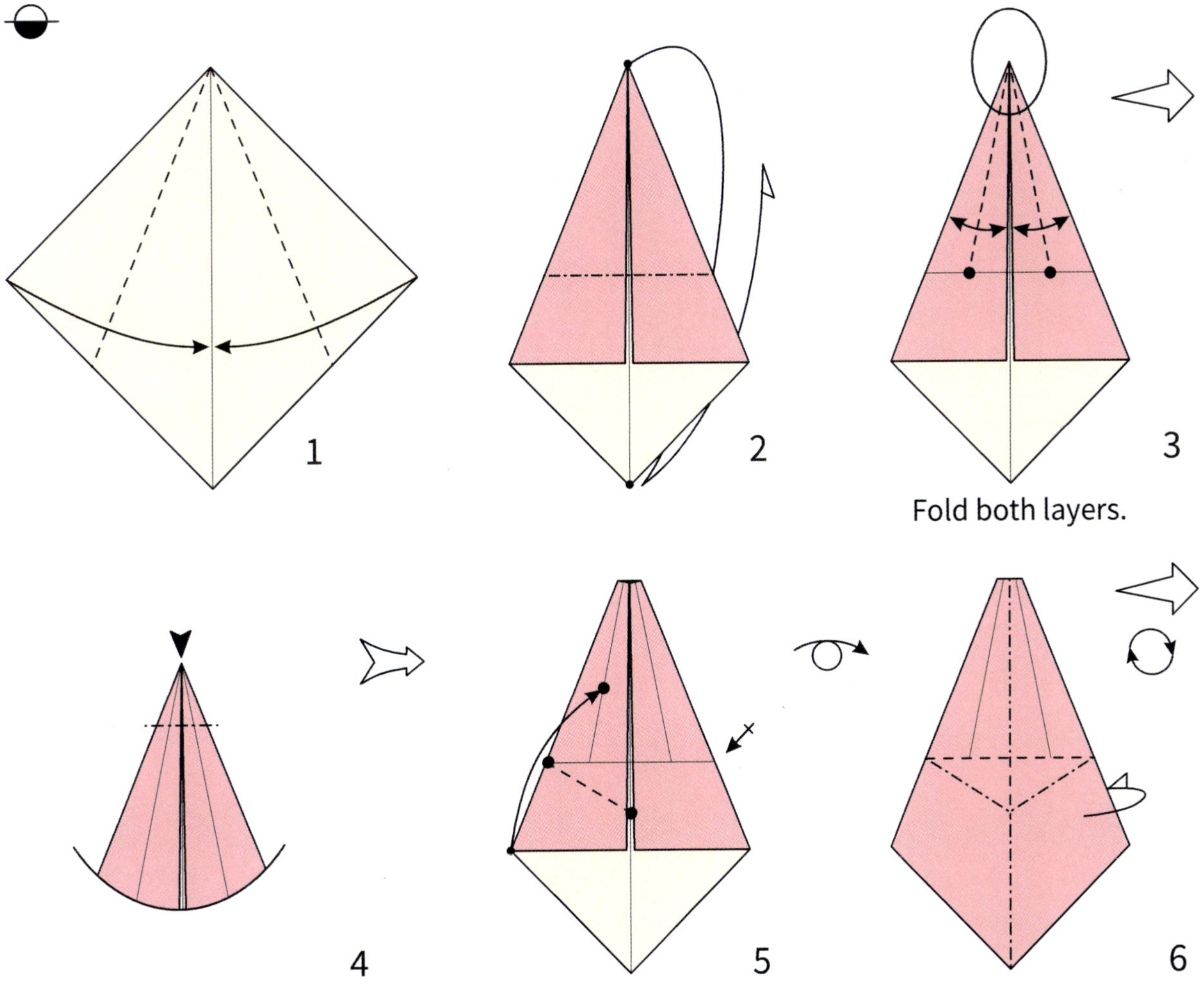

1

2

3

Fold both layers.

4

5

6

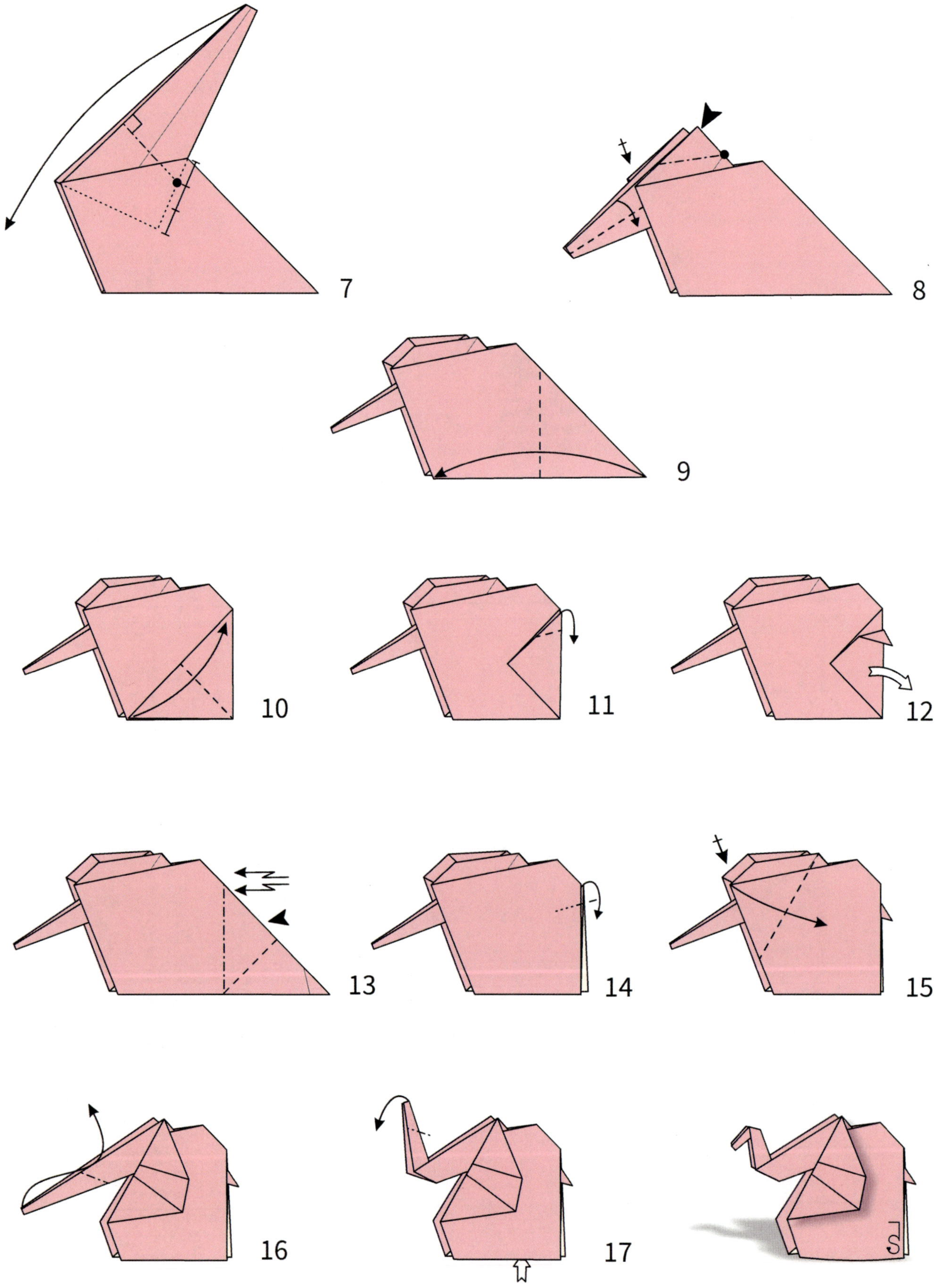

7

8

9

10

11

12

13

14

15

16

17

# 3D Rosa-fant

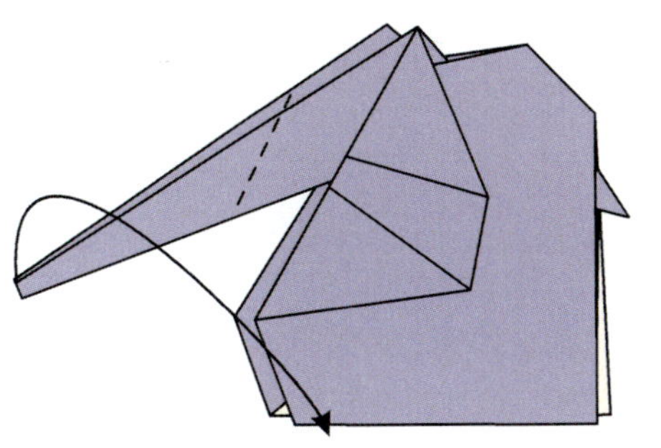

1

Fold steps 1-15

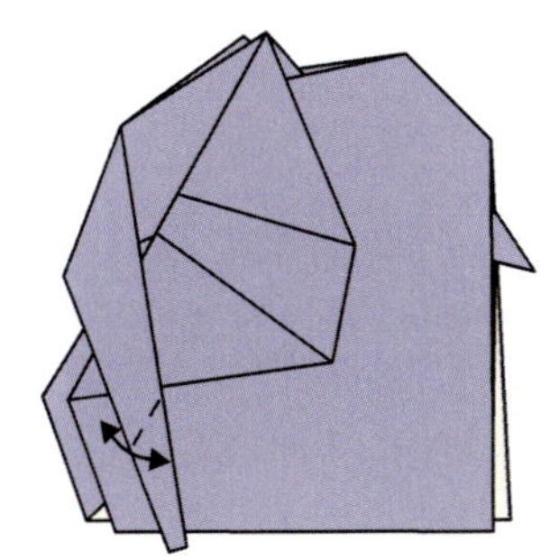

2

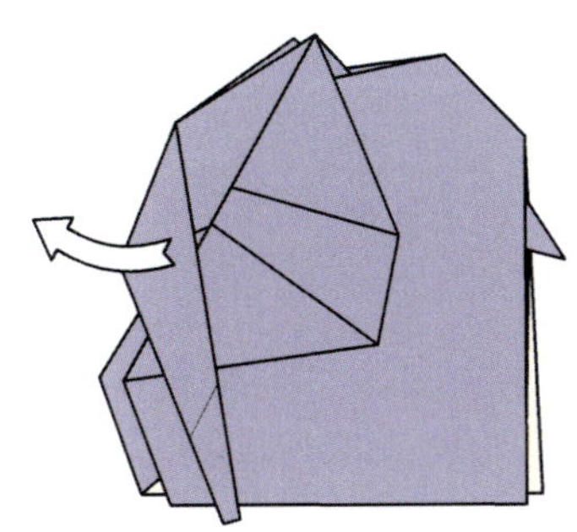

3

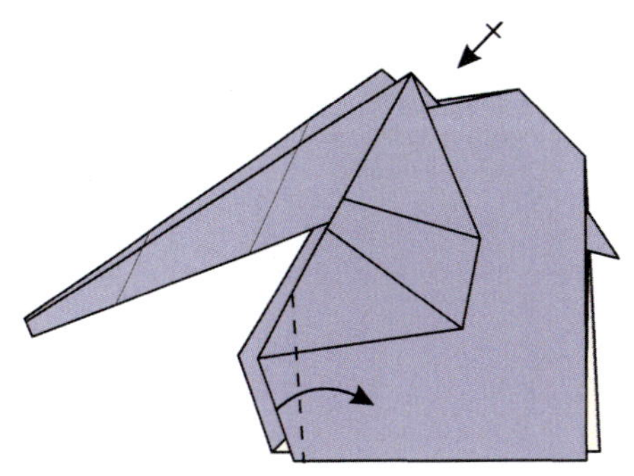

4

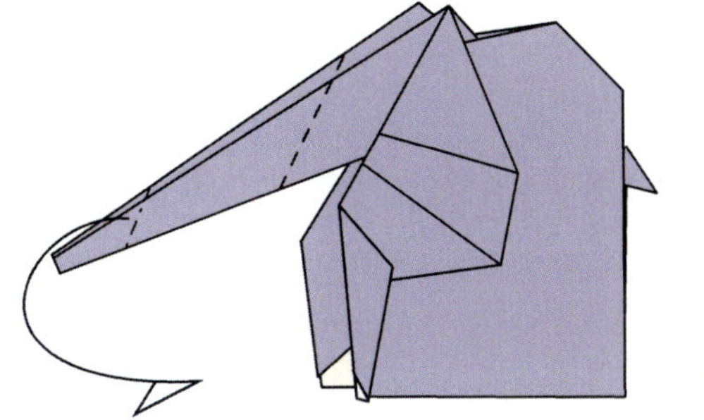

5

6

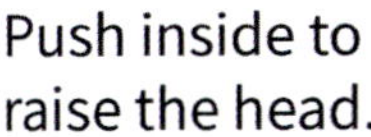


Push inside to raise the head.

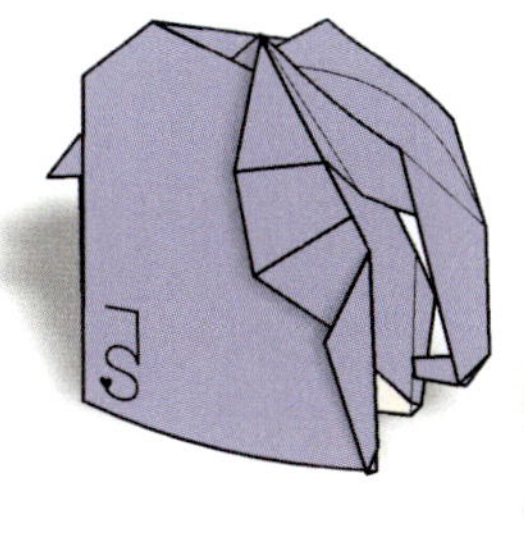

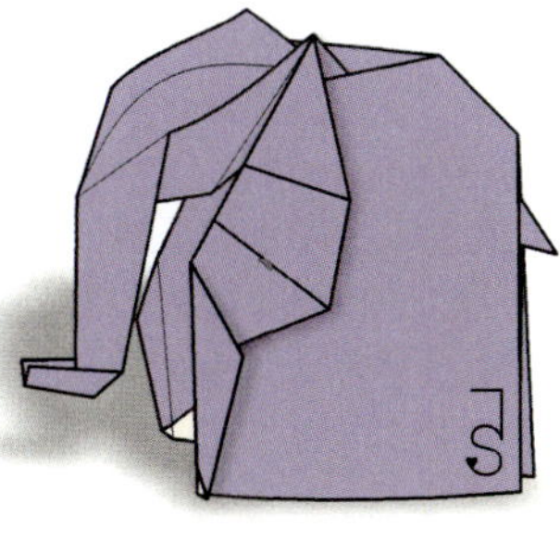

# Butterfly Kisses

17-07-2024

This cute model has only recently been designed. I came up with it as a treat for the maternity visit for our 6th lovely grandchild, Teddie Louise. It was important for the parents that the box could be opened, filled, and then closed again without any origami skills needed. So I ended up with this easy and cute model. A small label can be attached for the name and date of birth.

Paper:
- 15x15 cm Duo color
- Label 0,8x15 cm

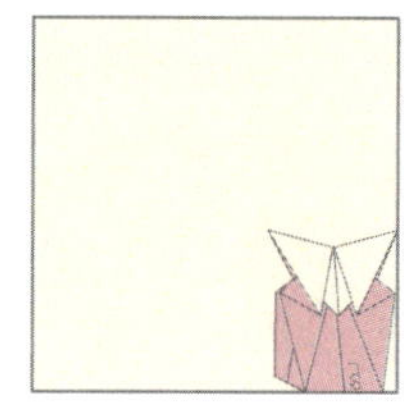

The light side is the butterfly

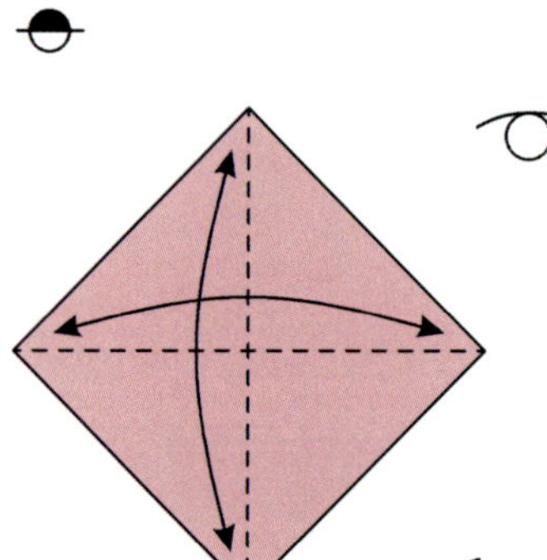

1

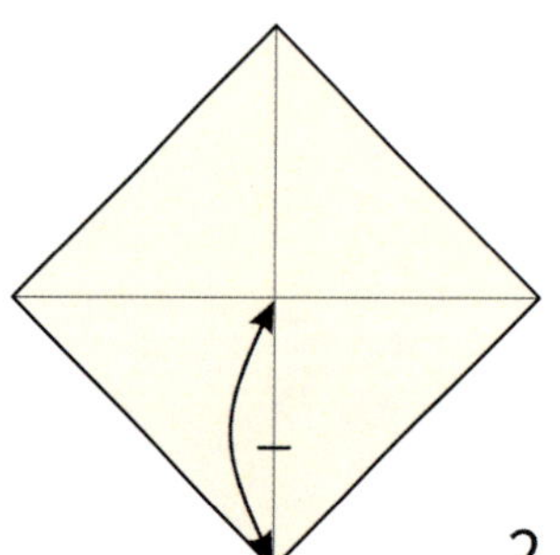

2

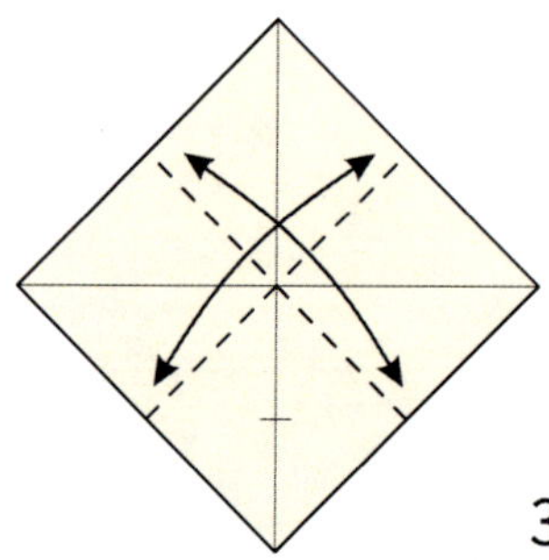

3

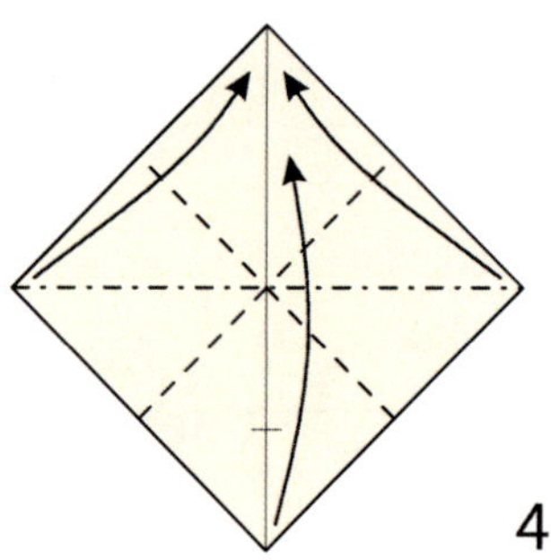

4

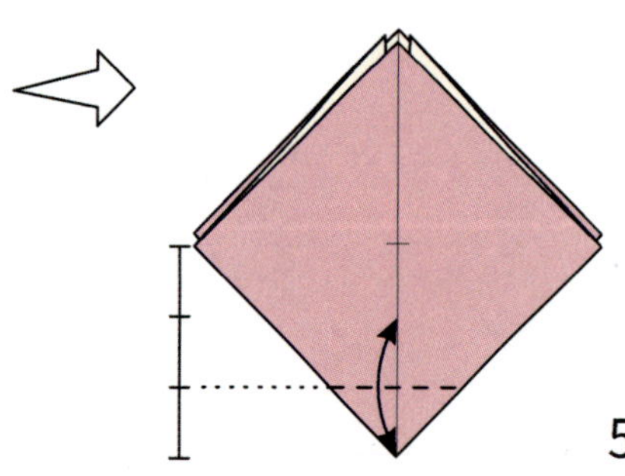

5

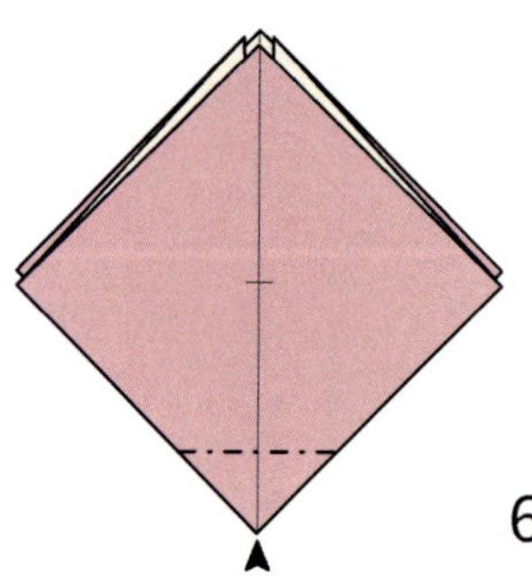

6

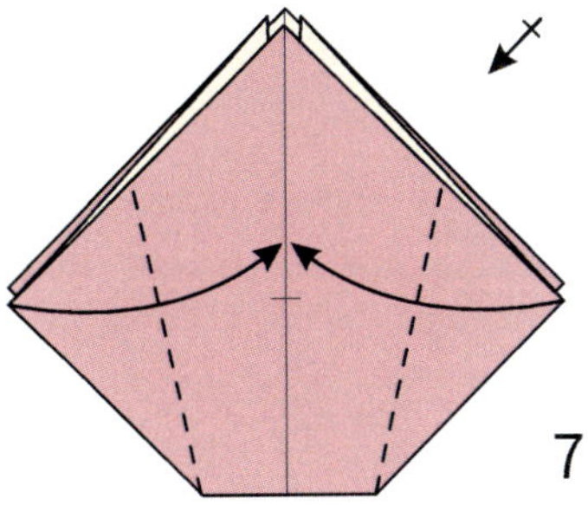

7

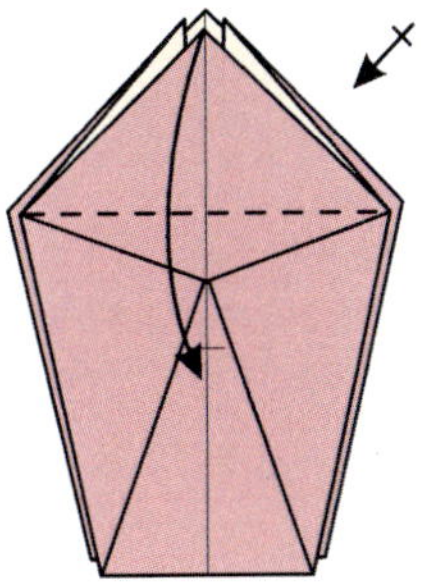

8

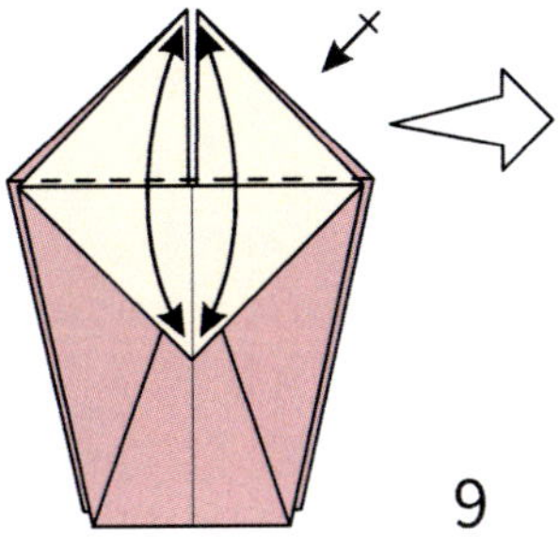

9

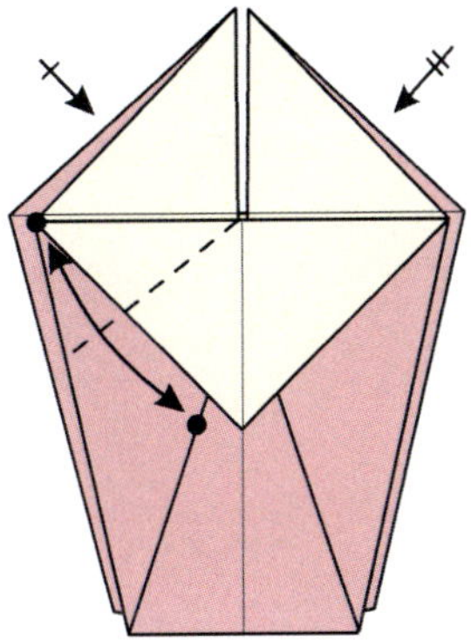

3D

10

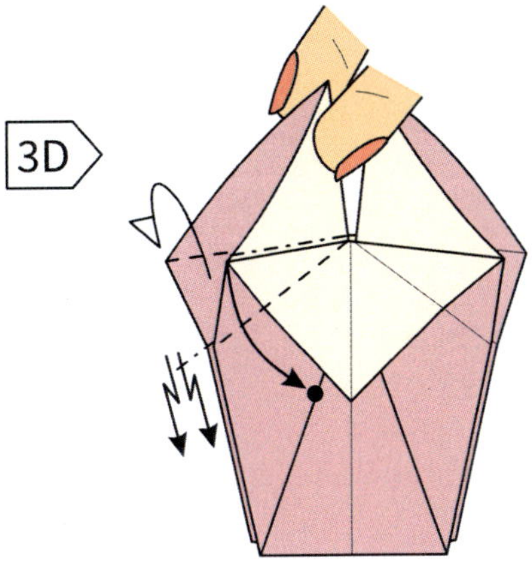

11

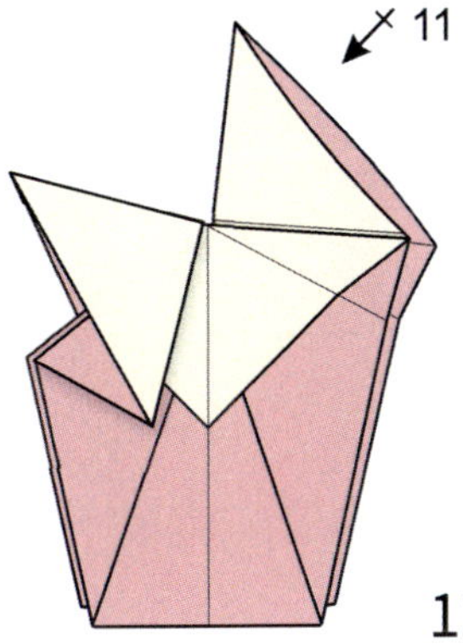

12

3D

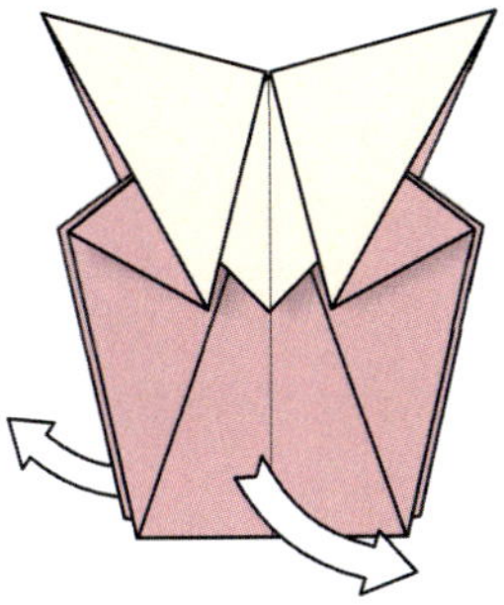

13

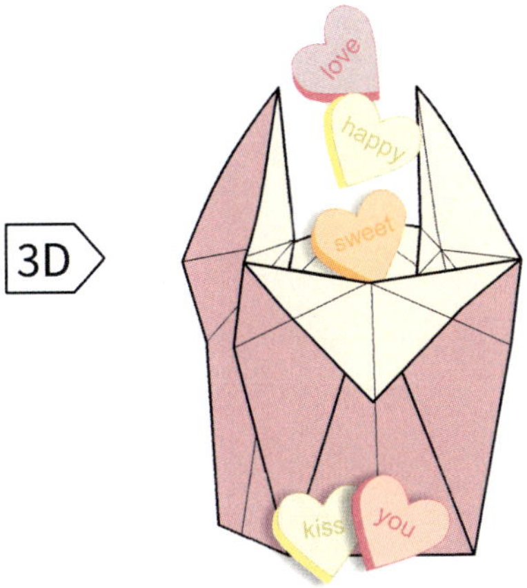

14

Unfold the wings to step 11 and open the front. Fill the box. Fold step 11-12 again to close the box.

*Variation*

Make the next step before step 8 to see more of the paper on the front. Continue folding as shown.

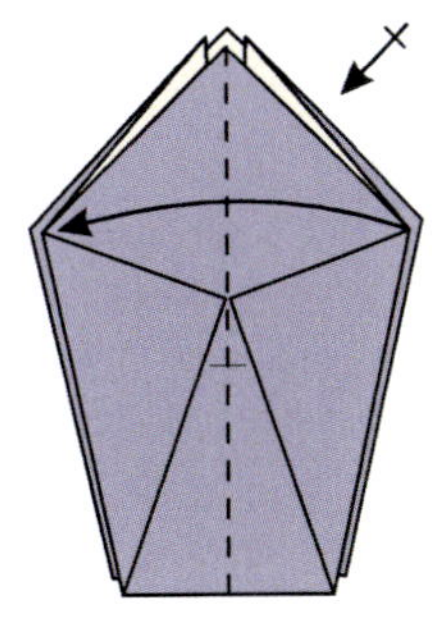

# Cradle of Love

04-01-2022

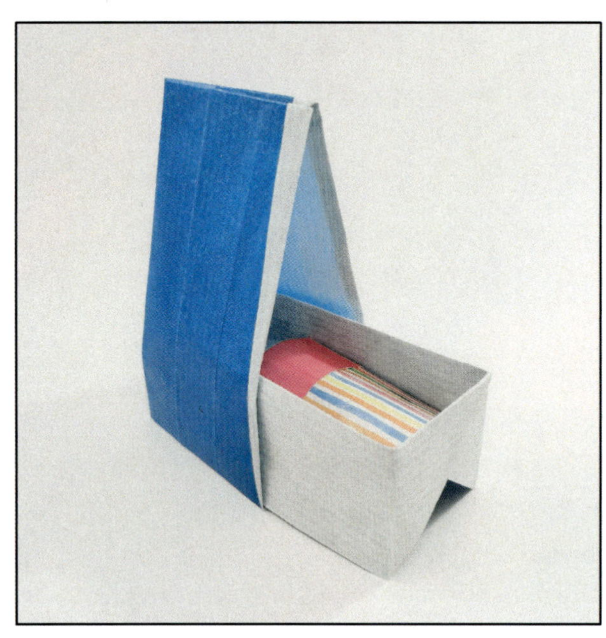

For me there is often a special reason to design a model. To celebrate the birth of our grandson, Joah Jaxx, I designed this Cradle of Love.
My goal was to develop a 3D cradle from one piece of paper, suitable for placing a wooden doll. A strip of paper with name and date can easily be attached without glue. This cradle was used as a maternity visit gift.

Paper:
- Duo color 24x12cm
- Label 9x1 cm

Colored side is the cradle

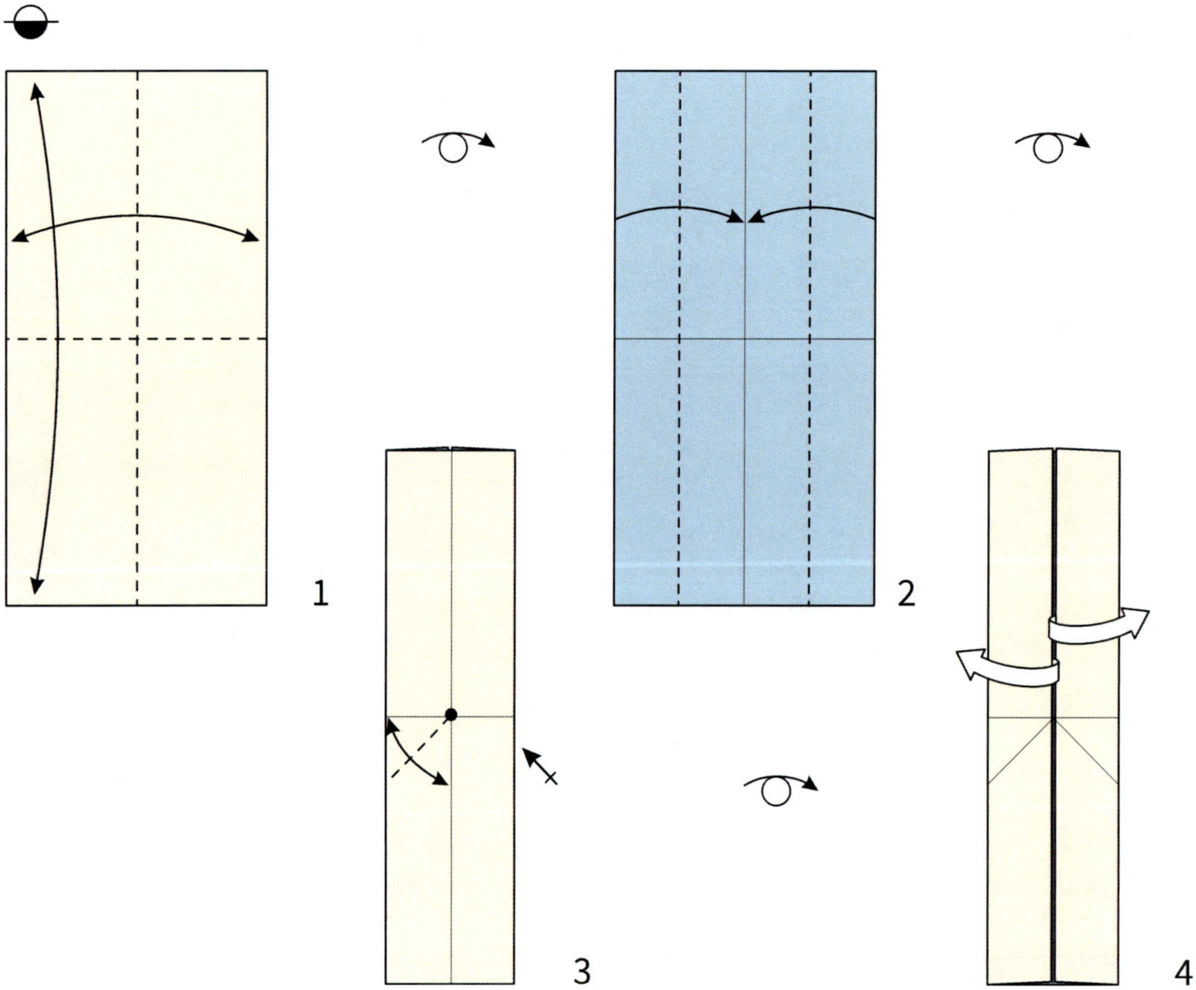

1

2

3

4

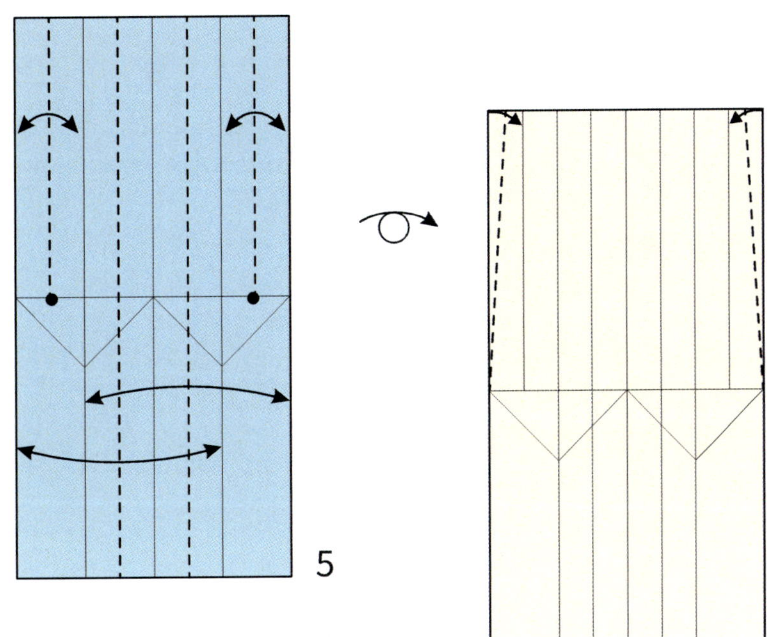
5
6

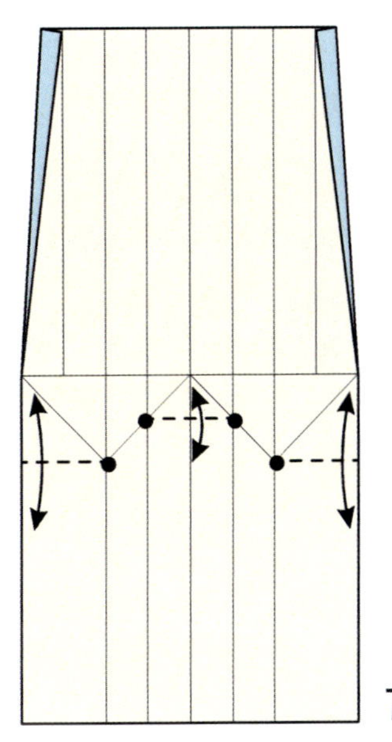
7

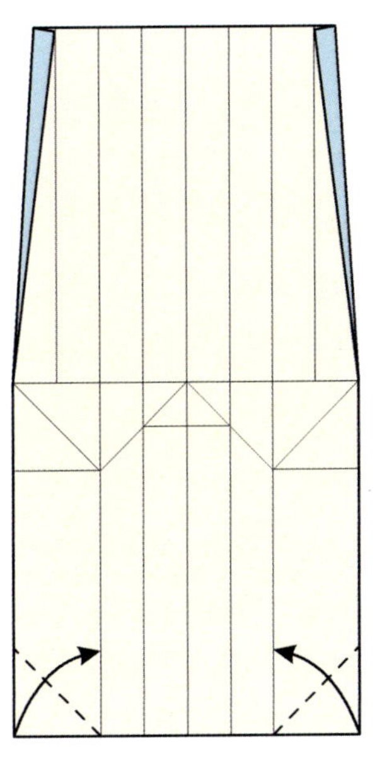
8

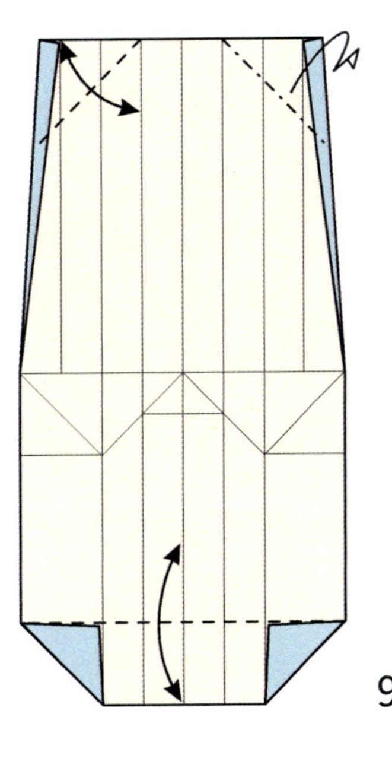
9

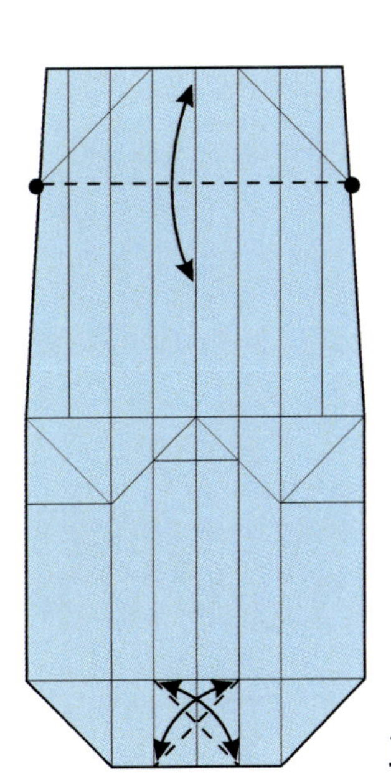
10

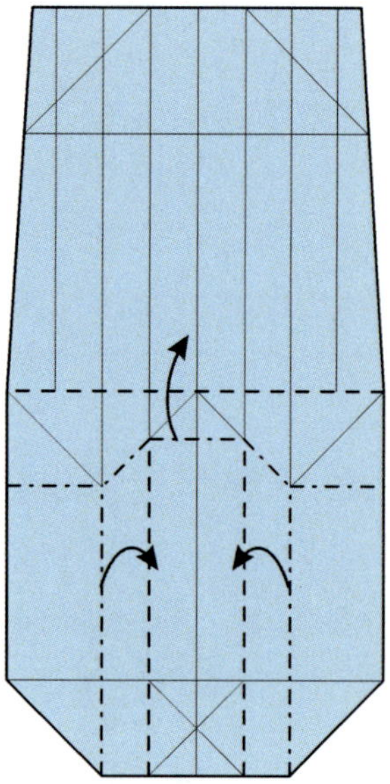

3D

11

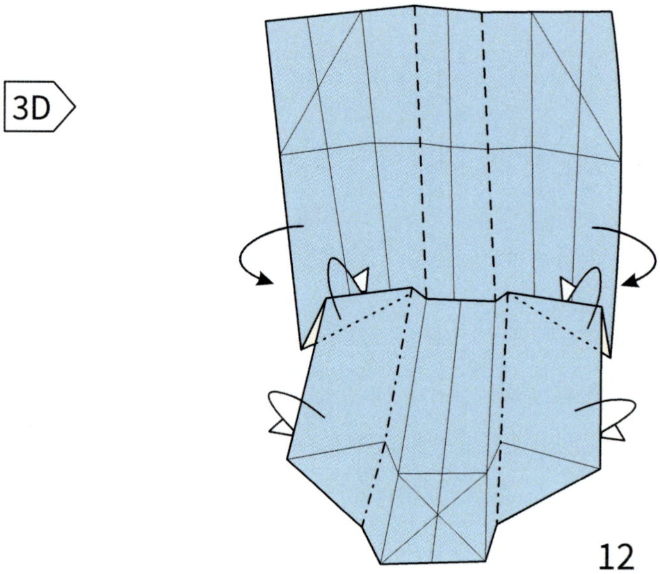

12

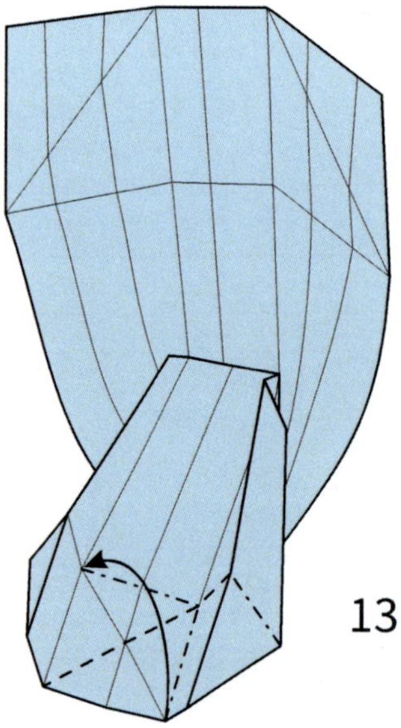

13

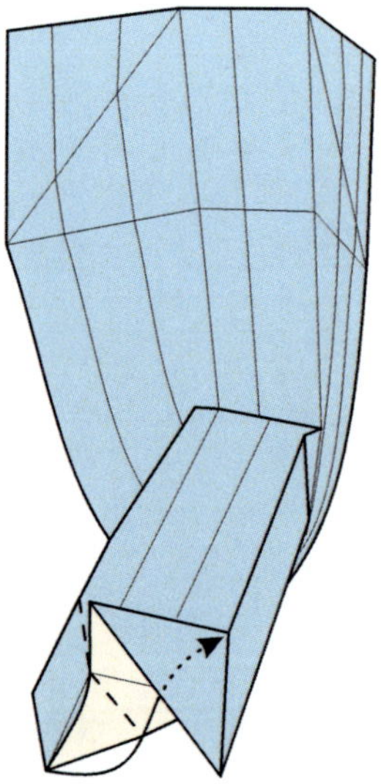

14

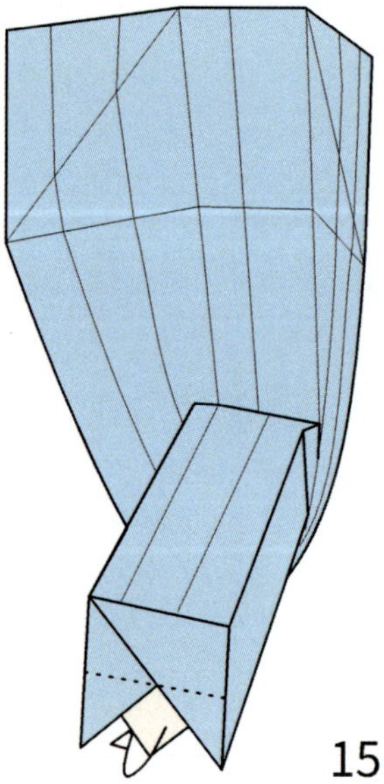

15

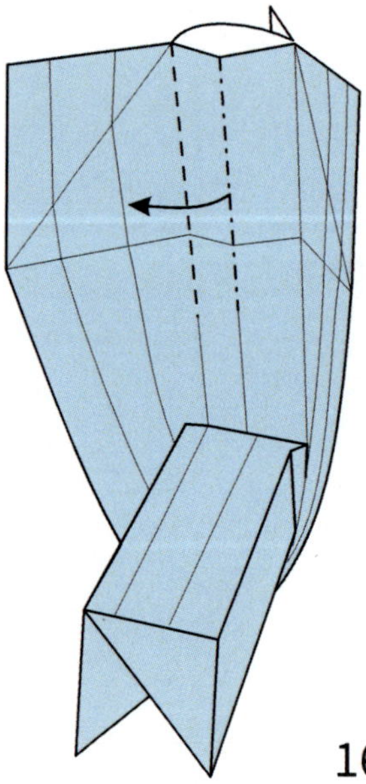

16

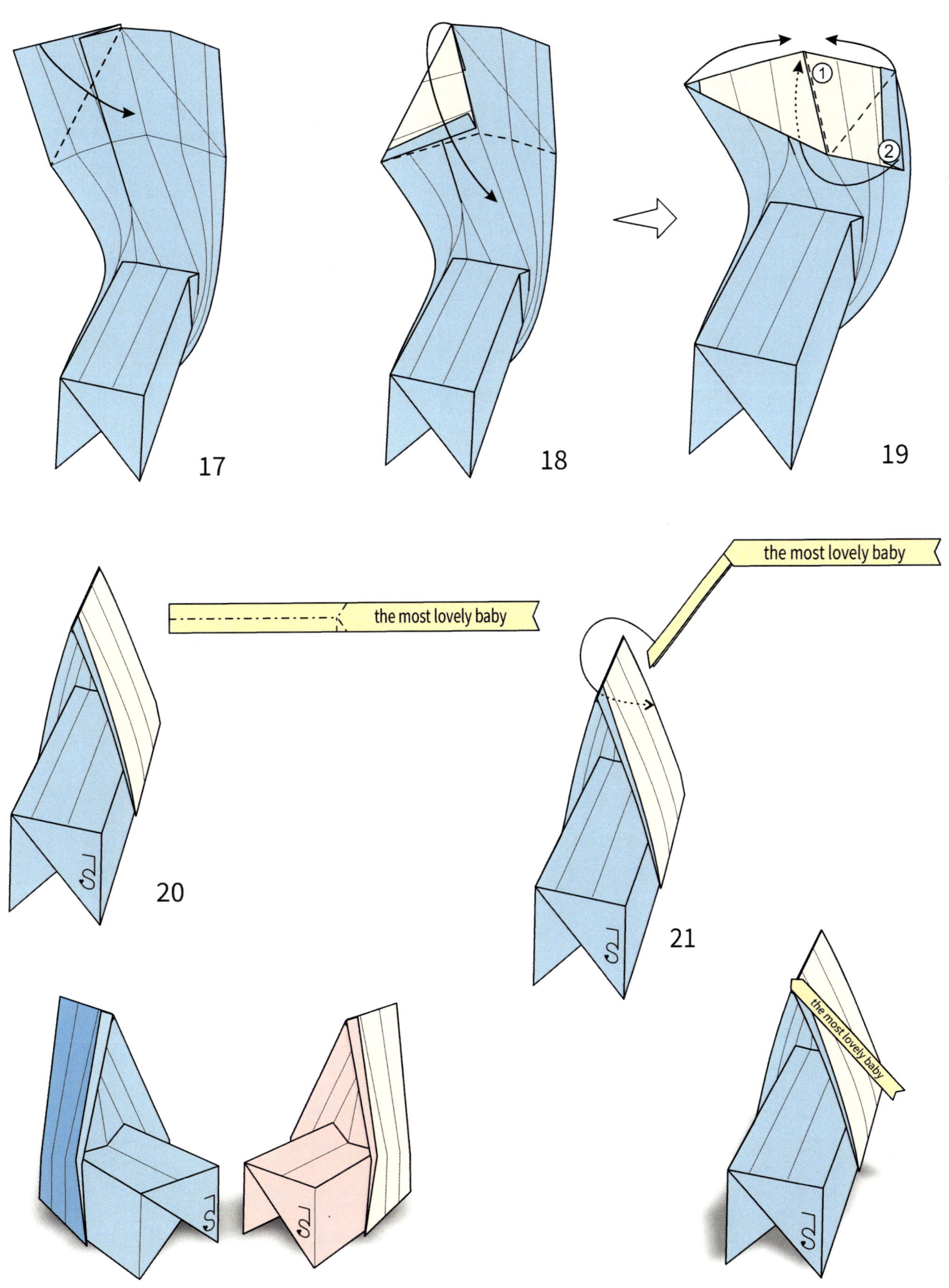
17
18
19
1
2
20
the most lovely baby
21
the most lovely baby
the most lovely baby

# Little Mousy Josh

04-07-2022

In 2022 I was designing a flower with variations. (You will find them in my next book.) Every time I saw its petals, the ears of a mouse came to my mind. After some puzzling, the flower heart became the body and head, and then a set of petals became the ears. I named it after our grandson, Joshua, who is so crazy about cuddly toys and plays with everything I fold.

Paper:
- Body: 15x15 cm duo paper
- Ears: 7,5x7,5 cm duo paper

## Body

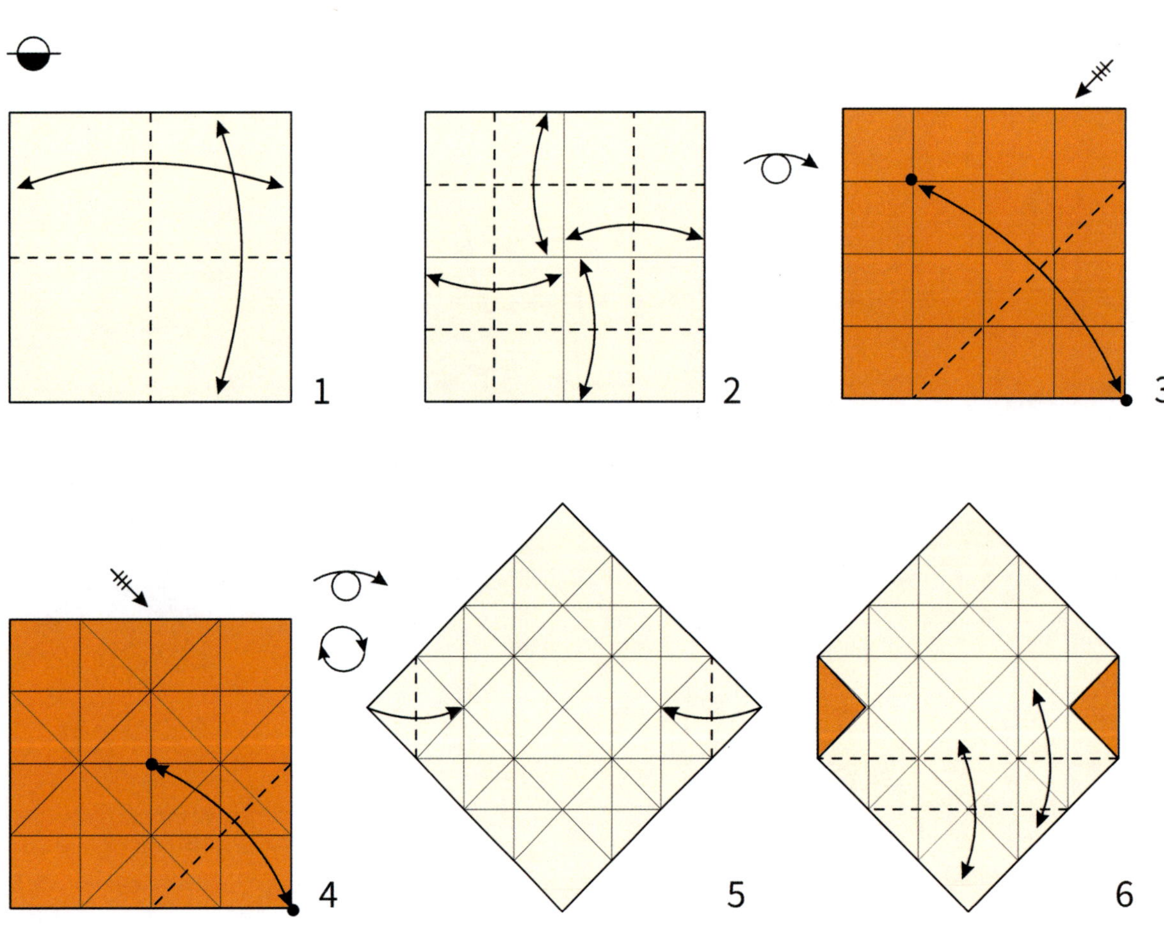

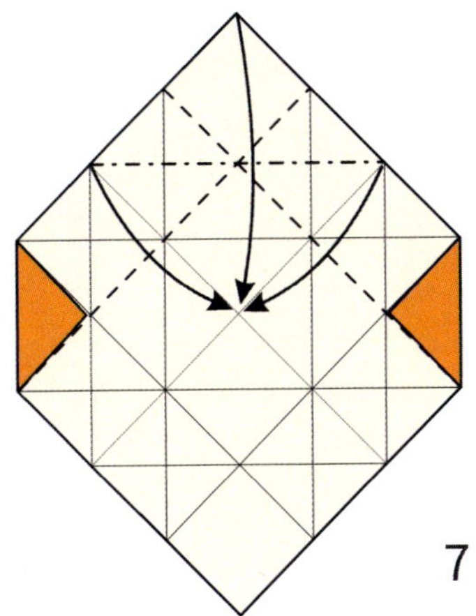
7

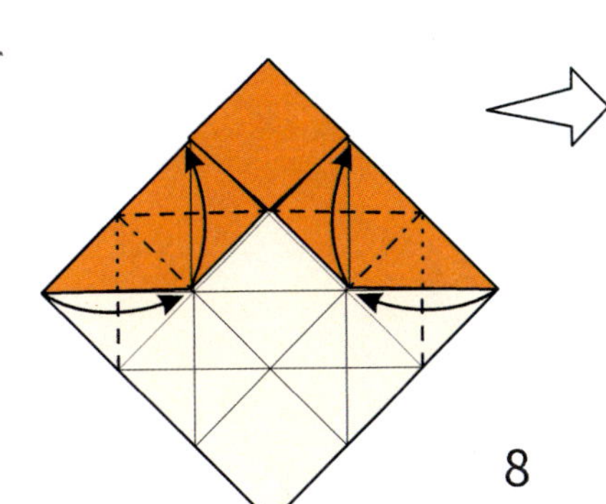
8

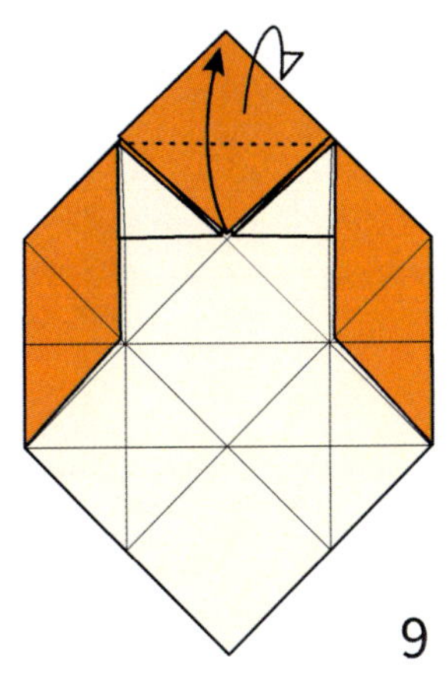
9

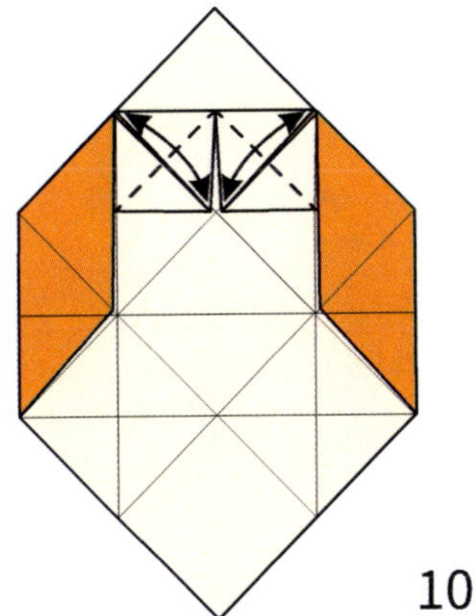
10

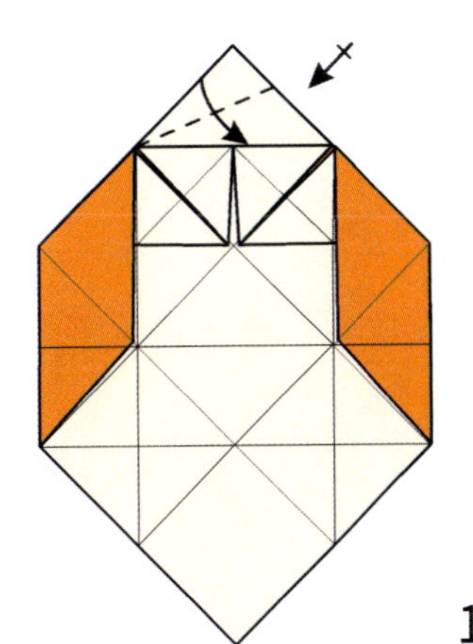
11

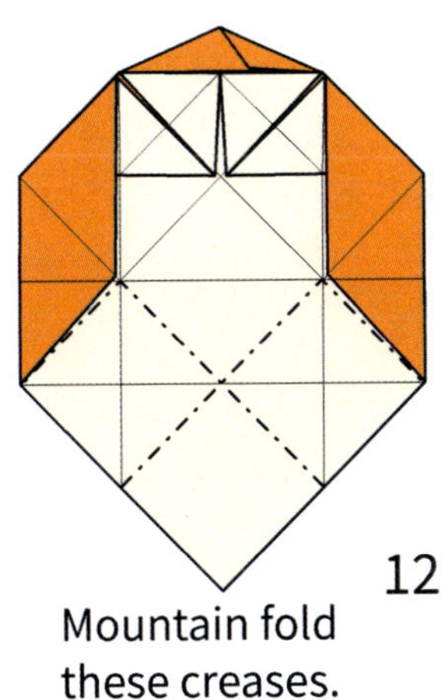
12

Mountain fold these creases.

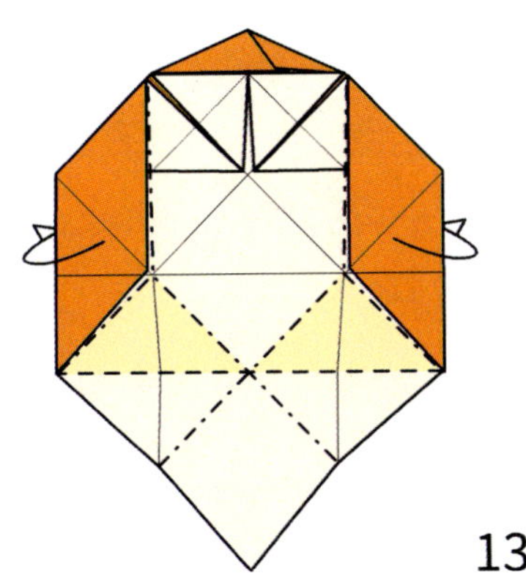
13

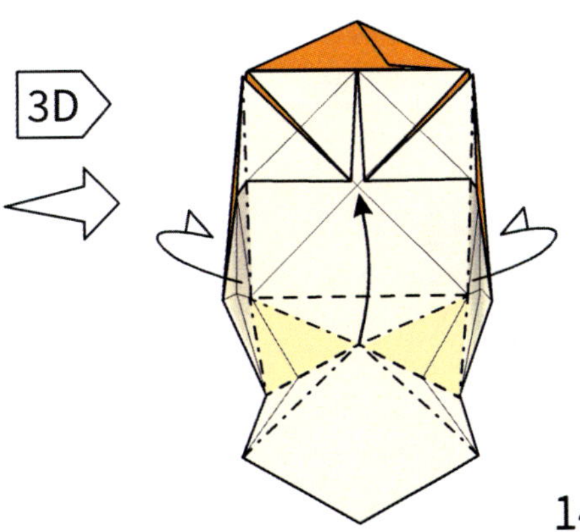

14

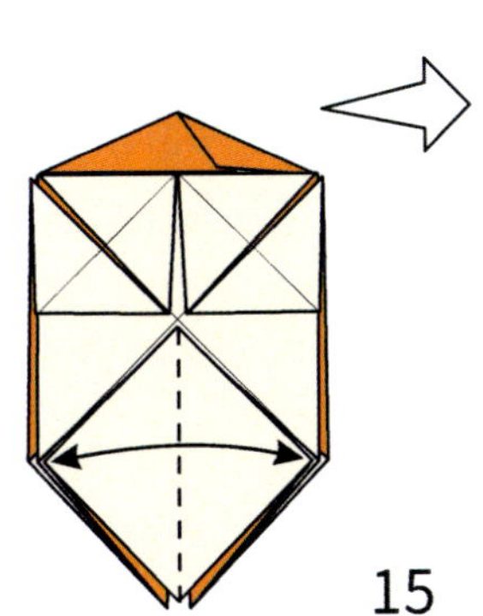
15

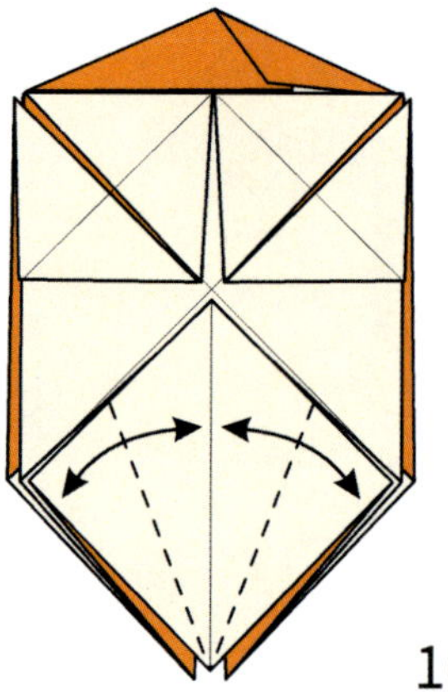

16

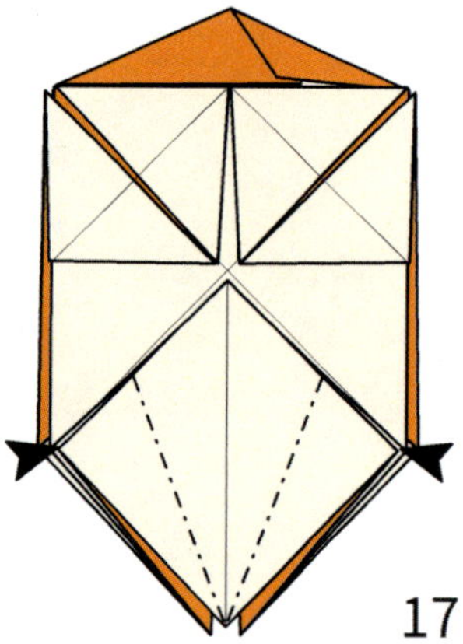

17

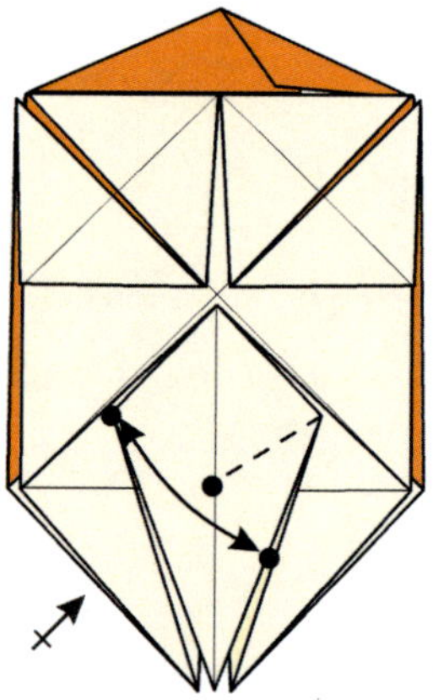

18

19

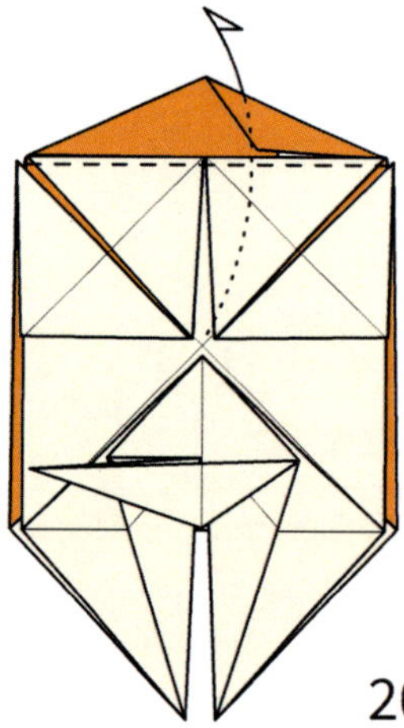

20

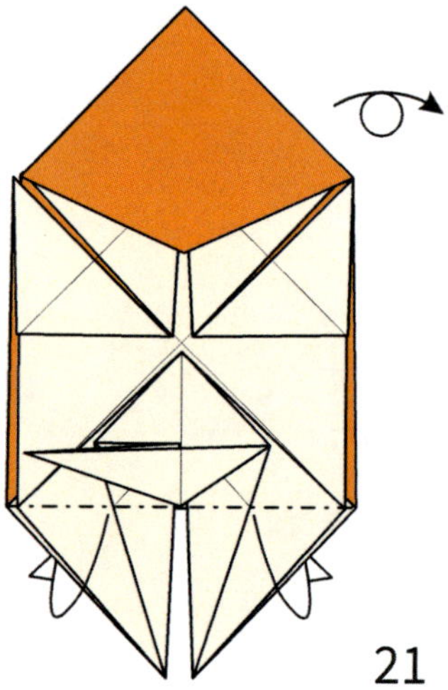

21

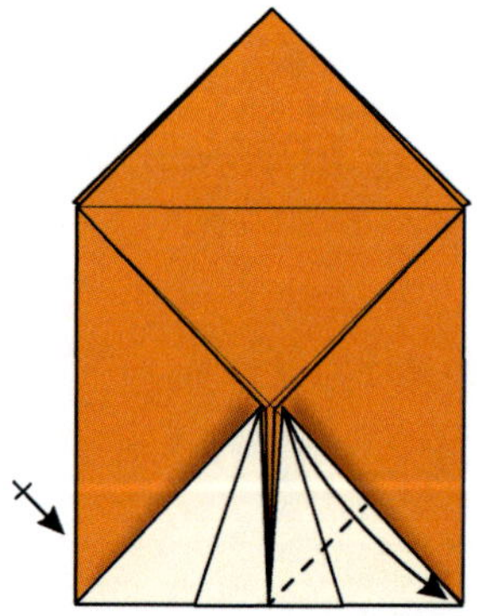

22

23

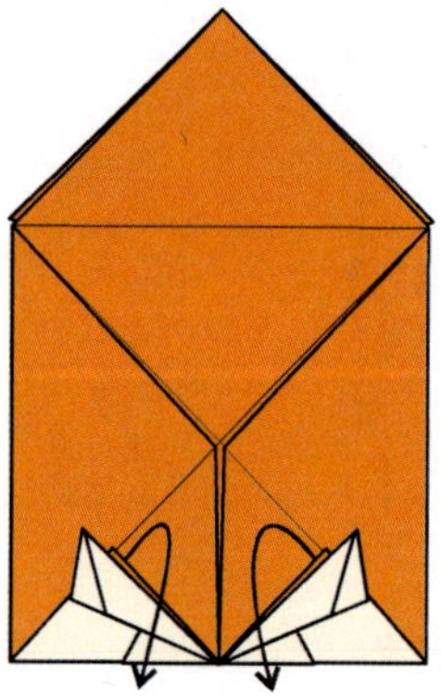

24

3D

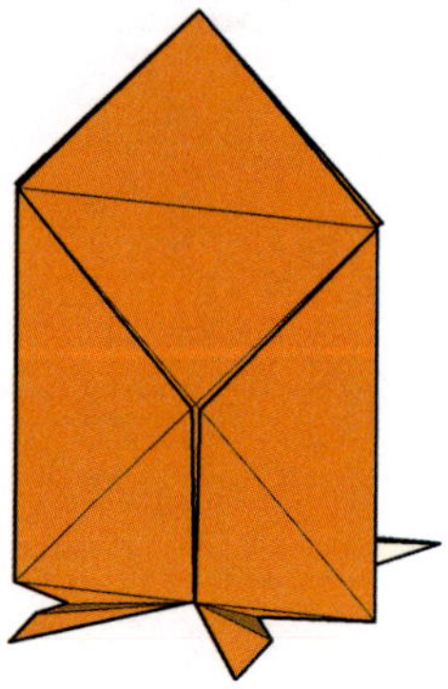

## Ears

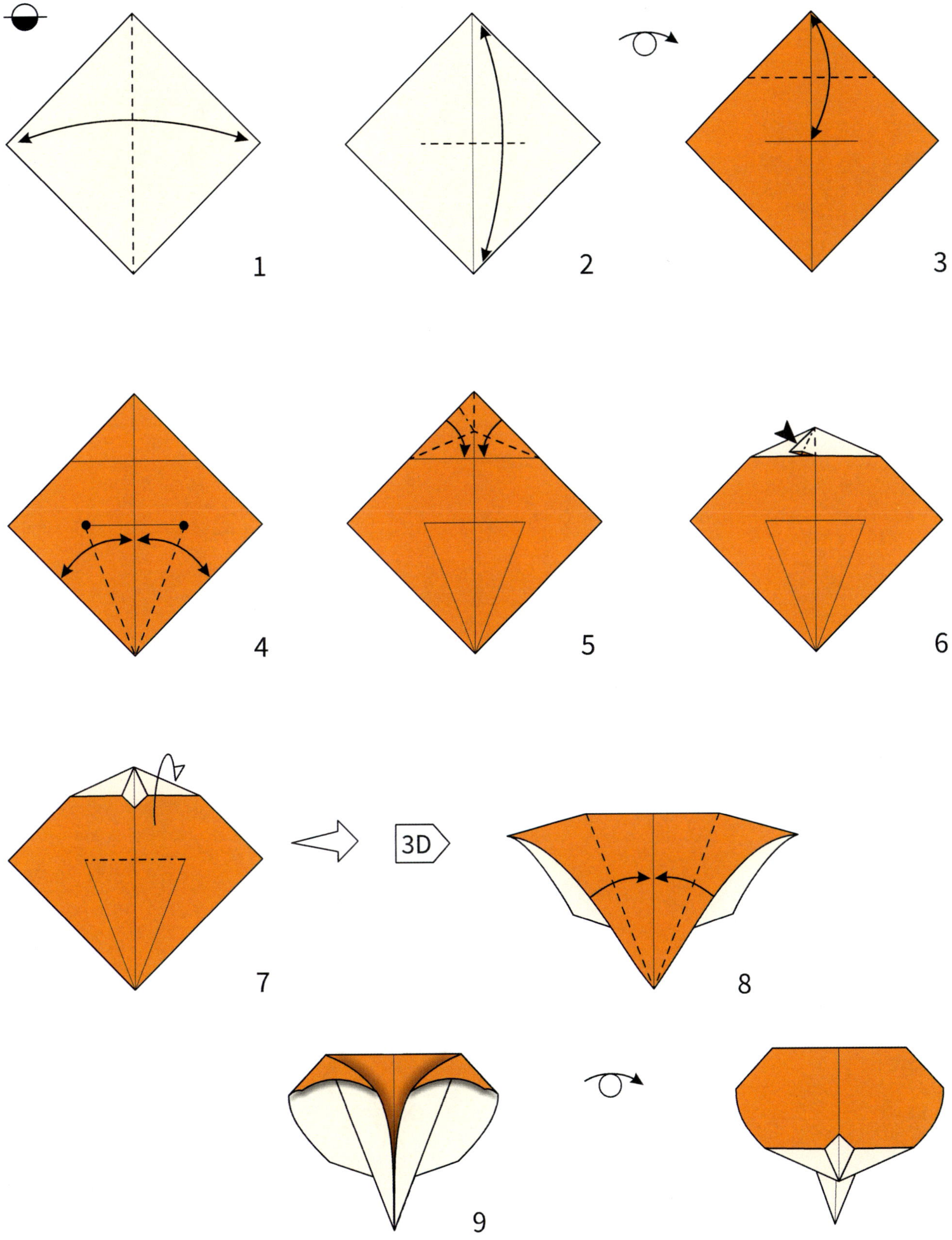

1

2

3

4

5

6

7

3D

8

9

## *Assembly*

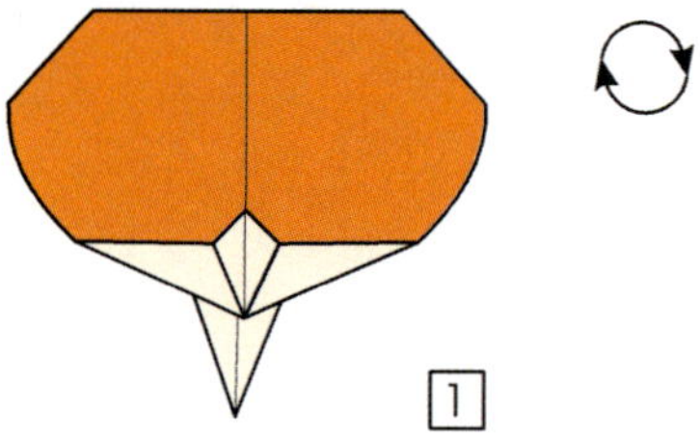

1

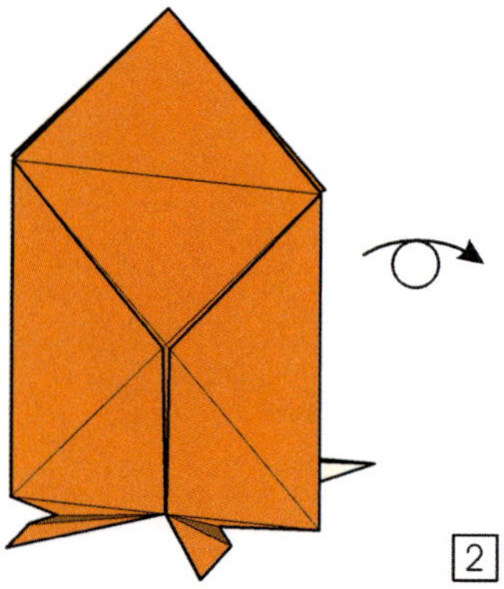

2

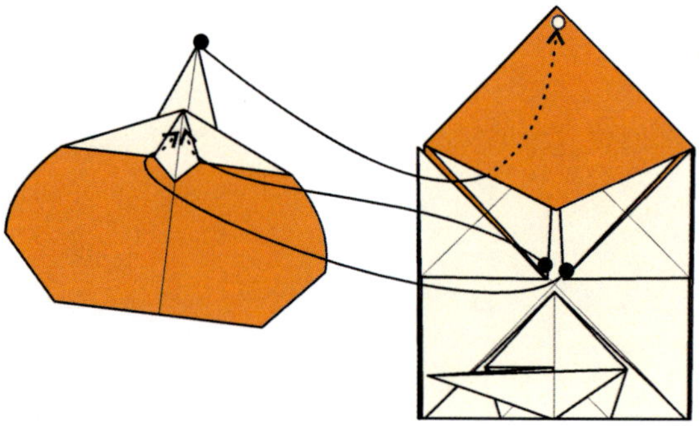

3

Turn over the ears. Slide the point under the diamond shaped paper layer.
The little kite shape slides under the two squares .

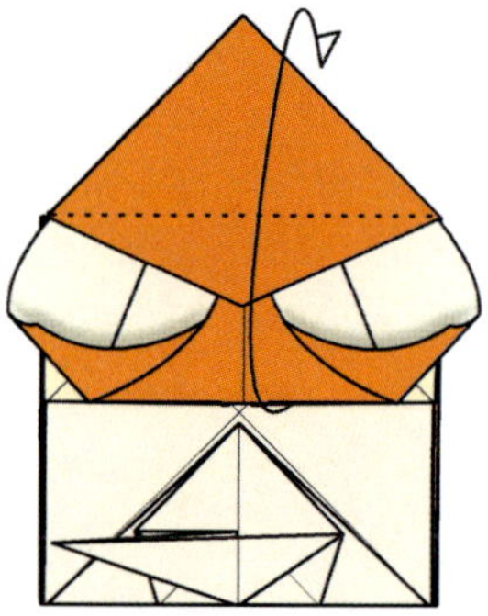

4

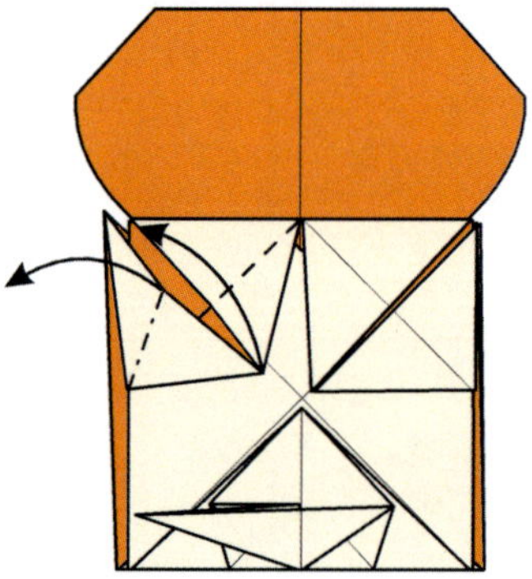

5

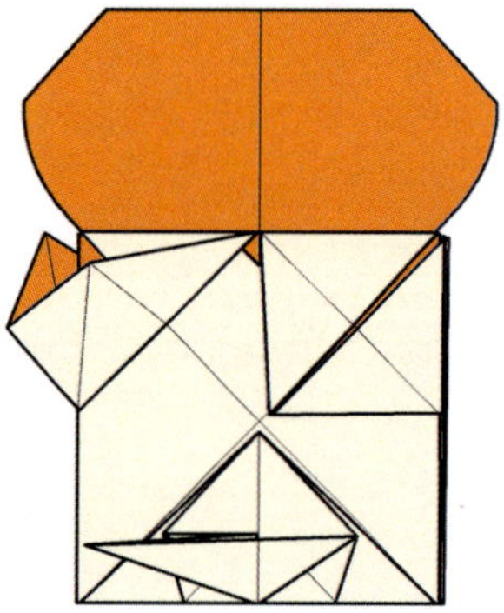

6

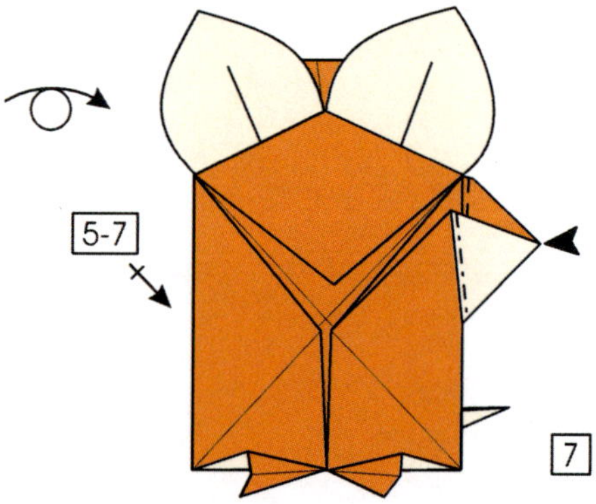

5-7

7

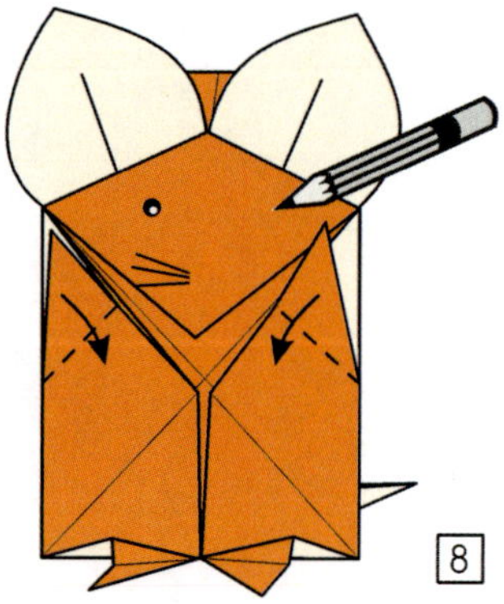

8

# Norah Amélie Box

03-06-2022

This box was designed a few weeks before the birth of our granddaughter, Norah Amélie. It was meant as a maternity gift for the visitors. I glued a name strip on the opening point. The box, made from one piece of paper, can easily be opened and closed because of the hinge. Punch holes in it with a pin, fill it with lavender, and you have a perfect scented sachet.

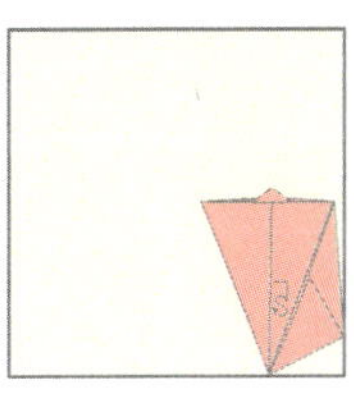

Paper:
- 15x15 cm karft or duo paper
  Sturdy paper works better.

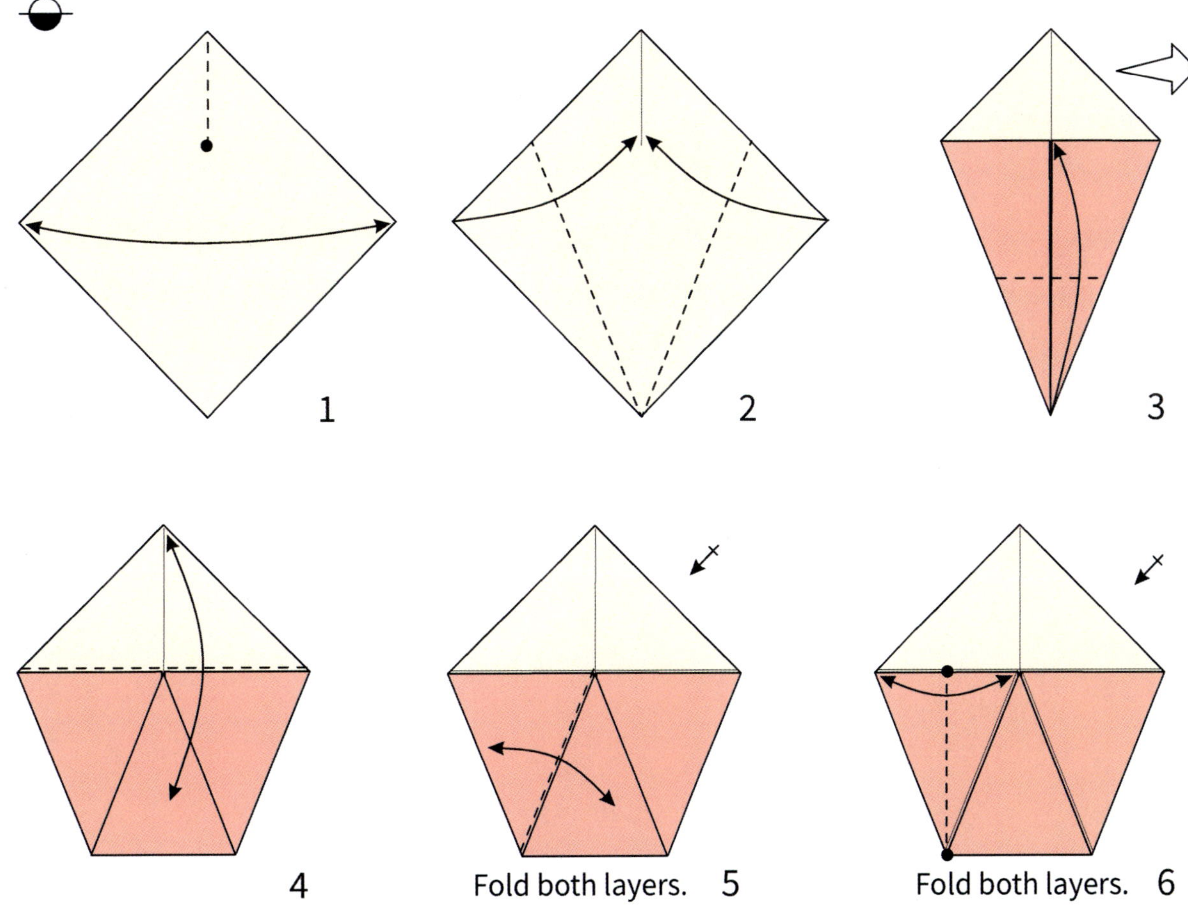

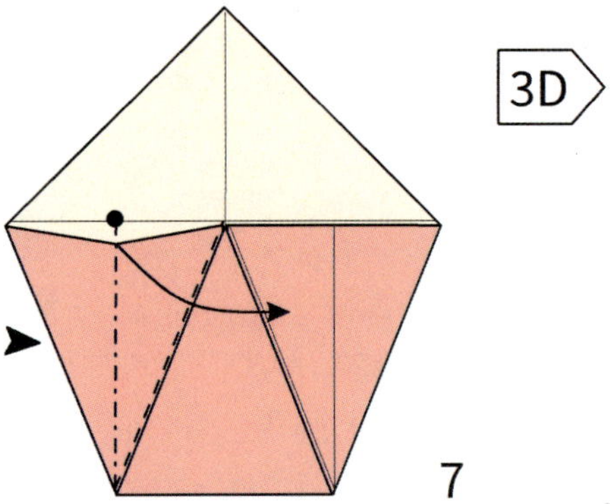

3D
7
8 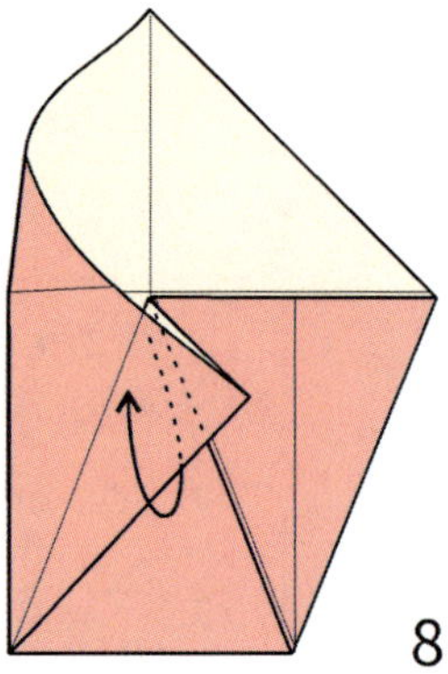
9 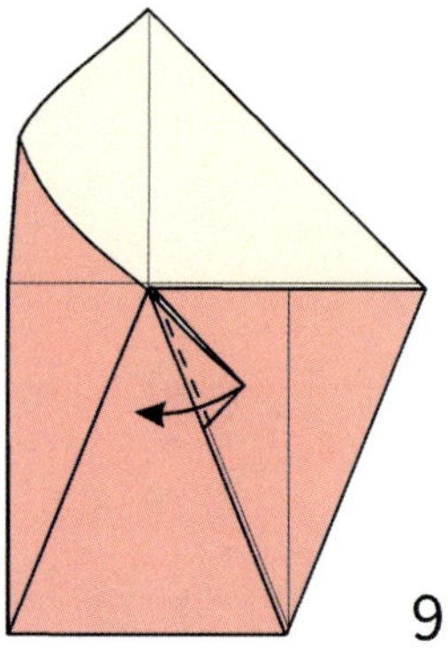
10 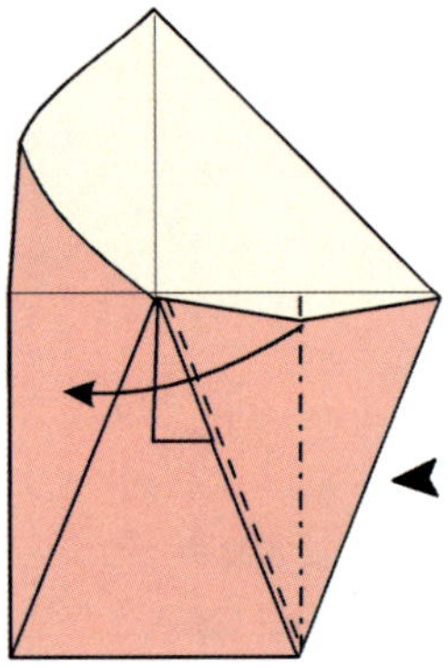
11 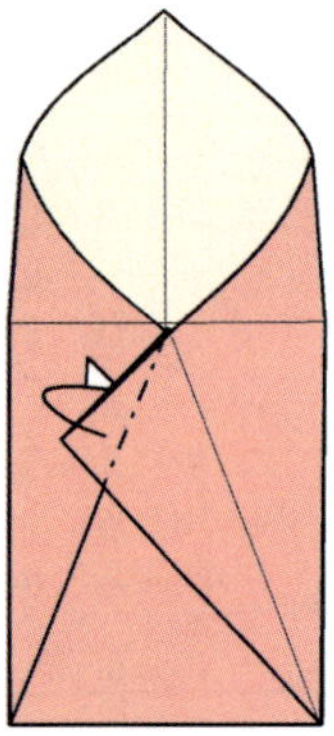
12 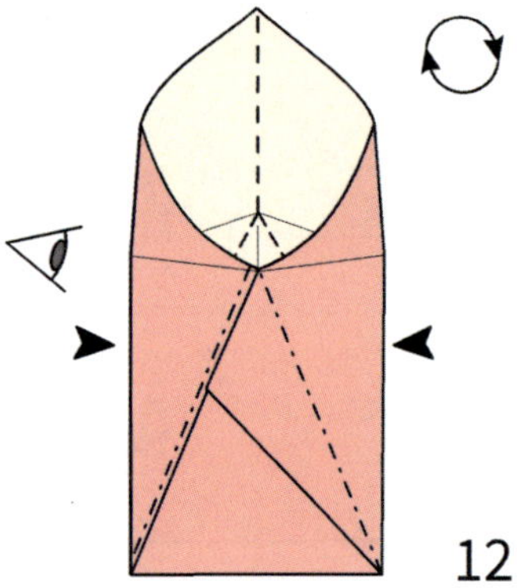
13 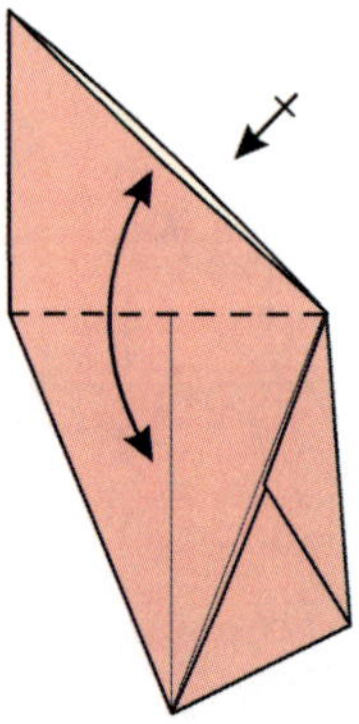
14 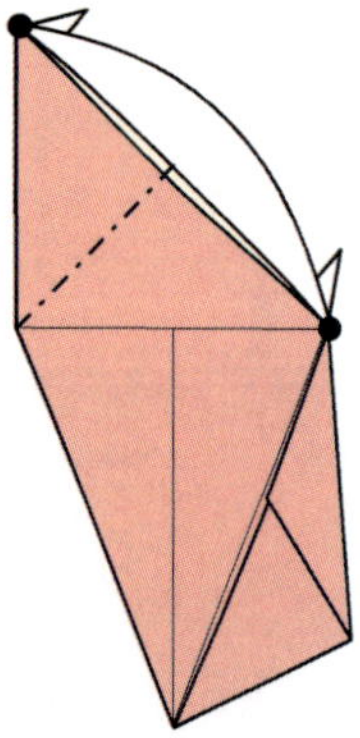
15 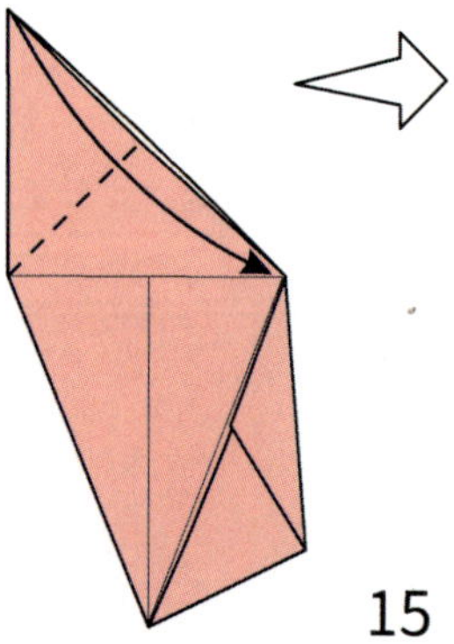
16 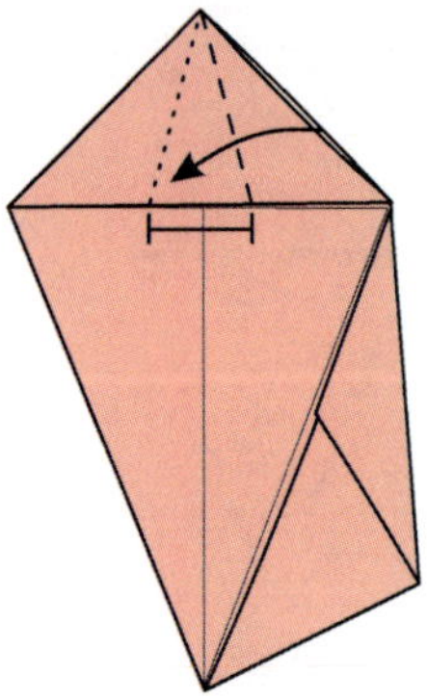
17 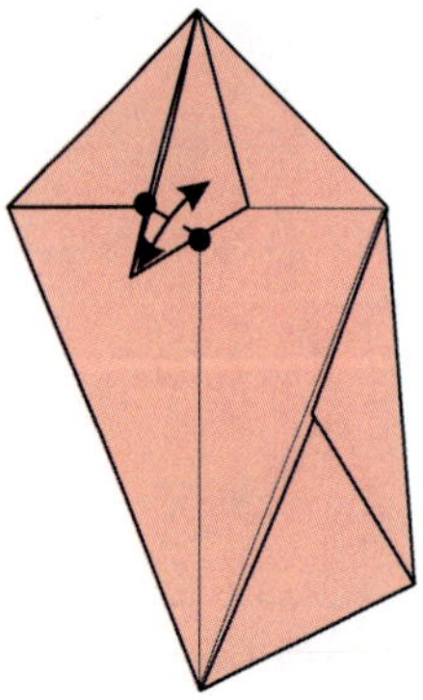
18

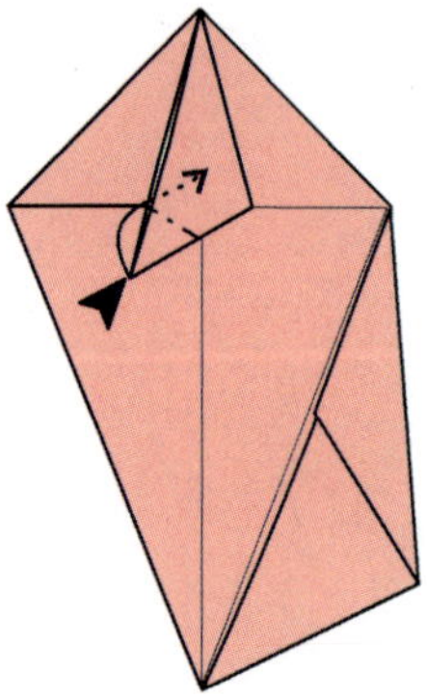

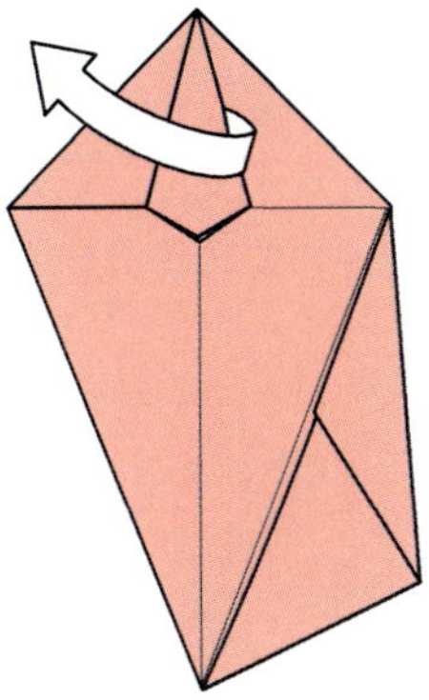

19

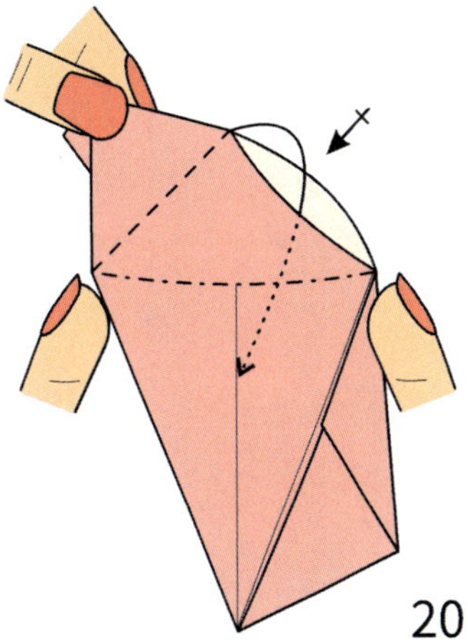

20

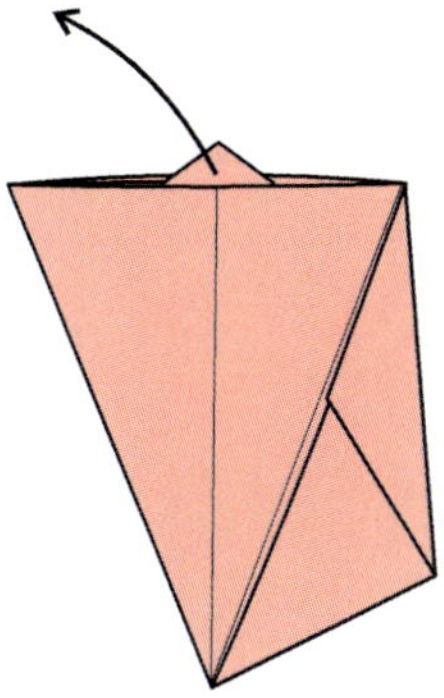

21

The first time closing the box, it needs a little help to get the folds in the right direction.

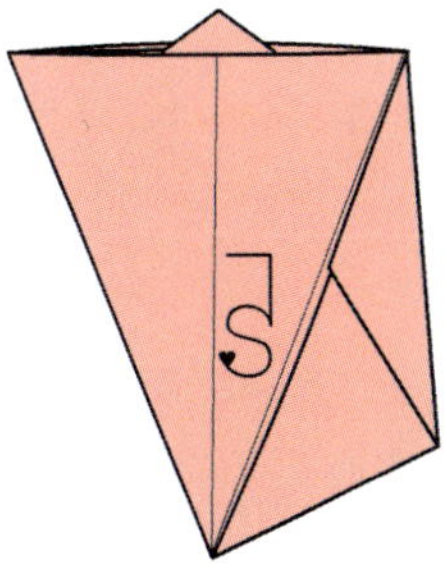

22

*Variation*
*for a colored handle*

Fold steps 1-15

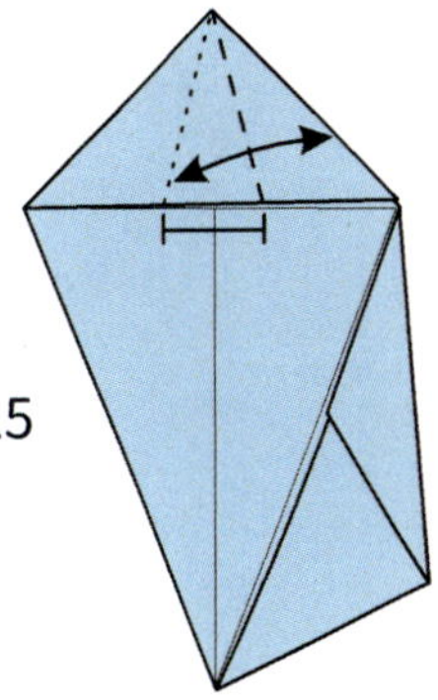

1

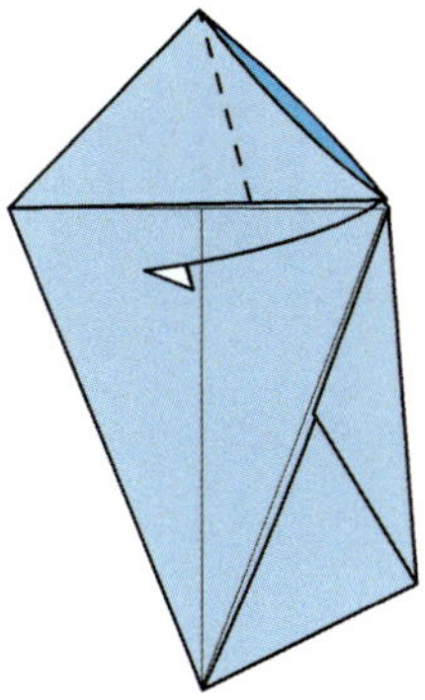

2

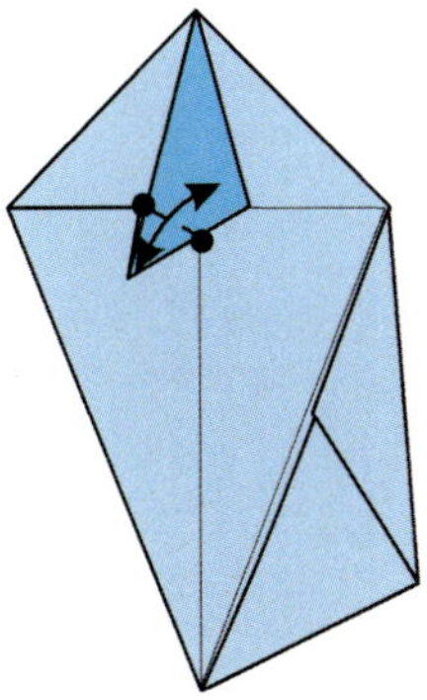

3

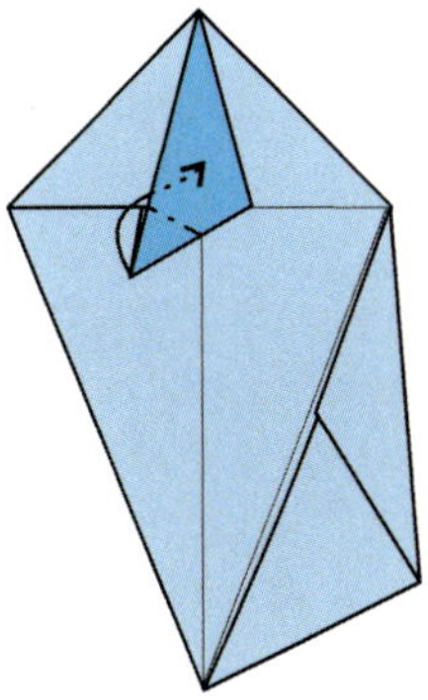

4

Continue with steps 19-22

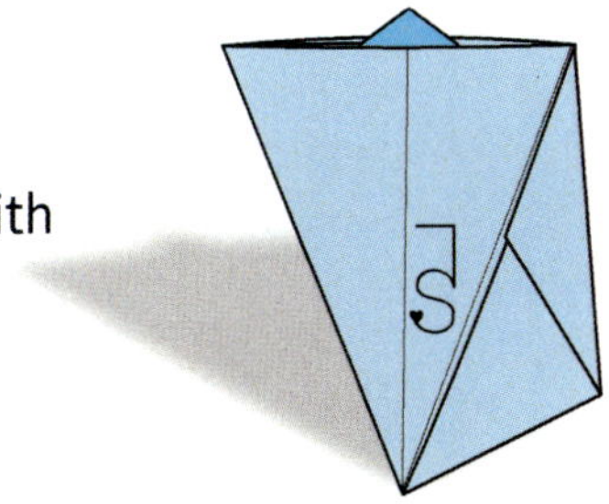

# Star Joëlle

15-01-2010

This star is a modification of one of my already existing baskets (2007). Flatten the basket, add some folds to close, and, voila a star is born. Because you can see both sides of the paper, it's worth using a nice double-sided paper. In 2014 I named this star after our granddaughter, Joëlle, who is a star on stage. I also used it as a Christmas wish. Fold two of them and attach them to each other without any glue. Use transculent paper, for instance baking paper, for a nice window decoration.

Paper:
- 2 squares 15x15 duo color or transculent paper

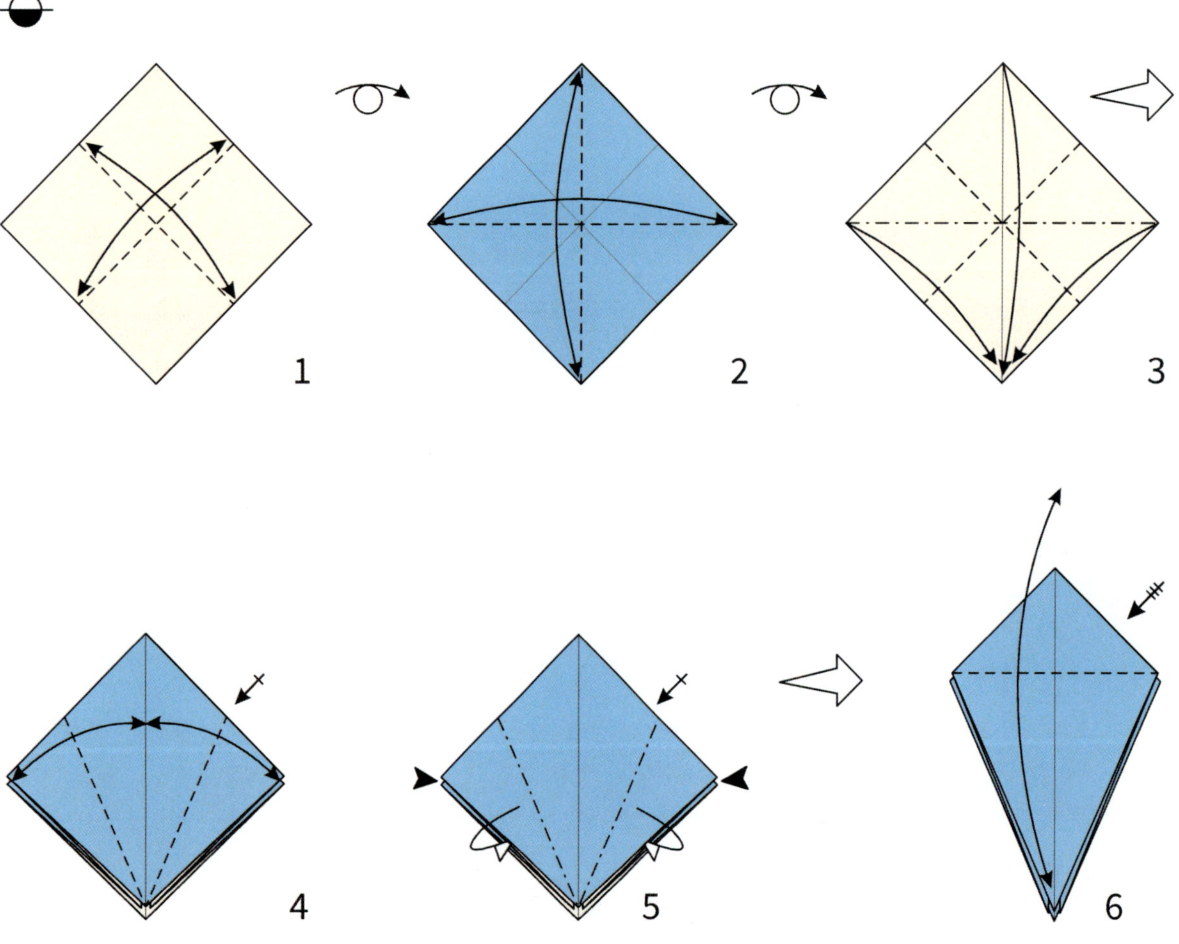

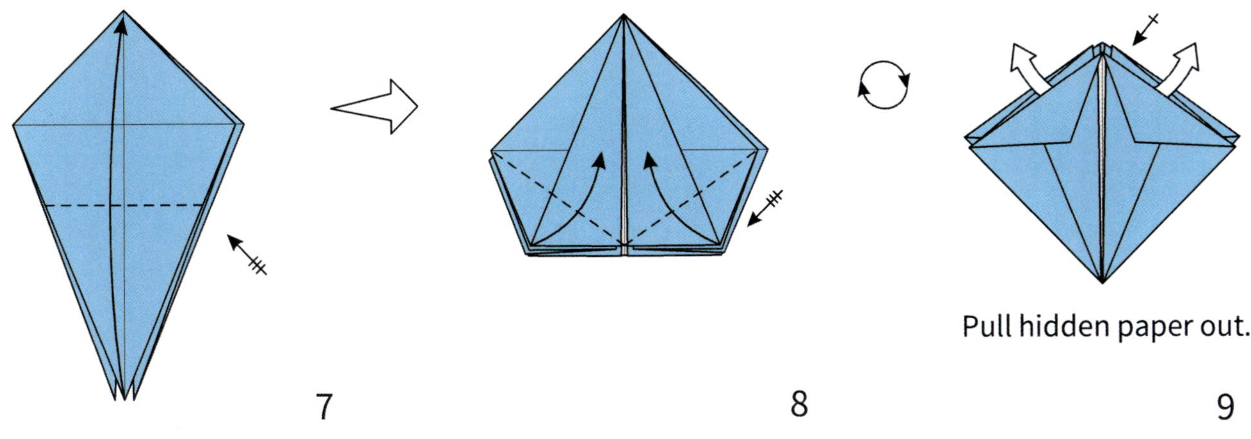


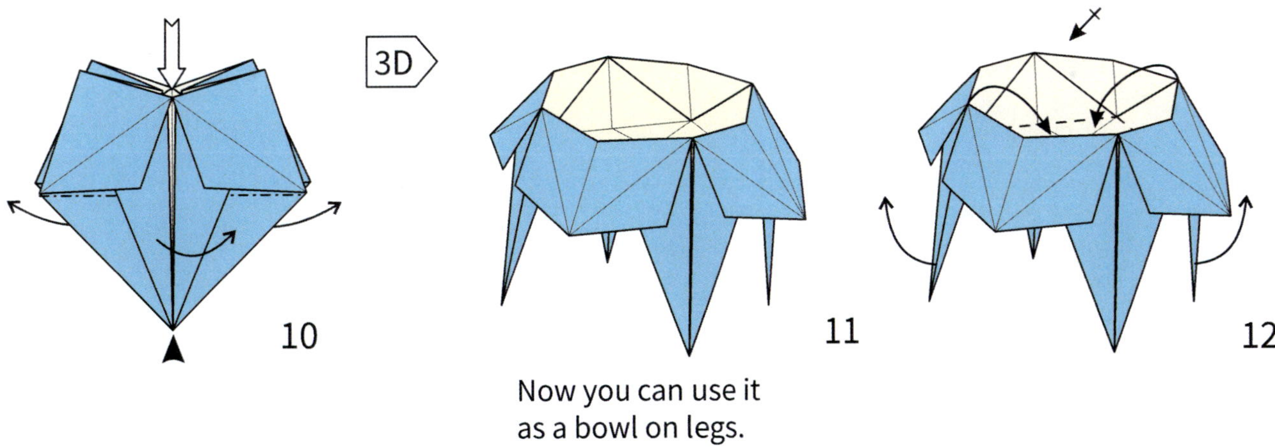


Now you can use it as a bowl on legs.

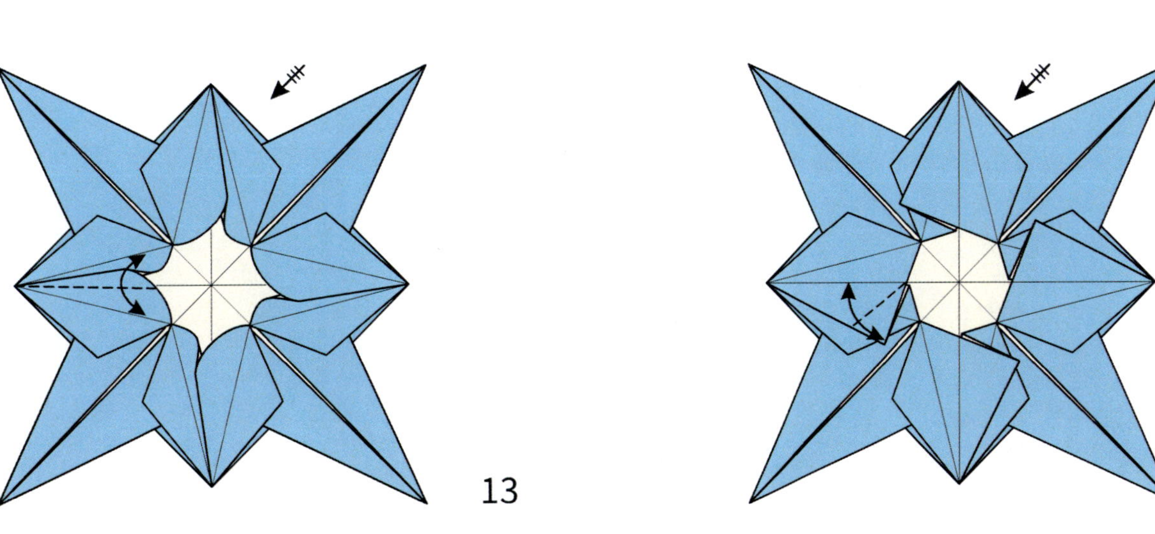

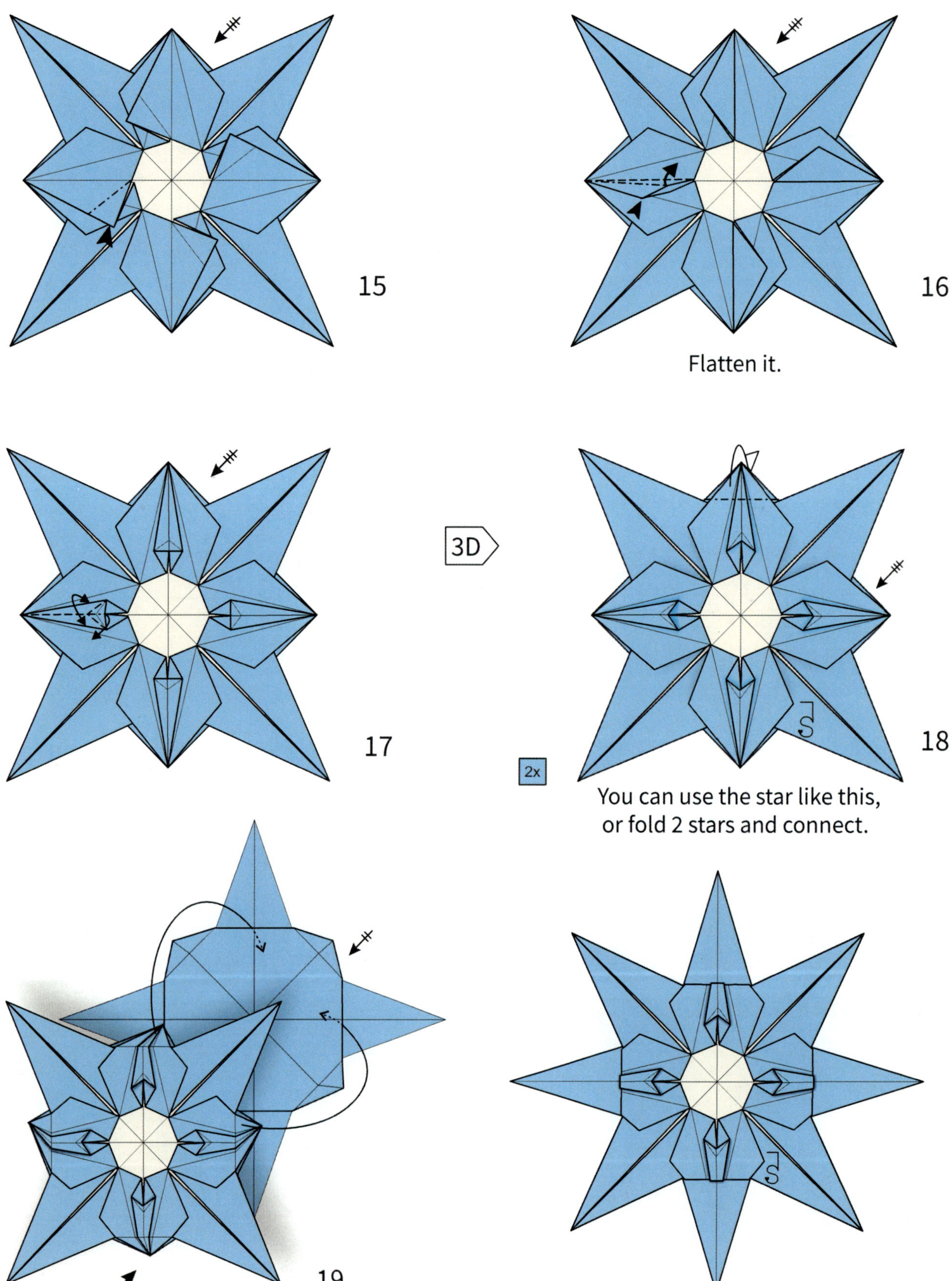
15
16
Flatten it.
3D
17
18
2x
You can use the star like this, or fold 2 stars and connect.
19

# Practical

Of course a practical chapter cannot be missed. I like to think of solutions for things that are difficult or could be different. In this chapter you can find a few things, such as the Handy Paperclip Box or the Ori-Paper-Saver. Enjoy folding the beautiful envelopes and the paperclips. Have fun.

# Jannie's Paperclip base

10-06-2007

When I designed the paper clips, the beginning turned out to be a basis that can be used in many directions. I remember how proud I was when Sok Song took a closer look at my 'paperclip' and said that it was a good and stable origami paperclip. I called the base 'Jannie's paperclip base'. Below I will show you the basics. Enjoy and let your imagination run wild.

Paper:
- 10x10cm or smaller

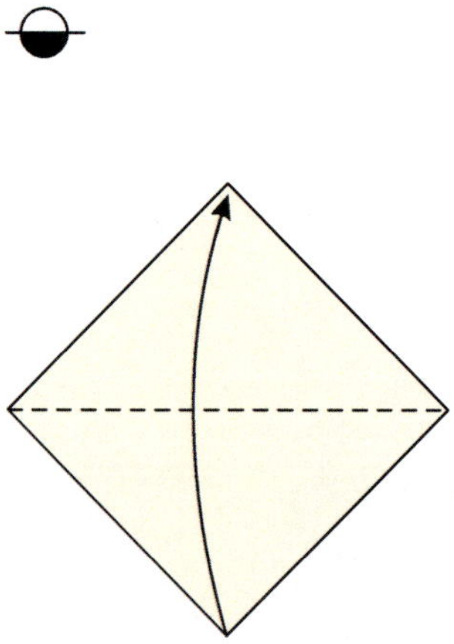

1

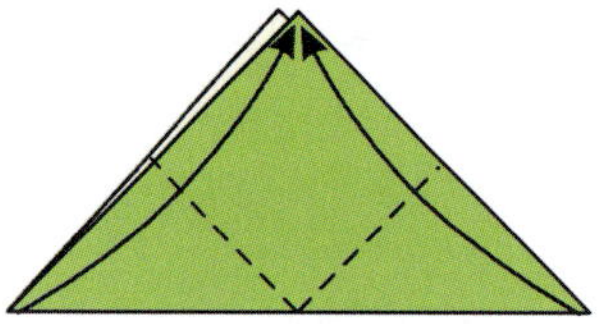

2

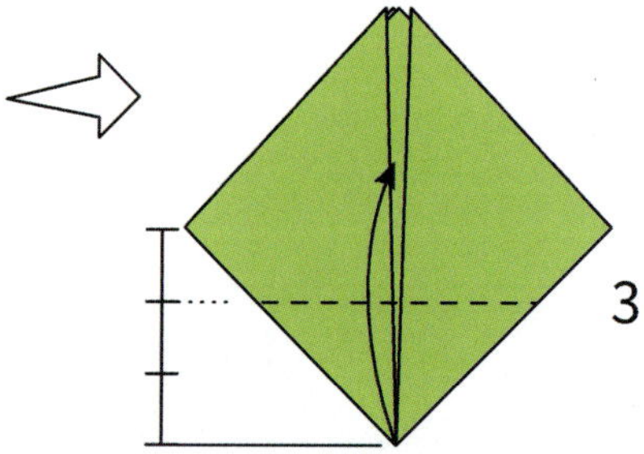

3

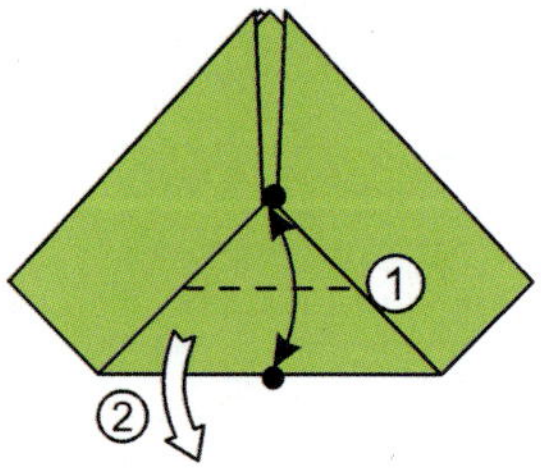

4

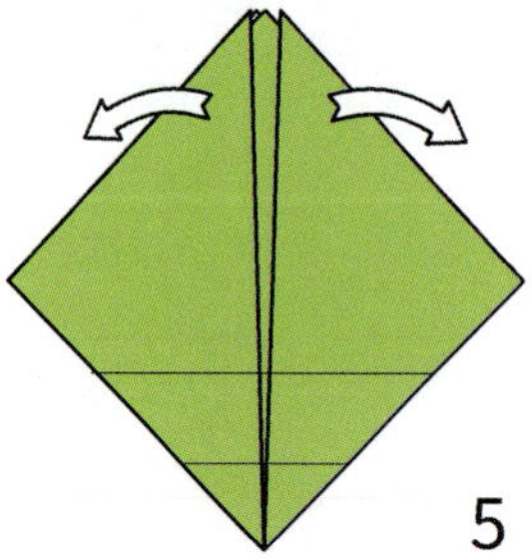

5

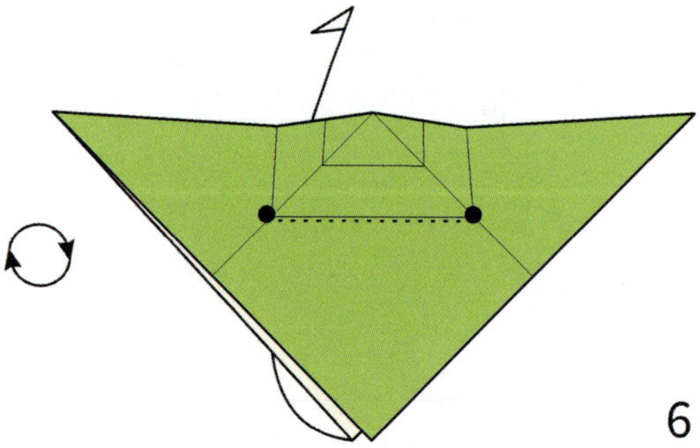

6

7

8

9

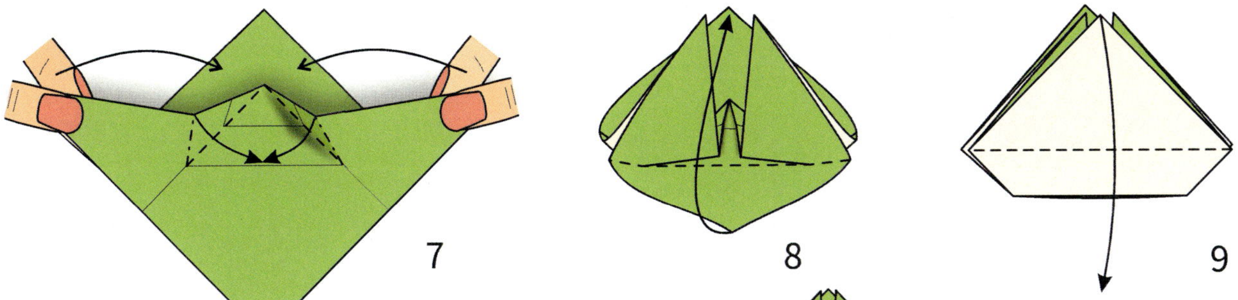

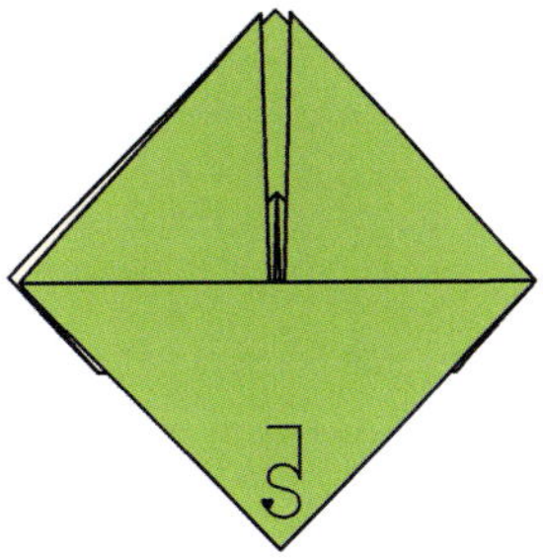

This is the base.
From here the models are created.

## *How to lock the paper in the paperclip*

1

2

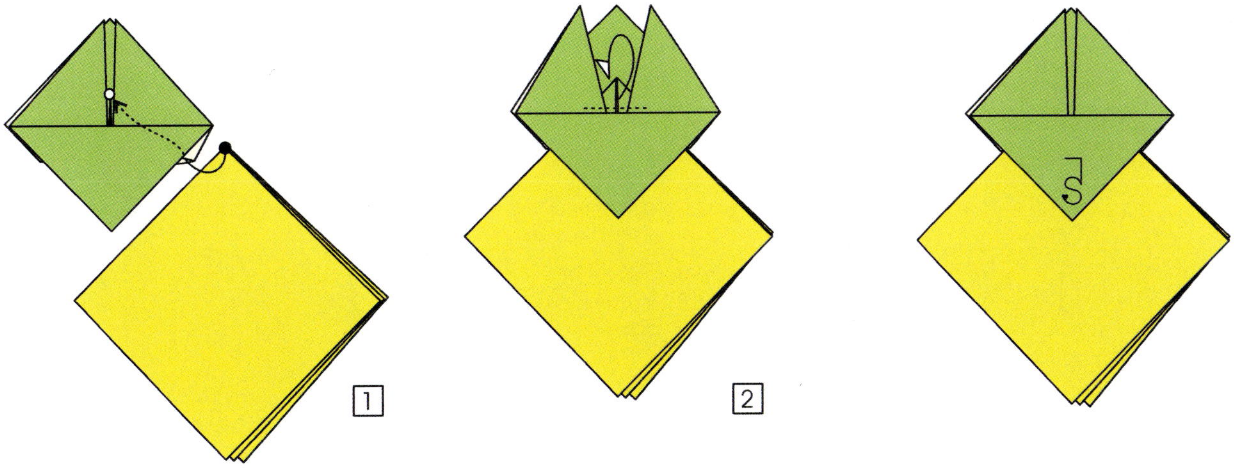

Options for clip heigh. (Or try others) Fold step 1-2

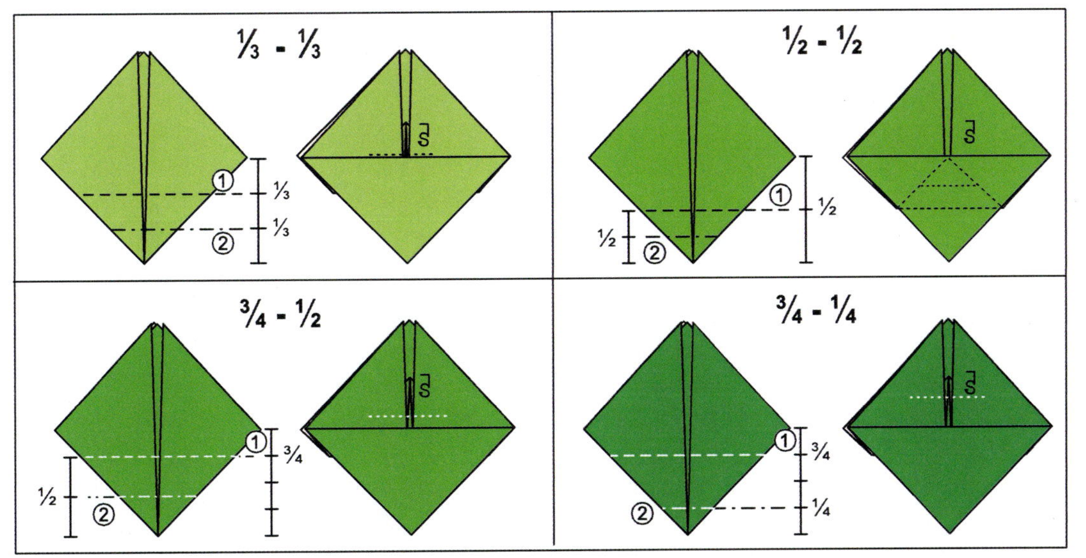

⅓ - ⅓
½ - ½
¾ - ½
¾ - ¼

# After-Bonn-Heart paperclip

10-06-2007

In June 2007 I attended my first foreign origami convention. I enjoyed it very much, saw beautiful things, and met many people who were just as crazy as I am (about origami). Because I was completely hyper, I designed this After Bonn Heart during the return journey by train. (The first model in the origami paper clip series.)
It was then that I decided to design a model after every convention.

Paper:
- 10x10cm or smaller

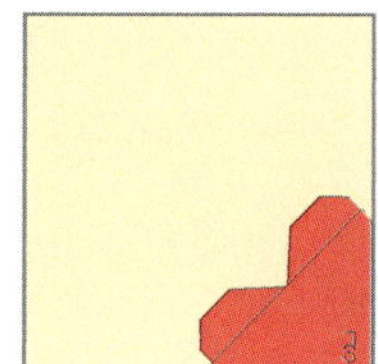

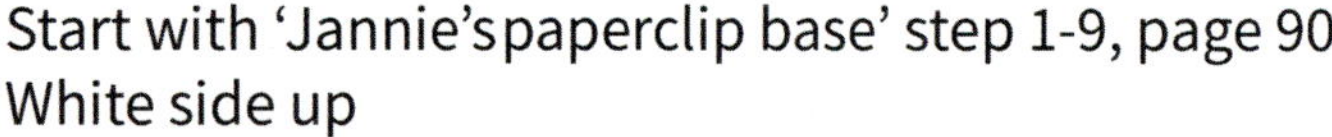

Start with 'Jannie'spaperclip base' step 1-9, page 90
White side up

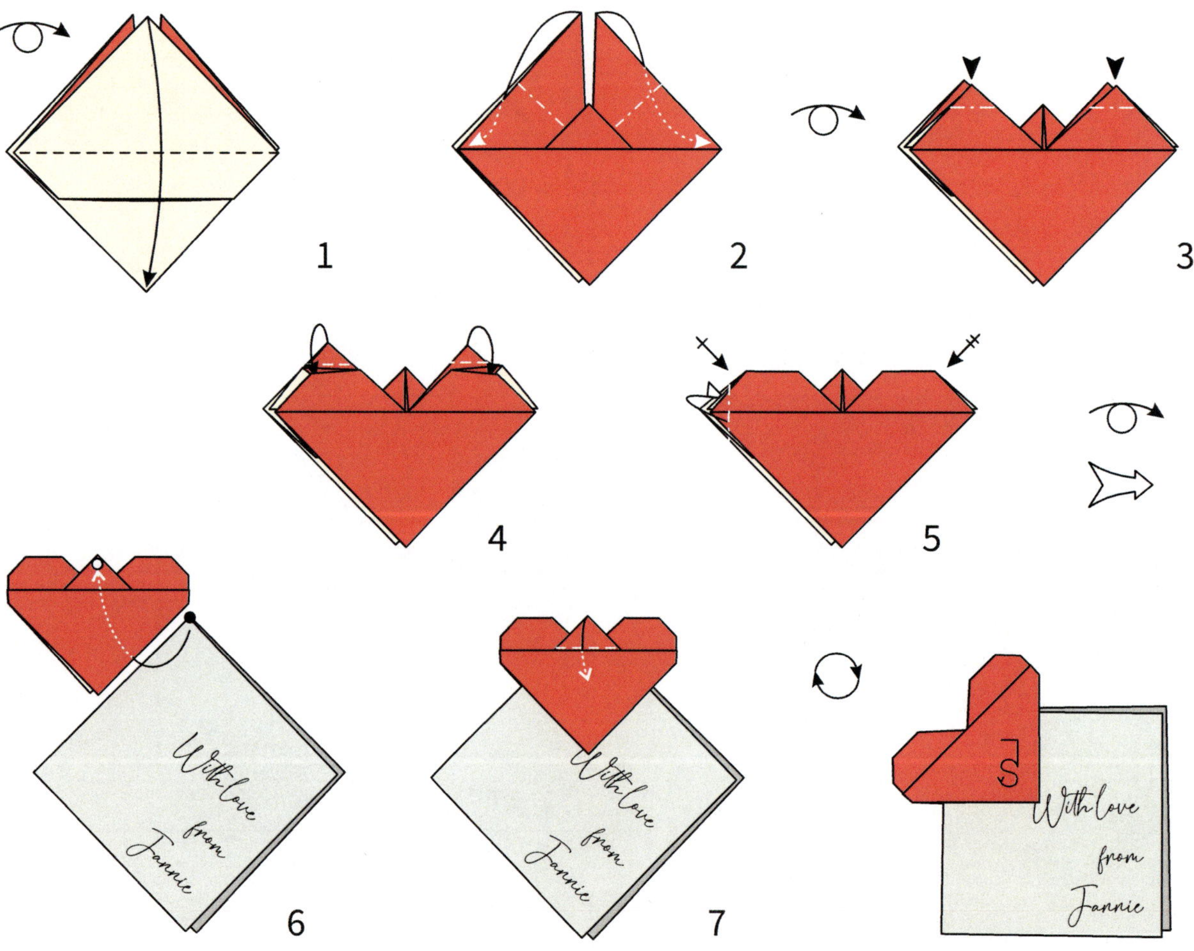

# Orchid paperclip

10-06-2007

Happy Birthday
Jannie

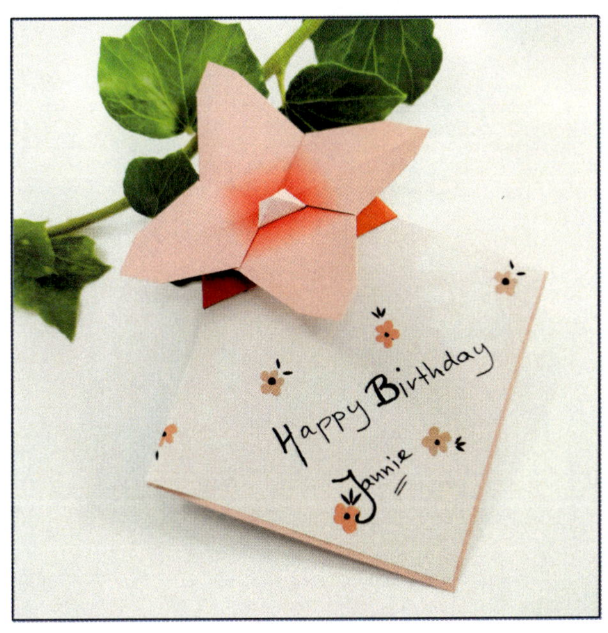

This Orchid is one of the flowers in my paperclip series. I really like the closure through the heart as well as it's small heart variation in the center.
And like all the other paperclips, it holds paper very well. It's a nice gift when attached to a little message or card, especially for orchid lovers.

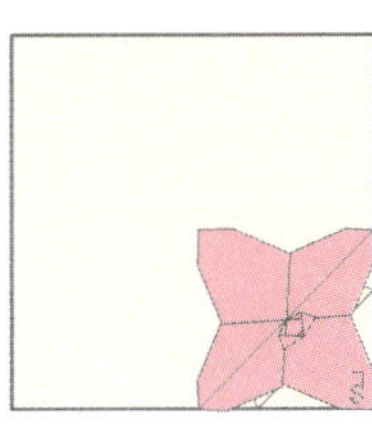

Paper:
- 10x10cm or smaller

Start with 'Jannie's paperclip base' step 1-8, page 90
White side up

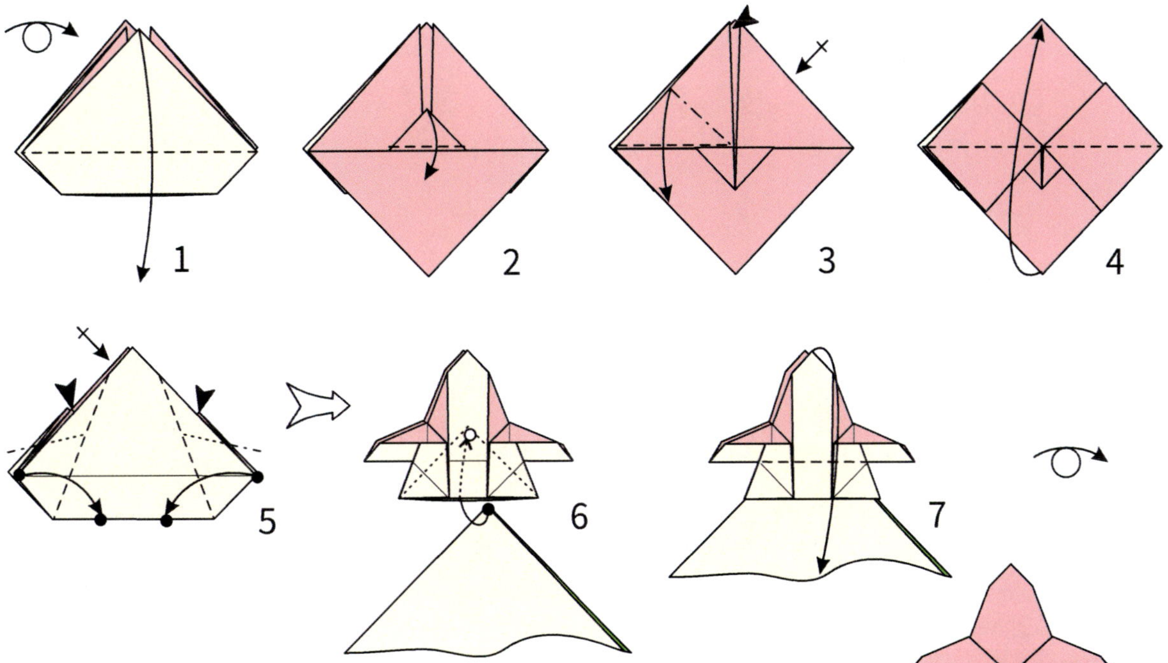

1
2
3
4
5
6
7

Happy Birthday
Jannie

*Variation center:*

8'
3D

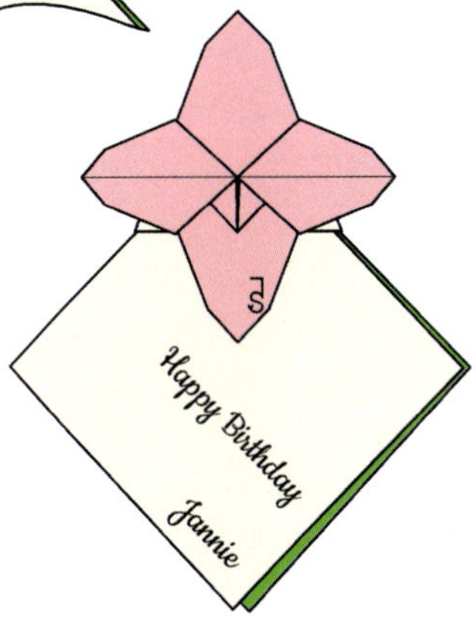

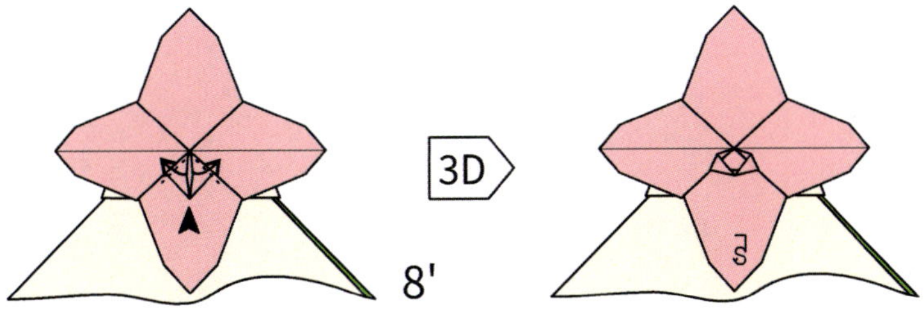

# Handy Paperclip Box

11-08-2015

Sometimes I design models not only for the beauty of it but also for practicality. That is how this box came about. It is annoying that there are always paperclips, beads, or pins in the corner of a box that I can't get out. With this rounded inside that problem now is a thing of the past. So enjoy tidying up. The variation gives a colored edge. Make the lid and you can store all kinds of things safely.

Paper:
- box: 20x20 cm kami/duo color gives a 5x5 cm box
- lid: 15x15 cm

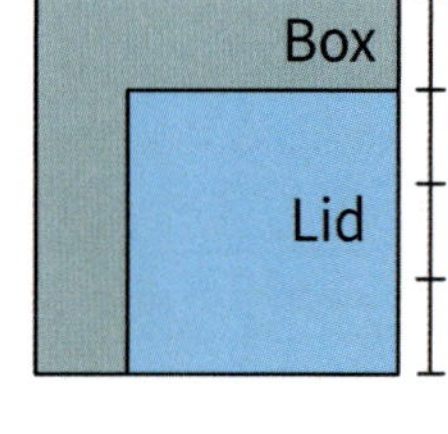


## Box

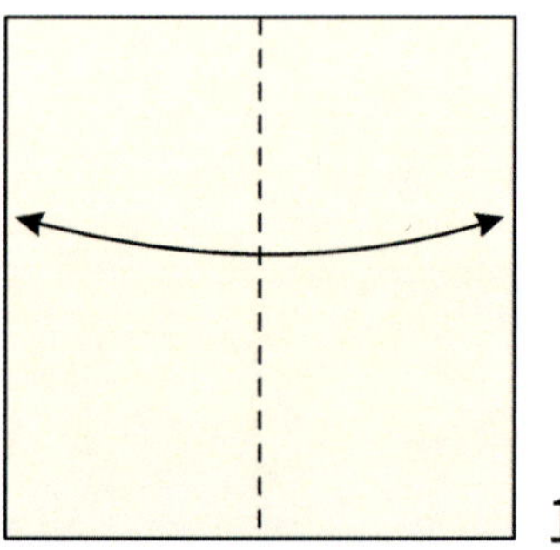

1

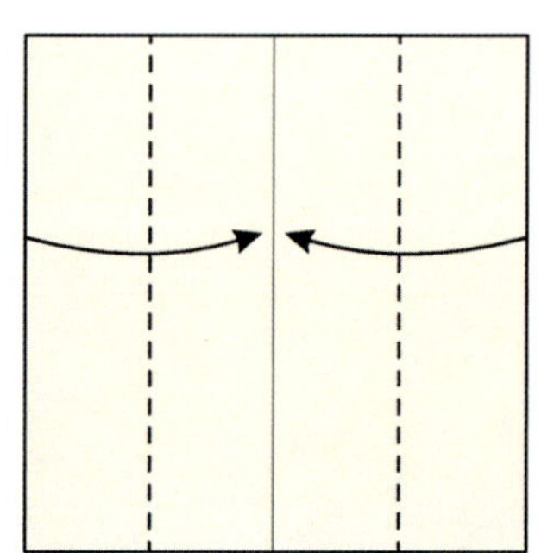

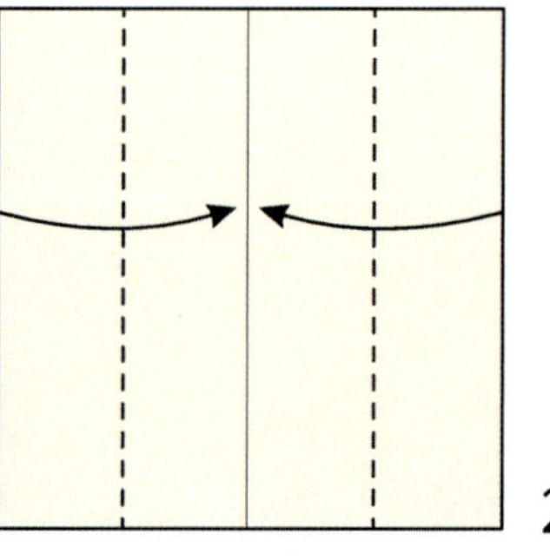

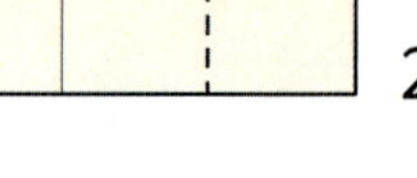

2

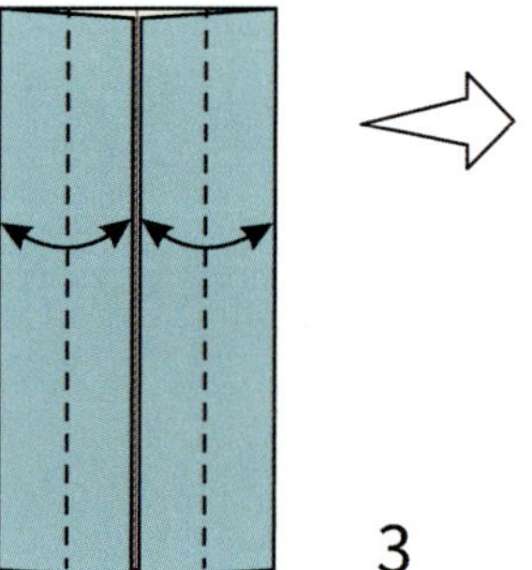

3

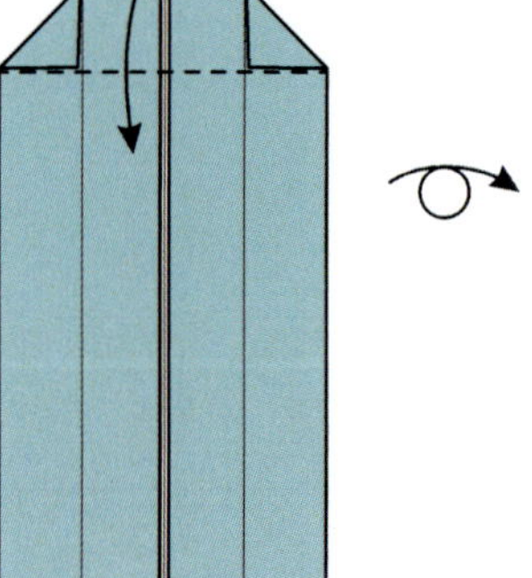

4

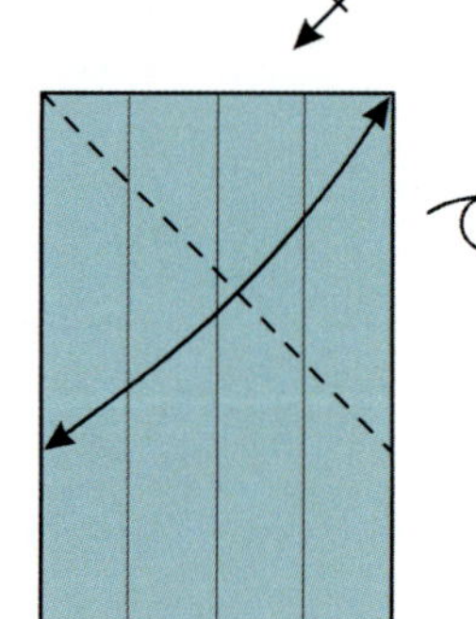

5

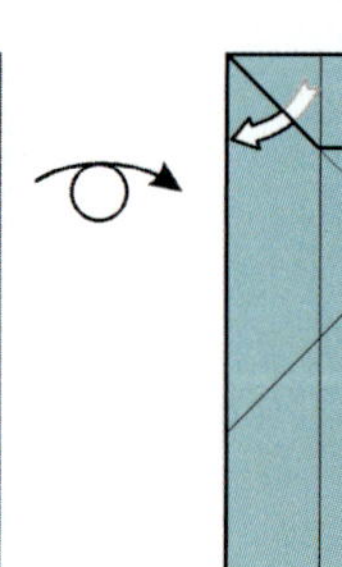

6

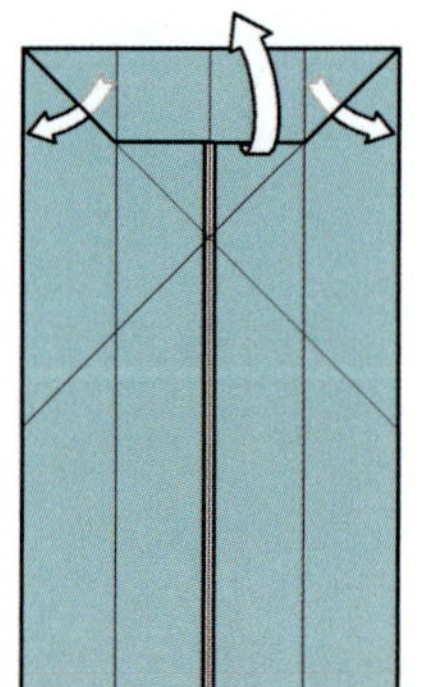

7

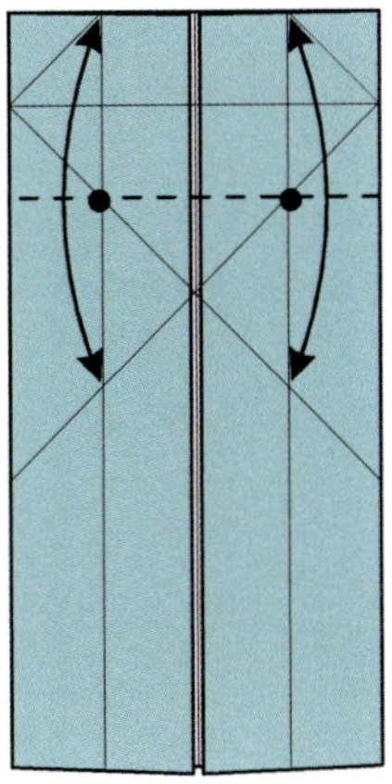

8

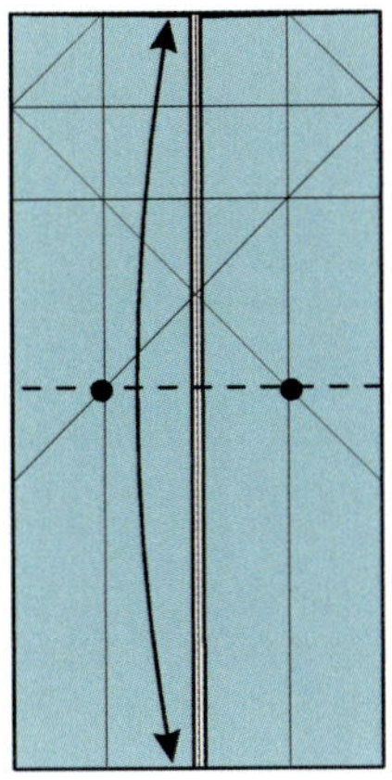

9

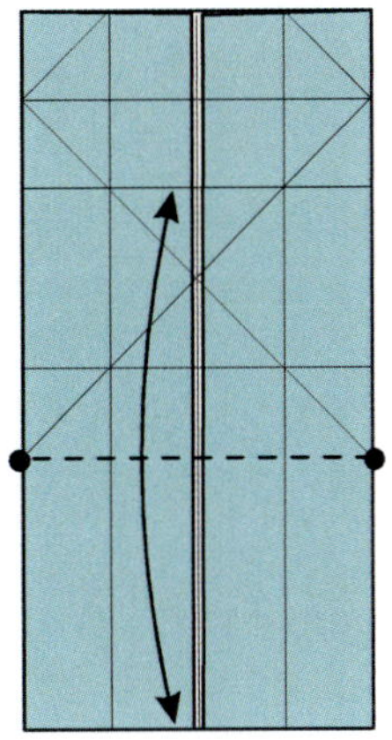

10

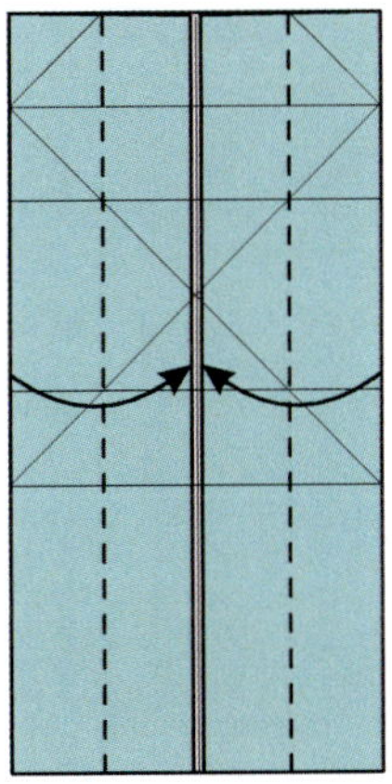

11

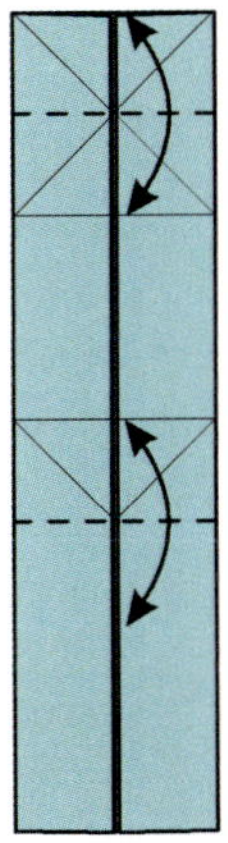

12

Make these creases extra sharp.

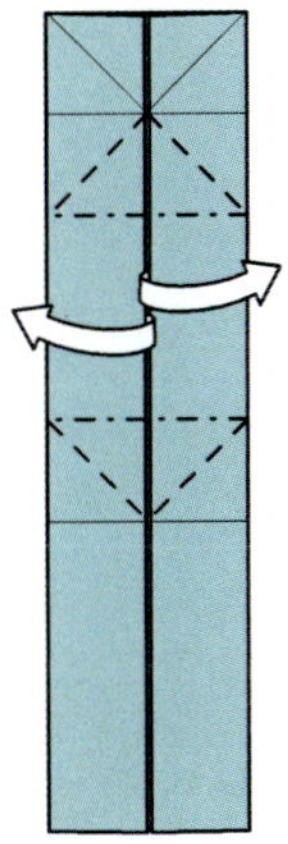

13

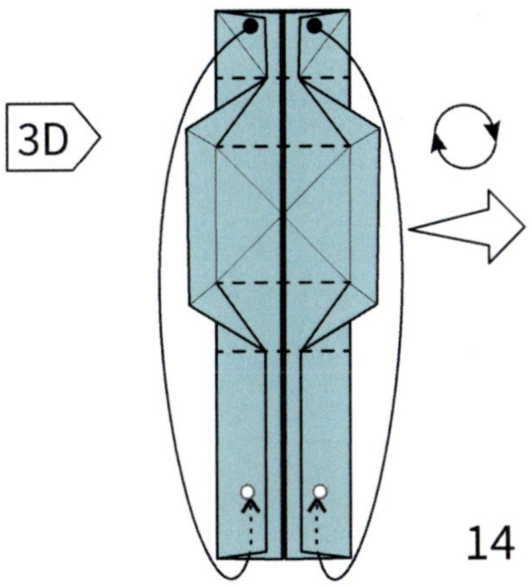

3D

14

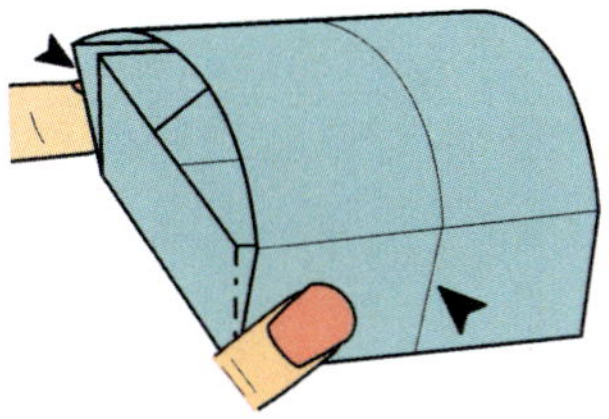

15

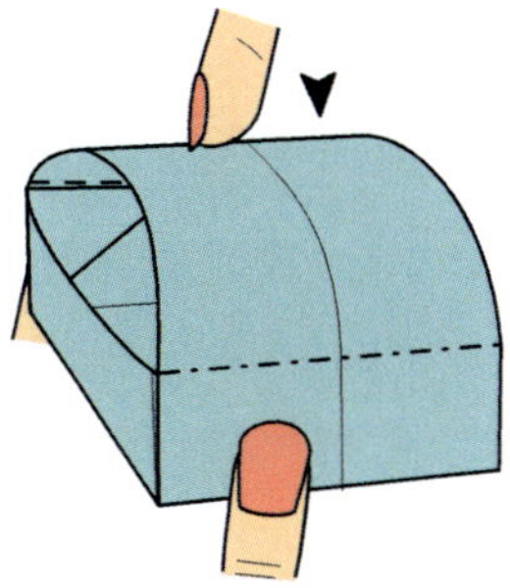

16

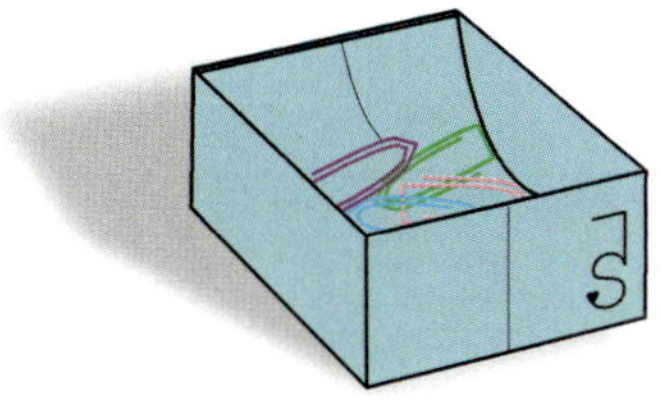

## *Variation with color change*

Fold steps 1-2

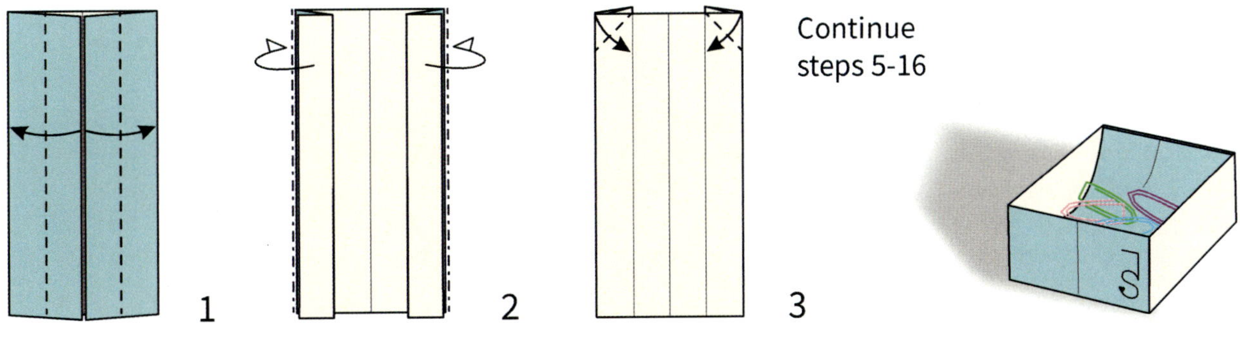

# Handy Paperclip Box Lid

03-08-2024

## Lid

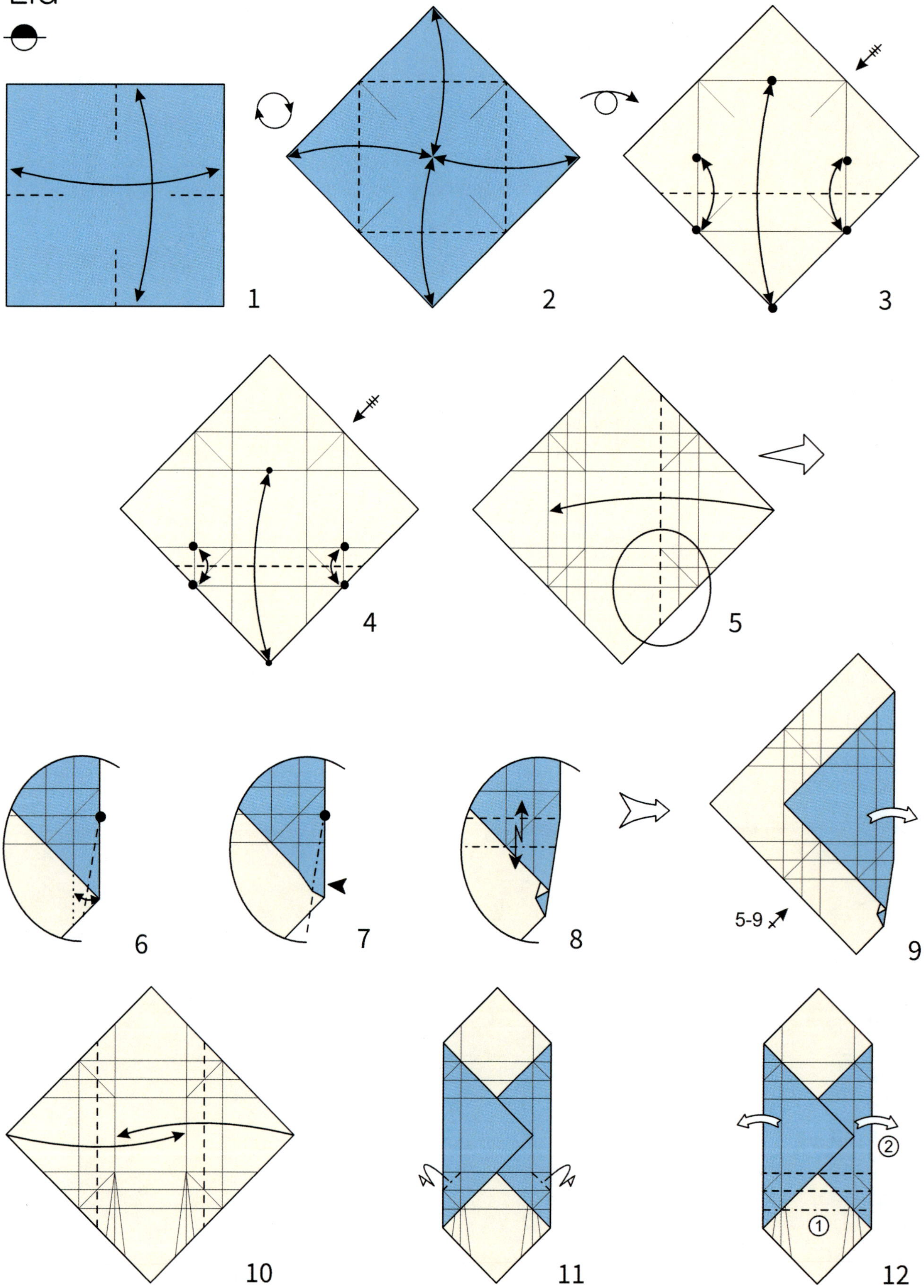

1 2 3

4 5

6 7 8 9

5-9

10 11 12

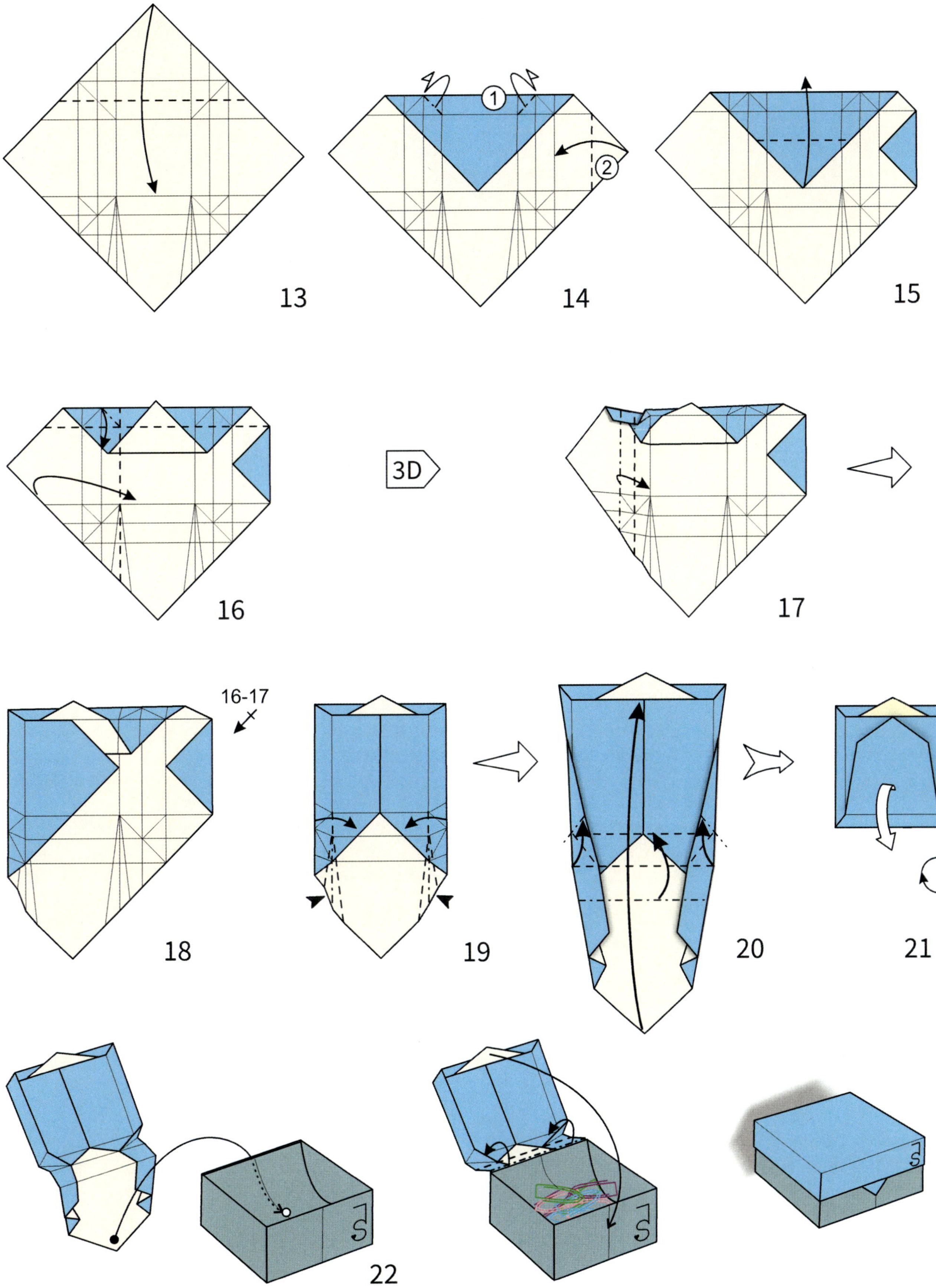

13

14

15

16

3D

17

16-17

18

19

20

21

22

# Ori-Paper-Saver

18-04-2021

During a workshop by Jolette Flapper we made an easy bookcover model of bookbinding artist Roberta Lavadour. This inspired me to develop a completely folded box, uncut, from one sheet of paper, with a closure and sturdy enough to store paper. This box has it all, including a solid bottom. Also, you can add a label holder to see what it contains. It's possible to make it for all sizes of square paper.

Paper:
Box: kraft paper or other sturdy paper
Labelholder: use the same size paper you make the box for

This is the paper advice for an Ori-Paper-Saver for 5 cm and 7,5 cm paper pack
Other sizes and information you can find in the calculation table at page 11

*Paper:*
for a ***5 cm*** square paper pack: **37 x 13 cm**
length: (6 x 5,5 cm =) **33 cm +** (lock =) **3 cm +** (reinforcement =) **1 cm = 37 cm**
width: (2 x 5,5 cm =) **11 cm +** (depth box =) **2 cm** = **13 cm**

for a ***7,5 cm*** square paper pack: **53 x 18 cm**
length: (6 x 8 cm =) **48 cm +** (lock =) **4 cm +** (reinforcement =) **1 cm = 53 cm**
width: (2 x 8 cm =) **16 cm +** (depth box =) **2 cm** = **18 cm**

White side up. Look at the diagram, when you have a directional pattern.
Start making small marks with a pencil for an easier way of folding. It's easier to fold against a mark than to fold the mark itself. These diagrams are based on 7,5 cm square.

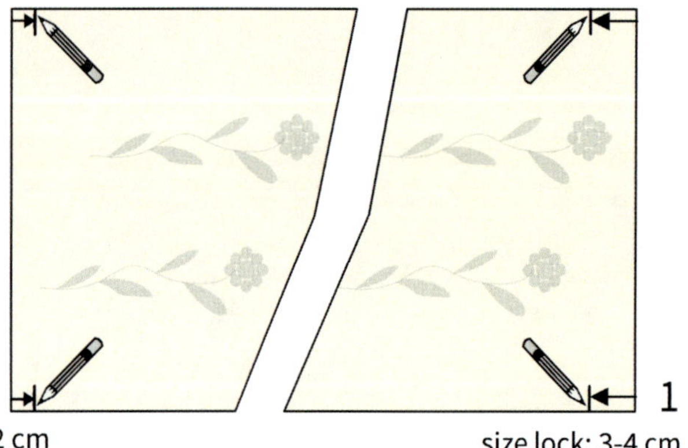


On the left side make a mark twice the size of the reinforcement (2 cm)
On the right side mark the size of the lock (3 or 4 cm)

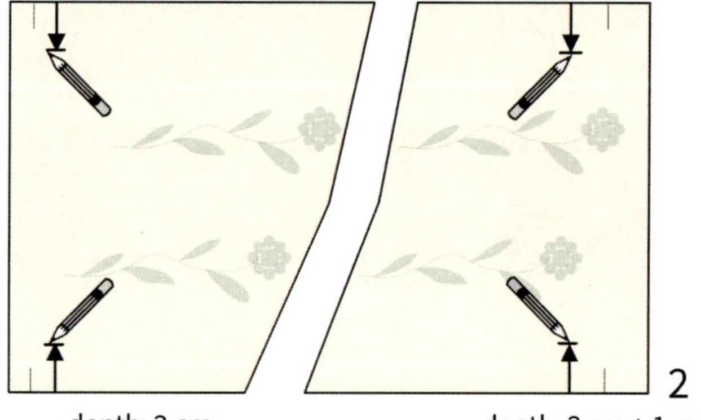


Mark on the top and bottom left side the depth (2 cm)
Mark on the top and bottom right side the depth + 1 mm (2,1 cm)
The closure needs extra space to put the paper inside

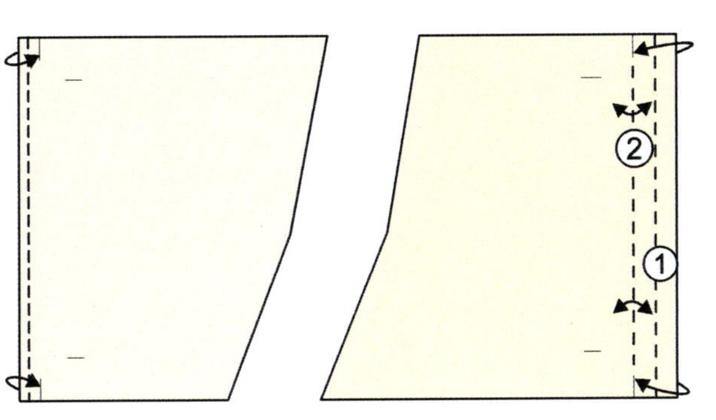


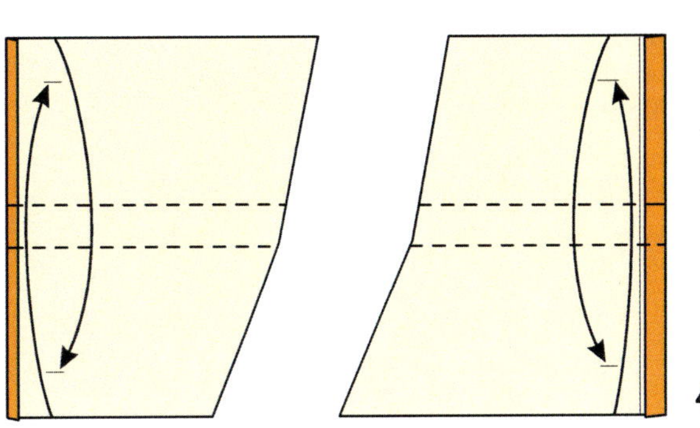


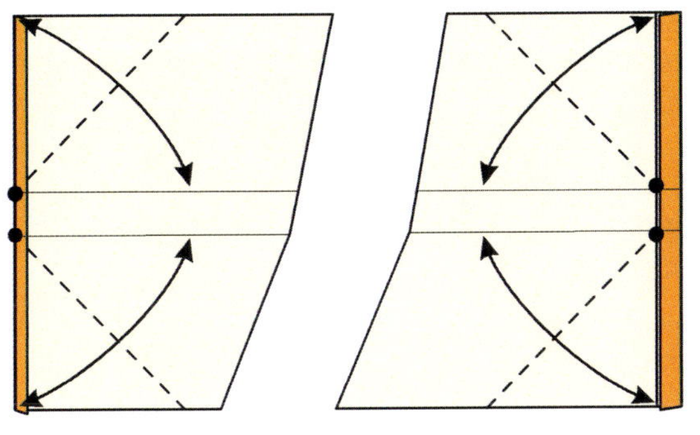


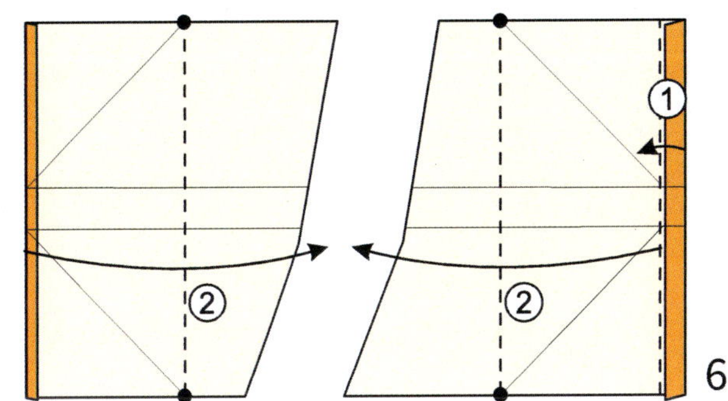


Pay attention to the folding proces at the right side.
Don't fold over the vertical creases.

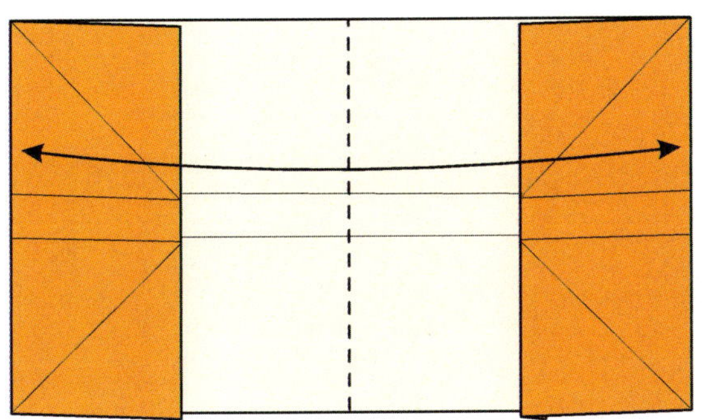


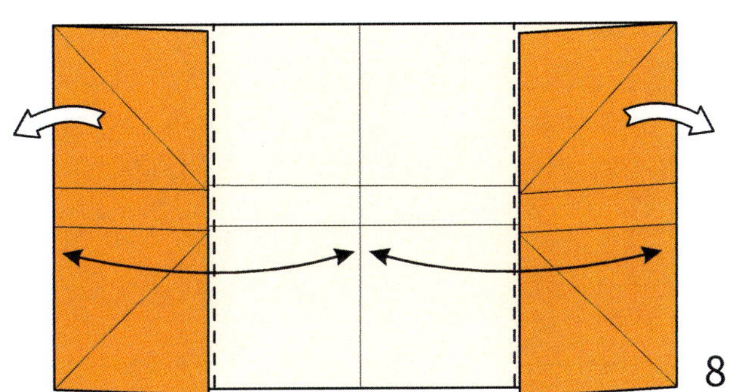


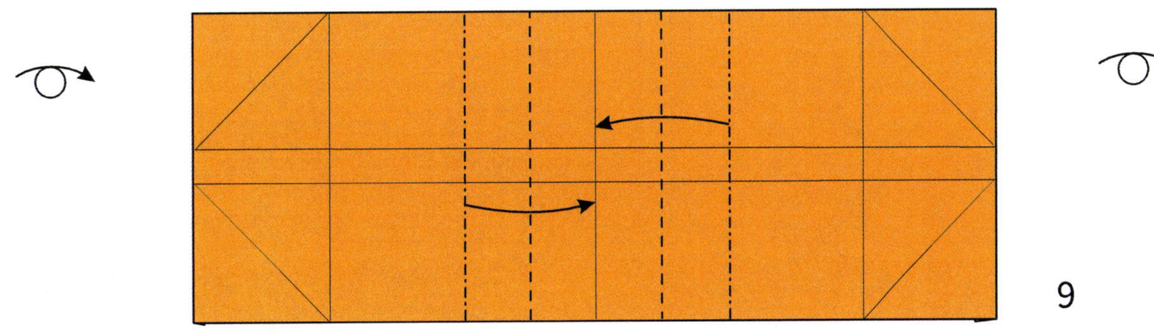

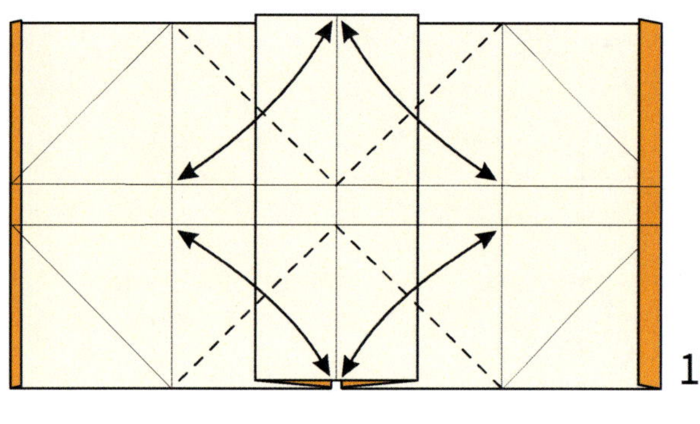

10

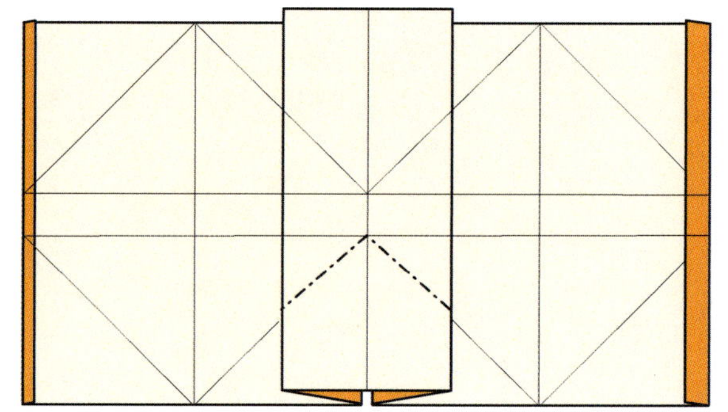

11

Change the top layer crease into a mountain fold.

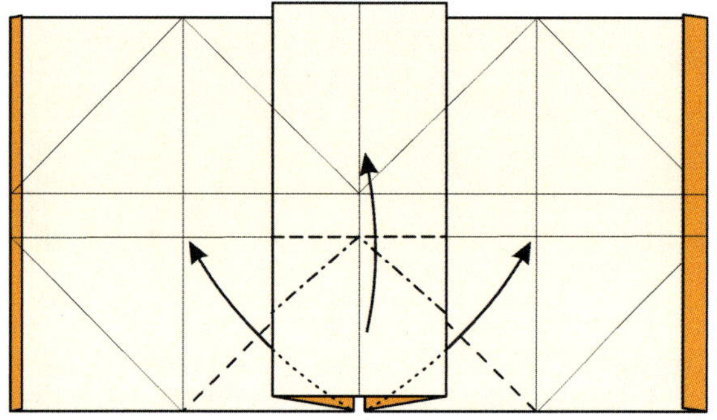

12

Make a horizontal valley fold on the top layer. The 2 diagonal creases under these layers will be all valley. Squash the paper carefully, step by step. The model is 3D. It looks a bit like making a butterfly or box.

3D

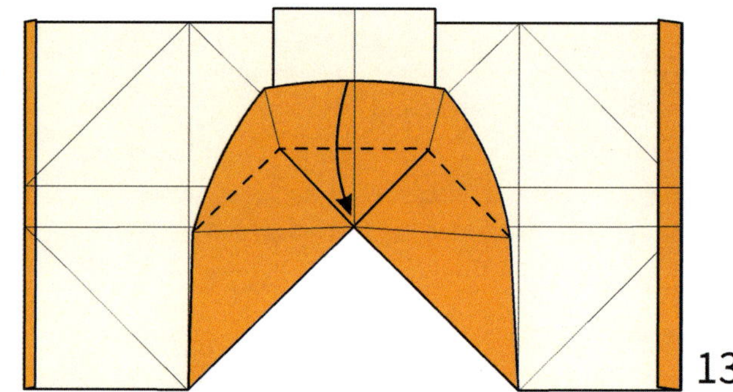

13

Flatten carefully by folding the top layer downward.

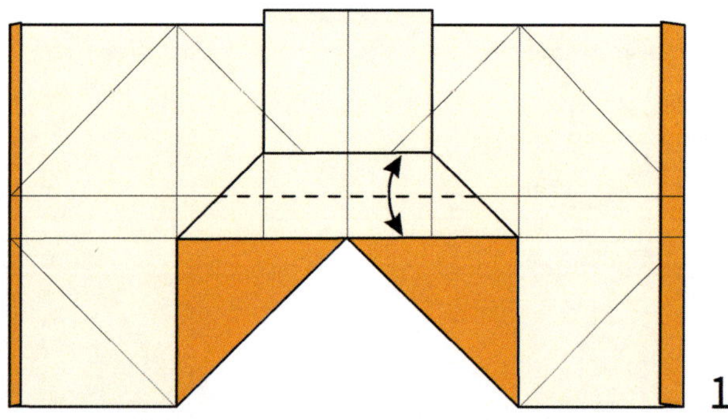

14

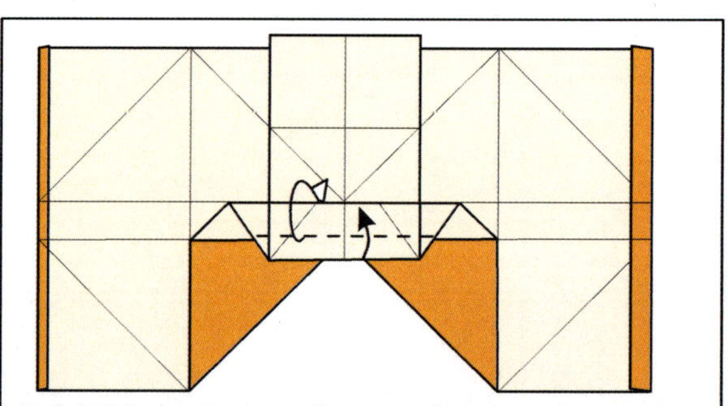

14'

Fold this bottom twice, as shown, when there is more paper. That will happen when a box is for bigger paper then 8 cm.

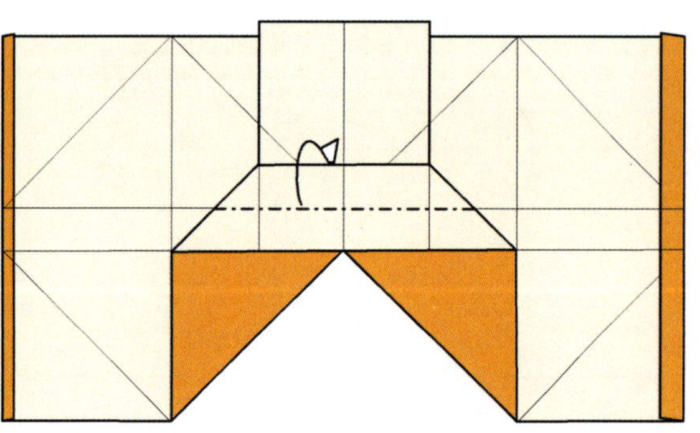

15

11-14

16

Repeat steps 11 - 14. The paper from step 15 tucks into the pocket of the first squash fold.

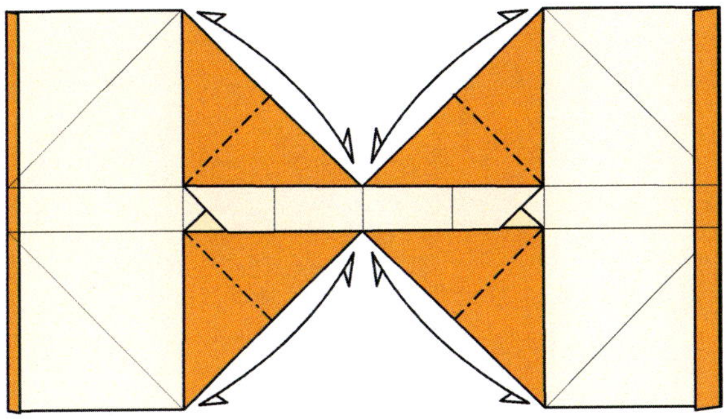

17

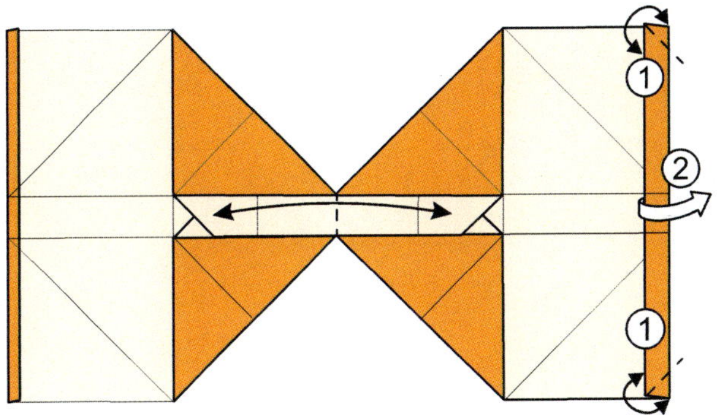

18

1 2

3D

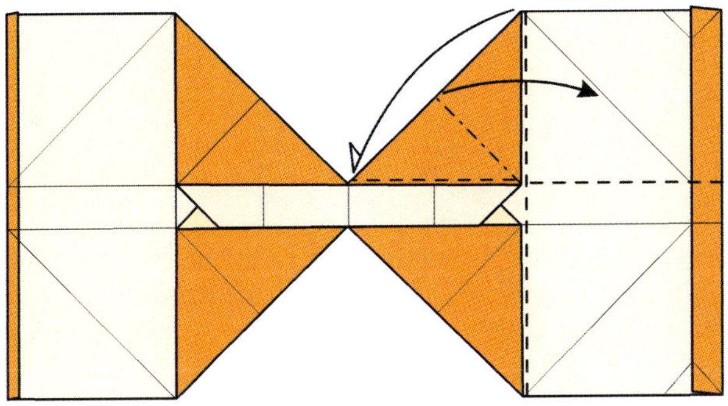

19

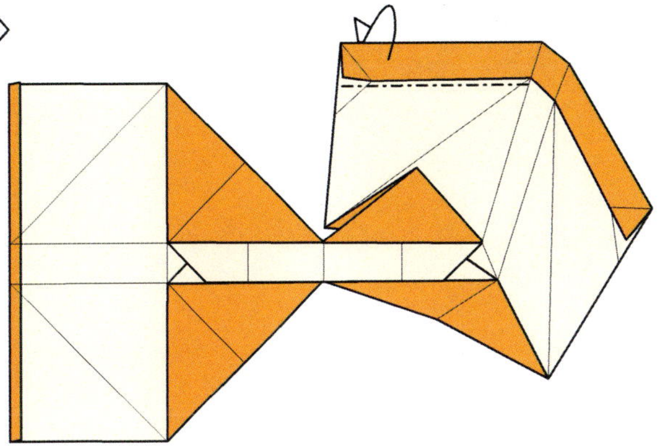

20

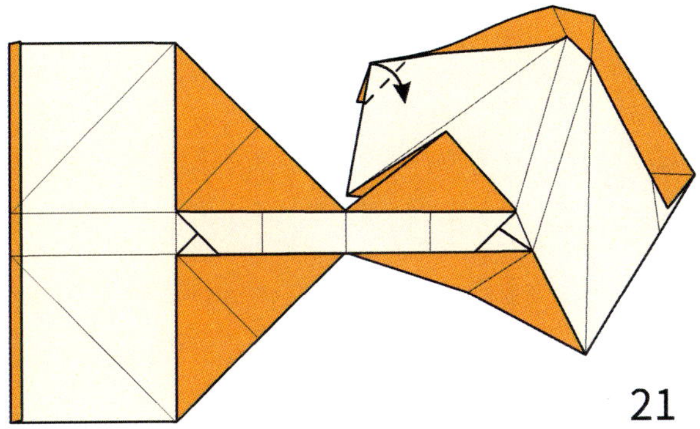

21

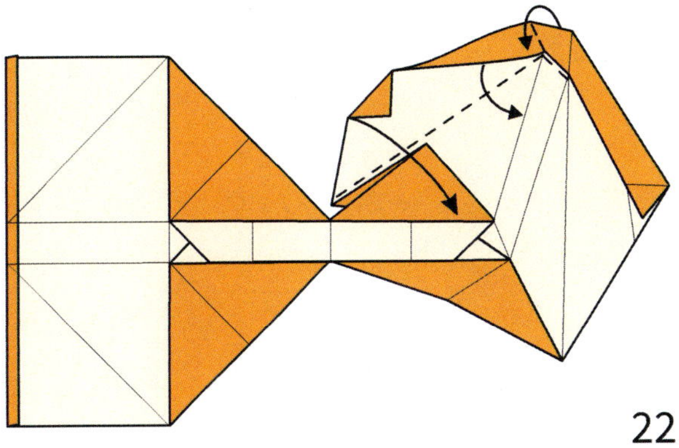

22

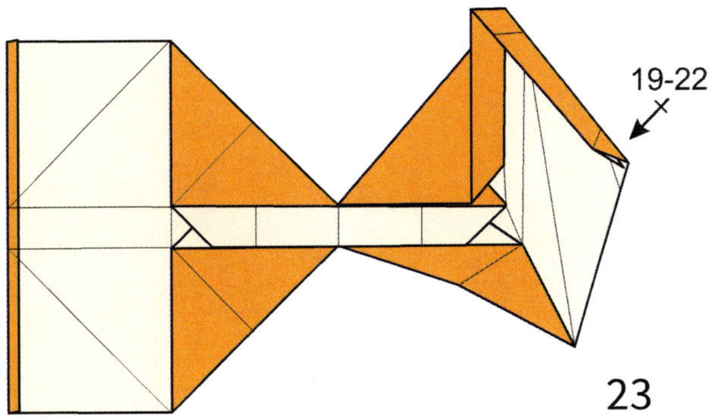

23

19-22

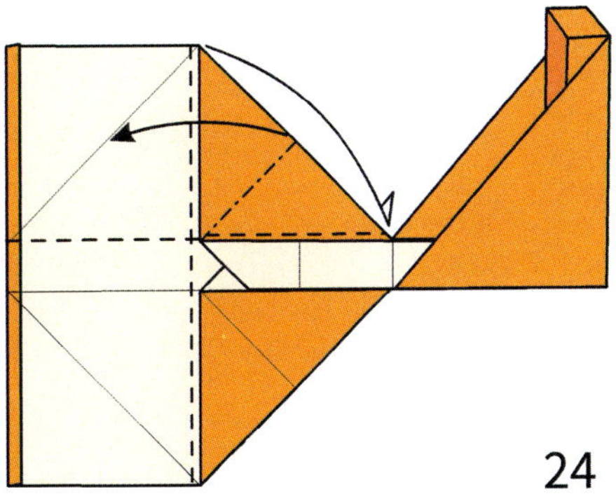

24

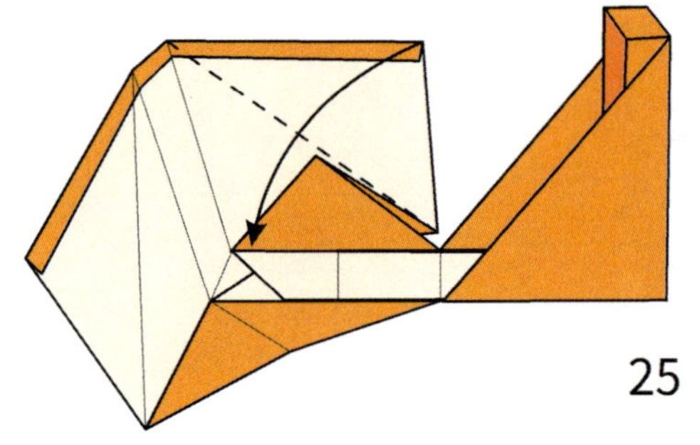


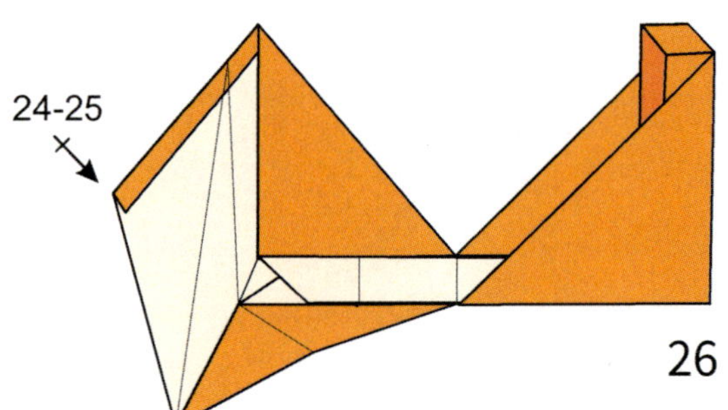


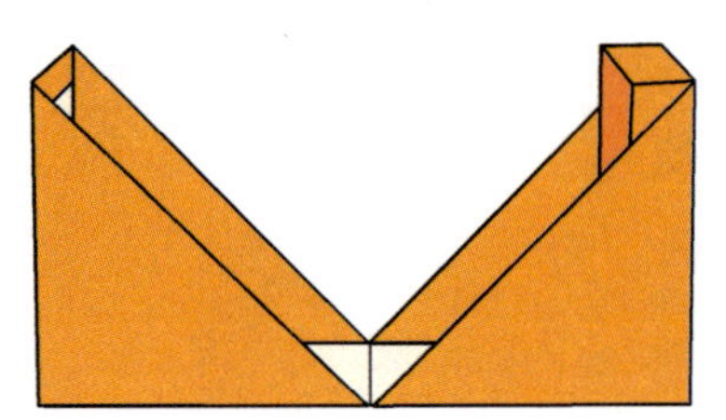

27

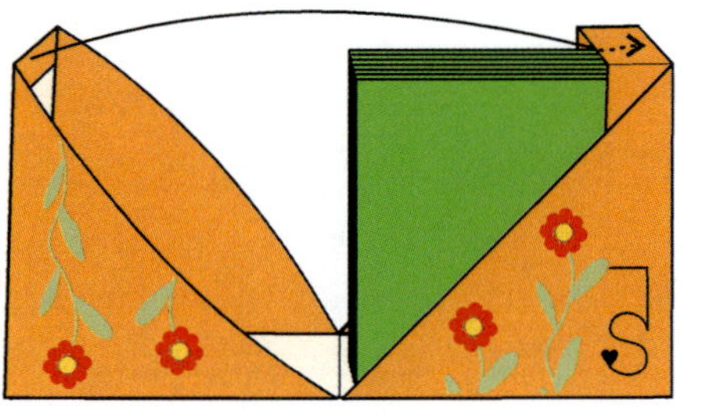

28

Store the paper in het part with the band. Widen the left diagonal sides a bit to make the box easier to close. The left top comes under the right band.

If you want a color change of the lockband, then mountain fold the right strip in step 3 ①

## Labelholder

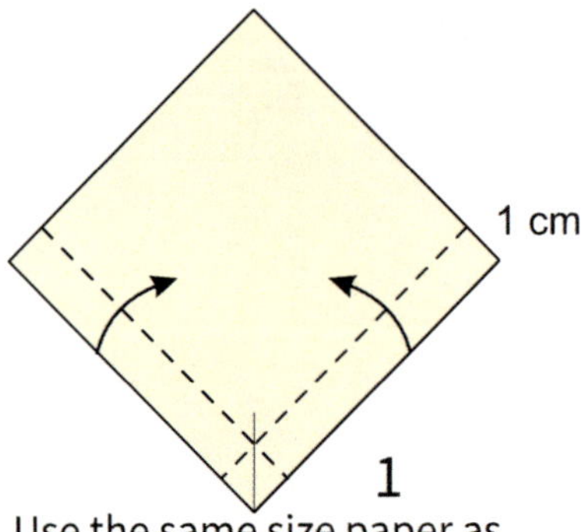


Use the same size paper as the box is intended for.

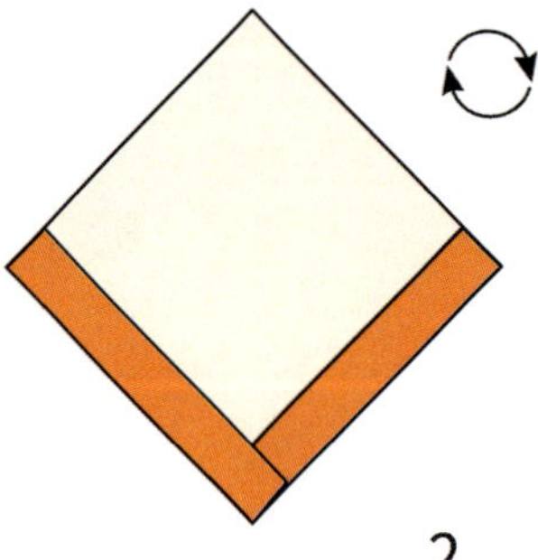


3

Put the colored point of the diamond in the pocket of the hinge as far as possible.

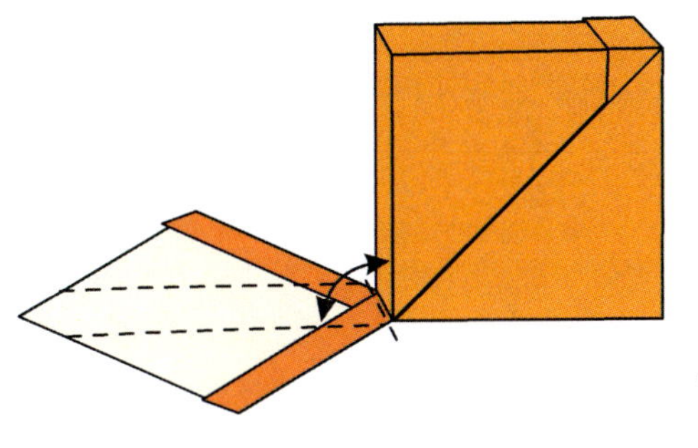


Fold up the paper up against the hinge to make a valley fold. Fold the paper around both vertical corners of the box, as a mark.

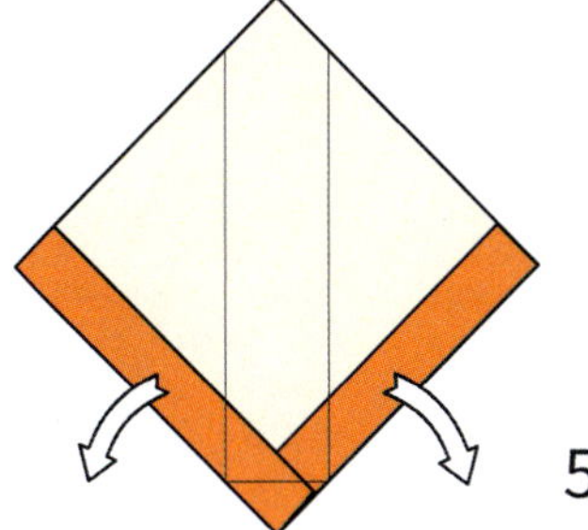


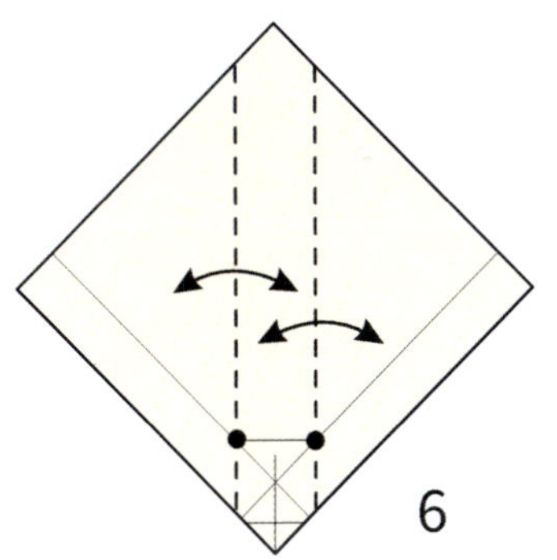


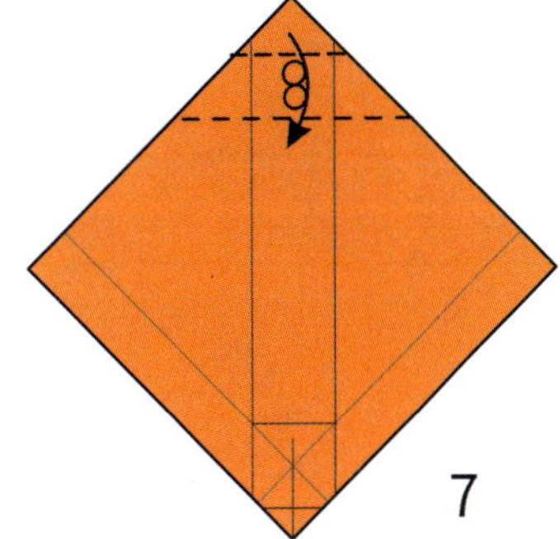


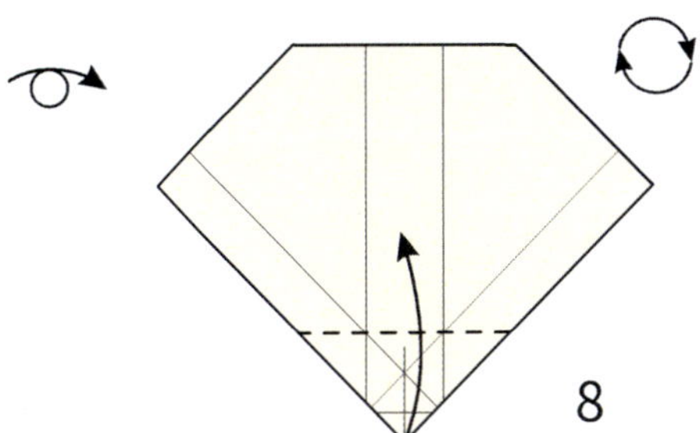


## *Assembly*

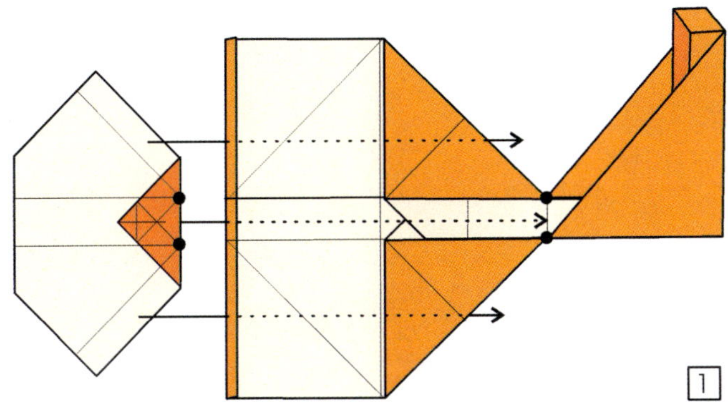


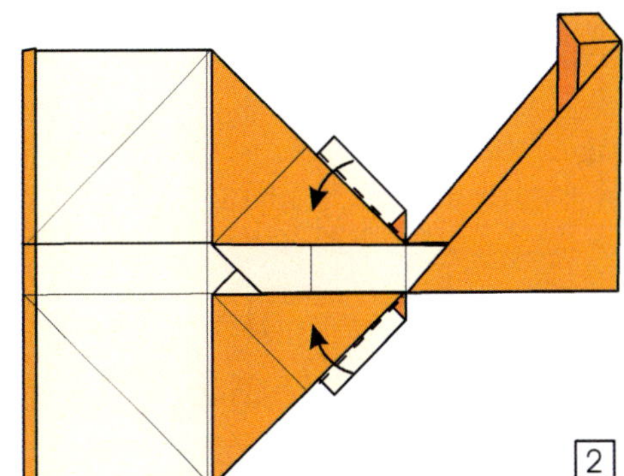


Unfold the box till step 24. Place the paper under the box. The folded edge comes as far as the hinge.
Both diagonal creases are aligned with the diagonal folded edges.

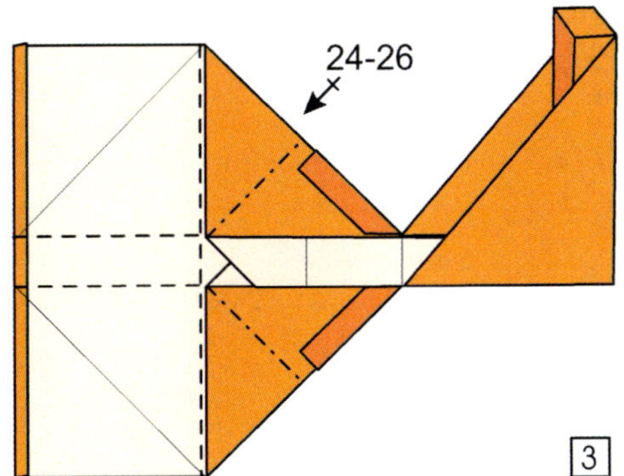

# Rosalina's Envelope

18-08-2015

My granddaughter loves playing with paper. She was only 4 years old when she gave me an A4 sheet folded as in step 4. The folds fit perfectly. I just had to add a few creases to get this great and simple letter fold/envelope. Both Rosalina and I are the designers of this beautiful model and of course I named this model after her. I use this model often and it's nice to put a small gift in it.

Paper:
- A4 size or smaller
- Making A4 size from Letter size: cut off about 3/4" of an inch off the long side

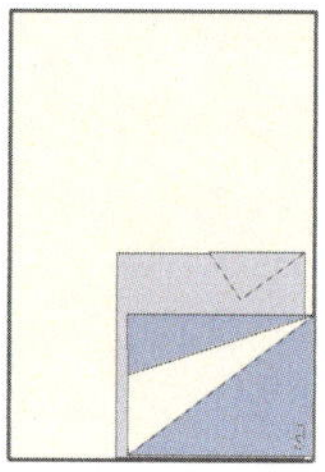

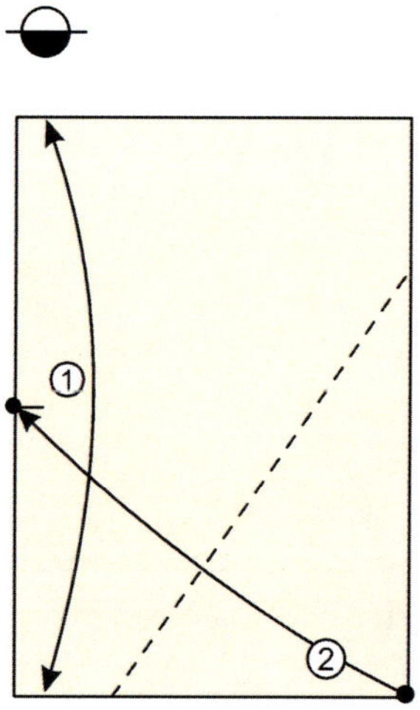

1

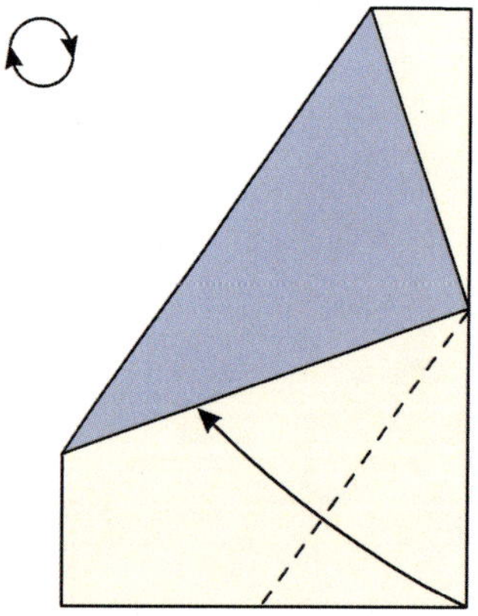

2

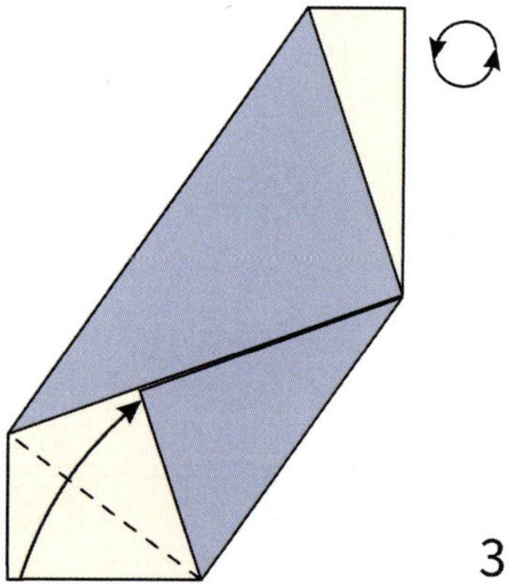

3

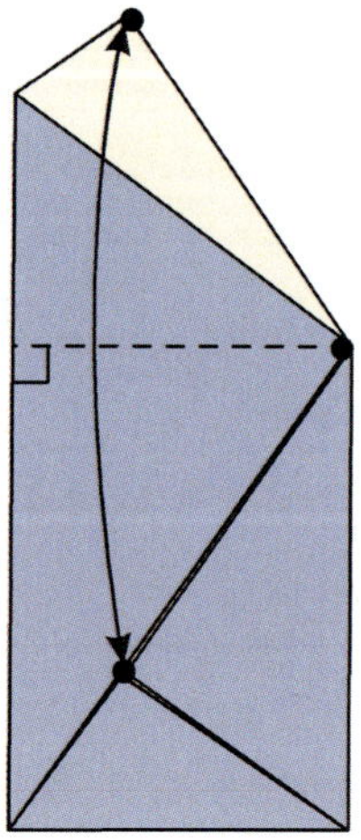

4

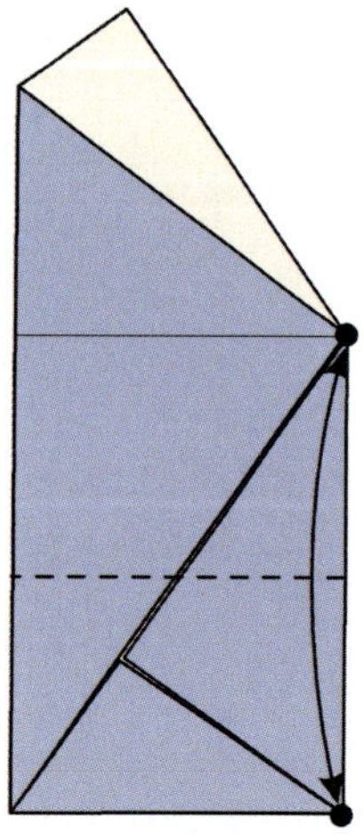

5

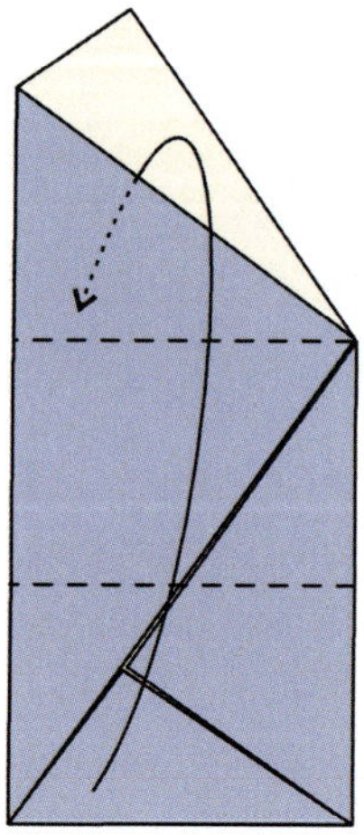

6

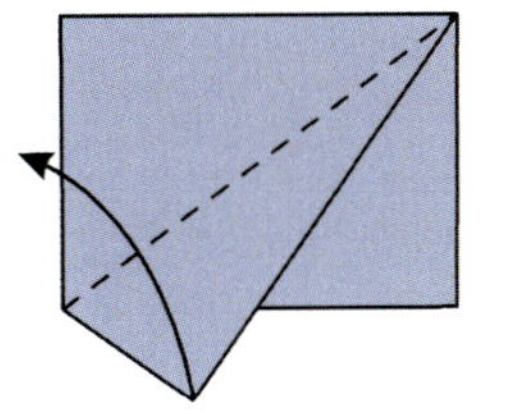

7

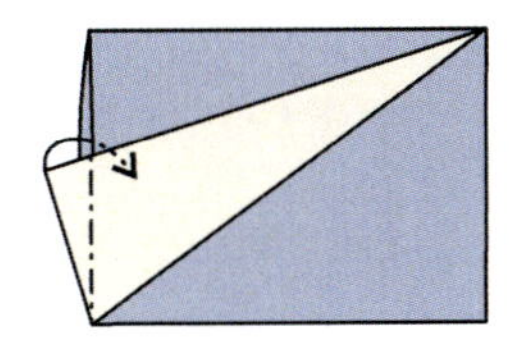

8

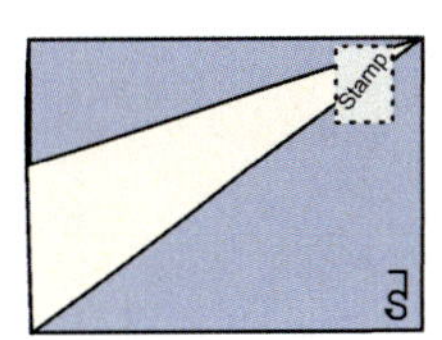

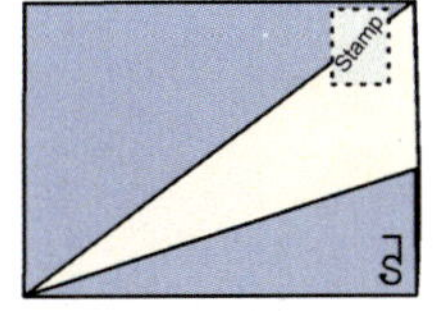


*Variation without color change*
*Locked with a stamp*

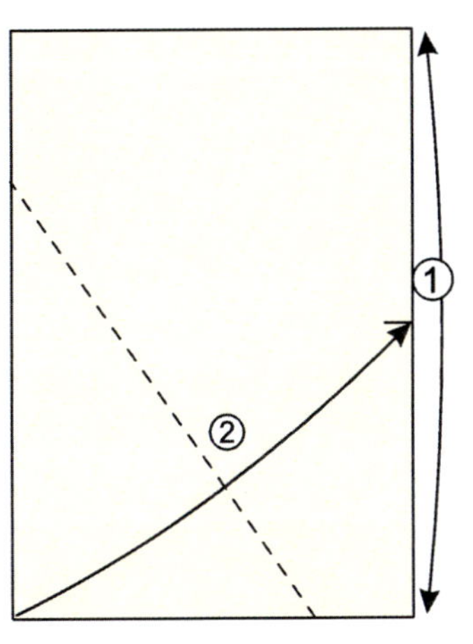


1

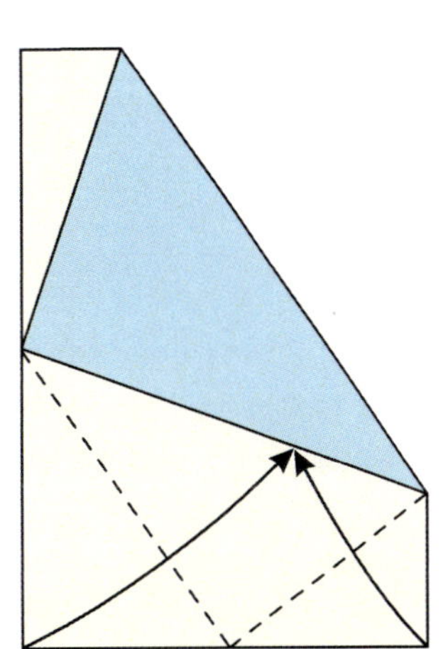

2

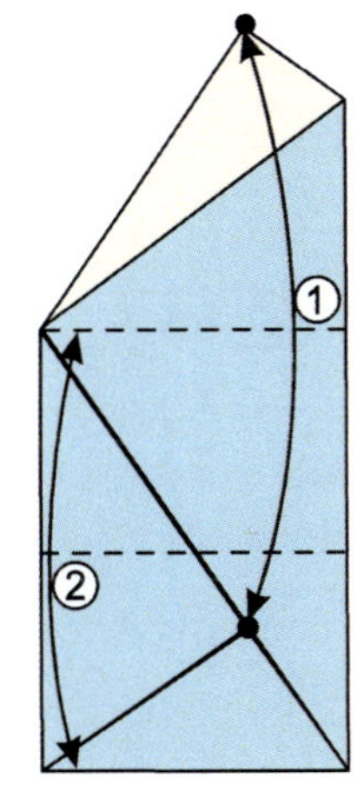


3

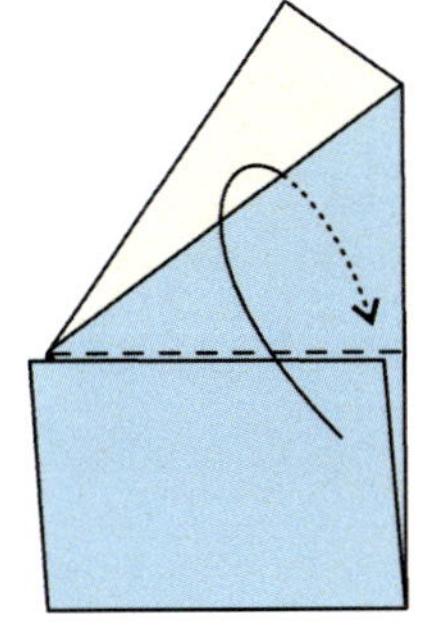

4

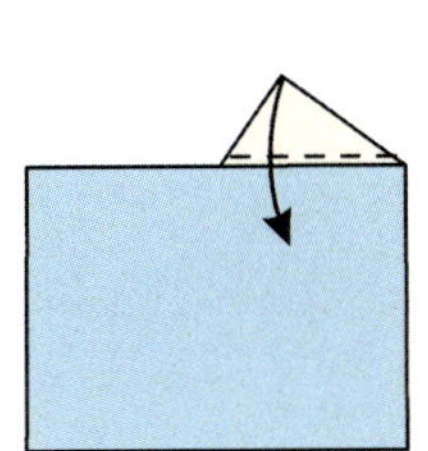

5

*Variation square shape*
*Locked with a stamp*

fold step 1-2 above

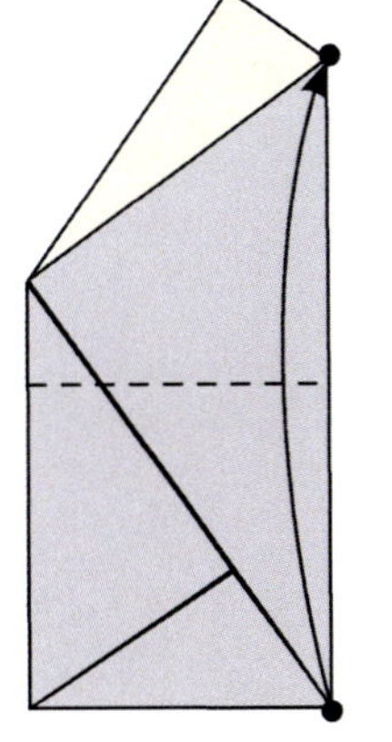

1

2

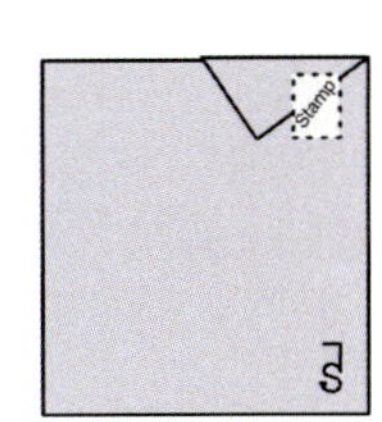

# Heart Envelope

13-03-2006

Envelopes are always useful. If not for just the pleasure of folding them at least to use them for sending a friendly greeting.
Of course you can also use them to wrap a small gift.
I am sure everyone can use a heartfelt one, so I recommend this chapter for that purpose.
You can find this model on my YouTube channel.

Paper:
- 15 x 15 cm Duo color

Colored side becomes the heart

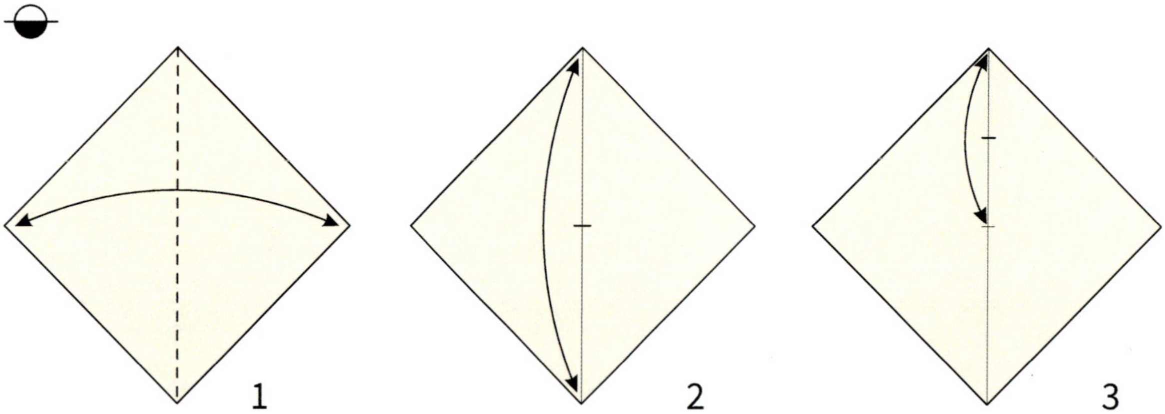

1

2

3

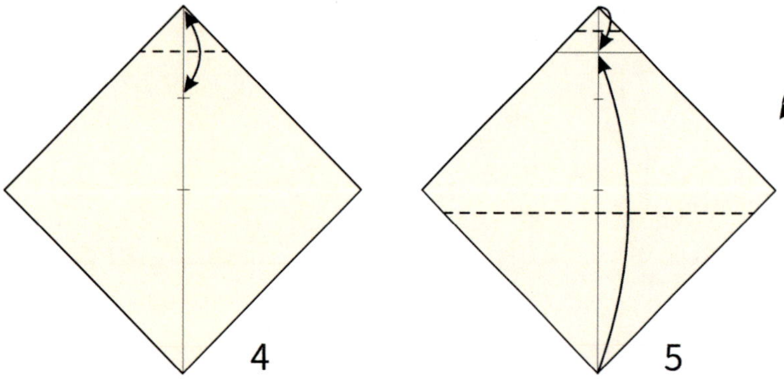

4

5

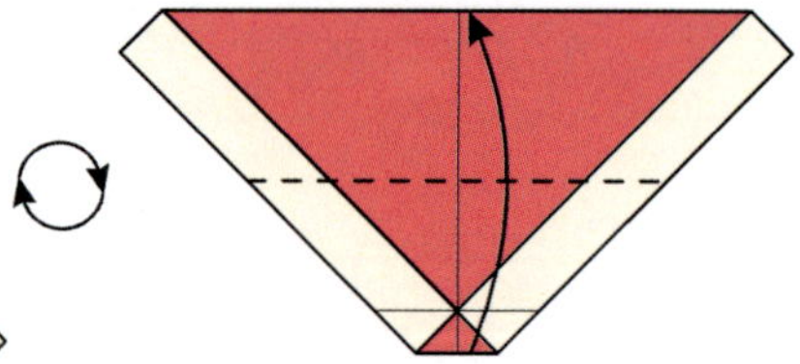

Hold both paper layers securely before folding.

6

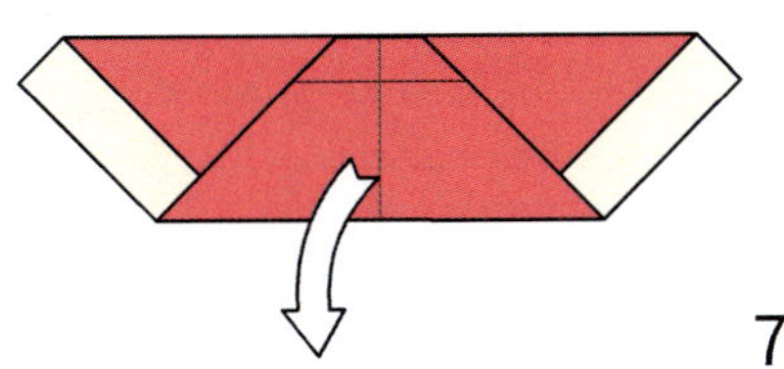

7

Hold both paper layers securely before Folding.

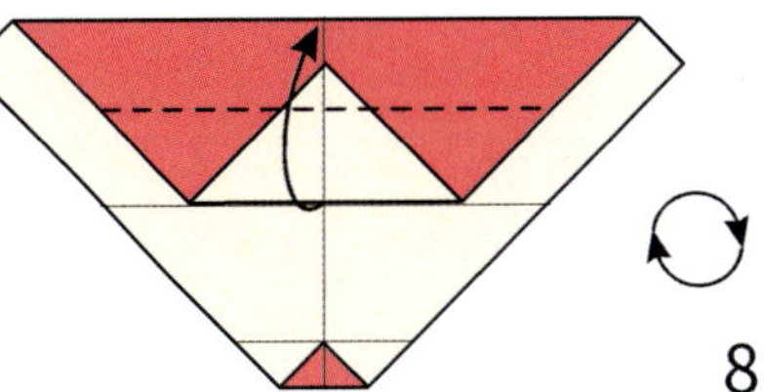

8

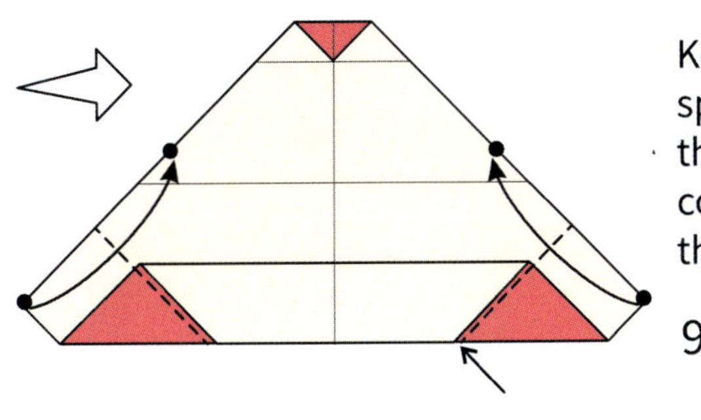

9

Keep a little space between the white and colored side of the paper.

10

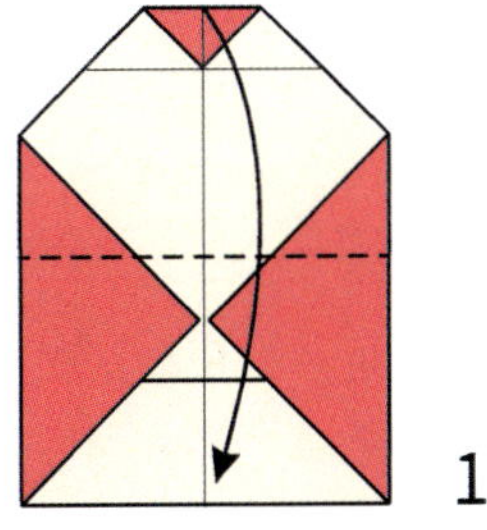

11

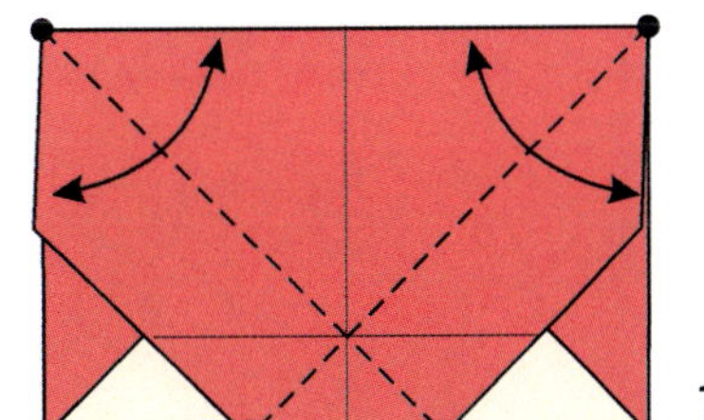

12

13

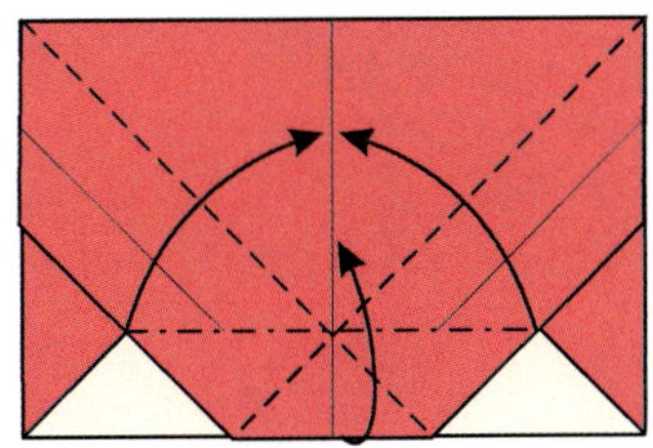

14

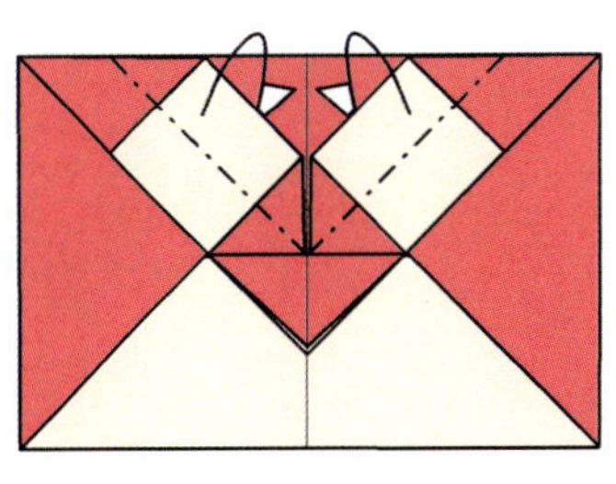

15

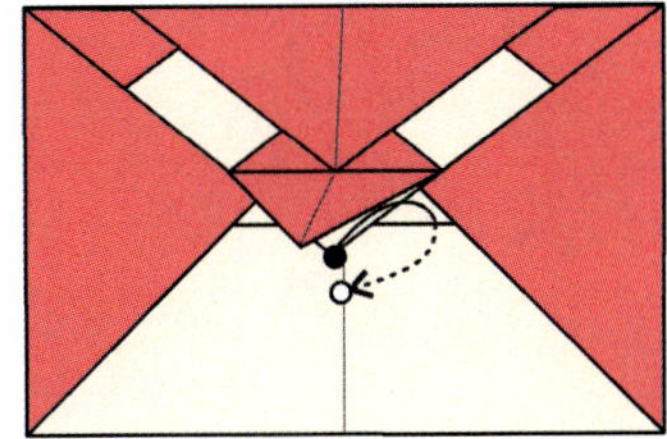

16

# Willem's Vaart Envelope

03-02-2023

This envelope is a tribute to my beloved father, Willem. He was a skipper and sailed away from this world January 2023. In the Netherlands there is the canal called (Zuid-) Willems Vaart. My dad used to sail there also. In Dutch the term 'Goede Vaart' means 'Farewell'. So that's why I choose the name to honour my father. A great envelope for a great dad!
I love this model too because of the very nice move in steps 10 - 12 that makes a closed sink in a very easy way.

Paper:
- 15x15 cm white/color Kami

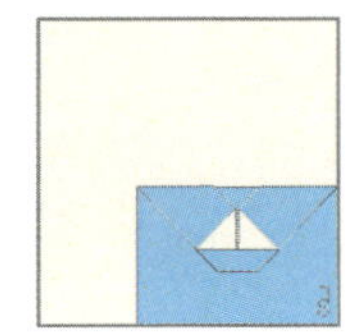

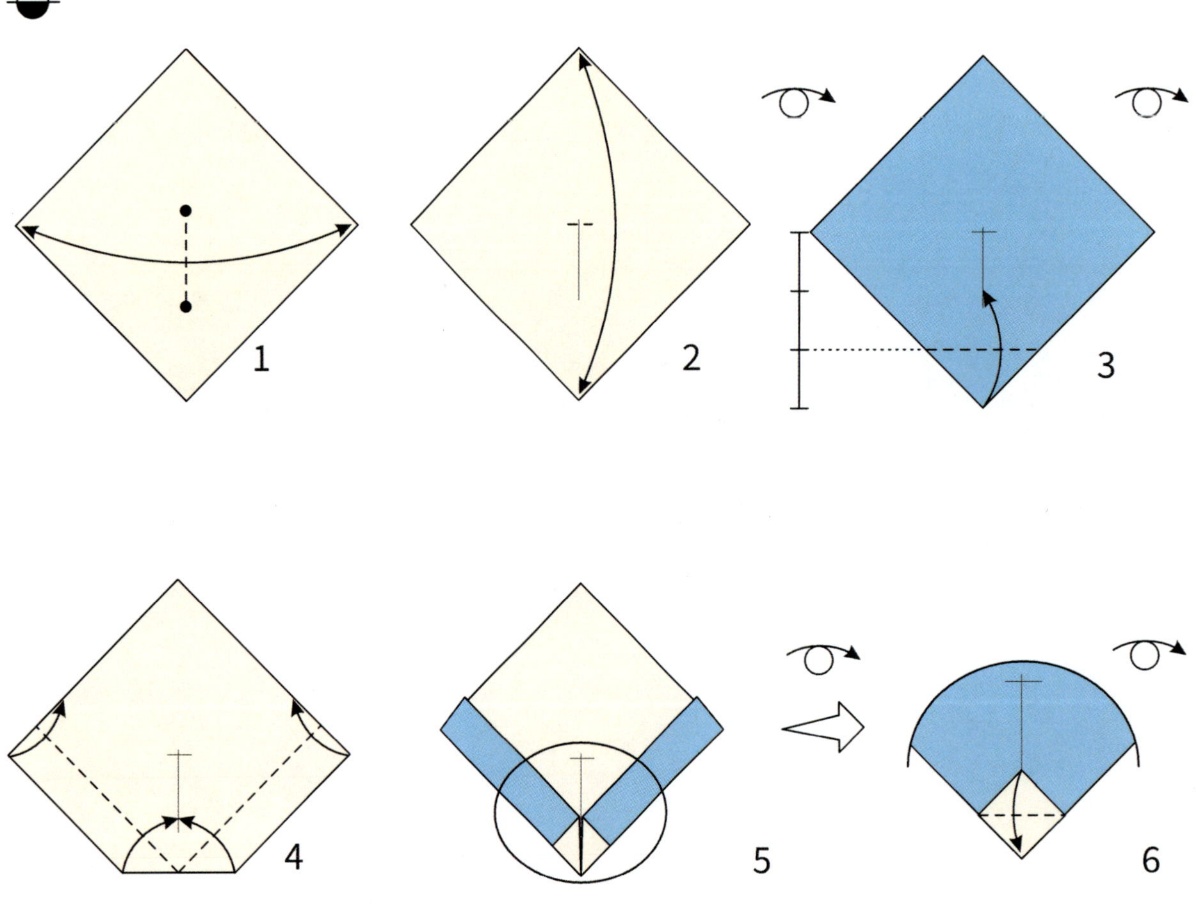

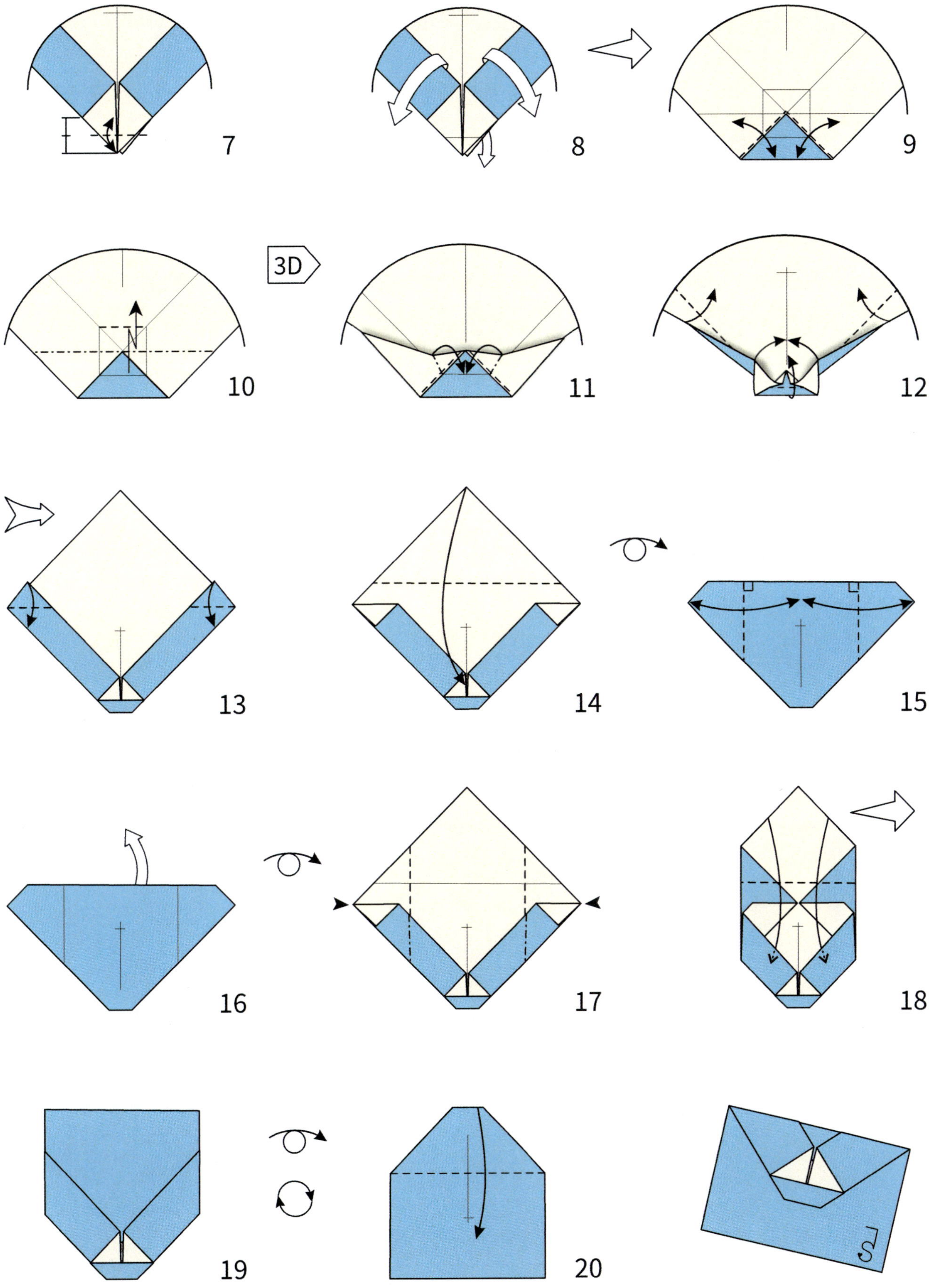

7

8

9

3D

10

11

12

13

14

15

16

17

18

19

20

# Christmas

Christmas is also something to be happy about. There is a lot of folding for the advent and Christmas days. That's why this book contains eight beautiful models you can use to send a greeting or to celebrate Christmas. The wreaths can be folded small and mailed or hung large in front of the window. The angel is beautiful on the table with a small battery light underneath. You can attach the star paperclip to a name card. Put down a bowl of water and fold the swan from waterproof paper. With a light in it you will certainly reap a lot of admiration. The Snowy Christmas Tree can be hung as an ornament, used as box with something tasty inside, or made from translucent paper and displayed as a decoration.

# Preacher's Wreath

21-05-2023

During a Zoom meeting Ayumi Hayatsu asked if anyone had an idea for the cut-off triangular points that are left overs when you make an octagon. My brain immediately went into 'design' mode.
The next morning, while following our church service online, the Preacher's Wreath was created. Later that year, 11-11-2023, I developed the variations, as our Christmas wish for 2023. It's a very easy but stable unit, so give it a try.
You can find this model on my YouTube channel

Paper:
- 8 sheets 5x5 cm kami or duo color
- You can choose 1 color or 2 different colors
- 5x5 cm Paper gives a 12,2 cm ring
- 10 Units make a nice candle holder for a battery light

## Unit

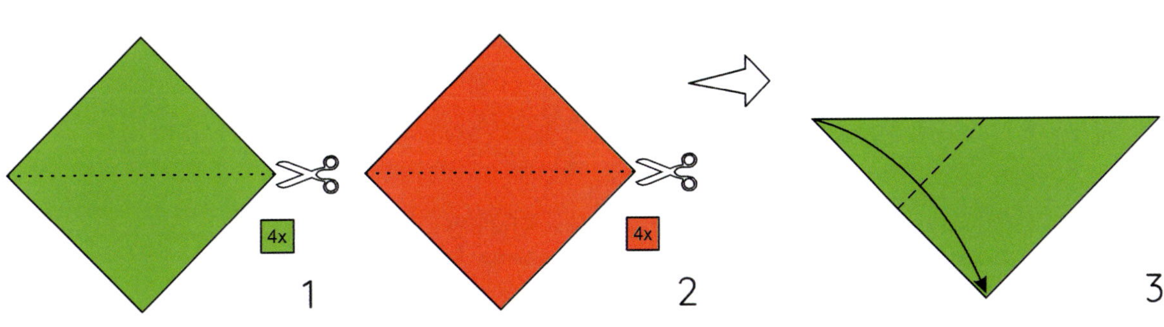


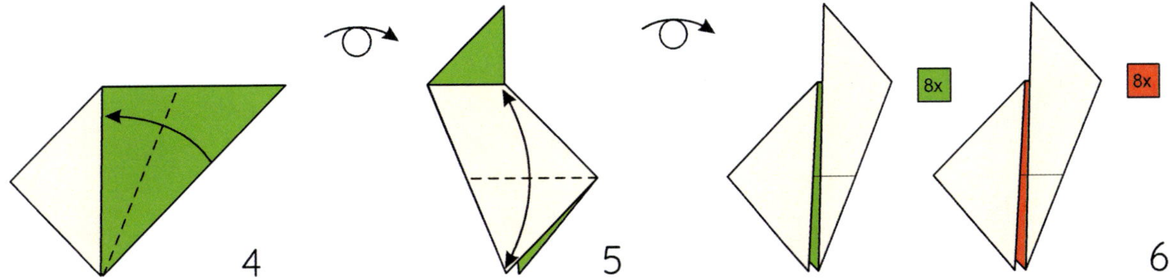

## *Assembly*

When I taught this model I found out that not everyone knew how to hold the element. when I had to explain it to a blind lady I made up this story to help the assembling. Now this is easier for all to do.

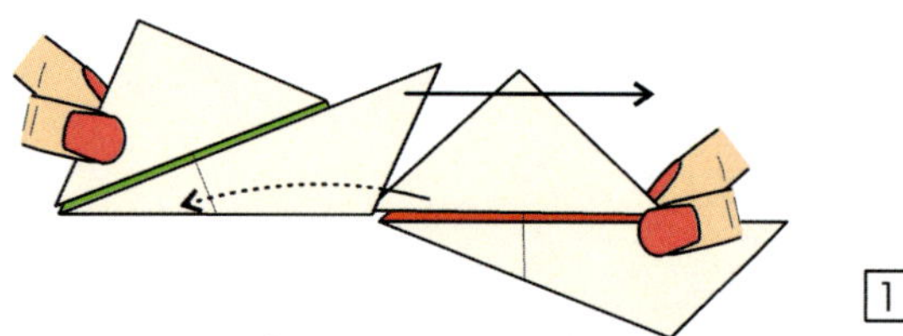

1

Do you see that ship sailing over there on the left? It looks like the Titanic. Oh my, over there on the right is a mountain. Is it an iceberg? Careful...

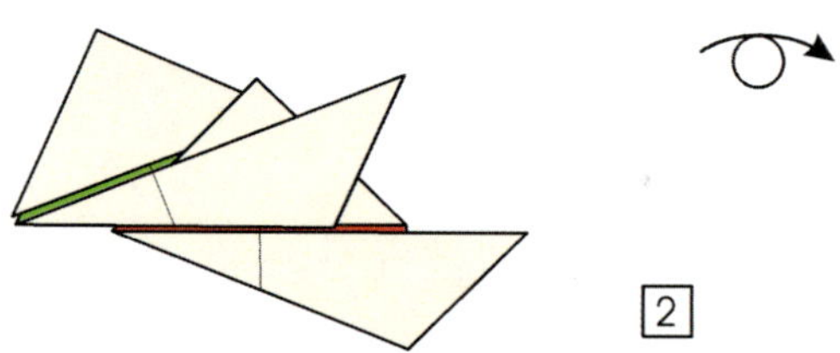

2

Oh no, collision ahead. He's going to sail right to the iceberg. Ahh, the iceberg has gone all the way into the hull. He really can't go any further. What would his other side look like?

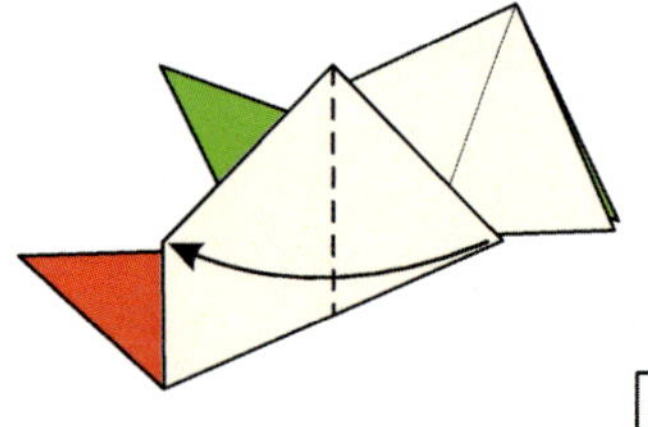

3

The first part can be folded from right to left. Then we can look into the engine room.

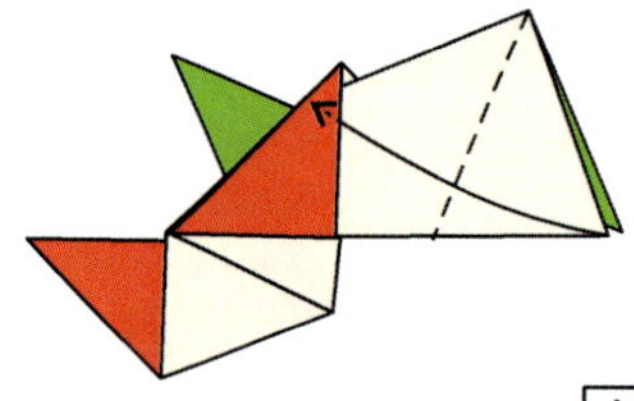

4

Oh, there's a door on the right that's slanting. Let's lock that one on the top left.

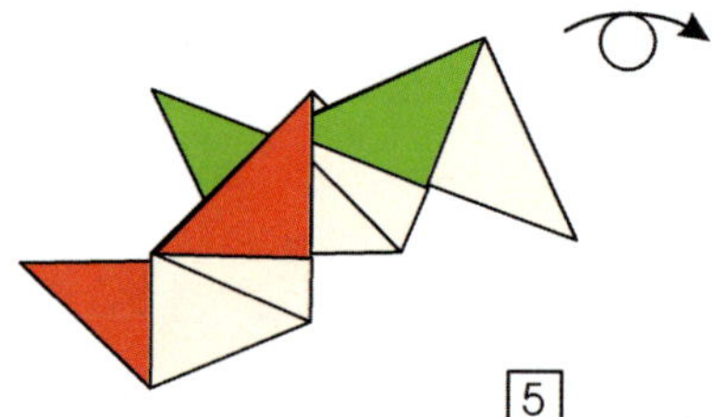

5

We're turning it back.

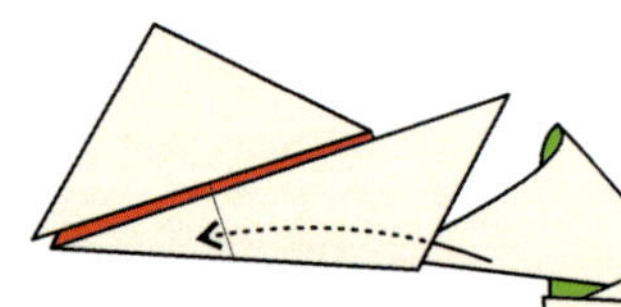

6

Here comes another ship on our left. On our right there is another iceberg... Be careful or the same thing will happen as with the previous ship. This ship lifted the iceberg a bit and then sailed further.

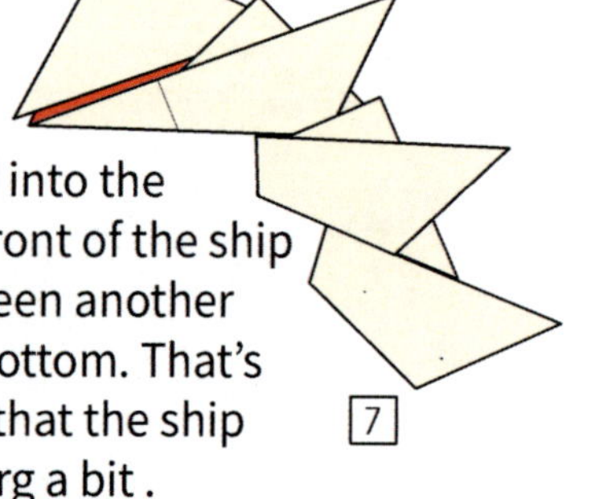

7

Again it still sailed into the iceberg. And the front of the ship is also stuck between another mountain at the bottom. That's possible because that the ship lifted up the iceberg a bit . Let's look at the other side.

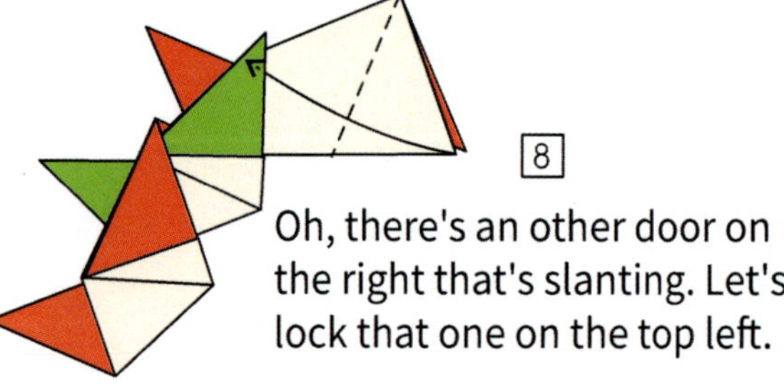

8

Oh, there's an other door on the right that's slanting. Let's lock that one on the top left.

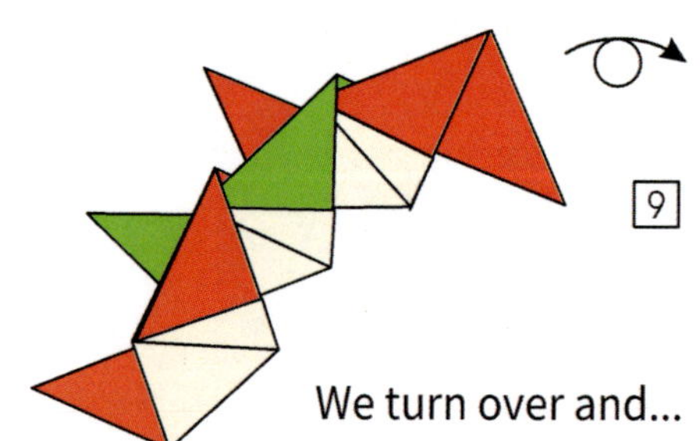

9

We turn over and...

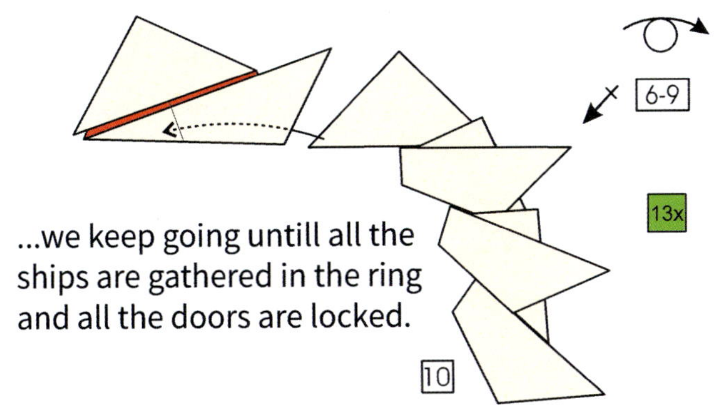


...we keep going untill all the ships are gathered in the ring and all the doors are locked.

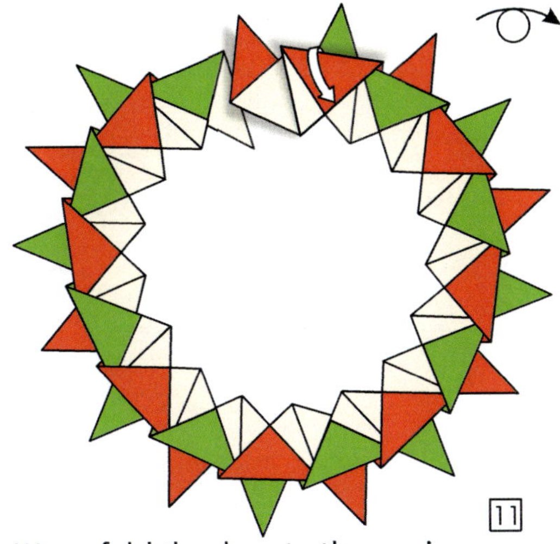


We unfold the door to the engine room, from step 3, and turn over to the other side.

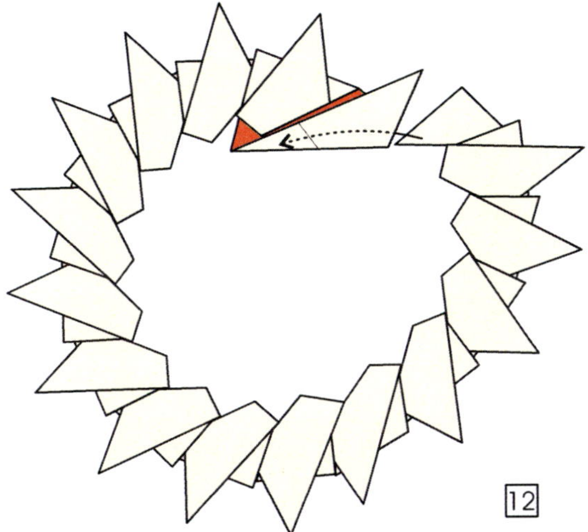


Ah, there we find on the left, one last ship and on the right an iceberg. The iceberg must also slide into the ship, like all the others.

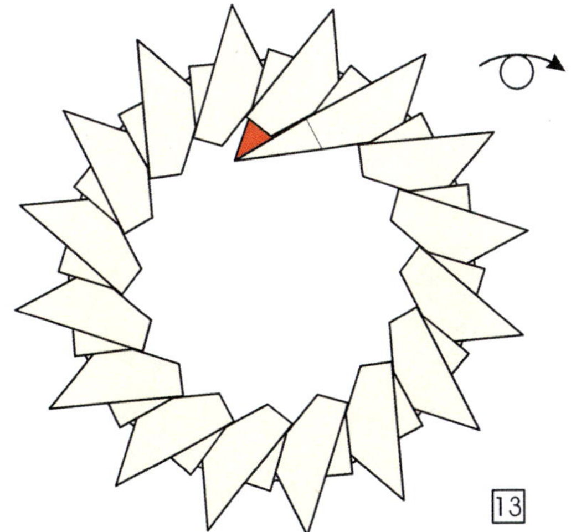


We turn over the wreath.

We close the last slanting door and lock that under the top left. And then...

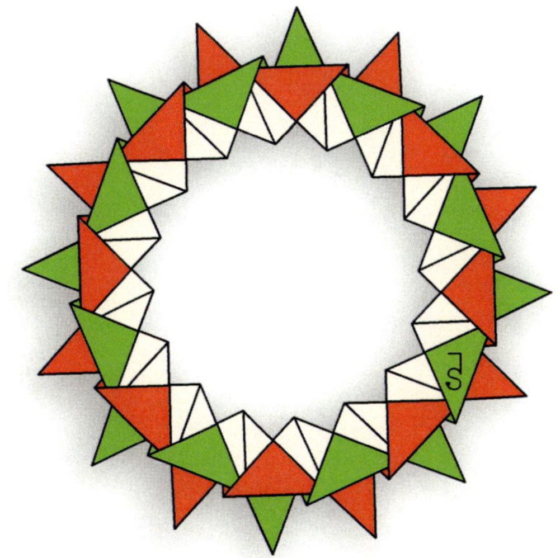

...our Preacher's Wreath is ready.

# Preacher's Wreath V-1

12-11-2023

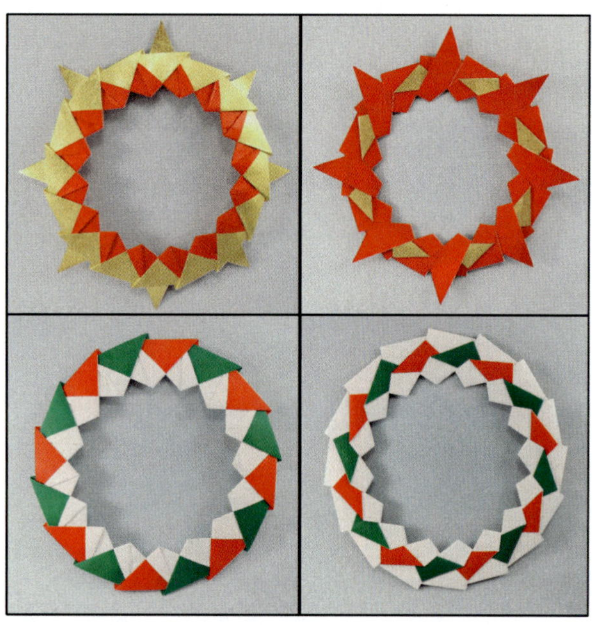

With the folded wreath a lot of variations are possible. I like it when a base is good and you can 'play' with it. Try it. Variation 1 becomes either a ring, with less points than the Original, or even a flat ring. Both sides of the models look nice.

Paper:
- 8 sheets 5x5 cm kami or duo color
- You can choose 1 color or 2 different colors
- 5x5 cm paper gives a 12,2 cm ring with spikes
- 5x5 cm paper gives a 10,5 cm ring without spikes

Fold steps 1-6 and assemble like Preacher's Wreath, page 111. Turn over.

1

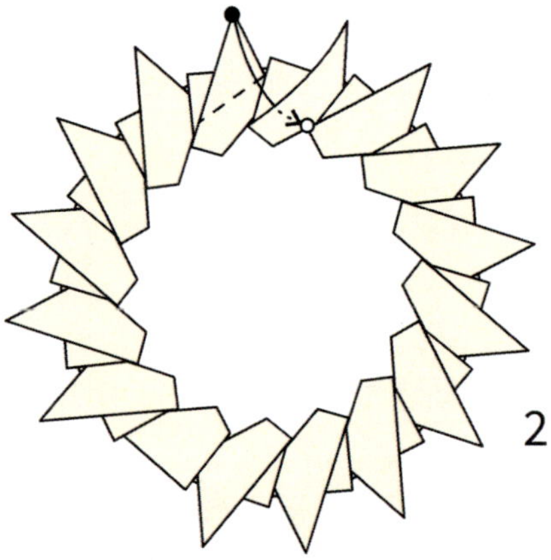

2

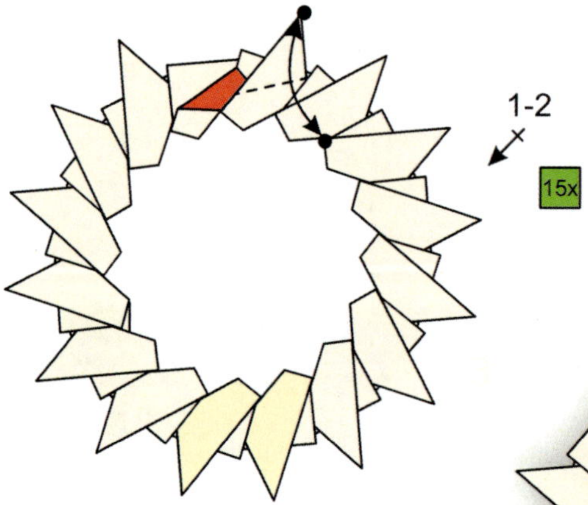

1-2

15x

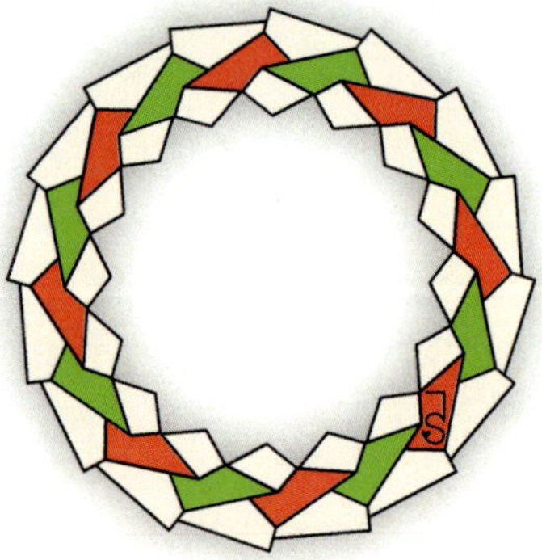

If you fold steps 1-2 alternately on the points you will also get a nice result.

# Preacher's Wreath V-2

12-11-2023

When you fold this variation of the Preacher's Wreath, it looks like there are little leaves on top of the wreath. It is also beautiful from transparent paper. Or make a large one for your door or window.

Paper:
- 8 sheets 5x5 cm kami or duo color
- You can choose 1 color or 2 different colors
- 5x5 cm paper gives a 10,5 cm ring

Fold steps 1-6 and assemble like Preacher's Wreath, page 111. Turn over.

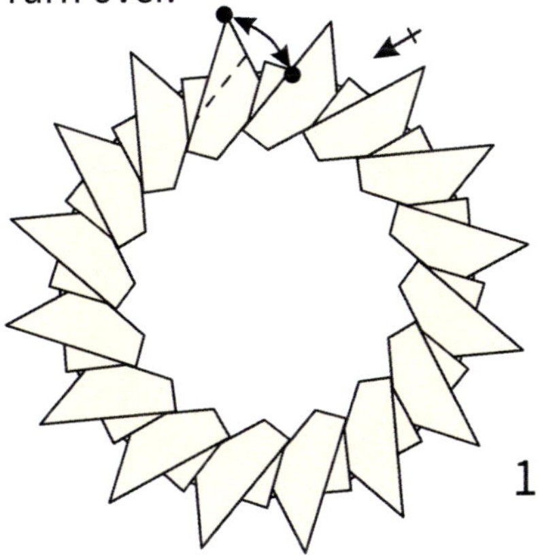

1

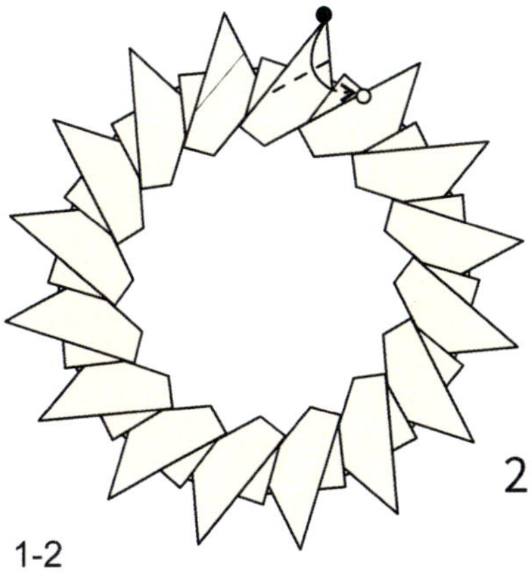

2

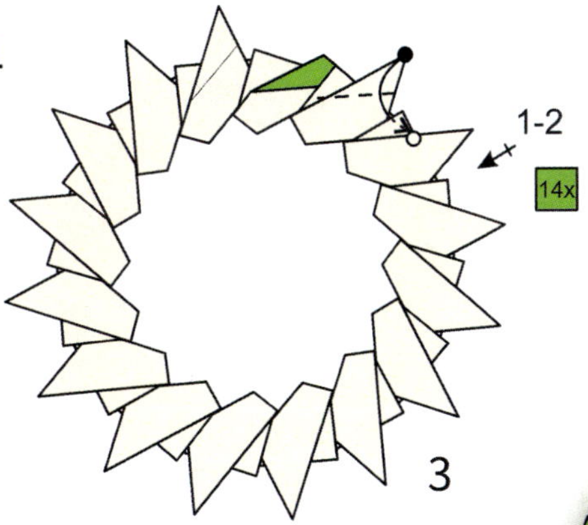

1-2

14x

3

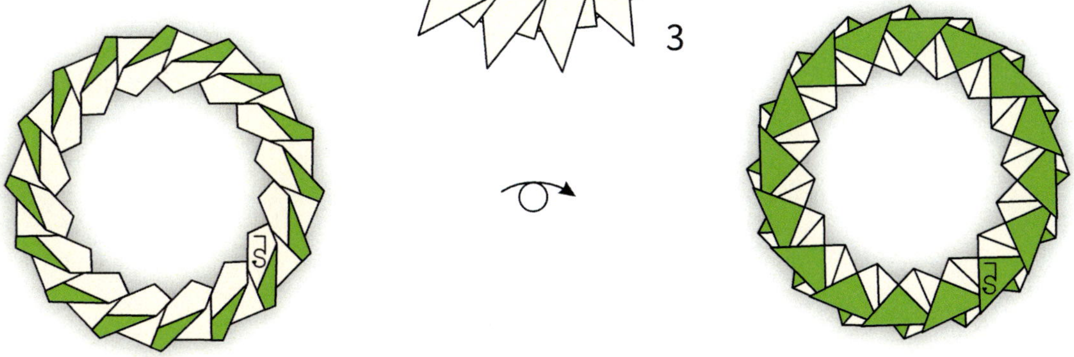

# Double Christmas Tree

05-12-2012

Every year at the end of November beginning of December, I design a new model for my Christmas wish. I´m always looking for something original, not the usual, like a 3D model that can be send flat. This Christmas tree is very nice because it is visible on both sides of the card. It is also possible to remove the tree from the card and place it as a decoration. Just give it a try.

Paper:
- 15x15 cm duo color paper

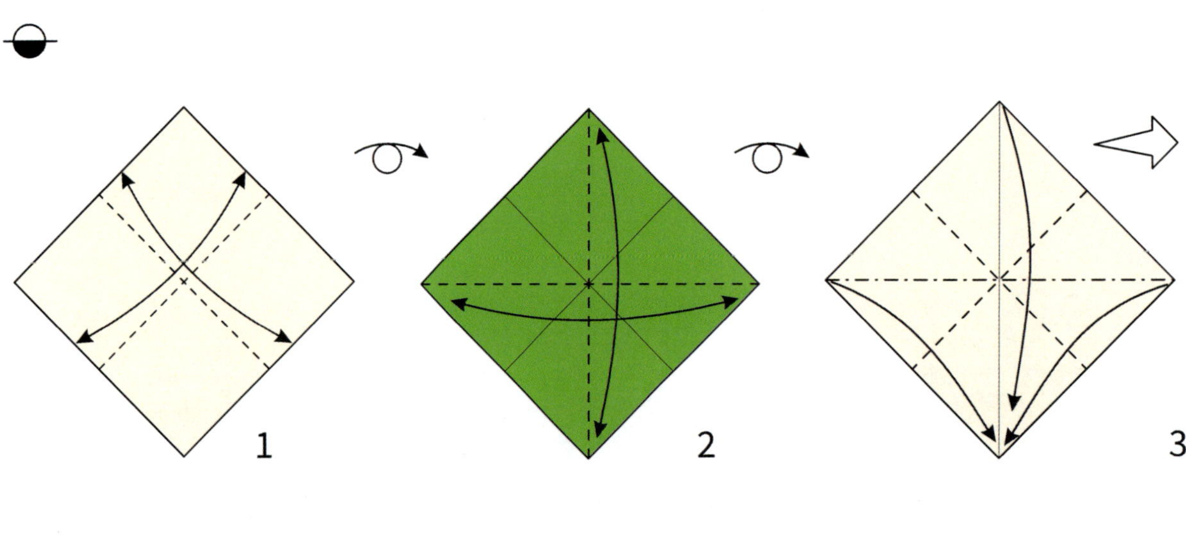


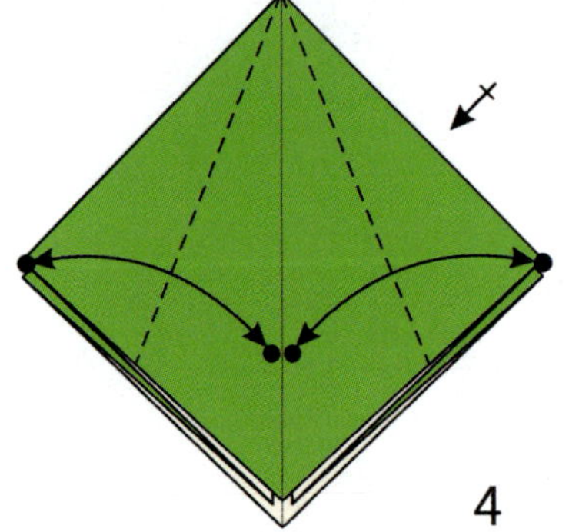


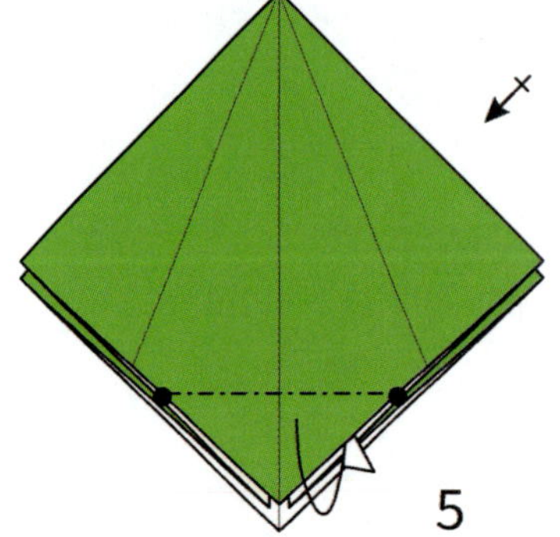


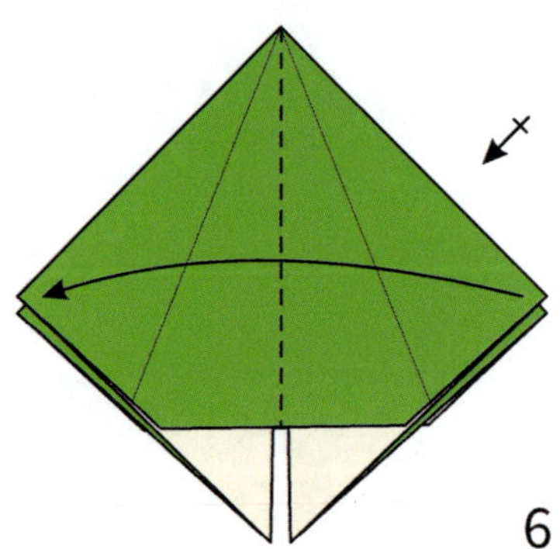

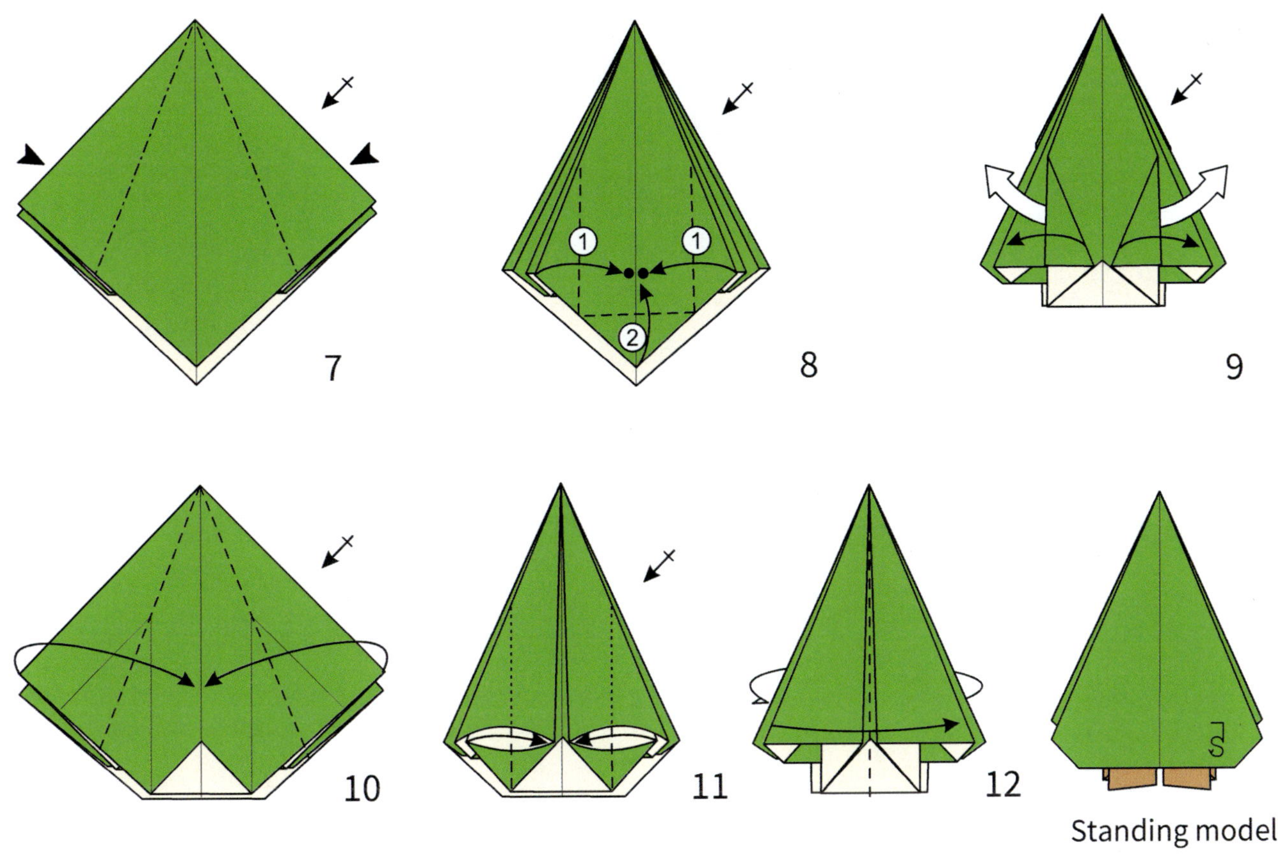


*Attach to a card*

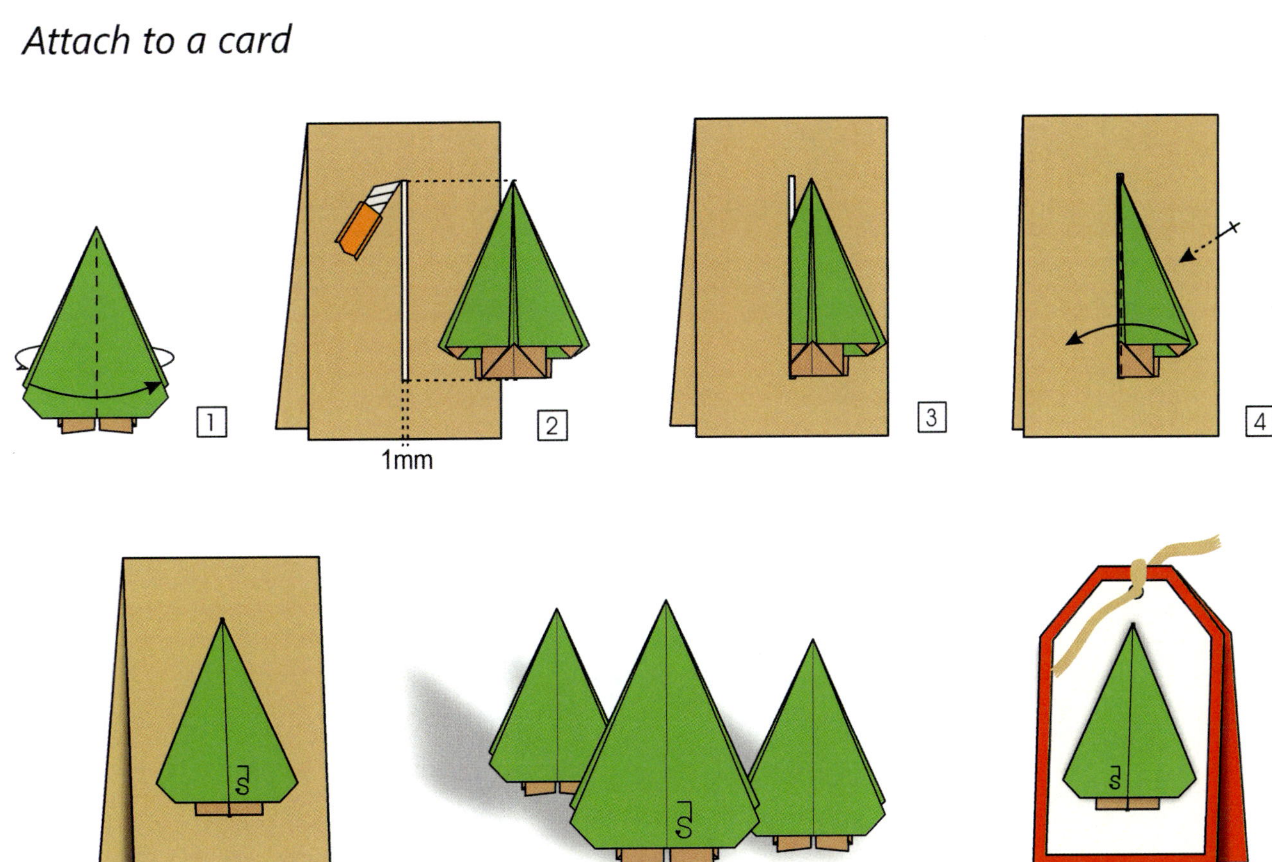

# Angel Emma

10-12-2010

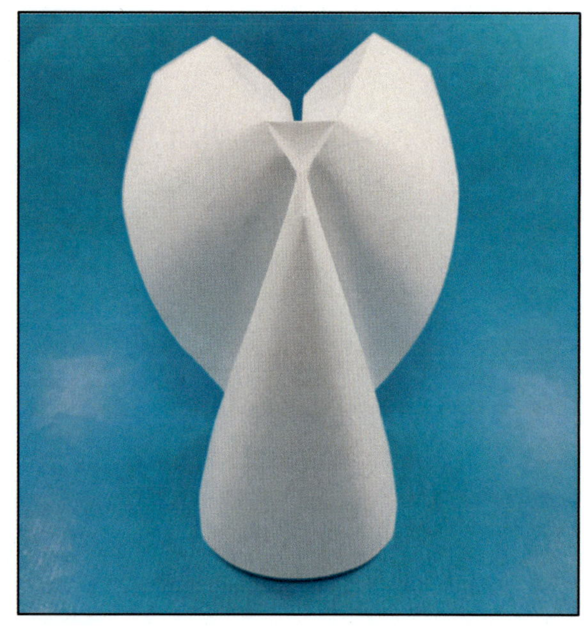

When designing this angel, I had in mind to make a model with a minimum of lines and folds. Stylistic, but clearly recognizable. It was a technique I had not tried before. It was exciting to do it this way and I think it definitely worked. In January 2019 I named this angel after my beloved sister.

Paper:
- 15x15 cm sturdy white paper
- 20x20 cm for the first time

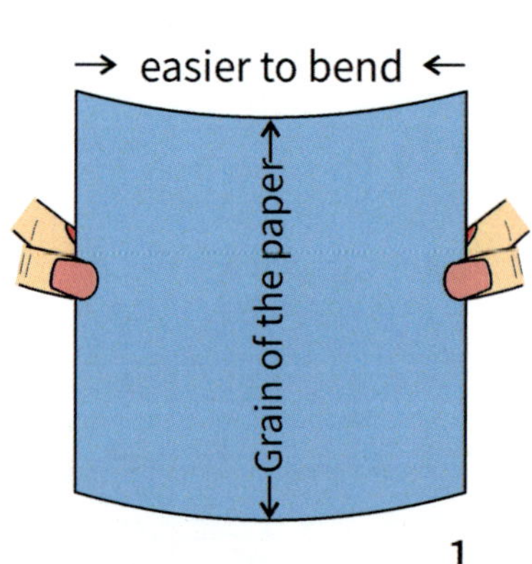


1

Look carefully at the grain of the paper. The sides should bend toward the centre more easily than the top and bottom.

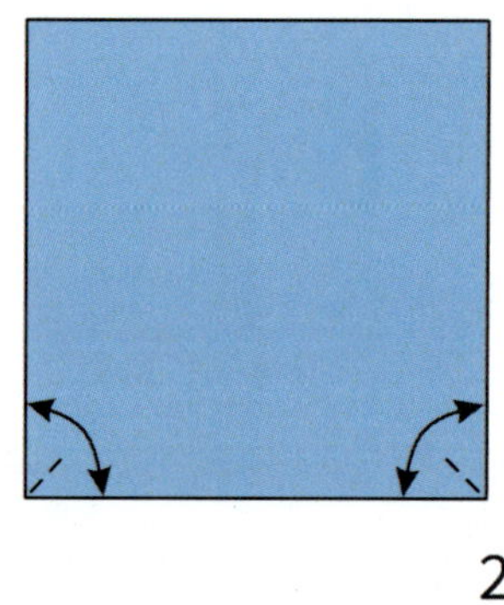

2

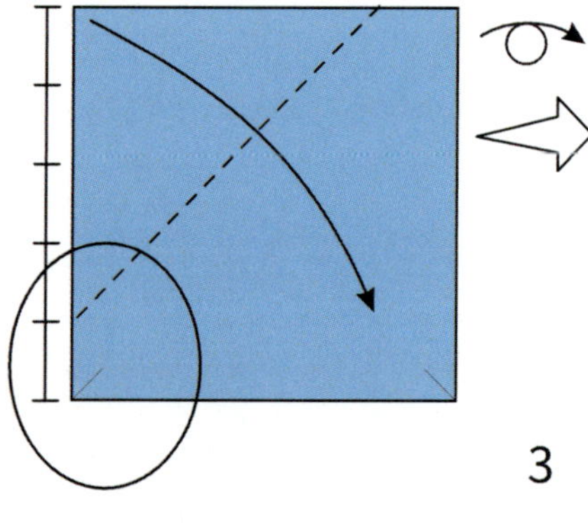

3

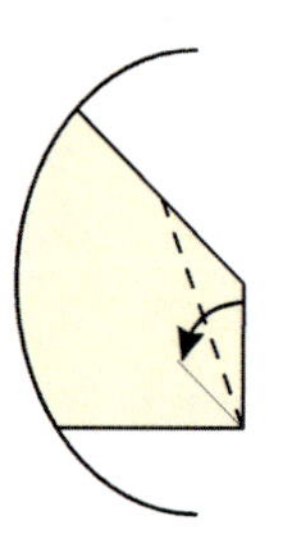

4

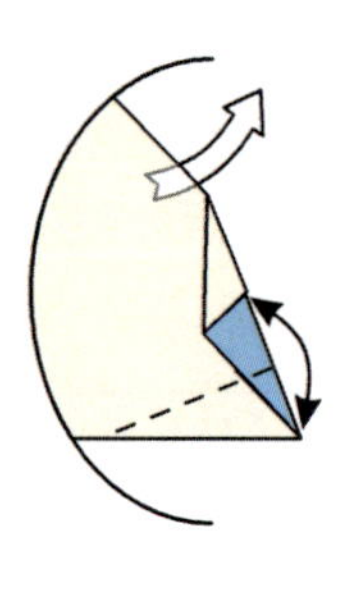

5

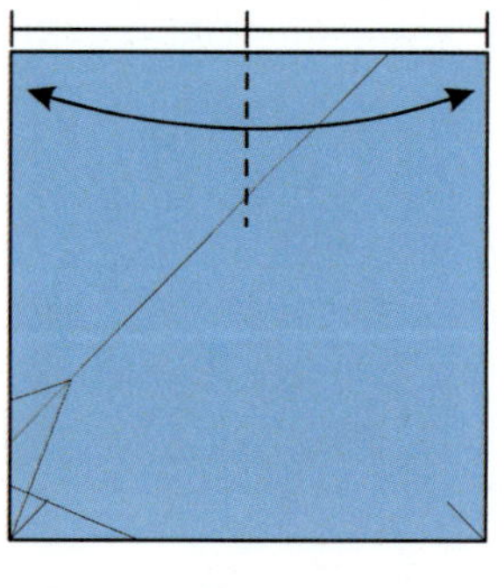

6

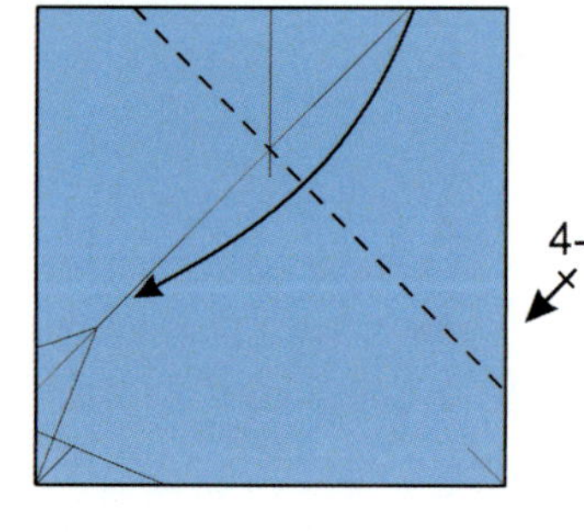


7

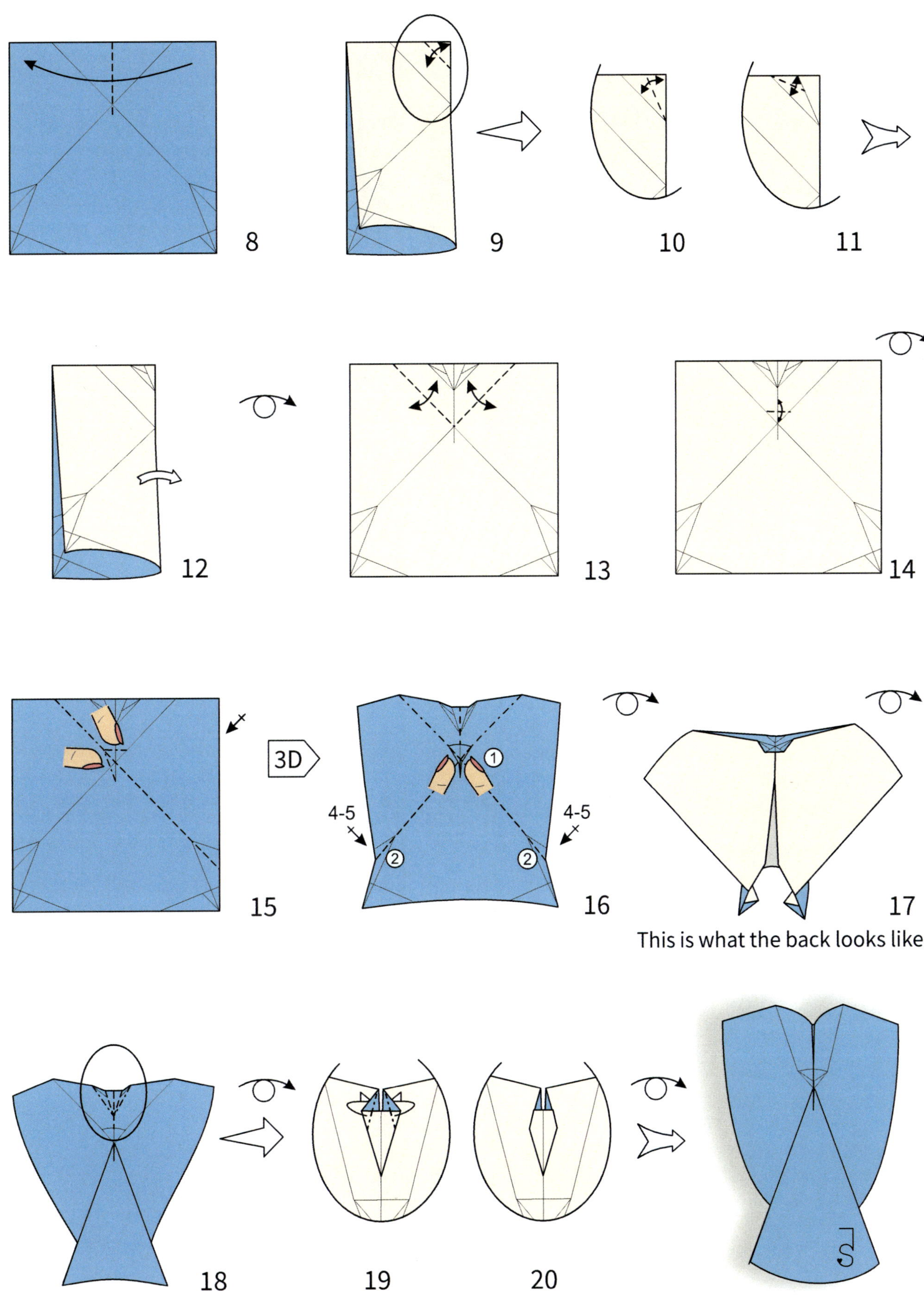


This is what the back looks like.

# Snowy Christmas Tree

15-05-2023

This tree is a variation on my basic model 'Hydrangea-/Mount-Fuji box' from 2015. The bottom becomes slightly smaller and the tree higher thanks to the extra pinch (step 4) from Vanda Battaglia. Thank you, Vanda, for your good idea. Furthermore, the folding remained the same. Use this Snowy tree as a gift box, a hanging ornament, or a table decoration with a star on top of it. Hanging or standing, made of translucent paper with a battery light inside it is a beautiful room decoration. Try using double-sided patterned paper for a surprising result. You can find this model on my YouTube channel.

Paper:
- 15x15 cm kami or duo color
- 20x20 transculent paper and a balloon light for a light tree
- 1 bead and 10 cm wire for a hanging tree

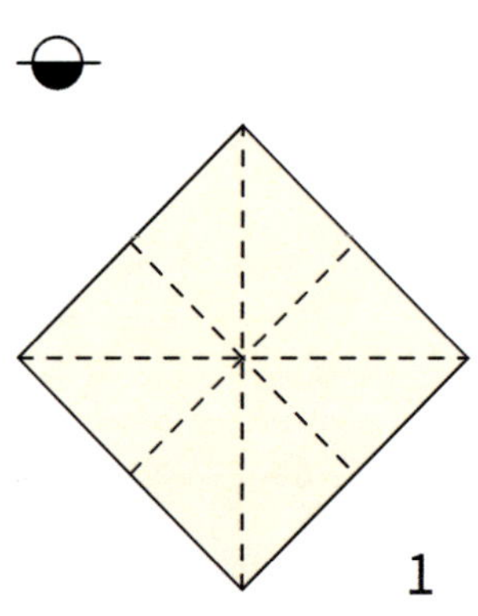

1

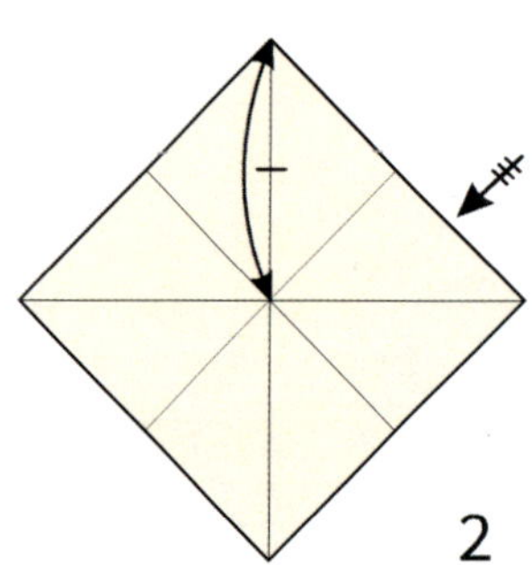

2

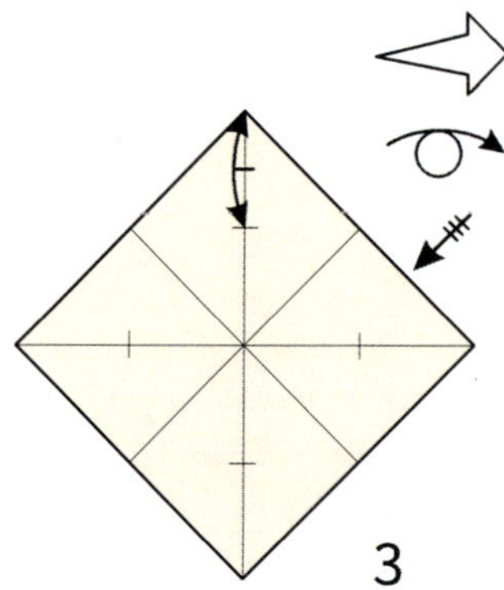

3

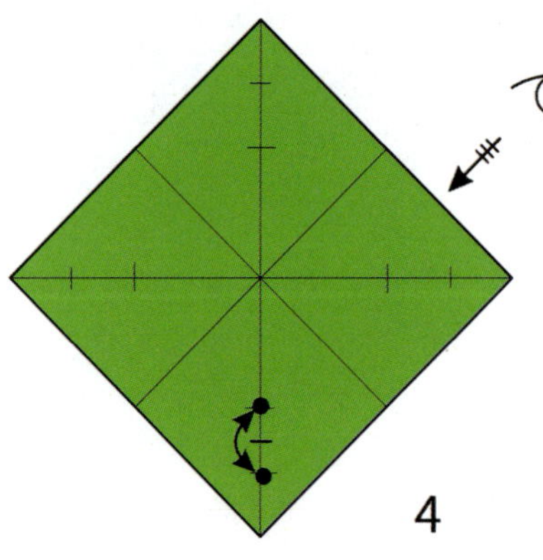

4

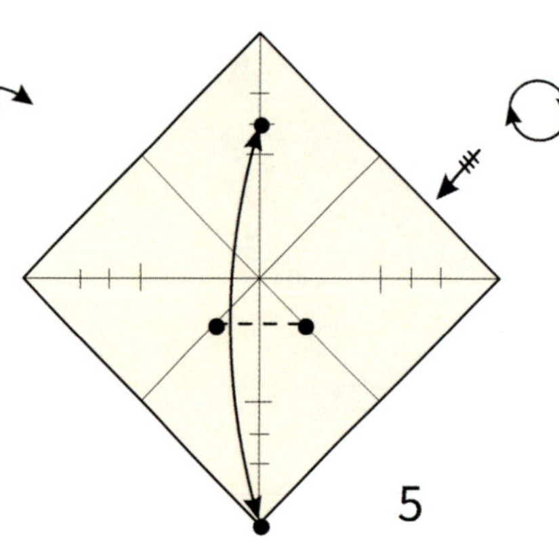

5

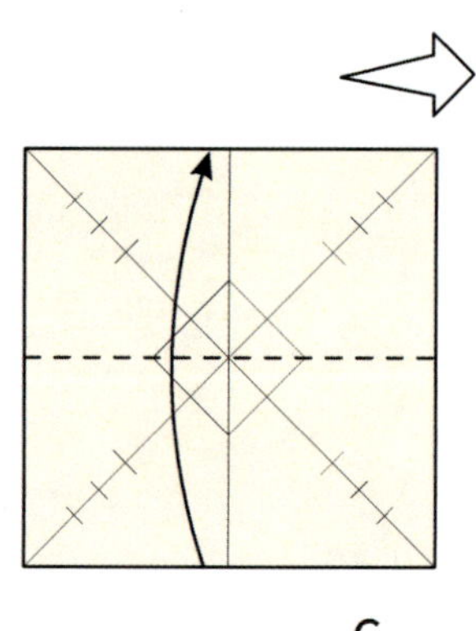

6

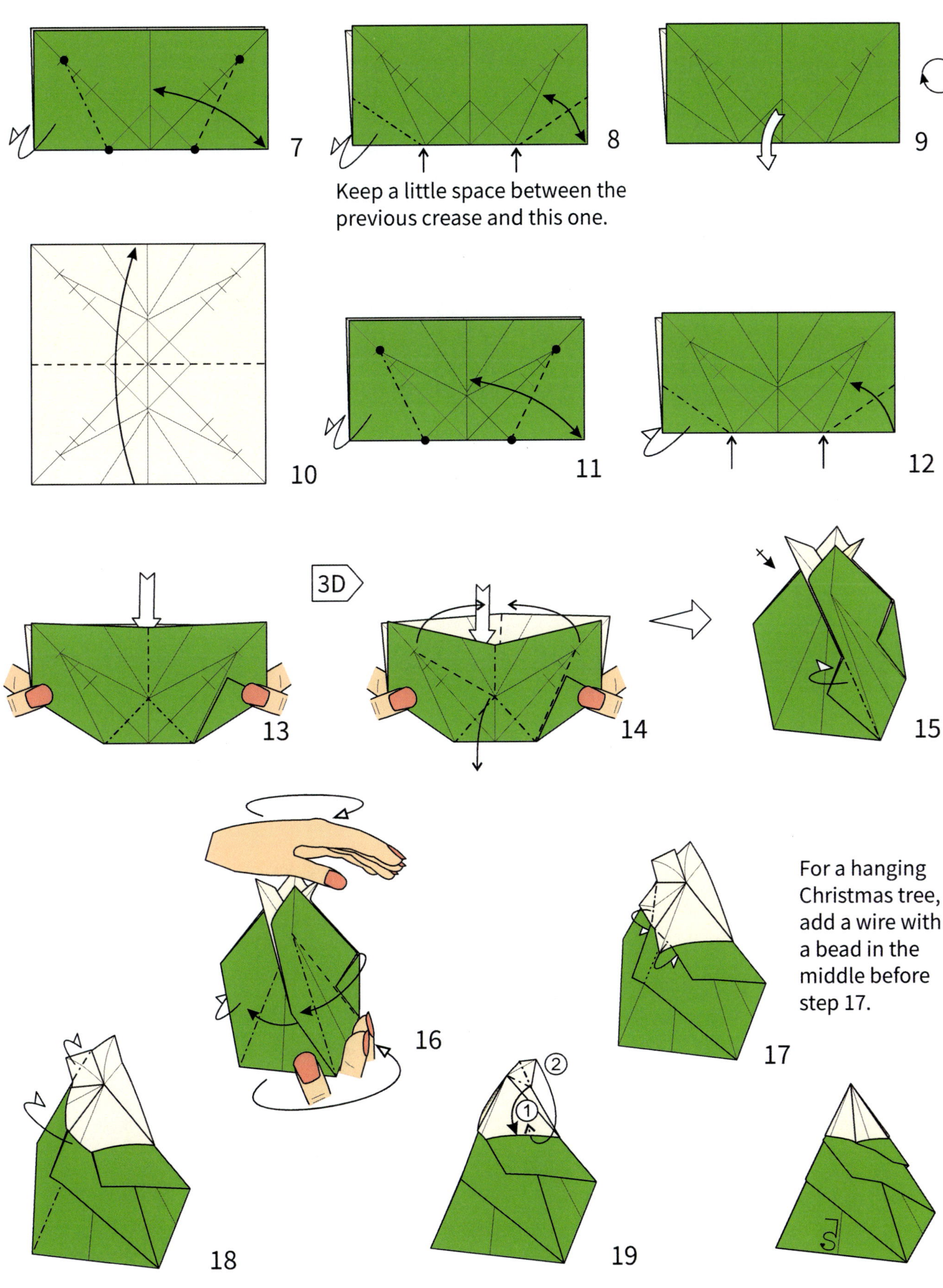
7
8
Keep a little space between the previous crease and this one.
9
10
11
12
13
3D
14
15
16
For a hanging Christmas tree, add a wire with a bead in the middle before step 17.
17
18
2
1
19

# Star Paperclip

10-04-2011

This paperclip was originally designed in 2011. While making this book I made some adjustments to make an even prettier star. (13-08-2024)
You can use the paperclip to send someone a star wish. It can be used as a table arrangement for the holiday festivities or just as a decorative paperclip. So many practical possibilities.

Paper:
- 10x10cm or smaller

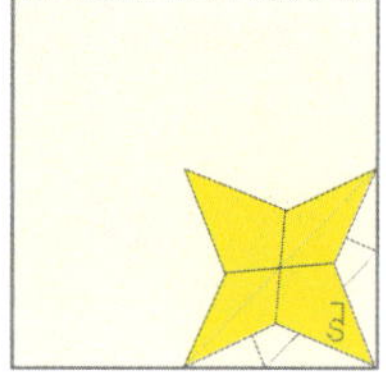

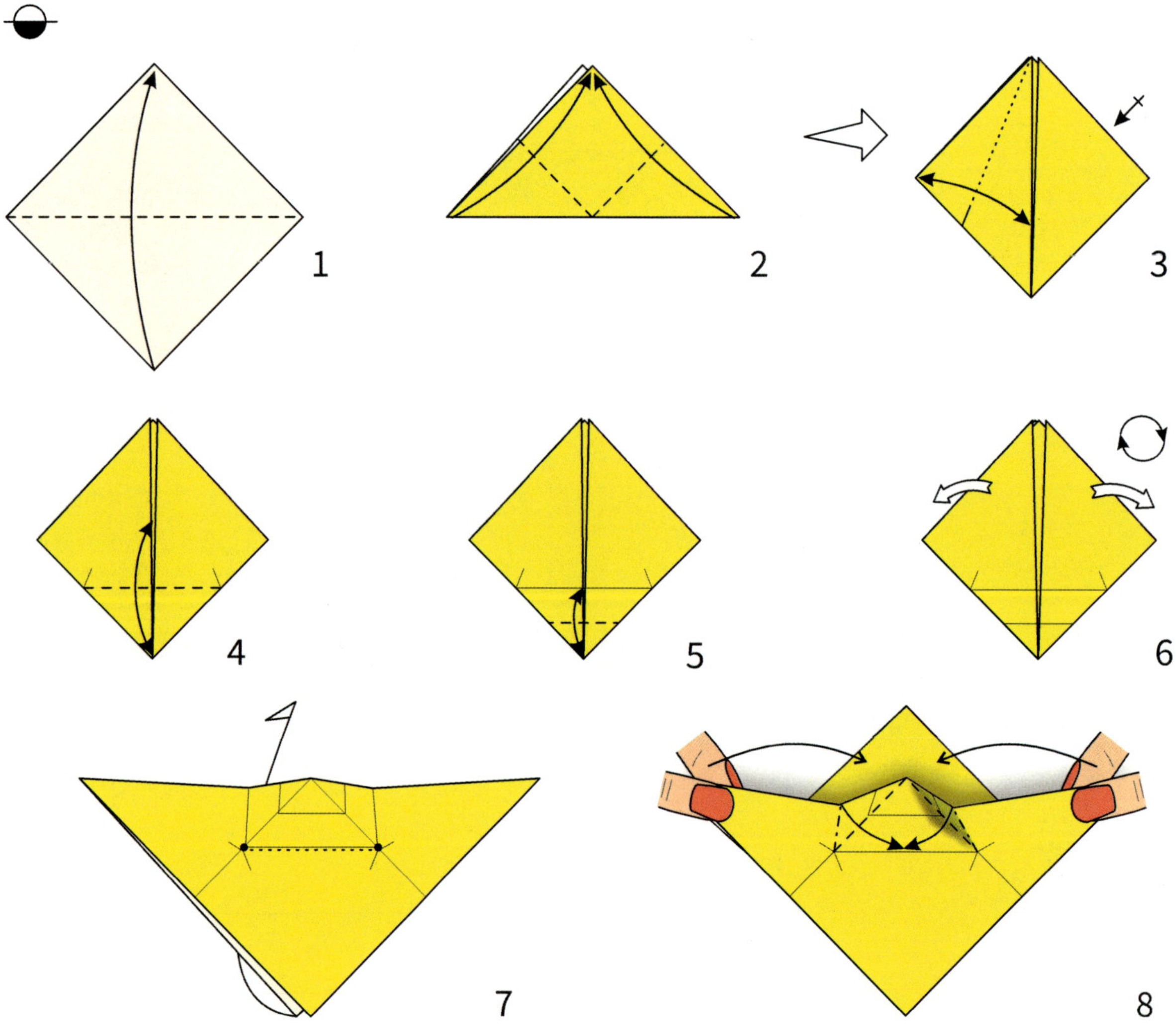

1

2

3

4

5

6

7

8

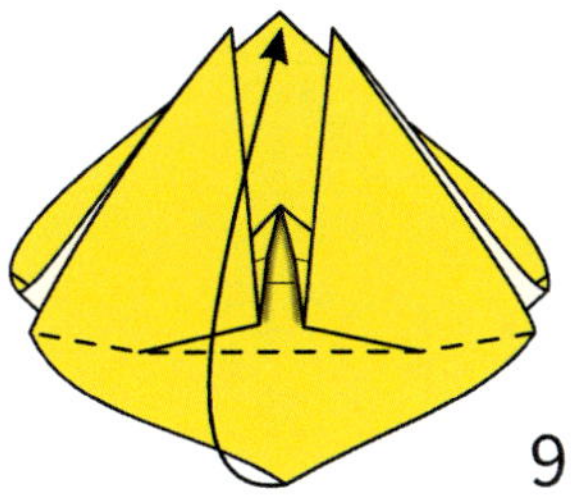

9

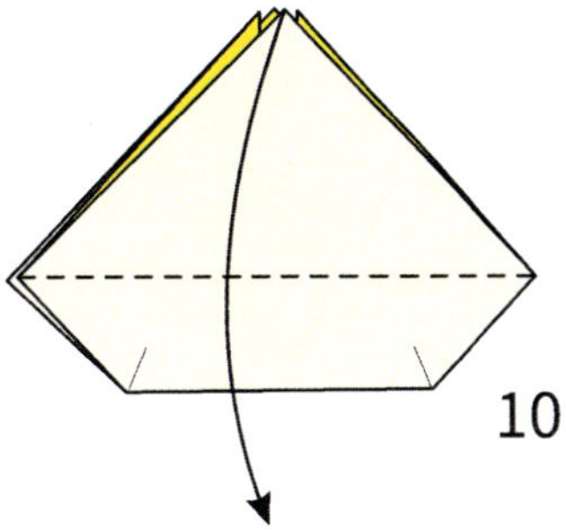

10

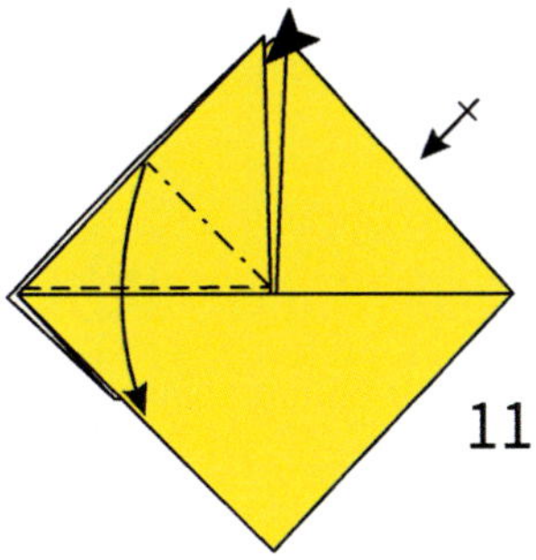

11

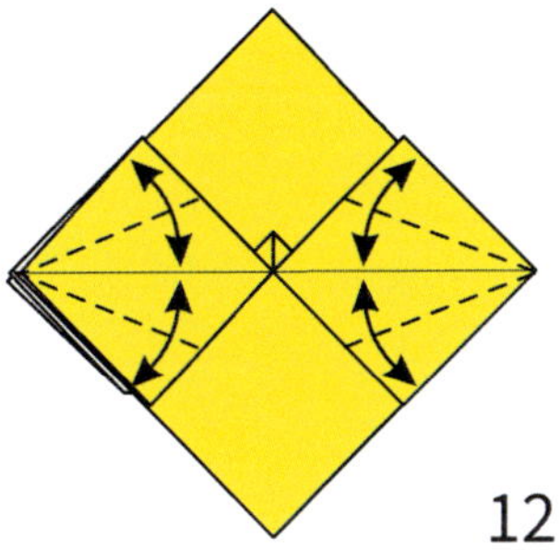

12

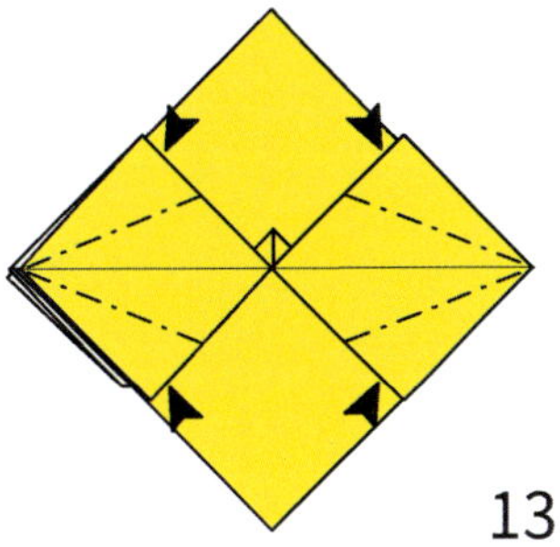

13

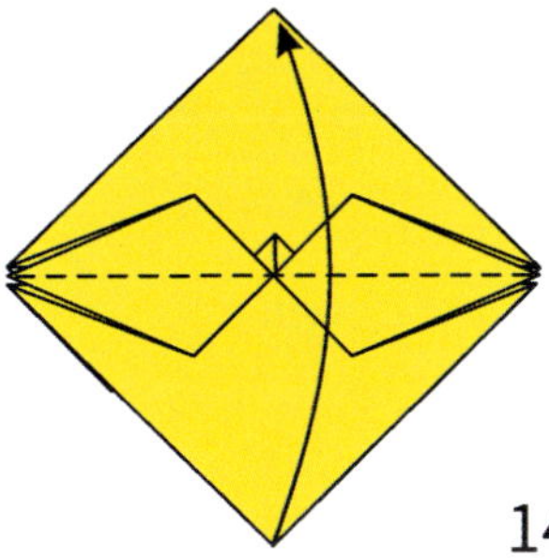

14

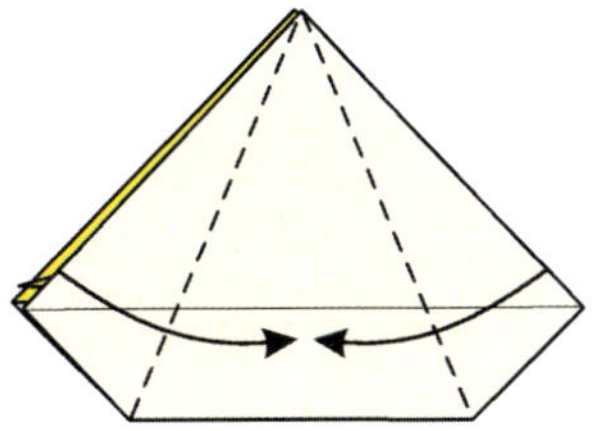

15

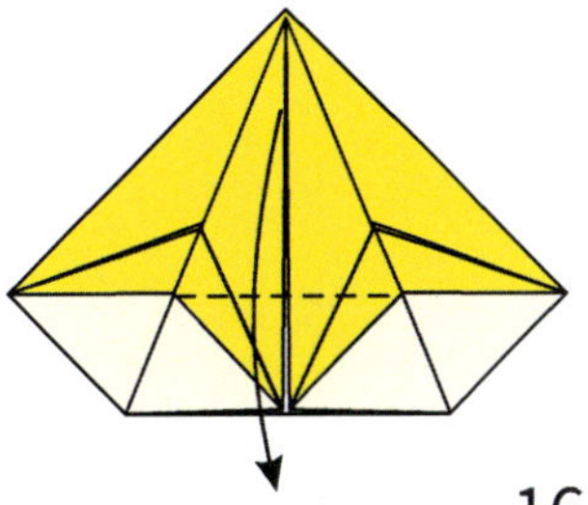

16

17

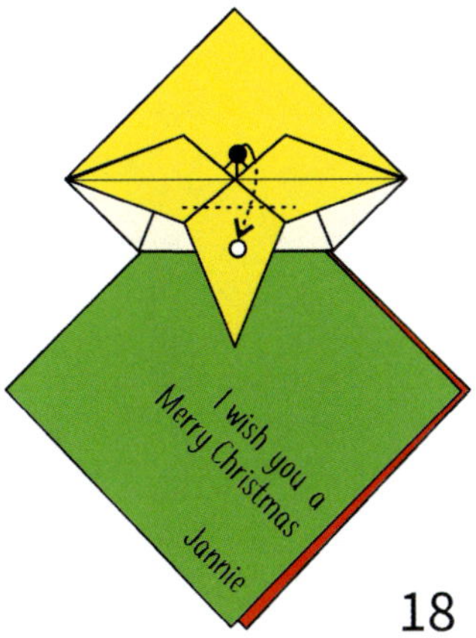

18

19

# Swimming Swan

16-02-2009

This swan was initially designed for Aqua paper, a waterproof paper, very suitable for floating models. Between the wings there is enough space for a (battery) tea light. Using this, the stable swan will become a very special floating light. Besides Aqua paper the model is beautiful folded from a lot of other (duo color) papers.

Paper:
- 15x15 cm duo color paper
- Aqua paper for a swimming Swan
- 30x30 cm for a light inside

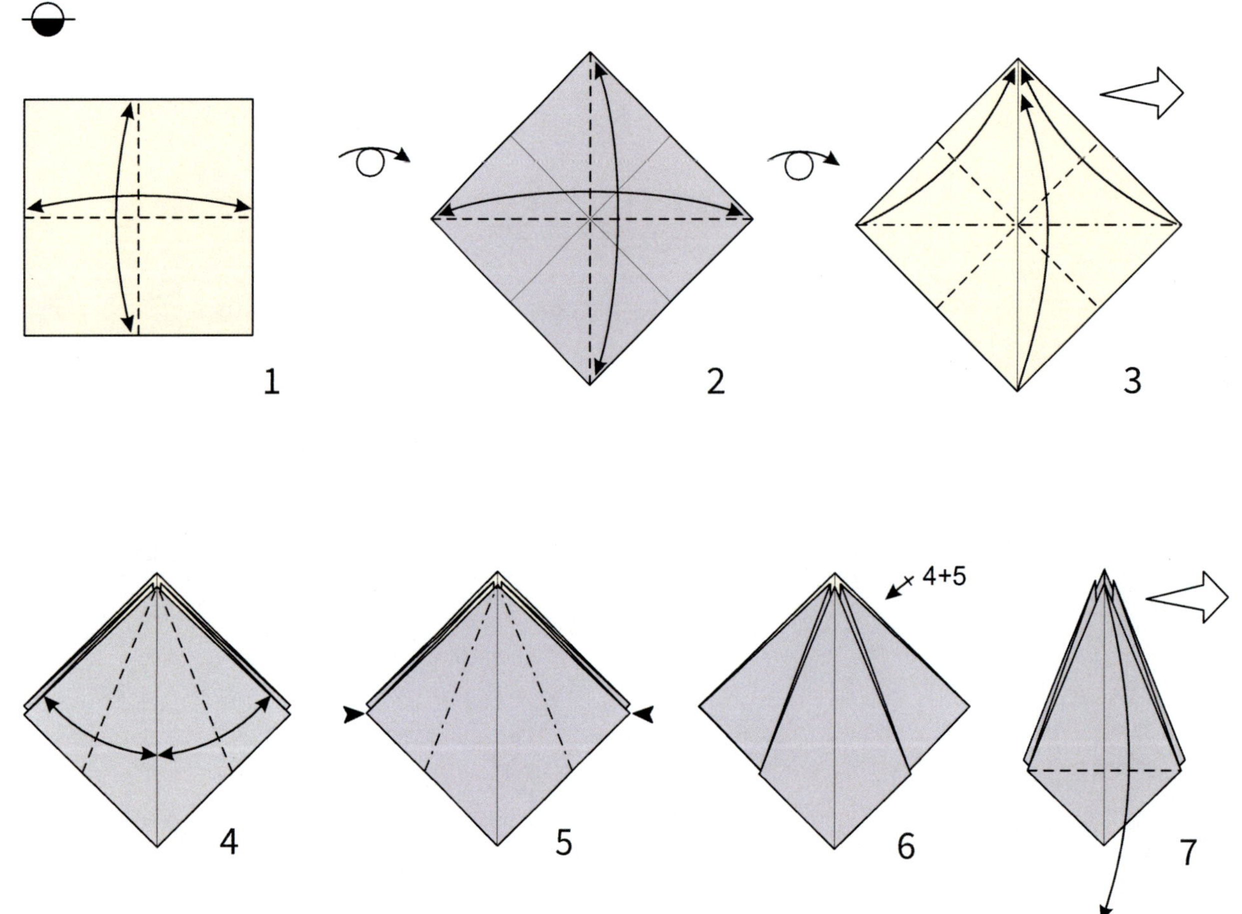

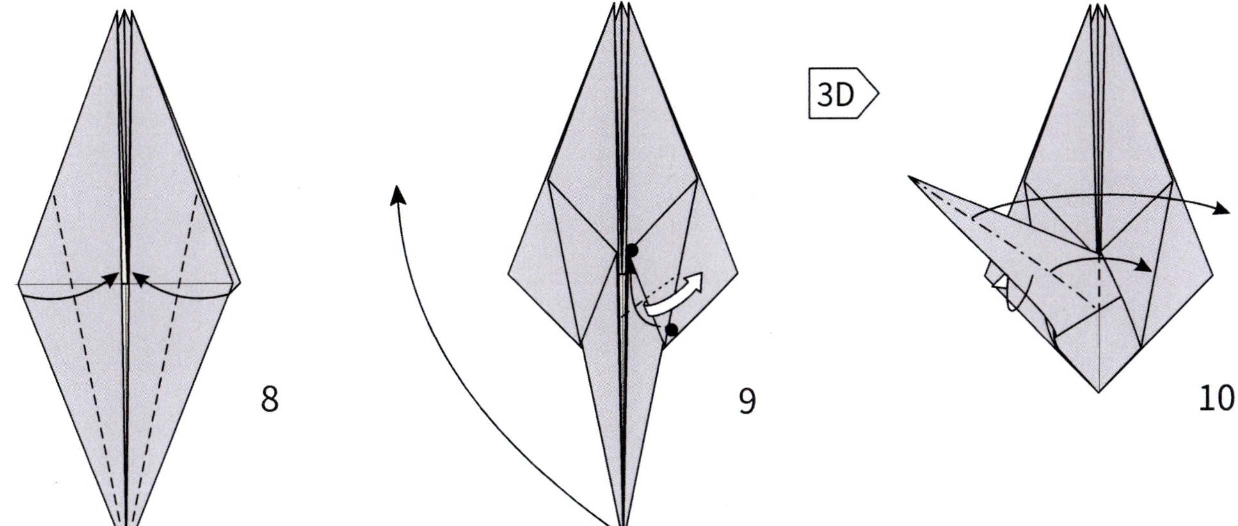


Open the top layer a bit. Now you can valley fold the paper underneath as far as it goes.

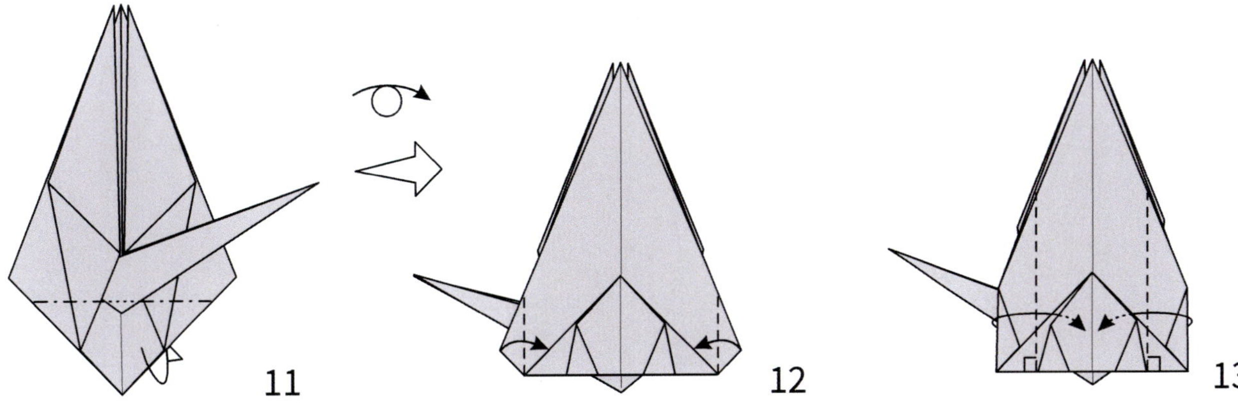


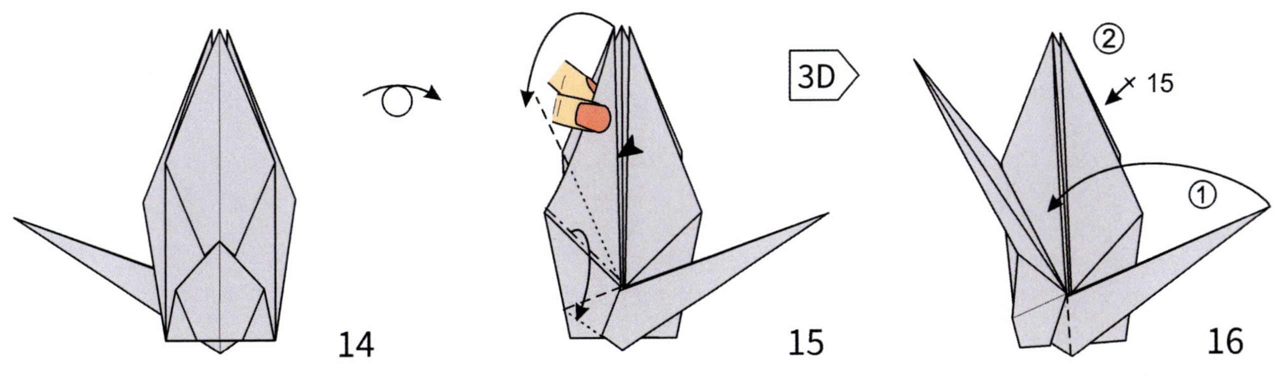

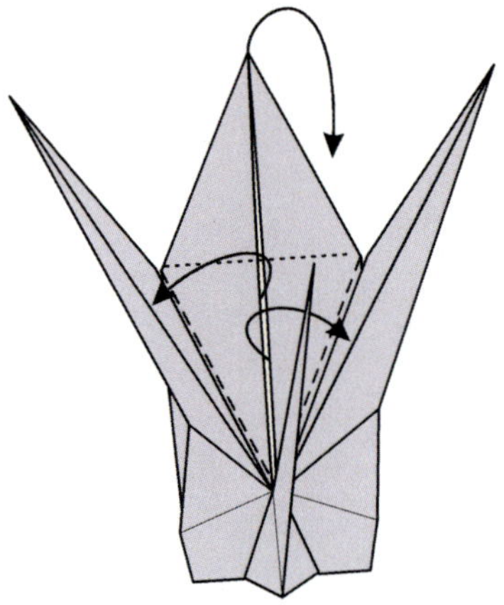

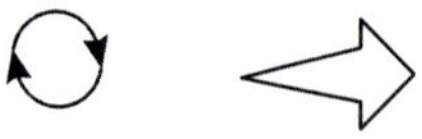

17

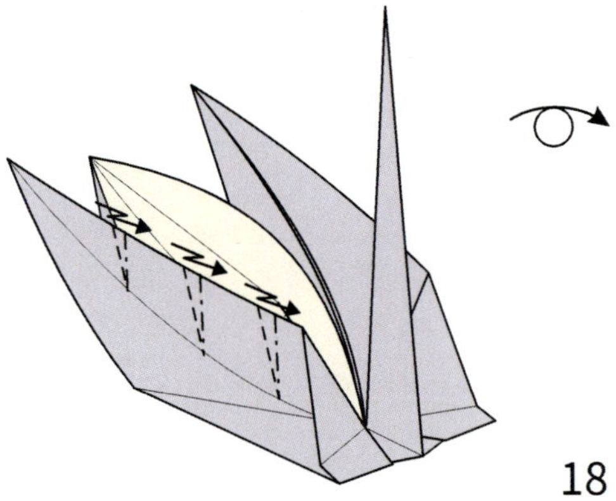

18

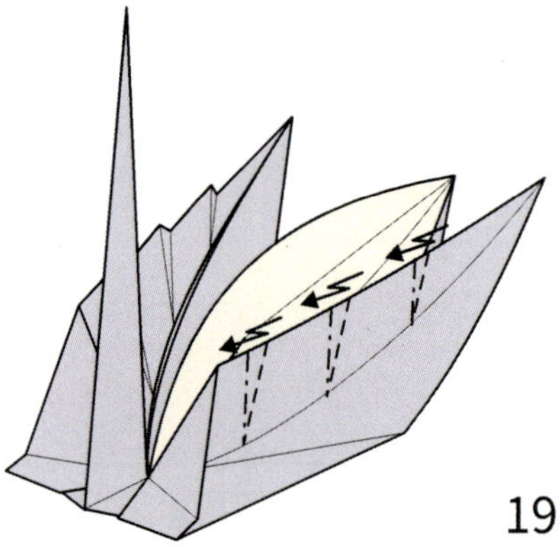

19

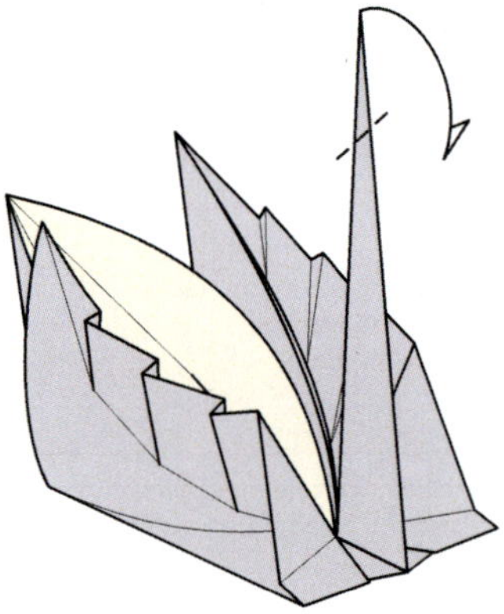

20

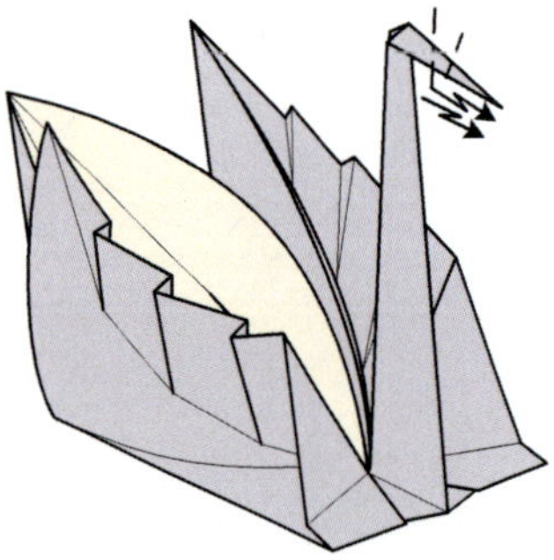

21

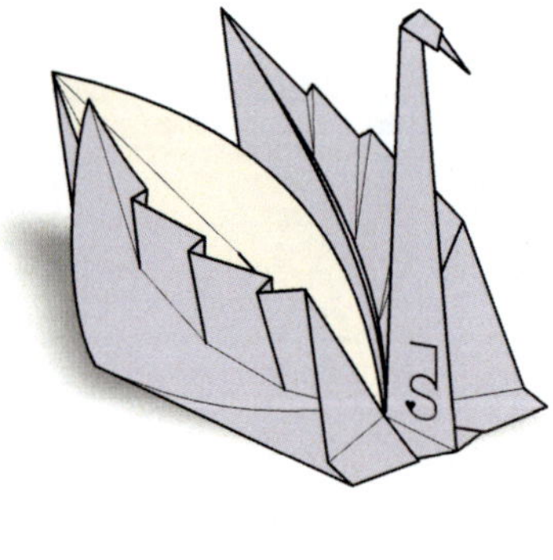

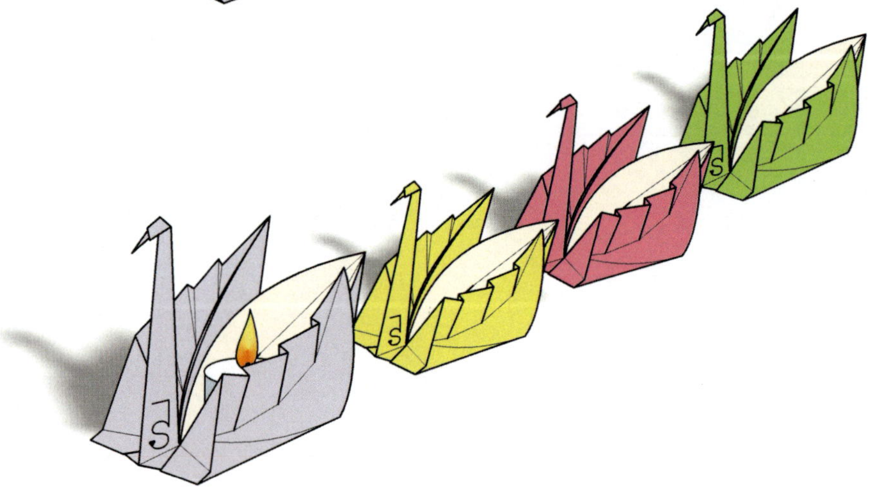

# Challenge

Thank you for buying this book.

Hopefully you have already folded several nice models. I have a challenge for you. It is possible to make a stable kusudama from the double sunflower on pages 46-48. Do not use glue - only a connecting element, with the measurement of the petals. Will you succeed? Let me know.

Can you also make a kusudama from Star Joëlle on pages 86-88?

Give it a try.

# Origami Associations

Here is a small selection of origami associations and paper sellers. Look on the origamiusa.org/groups/international or CFC-site for more.

www.origami-osn.nl

origamiusa.org

origamisrael.com

cfcorigami.com

www.origami-cdo.it

www.papierfalten.de

www.mfpp-origami.fr

origamioritai.com

www.britishorigami.org

Instagram.com/
asosiasiorigamiindonesia

pajarita.org

www.origami-noa.jp

amigosplegadores.blogspot.com

origami.jp

ori-gami.hu

ifoldedit.org

origami-shop.com

origami-papier.eu

# Other books of Jannie

2000 2002 2005 2006-2008 2008 2009

2010 2012 2013 2014 2014

## How publishing started

In 2000 I made a small book,"Kaart-o-gami", after an origami playing card exhibition with 3 friends. The Origami Sociëteit of The Netherlands would publish the book, but I wanted to draw it myself. I knew nothing about that and the book, "Corel Draw for Dummies", was a godsend. This was my first step on the road of making digital diagrams.

I drew the origami magazine, "Orison", for the OSN. Later, Nice-Papers, in Germany, also asked me to draw their books. When they saw my origami models, they published books with my models. For example, two boat books and "Dass Grosse Lichterbuch no. 2" were published. A part of the content of the boat books was published in Hungarian, Romanian, and Yugoslavian. Various Dutch publishers and an English publisher also saw potential in origami books. In 2014 I published a booklet myself, which was popular in the Netherlands. Most of the books can only be found in second-hand bookstores.

The booklets, "Send a Garland full of wishes", and "Geldvouwen-Cadeau ideetjes" are still available from me. Send an email to jannievanschuylenburg@gmail.com.

It is special to see how my origami journey has gone in the past years. I plan to continue my passion for origami and look forward to the future.

Made in the USA
Monee, IL
22 October 2024

68470451R00079

# Big Cats

Jonathan Sheikh-Miller and Stephanie Turnbull

Designed by Neil Francis
with Jayne Wilson, Glen Bird
and Stephanie Jones

Illustrated by John Woodcock

Consultants: Pat Mansard, Ridgeway Trust
for Endangered Cats and LiFeline,
Dr Nobuyuki Yamaguchi and Dr Andrew Kitchener

Series editor: Gillian Doherty

SCHOLASTIC INC.

New York Toronto London Auckland Sydney
Mexico City New Delhi Hong Kong Buenos Aires

Cover picture: tiger
Title page: leopard
This page: young cheetah

# Contents


4 What is a big cat?
6 Cat bodies
8 On the move
10 Senses
12 Coats and camouflage
14 Hunting
16 Killer bites
18 Cat talk
20 Getting together
22 Growing up
24 Cat habits
26 Tigers
28 Lions
30 Leopards
32 Asian leopards
34 Cheetahs
36 American big cats
38 Small wild cats
40 Under threat
42 Caring for cats
44 Myths and legends
46 Using the Internet
47 Index
48 Acknowledgements

A puma

**Internet links**

Look for the Internet links boxes throughout this book. They contain descriptions of Web sites where you can find out more about big cats. For links to these Web sites, go to **www.usborne-quicklinks.com** and type in the keywords "discovery big cats".

★ Some of the pictures in the book have a star symbol beside them. It means you can download the pictures from the **Usborne Quicklinks Web site**. For more information, and for safety guidelines for using the Internet, and downloading Usborne pictures, see inside the front cover and page 46.

# What is a big cat?

Not everyone agrees about what a big cat is, as it's not a clearly defined scientific term. Although there are 37 kinds, or species, of cats, only a few of these are usually described as big cats.

## Cat characteristics

All cats belong to a group of animals called mammals. Like most mammals, they have fur on their bodies and give birth to live young.

Cats are also carnivores, which means they eat meat or fish. They have sharp claws and teeth, which help them to catch and kill the animals they hunt for food (their prey).

Internet links

For a link to a Web site with dramatic photographs and information about cats from all over the world, go to **www.usborne-quicklinks.com**

## Big cat or not?

Scientists rarely use the term "big cats" without saying which cats they mean. They often include lions, tigers, jaguars, leopards, snow leopards and clouded leopards, which all belong to the "panther" group of cats. But, many people call other large cats, such as cheetahs and pumas (also called cougars, mountain lions or panthers), big cats too.

Lions are most definitely big cats. This young male is padding lazily across the grasslands of East Africa.

Fact: Cats are descended from small meat-eating mammals called miacids that lived about 60 million years ago, at around the time the dinosaurs died out.

## Cat differences

This is how a small cat usually eats.

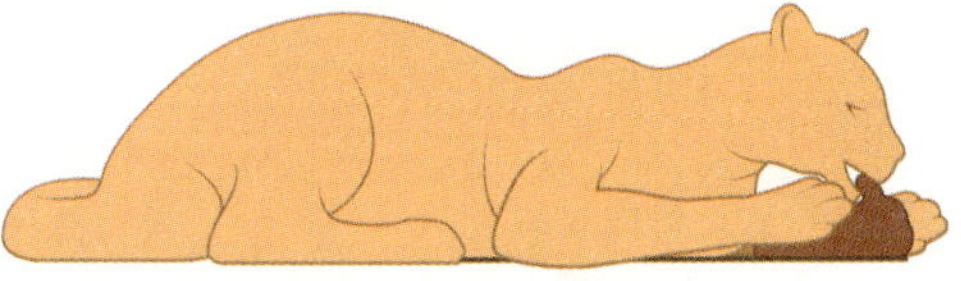

This is how a big cat usually eats.

Big cats and small cats have a lot in common, but there are also some interesting differences between them. Some big cats can roar, while no small cats can. Most big cats also tend to feed lying down, while small cats generally feed in a crouching position.

## All over the world

Cats live in a variety of places, or habitats, including tropical rainforests, grasslands and high up on mountains. But there are no cats in the wild in either Australia or Antarctica. Wherever they are, most cats have individual areas, or territories, where they hunt and have their babies.

This puma is running across a snowy forest clearing in North America. Pumas live in both hot and cold places.

## Are big cats dangerous?

Although some big cats could easily kill people, they very rarely do. However, sometimes individual cats develop a taste for human flesh and begin hunting people regularly. Lions, leopards and tigers are the most dangerous to people.

This angry leopard would have no trouble killing a person if it decided to attack.

# Cat bodies

Apart from their size and weight, there is little physical difference between a small pet cat and a large, powerful tiger. Here you can find out what they have in common.

## Designed for hunting

All cats have agile, athletic bodies, which are perfect for hunting. They need to be fast enough to catch prey and strong enough to pounce on it and kill it. They use their powerful back legs to push off when they run or jump, and their front legs to grab and hold prey.

## Dog-like cat

Cheetahs have slimmer bodies and longer legs than other cats. In fact, they are shaped more like a greyhound, a breed of dog, than like a cat. They are not as strong as other big cats, but they are the fastest land mammals in the world.

Here you can see how a cheetah's long, athletic body is very similar to that of a greyhound dog.

This is a leopard. The labels around it indicate some of the features that cats have in common.

A cat's upright ears can detect very quiet sounds. They can be rotated to pick up sounds from different directions.

Stiff hairs called whiskers on a cat's face help it to feel its way.

The area around a cat's nose and mouth is called a muzzle.

## Claws in close-up

Cats have five claws on their front paws and four on their back paws. The fifth claw on the front paws, called the dew claw, is high up on the paw and doesn't touch the ground when cats walk. Cats use their dew claw like a thumb, to help them hold their prey. All big cats, apart from cheetahs, can pull their other claws back into pockets in their toes when walking, so that they don't wear down. On the bottom of the paws there are pads of skin which help cats to move quietly when hunting.

This picture shows where the dew claw is on a cheetah's leg.

Most cats have long tails, which they use to help them keep their balance.

Cats' bodies are covered in fur. Some cats have patterns such as spots or stripes on their fur.

Cats have loose skin under their fur. This makes it harder for rivals to cause bad bite wounds in fights.

Fact: A cat's claws are made of keratin, the same substance as your fingernails.

# On the move

Big cats are fast and graceful movers. Their powerful legs help them take big strides, and their muscular bodies give them the strength to jump long distances or climb high trees.

A cheetah sprinting. When it runs as fast as it can, it takes almost three strides every second.

## Built for speed

Cheetahs are excellent sprinters, able to reach 115kph (70mph). They have a flexible backbone that stretches to cover as much ground as possible, and then bends to provide the spring for the next stride.

Cheetahs also have very long tails that act as stabilizers. They help cheetahs to keep their balance while changing direction at high speeds. Cheetahs often need to do this when chasing prey.

## Firm footing

Cheetahs use their extended claws to help them grip the ground. The claws act like the spikes on running shoes. Some cheetahs' paw pads are deeply ridged and this can help improve their grip, because they don't slip when they make sudden turns while racing along.

Internet links

For a link to a Web site that shows cats running and jumping, go to **www.usborne-quicklinks.com**

A cheetah starts to run by pushing up with its back legs.

It stretches right out with each bound, lifting all four legs off the ground.

It then draws its legs in, ready to spring again.

Fact: Cheetahs have extra-wide nostrils. These help them to breathe easily, so that they can run faster and cool down quicker.

## Climbing high

Leopards have large, muscular bodies that are ideal for climbing trees. They hold on to the trunk with their short, strong front legs, and push themselves up the tree using their powerful back legs. As they climb they dig their claws into the trunk for extra grip.

See how this leopard climbs a tall tree, using its tail to keep its balance.

## Long jumpers

A puma crouches down, ready to spring.

It pushes off with its back legs and stretches its body out.

Pumas and snow leopards have a stocky build and muscular back legs that are proportionately longer than those of other cats. They can jump long distances, which is useful for crossing from rock to rock in mountainous areas. Their jumping skills also enable them to hunt effectively, as they can spring onto unsuspecting prey.

# Senses

All cats have well-developed senses that help them stay alert. Their sight and hearing are excellent, which makes them good hunters. Cats also have keen senses of smell and touch.

## Good listeners

Cats' ears are very sensitive to vibrations, and detect sounds far beyond the range of human hearing. Their wide, funnel-shaped ear flaps channel sounds effectively into the ears.

## Cat vision

Cats see so well because the size of their pupils (the dark circles in the middle of the eyes) can change dramatically to let in more or less light. In bright sunlight, a big cat's pupils close to tiny dots so that it can see without damaging its eyes. In dim light, the pupils open wide to let in as much light as possible.

Cheetahs hunt during the day. This cheetah's pupils have shrunk to small dots, so the cat isn't dazzled by the light.

**Internet links**

For a link to a Web site with lots of fascinating facts about cat senses, go to **www.usborne-quicklinks.com**

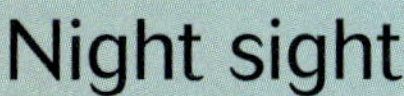

## Night sight

Cats have a reflective layer, called a tapetum lucidum, at the back of their eyes, which improves their night vision. This layer reflects light back through the eye, so that the cat sees with twice as much light.

The reflective layer in this leopard cub's eyes glows when a light is shone on it.

This is a diagram of a cat's eye from the side. The retina detects light twice – first as it enters the eye, then when it is reflected by the tapetum lucidum.

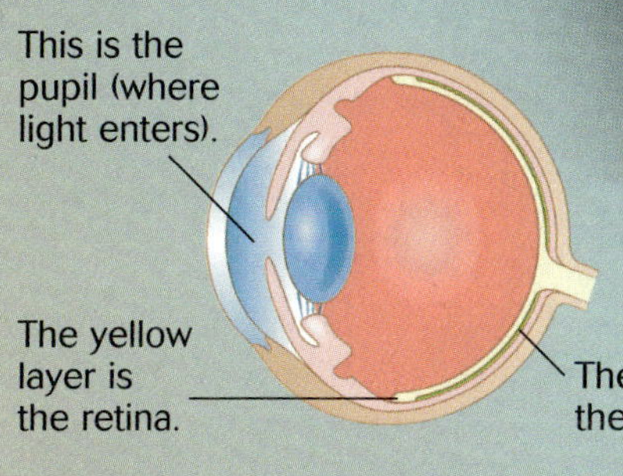


## Sensitive whiskers

The long whiskers on a cat's face are very sensitive. If something touches the whiskers, or even moves nearby, cats sense it at once. Cats use their whiskers to feel their way in the dark or to investigate objects up close.

Normally a cat's whiskers stick straight out.

The whiskers can tilt down to sense objects ahead.

## Smell detectors

Cats can smell using their noses, but they are also able to detect scents using a sensitive area, called the Jacobson's organ, in the roof of the mouth. To allow scents to reach it, a cat opens its mouth and wrinkles its nose. Scientists think that cats may need to be very close to something in order to pick up its scent like this.

A cat opens its mouth like this to detect a scent nearby.

# Coats and camouflage

All cats have fur coats to keep them warm. Some have markings on their fur, and others have plain coats. Their appearance can help them to blend in with their surroundings. This is called camouflage, and it enables cats to remain hidden when hunting.

## Hidden cats

Jaguars and leopards have patterns called rosettes which make them hard to see among trees, while tigers' stripes help them to hide in long grass. Lions have plain yellowish fur, which provides camouflage on the dry African grasslands.

## Spot the difference

Although some species of cats have markings which make them look very similar to each other, no two cats ever have exactly the same markings.

The faces of these leopards look almost identical, but there are slight differences between them.

The markings on this tiger's head enable it to remain well hidden while choosing its moment to attack its prey.

## Black cats

Most leopards and jaguars have patterned yellowish-brown fur, but some are born with black fur instead. Their fur is patterned too, but because they are black the markings are hard to see. Black leopards are often called "black panthers". Black leopards and jaguars spend most of their time in shady forests, where their dark fur gives them good camouflage.

This black leopard's camouflage is well-suited to a shady forest, but here in the open it is easy to see.

## Keeping warm

Cats that live in cold places, such as snow leopards and Amur, or Siberian, tigers, have thick fur to keep them warm. Snow leopards also have long furry tails, reaching up to 90cm (3ft) in length. When resting, they curl their tails around their bodies to give them extra protection against the cold.

## Furry feet

Fur is not just good for keeping out the cold. Snow leopards have thick fur between the pads on their feet. While it gives protection in snowy weather, the fur also cushions their feet as they walk over hot, jagged rocks during the summer.

This picture shows the thick fur on a snow leopard's paw.

This snow leopard's furry tail is almost as long as its body.

# Hunting

Big cats are good hunters. They use a combination of cunning, patience and strength to track down and capture gazelles, antelopes, wildebeests and other prey.

A lioness creeps up on her prey, keeping her body close to the ground. She is careful not to make any sound at all.

## Stealthy stalking

In places with lots of trees or long grass, big cats can sneak up on prey without being seen. This is called stalking.

When a big cat has spotted the animal it wants to catch, it inches slowly along, crouching so low that its body almost touches the ground. It gets as close to the prey as possible, then runs out of its hiding place and pounces on the animal before it can escape.

## Working together

Lions sometimes hunt in groups to increase their chances of catching prey. Often they spread out and surround animals, and then run at them from different directions. This forces the animals into the paths of other lions.

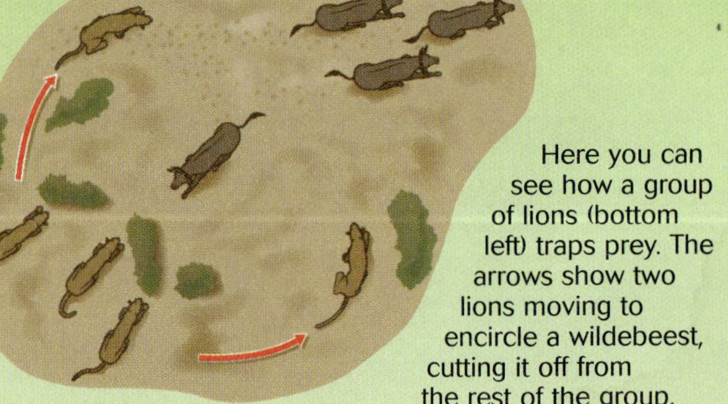

Here you can see how a group of lions (bottom left) traps prey. The arrows show two lions moving to encircle a wildebeest, cutting it off from the rest of the group.

Fact: Lions often steal prey from other cats. They wait until the prey animal has been caught and killed, then grab it for themselves.

## The big chase

Cheetahs are such fast sprinters that they often chase their prey over open ground. They don't make much effort to hide as they slowly begin to approach their prey, but will sometimes freeze if the animal turns to look at them. Cheetahs only start to sprint when they get fairly close to their prey.

A mother cheetah and her cub chase a young gazelle. The mother is teaching the cub how to hunt.

**Internet links**

For a link to a Web site where you can watch a video clip of a cheetah chasing and killing a wildebeest, go to **www.usborne-quicklinks.com**

## Lying in wait

Sometimes a big cat simply hides and waits for prey to come along, rather than tracking it down. For example, a tiger will often hide next to a waterhole. When an animal comes there to drink, the tiger springs out and catches it.

# Killer bites

Big cats are swift and efficient killers. They can pounce on and kill an animal in less than a minute, and are strong enough to attack prey much bigger than themselves.

## Capturing prey

A cat keeps its back paws firmly on the ground to help it drag down prey easily.

The cat forces the prey to the ground, making it fall on its side.

Big cats usually approach large animals from the back or side, to avoid being hurt by their hoofs or horns. To attack, they use their strong front legs and claws to drag an animal down.

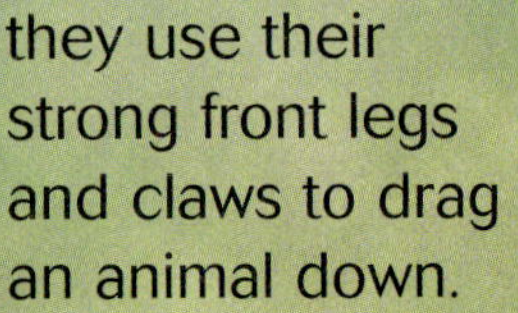

## Deadly neck bite

Big cats usually kill their prey with a single bite. The technique they use depends on the victim's size. Small animals are killed with a bite to the back of the neck. The cat slides its long teeth between the bones of the animal's neck, cutting the spinal cord leading from the brain. This kills the prey instantly.

## Going for the throat

Large prey animals are too big and heavy to be held in the right position for a neck bite. Instead, the big cat bites the animal's throat and holds on tightly. Air can't get into the victim's lungs, so it is unable to breathe and soon dies.

A lioness holds down a zebra and bites into its throat, suffocating it.

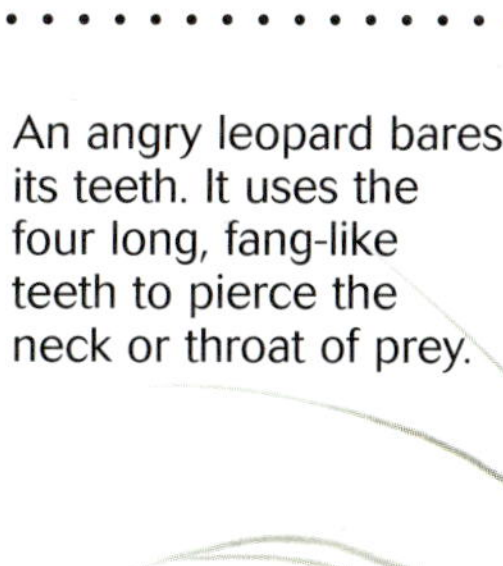

An angry leopard bares its teeth. It uses the four long, fang-like teeth to pierce the neck or throat of prey.

## Terrifying teeth

Big cats normally have thirty teeth. The four long, pointed front teeth are called canines. These are used for biting and killing prey. The twelve smaller front teeth are called incisors, and are used for stripping off fur or feathers, and tearing meat from bones.

At the sides of the jaw are large, wide teeth called premolars and molars. Humans have teeth that look a bit like this. But whereas ours are rounded for chewing, cat molars and premolars have sharp edges for slicing through flesh.

**Internet links**

For a link to a Web site where you can learn all you need to know about tigers' teeth, go to **www.usborne-quicklinks.com**

Fact: Tigers have the longest canine teeth of all big cats. The visible part can be over 5cm (2in) long.

# Cat talk

Cats have a number of ways of communicating with each other, but not all of them involve making sounds. Slight body movements by one cat can send out clear signals to another, while smells are also a part of communication.

This male lion is roaring to tell other lions to keep their distance.

## How cats roar

A roar is a deep, vibrating noise made by some big cats. Lions, leopards and jaguars can all roar, but lions are the only big cats that roar frequently. Experts aren't sure how cats roar. Most think the sound is made by air passing through the cat's voicebox, or larynx, as it breathes out forcefully. The air causes fleshy folds in the voicebox to vibrate.

## When do cats roar?

Big cats often roar to warn other cats to keep away from their territories. They also tend to roar at sunrise and sunset. Sometimes cats roar when they have finished eating.

Internet links

For a link to a Web site where you can hear a lion's roar, and other animal sounds, go to **www.usborne-quicklinks.com**

## Quiet tigers?

Tigers make many kinds of noises, but they can't roar like lions. Some sounds they produce are so low-pitched that humans can't hear them. Low-pitched sounds can travel long distances, so they may help tigers to communicate with each other in large, dense forests.

These jaguars are poised for a savage fight. They are growling at each other and are ready to pounce.

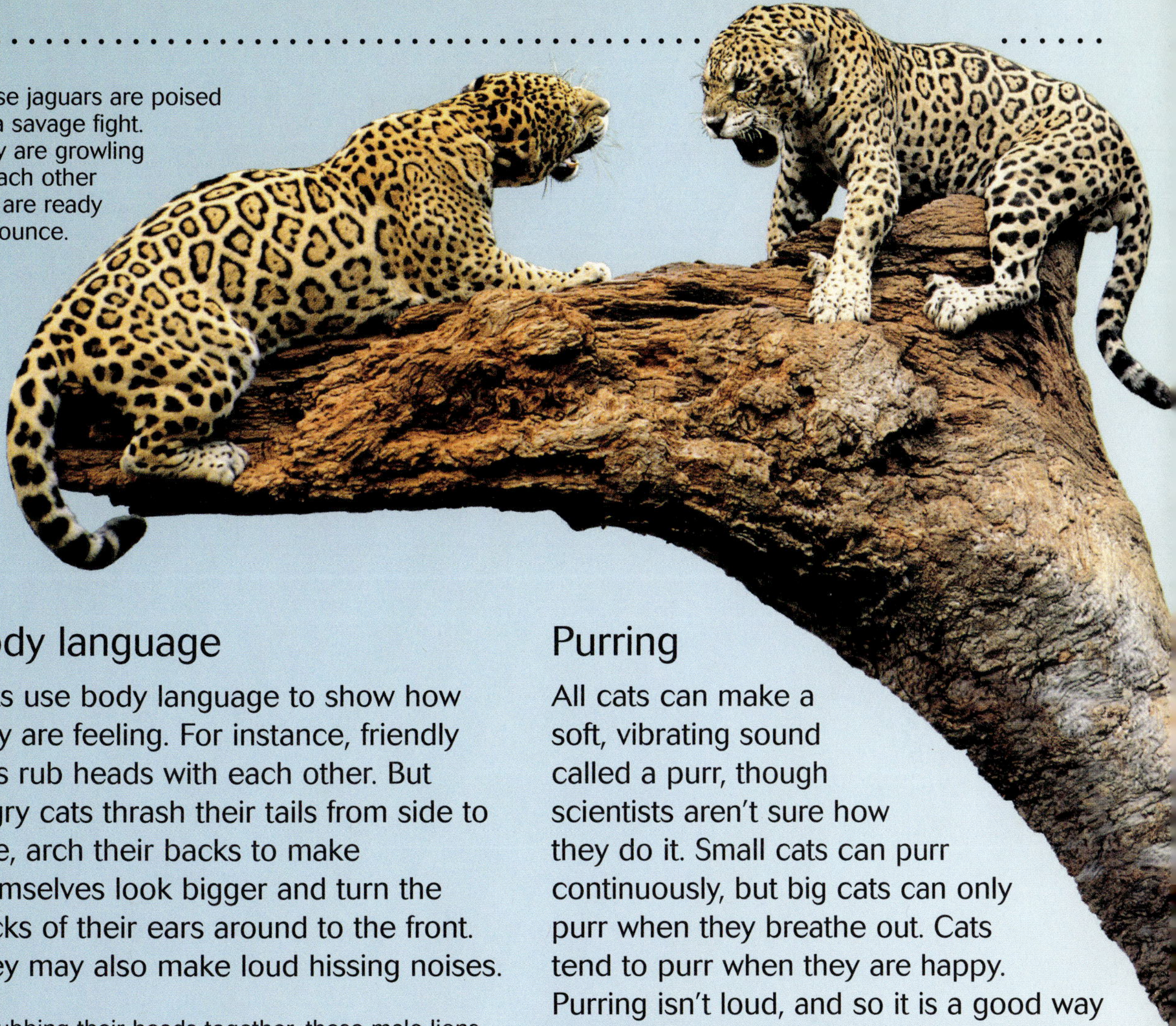

## Body language

Cats use body language to show how they are feeling. For instance, friendly cats rub heads with each other. But angry cats thrash their tails from side to side, arch their backs to make themselves look bigger and turn the backs of their ears around to the front. They may also make loud hissing noises.

By rubbing their heads together, these male lions are showing that they like each other.

## Purring

All cats can make a soft, vibrating sound called a purr, though scientists aren't sure how they do it. Small cats can purr continuously, but big cats can only purr when they breathe out. Cats tend to purr when they are happy. Purring isn't loud, and so it is a good way for mothers and cubs to communicate, without attracting interest from predators.

## Scent marks

All cats use urine to mark out their territories, often spraying it against trees and rocks as they wander around. The urine has a strong scent, which is easily detected by other cats. It tells them they have entered another cat's territory.

Fact: A male lion's roar can be heard nearly 8km (5 miles) away.

# Getting together

To have baby cats, known as cubs, a male and female big cat must mate with each other. Females give clear signals when they are ready to mate.

## The smell test

Male cats use their sense of smell to find out if females want to mate. When females are interested, their urine contains special chemicals that tell males they are ready.

A female leopard lifts her tail up like this to spray her urine against a tree.

When a male sniffs the tree, he can tell from the smell if the female wants to mate.

## Waiting for mating

It is the female cats that decide when mating occurs. Males have to be patient and keep their distance until the time is right. If a female isn't ready, she will snarl and slap the male away with her paws.

This lioness is warning a male lion to keep his distance.

## Gentle persuasion

Males call to females to try to persuade them to mate. When a female is ready, she may show this by roaring, waving her tail or rolling on the ground. During mating, big cats often snarl and bite one another, making it look more like fighting than mating.

## Brief encounters

Mating between big cats usually lasts just a few seconds, although they may mate many times a day. Smaller cats don't mate so often, perhaps because during mating they are more vulnerable to attack.

## Safe den

When female cats are almost ready to give birth, they look for a well-hidden place, or den, where they can have their cubs in safety. This might be in a cave or under bushes. It is vital that the den is well out of sight of predators.

During mating, male cats often bite the fur on the back of a female's neck like this.

Fact: Lionesses within the same pride often produce cubs at around the same time.

# Growing up

In their first year or two, cubs are dependent on their mother. She not only provides them with food, but also teaches them how to hunt and survive in the wild.

## Helpless babies

Cubs are blind for a short time after their birth and are totally helpless. During their first few months, they feed mostly on milk produced by their mother. They suck the milk through small teats on their mother's belly.

This female leopard is showing her cubs affection by licking them, as they fight to get to her teats.

## Moving dens

If a mother fears that her cubs are in danger from predators, she will move them to a new den. She does this by carrying them, one by one, between her teeth. This doesn't hurt the cubs, as she holds the loose skin at the back of the neck. Cheetahs move their dens every few days to stop predators from finding them.

A lioness carrying her cub by the skin on the back of its neck



Fact: After mother cats have moved their cubs to a new den, they sometimes make a final trip to their old den to check that they haven't left any behind.

## Fighting and learning

These tiger cubs are not trying to hurt each other, but are enjoying a play fight.

Cubs spend a lot of their time play-fighting. The fights help to develop their strength and technique for when they are older and need to defend themselves against other cats, as well as catch and kill prey. If a cub doesn't have a brother or sister to fight with, its mother will sometimes play with it instead.

## The first kill

Cubs instinctively know how to kill, but they need to get used to doing it, and to learn to recognize their prey. At first, their mother may bring them dead prey to eat. As they get older, cubs go hunting with their mother to learn what to do. She may catch and injure prey, but leave the cubs to kill it.

This female lion and her cubs are eating a buffalo that she has killed.

# Cat habits

Cats have a lot of habits in common. For instance, they all like to keep their claws sharp for hunting, and their bodies clean. They are also very protective of their territories.

## Day dreamers

Most cats sleep or rest during the day and become active at sunset. This allows them to take advantage of their excellent night vision to attack animals that can't see as well in the dark. They are also able to surprise animals that are sleeping.

## Up to scratch

To keep their claws clean and sharp for hunting, big cats regularly scratch tree trunks. This also leaves a scent on the tree, which tells passing cats they have entered another cat's territory. Pet cats often try to sharpen their claws in the same way, by scratching furniture.

To sharpen its front claws on a tree trunk, a cheetah stretches up onto its back legs like this.

★

Most of the lions in this group are either dozing or yawning. Lions can spend up to 20 hours a day resting.

## Spiky tongues

Cats often lick their fur to clean it. Their tongues are covered in small spikes, which make them feel rough. When a cat licks itself, the spikes act like a comb, helping to remove any loose hair. Big cats' tongues are so rough that they can lick flesh from the bones of their prey.

These tigers are fighting viciously in a river and could hurt or kill each other.

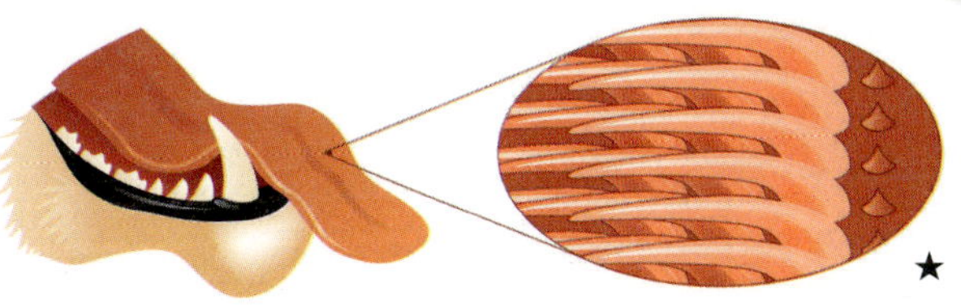

This close-up diagram shows the tiny comb-like spikes on a cat's tongue. The spikes point into the mouth.

## Cat fights

A big cat's territory can be so vast that it takes three weeks to walk around it. Big cats don't like other cats moving into their territories, and will often challenge intruders aggressively. This can result in ferocious fights, which can cause serious injuries or even death.

# Tigers

Tigers are huge, powerful animals that live only in Asia. Hunting and the destruction of their habitats have reduced the number of tigers in the wild, and they are now very rare.

An Amur tiger running across snow-covered ground in Russia

## King of the tigers

The Amur, or Siberian, tiger, is one of the biggest cats. The males can reach up to 3m (10ft) in length, and can weigh three times as much as a person.

Amur tigers live in cold, remote areas of Russia and northern China. As protection against the biting cold, they have longer fur than other tigers. They also have a special layer of fat under the skin, which gives them extra insulation.

## Big eaters

Tigers have big appetites. They can eat up to 40kg (90lb) of meat (the equivalent of a whole adult deer) in one huge meal. When looking for food, it is not unusual for tigers to walk more than 25km (15 miles) in a day.

Internet links

For a link to a Web site where you can see a video clip of tigers in the wild, study a map of where they live and send an electronic postcard of a tiger to a friend, go to **www.usborne-quicklinks.com**

Fact: Since 1900, the Caspian tiger, the Bali tiger and the Javan tiger have all died out.

## Cool cats

Most tigers live in warm places, although they can find very hot weather uncomfortable. But, unlike most cats, they enjoy being in water. In India, where the summers are very hot, Bengal tigers often cool off in rivers. Tigers are good swimmers too – they are capable of crossing rivers 29km (18 miles) wide.

## Man-eaters

Tigers do sometimes eat people. In the Sunderbans forest in Bangladesh and India, they kill up to a hundred people a year. To prevent attacks, people in the forest wear face masks on the backs of their heads. Tigers usually attack from behind. So if they see a face, they are unlikely to pounce because they think their prey is facing them.

By wearing a face mask on his head, this man can fool a tiger into thinking he is facing it.

## White tiger

One of the rarest tigers is the white tiger from central India. These tigers are in fact Bengal tigers but, instead of having reddish-brown fur with dark stripes, they are mostly creamy white. No white tigers have been seen in the wild since 1951, although many live in zoos.

This white tiger lives in a zoo in the U.S.A. White tigers are a popular attraction for zoo visitors because of their striking appearance.

# Lions

Lions are among the most fearsome animals in Africa. They live together in groups and have no predators to fear. A male lion with a mane of bushy, golden hair around its head is an impressive sight.

## Pride of lions

Most big cats live alone, but lions usually live together in groups called prides. They often hunt together, so that they can each get a regular share of food. Large prides can contain more than 30 cats. Prides are biggest in places where there is plenty of food. In areas where prey is harder to find, prides can contain as few as two or three cats.

A group of lionesses hunting together. The one at the front is using her front legs to drag down a wildebeest.

Fact: In the space of nine months in 1898, two lions killed and ate more than a hundred workers who were building a railway bridge at Tsavo, in Kenya.

## Busy females

Females do most of the hunting for the pride, but males are always the first to eat. The females eat once the males have finished and the cubs eat last of all. If food is short, cubs can starve to death.

## Mane attraction

By the time a male lion is five years old, its mane is virtually fully grown. An impressive mane may help to attract the interest of females. It also makes a lion look big and fierce, and protects its neck during fights. As lions grow older, their manes become darker.

## Asian lions

Not all lions live in Africa. In fact, until 2,000 years ago, lions lived in parts of Europe. But now these lions, called Asian lions, are found only in the Gir Forest in western India. There are only about 300 of them in the wild.

The yellow area on this map shows where Asian lions lived about 2,000 years ago. The red dot is the Gir Forest, where they live today.

### Internet links

For a link to a Web site where you can see exciting live pictures of lions in Pittsburgh Zoo, in the U.S.A., go to **www.usborne-quicklinks.com**

A male and female lion keeping a watchful eye on the open grasslands. The male (on the right) is bigger and heavier than the female, and his mane makes him look bigger still.

# Leopards

Leopards are less than half the size of tigers, but they are very strong and can kill all kinds of prey. They are good climbers and, camouflaged by their patterned fur, can be hard to see resting in trees.

This young leopard is developing its climbing skills.

## Unfussy eaters

Leopards live in many parts of Africa, as well as throughout southern Asia. No other big cat is found over such a wide area. One reason why leopards can survive in so many places is because of their varied diet. These cats will eat almost anything, from antelopes and zebras to insects and prickly porcupines.

## City stalkers

Leopards are naturally shy animals. However, in parts of Africa they have become very bold, and sometimes hunt close to where people live. For example, on the edges of the city of Nairobi, in Kenya, leopards occasionally hunt very close to houses, and have even snatched pet dogs as their prey.

A leopard lazing on a large rock. Like most other big cats, leopards usually rest during the day.

Fact: Using their teeth, leopards can drag baby giraffes weighing 90kg (200lb) into trees.

## A meal in a tree

When a leopard has killed its prey, it will often use its strength and climbing ability to drag the body into a tree before settling down to eat. It does this to avoid attracting the interest of other animals that might want to steal its food. If the leopard is unable to eat the kill all at once, it will keep returning to it until it is finished.

The leopard climbs a tree, holding its victim firmly by the neck.

After draping the animal over a branch, the leopard is able to eat its meal undisturbed.

### Internet links

For a link to a Web site where you can see a selection of fascinating video clips of leopards in the wild, go to **www.usborne-quicklinks.com**

## Rare leopard

There are only about fifty Amur, or Korean, leopards left in the wild. They live in forests near the border between Russia and China. But their habitat is being destroyed by farming and forest fires, making it hard for them to find shelter. Food is also scarce because their prey is struggling to survive too.

The patterns on this Amur leopard's fur blend in well with the dead leaves on the forest floor.

# Asian leopards

Although they are both called leopards, snow leopards and clouded leopards aren't closely related. They both live in parts of Asia, but in very different places. Snow leopards live in mountainous areas, while clouded leopards are found in forests.

## Mountain hunters

Snow leopards' fur is mostly dark silver with black markings. This blends in well with the rocks and snow in their habitat, giving them good camouflage when hunting. They often surprise their prey by jumping on it from above.

When hunting, a snow leopard crouches down on a ledge and waits for prey to appear below.

When an animal comes close, the snow leopard uses its powerful back legs to leap down onto it.

## Hot and cold cats

In winter, snow leopards face very cold weather, but in summer, they experience swelteringly hot conditions. To cope with the cold, snow leopards grow longer fur and move to lower ground, while in summer they often rest in the shade.

The wide, flat shape of this snow leopard's paws spreads out its weight, so it doesn't sink when walking in deep snow.

## Winter maters

Snow leopards mate during the winter, so that their cubs are born in the spring. At this time of year there is a good supply of food, and the babies grow stronger while the weather is milder. This gives them a better chance of surviving their first winter.

These healthy-looking snow leopard cubs are ten weeks old.

### Internet links

For a link to a Web site where you can watch a fascinating video clip of a snow leopard in the wild, and find out more about clouded leopards, go to **www.usborne-quicklinks.com**

## Clouded leopard

Clouded leopards live in the forests of Southeast Asia. They are not very big, but they have extremely long canine teeth – only slightly smaller than a lion's. Clouded leopards are good climbers and hunt monkeys and birds in trees. They are also capable of killing large prey, such as deer and wild pigs, on the ground.

Here you can see the distinctive cloud-shaped markings, from which clouded leopards get their name.

# Cheetahs

Cheetahs live on open grasslands in many regions of Africa and in parts of Asia. They aren't as strong as leopards and lions, which live there too, and find it difficult to compete with them for food.

## Big cat cheaters

Many people view cheetahs as big cats, but some experts think they shouldn't be included in this group because their bodies look very different from other big cats' bodies. Also, unlike most big cats, they can't roar but make high-pitched yelps instead.

## Fast but weak

Although cheetahs are fast movers, they can only manage to run at very high speeds for about 300m (1,000ft). By the time they have caught their prey, cheetahs are exhausted. As a result, lions, leopards, hyenas and even vultures can easily snatch away their meal.

Here you can clearly see the cheetah's slim, athletic body shape.

### Internet links

For a link to a Web site where you can find out many more facts about cheetahs, and hear what they sound like, go to **www.usborne-quicklinks.com**

Fact: In the sixteenth century, the Indian Emperor Akbar tamed cheetahs and used them to catch gazelles on hunting trips.

## On the lookout

Unlike many big cats, cheetahs hunt during the day. They do this to keep out of the way of lions and leopards, which tend to hunt in the evening or at night. When hunting, cheetahs try to find areas of raised ground which will give them a good view of the open grasslands.

This cheetah has climbed onto a mound made by insects called termites to look for prey.

## Hungry for gazelles

Gazelles are the most common choice of prey for cheetahs. They are smaller than cheetahs and are easily overpowered. But gazelles are fast runners and if they see a cheetah nearby, they can sometimes get away. Cheetahs usually target young or old gazelles which can't run very fast.

## Cubs in danger

Cheetah cubs face a battle to survive. Within three months of their birth, most of them die. Some are snatched by predators and others starve. Female cheetahs need to make a kill almost every day to feed their cubs, but hunting is difficult and they can't always find enough food.

This female cheetah is keeping a close eye on her cub. But, when she goes off to find food, it is in danger of being taken by predators.

# American big cats

Although some of the best-known cats live in Africa and Asia, North, Central and South America contain many types of wild cats, including jaguars and pumas.

## Jaguars

Jaguars are the third-largest of the big cats. They live in Central America and parts of South America, mostly in tropical rainforests and never far from rivers or lakes. Like leopards, they have spotted fur, but jaguars have shorter legs, larger heads and stockier bodies.

## Water lovers

Jaguars hunt on the ground, in trees and even in water. They are good swimmers and often attack turtles, alligators and snakes in rivers. Jaguars also catch fish, but they can do this by fishing from the bank.

To catch fish, a jaguar finds a spot close to the water and lies in wait, keeping very still.

When a fish comes near, it swipes at it with one paw and hooks it right out of the water.

This is an excellent close-up view of a jaguar prowling through a forest in Belize, in Central America.

Fact: Jaguars are the only big cats that regularly kill their prey by biting through the skull.

## Adaptable cats

Pumas, also called cougars, panthers or mountain lions, live all over America – from Canada all the way down to Argentina, at the southern tip of South America. Pumas live in a wide variety of habitats, including mountains, grasslands, rainforests and swamps.

## Big little cat

Pumas are not usually classed as big cats, but they are often bigger than leopards and can be well over 2m (6ft) in length. They are easily capable of killing large prey such as wild deer and horses.

You can clearly see this puma's large, powerful front paws. Pumas use their front paws to grab hold of their prey.

### Internet links

For a link to a Web site with amazing photographs of pumas and jaguars, and fact files about them, go to **www.usborne-quicklinks.com**

## Big leapers

Pumas are very athletic and have strong back legs. They can leap the length of a bus in one bound when chasing after prey, and can jump almost 5m (16ft) straight off the ground into trees or onto rocky ledges.

A puma leaps impressively over some rocks as it chases its prey.

# Small wild cats

There are many species of small wild cats living all over the world, some of which you won't have heard of before. Because of their size, many of these cats are very agile.

This is a serval. It is using its very large ears to listen out for prey.

## Leaping servals

Servals live in Africa. They have very good hearing, and can hear small animals rustling in the grass. From the noise, they can work out exactly where an animal is and pounce on it. Servals are also able to leap a long way off the ground, which means that they can catch birds in the air too.

A serval creeps up on birds while they are on the ground.

When the birds fly away, the serval leaps up and knocks one to the ground.

Fact: The rusty-spotted cat from Sri Lanka and India is the smallest cat in the world. It is only half the size of a pet cat.

## Lynxes

Lynxes live in North America, Asia and in parts of Europe. They have short tails, distinctive tufts of fur on the tips of their ears, and long fur around their faces. Their sense of smell is thought to be particularly good – they can detect the scent of their prey 300m (1,000ft) away.

**Internet links**

For a link to a Web site where you can see a video clip of a margay climbing around in a tree, go to **www.usborne-quicklinks.com**

Like snow leopards, lynxes have wide paws. Here you see how they help them to walk on deep snow.

## Athletic margays

Margays live in the rainforests of Central and South America. They are very athletic and are superb climbers. Their sharp claws grip branches firmly, and their flexible ankle joints enable them to move around trees almost as easily as monkeys. They can run headfirst down tree trunks, and can even run upside down along branches.

A margay crouching in a tree. These cats spend much of their time off the ground.

# Under threat

Over the past hundred years, people have killed large numbers of cats and destroyed their habitats. As a result, some species of big cats have become rare and may die out (become extinct) if the current rates of destruction continue.

## Panther in peril

In Florida, in the U.S.A., pumas known as Florida panthers are very rare. Towns and cities have taken over much of their habitat, and they now live a lot closer to humans than they did. They are sometimes killed by fast-moving cars as they try to cross busy roads.

## No home, no hope

Every year, millions of rainforest trees are cut down for their wood, or to make way for farming. This affects cats such as jaguars and clouded leopards. As the land is cleared, their prey is either driven away or destroyed. The cats are left with little food and shelter, and so very little chance of survival.

This Florida panther lives in a zoo, safe from the many dangers that threaten these cats in the wild.

This Bengal tiger is cooling off in a river. There are now only 2,000 of these tigers left in the wild.

## Tiger medicines

For thousands of years, different parts of tigers' bodies have been used in traditional Chinese medicine. For example, their tail-bones are used in creams for curing acne.

Hunting tigers is banned in most places, and few Chinese doctors still use tiger body parts. But some people do make medicines which contain them. This means that the hunters can earn a lot of money from killing tigers illegally.

These are packets of dressings containing tiger bone.

## Fur trade

Clothing made from animal fur is very expensive, and hunters can make a lot of money by killing cats and selling their fur. Cats with attractive, patterned fur are especially at risk. In many places, it is now against the law to kill big cats, but illegal hunting still goes on.

### Internet links

For a link to a Web site where you can find out more about many endangered animals, including tigers, go to **www.usborne-quicklinks.com**

# Caring for cats

Now that some big cats are in danger of becoming extinct, people are learning to protect and care for them. Scientists are researching how cats live, and endangered species are well looked after in zoos.

## Cat tracking

To find out more about a cat's habits, scientists study its movements. They can do this by attaching a special collar to the cat's neck. The collar gives off signals which are detected by radio receivers. These allow scientists to track the cat's movements, without having to follow close behind it.

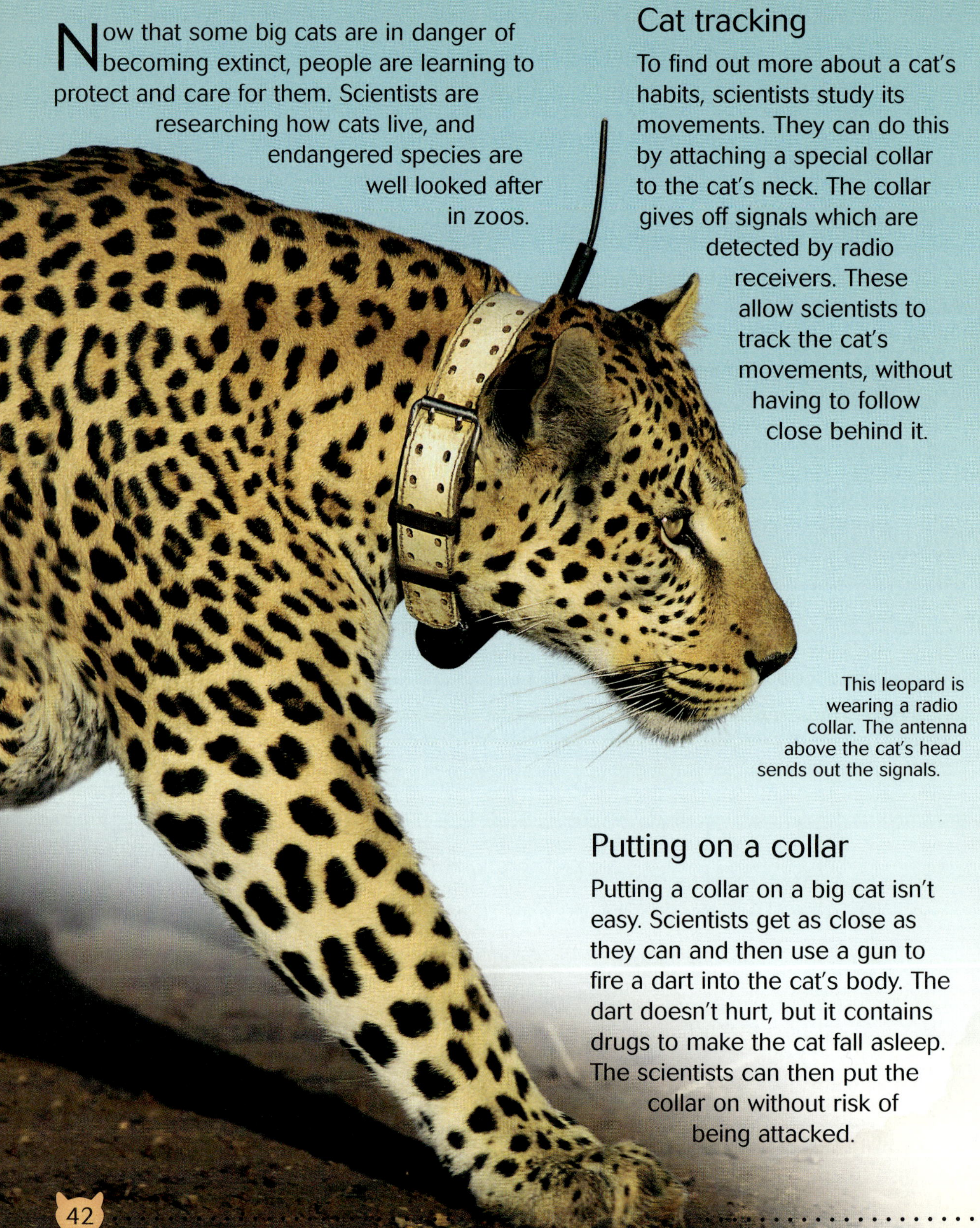

This leopard is wearing a radio collar. The antenna above the cat's head sends out the signals.

## Putting on a collar

Putting a collar on a big cat isn't easy. Scientists get as close as they can and then use a gun to fire a dart into the cat's body. The dart doesn't hurt, but it contains drugs to make the cat fall asleep. The scientists can then put the collar on without risk of being attacked.

## Captive cats

Zoos play an important part in caring for endangered cats and giving them a safe place where they can live and breed. For example, there are now more Amur (Siberian) and South China tigers living in zoos than there are living in the wild.

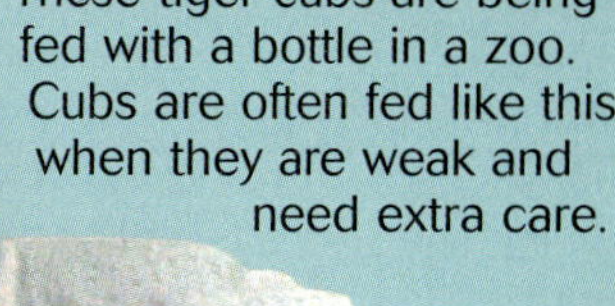

These tiger cubs are being fed with a bottle in a zoo. Cubs are often fed like this when they are weak and need extra care.

## Project Tiger

In 1972, Project Tiger was set up to protect Bengal tigers in India. Protected areas called nature reserves were created for them. The number of tigers almost doubled at one stage, but illegal hunting has started again and there could now be even fewer tigers than when the project started.

### Internet links

For a link to a Web site where you can find out more about tigers and how you can help to protect them, go to **www.usborne-quicklinks.com**

## On safari

Every year, thousands of people go on safaris where they travel into nature reserves to see wild animals. Countries make a lot of money from this type of tourism, and big cats are a very popular attraction. As a result, in some places, big cats are now much better protected from hunters.

These tourists are enjoying a close-up view of a male lion in Botswana, Africa.

Fact: Scientists think there are no more than 30 South China tigers living in the wild.

# Myths and legends

For thousands of years, cats have been respected for their power and beauty. In many places, they have been a central part of religious rituals and beliefs. In some societies, people wear the skins of big cats to show their own power and importance.

## The Sphinx

The Sphinx is one of the best-known statues in the world. It has a man's head and a lion's body. It is in Giza, in Egypt, and is at least 4,500 years old. The entire sphinx is 73m (240ft) long. Sphinxes also appear in several other ancient cultures. In Greek legend, the sphinx had the head of a woman, the wings of a bird and the body of a lion.

Here you can clearly see the Sphinx's long paws and human head.

Fact: In ancient Egypt, cats were so well respected, it was against the law to kill one. A person could be put to death for doing this.

## Cat gods

Some ancient Egyptian gods had cat features. For example, Bastet was a goddess of the Sun and Moon with the head of a cat, while Sekhmet, a goddess of war and punishment, had a lion's head.

A statue of the cat-headed goddess Bastet with several kittens at her feet

## Jaguar gods

The jaguar has been worshipped by different peoples of Central and South America. The Olmecs, who lived in Mexico over 2,500 years ago, believed that they were descended from jaguars, and their rain god was part man, part jaguar. Today, people in this area still occasionally wear jaguar masks during festivals.

A stone figure of an Olmec jaguar spirit

## Dressed to impress

Because big cats are regarded as powerful hunters, people sometimes wear their skins to emphasize their own power. In South Africa, kings of the Zulu people sometimes wear leopard-skin headbands and robes.

This Zulu prince is wearing a traditional leopard-skin robe.

# Using the Internet

Most of the Web sites listed in this book can be accessed with a standard home computer and a Web browser (the software that enables you to display information from the Internet).
We recommend:

- A PC with Microsoft® Windows® 98 or later version, or a Macintosh computer with System 9.0 or later, and 64Mb RAM
- A browser such as Microsoft® Internet Explorer 5, or Netscape® Navigator 4.7, or later versions
- Connection to the Internet via a modem (preferably 56Kbps) or a faster digital or cable line
- An account with an Internet Service Provider (ISP)
- A sound card to hear sound files

## Extras

Some Web sites need additional programs, called plug-ins, to play sounds, or to show videos, animations or 3-D images. If you go to a site and you do not have the necessary plug-in, a message saying so will come up on the screen. There is usually a button on the site that you can click on to download the plug-in. Alternatively, go to **www.usborne-quicklinks.com** and click on **Net Help**. There you can find links to download plug-ins. Here is a list of plug-ins you might need:

**RealPlayer®** – lets you play videos and hear sound files.
**QuickTime** – enables you to view video clips.
**Shockwave®** – lets you play animations and interactive programs.
**Flash™** – lets you play animations.

## Help

For general help and advice on using the Internet, go to **Usborne Quicklinks** at **www.usborne-quicklinks.com** and click on **Net Help**. To find out more about how to use your Web browser, click on **Help** at the top of the browser, and then choose **Contents and Index**. You'll find a huge searchable dictionary containing tips on how to find your way around the Internet easily.

## Internet safety

Remember to follow the Internet safety guidelines at the front of this book. For more safety information, go to **Usborne Quicklinks** and click on **Net Help**.

## Computer viruses

A computer virus is a program that can seriously damage your computer. A virus can get into your computer when you download programs from the Internet, or in an attachment (an extra file) that arrives with an e-mail. We strongly recommend that you buy anti-virus software to protect your computer and that you update the software regularly.

**Internet links**

For a link to a Web site where you can find out more about computer viruses, go to **www.usborne-quicklinks.com**

# Index

Words with several pages have a number in **bold** to show where to find the main explanation. Page numbers in *italic* show where to find pictures.


backbone 8
black panthers *13*, *17*
camouflage **12–13**, 30, 32
carnivores 4
cheetahs 4, *6*, 7, *8*, *10*, *15*, 22, *24*, ***34–35***
Chinese medicine 41
claws 4, ***7***, 8, 9, 16, 24, 39
dew claw *7*
climbing **9**, 31, 33, 39
clouded leopards 4, 32, ***33***, 40
communication 18–19
body language 19
growling 19
hissing 19
purring 19
roaring 5, ***18***, 34
scent 19, 24
cougars *see* pumas
cubs *11*, 20, 21, ***22–23***, 29, *33*, *35*, *43*
dens **21**, 22
ears 6, **10**, 19, *38*, 39
eyes *10*, ***11***
fur 4, 7, **12–13**, 21, 25, 26, 30, 31, 32, 36, 39
fur trade 41
gazelles 14, *15*, 34, **35**
gods (cat) 45
greyhounds *6*
habitats **5**, 26, 31, 32, 37, 40
habits 24–25
hunting **14–15**, 23, 30, 32, 33, 35, 36
stalking 14
Jacobson's organ 11
jaguars 4, 12, 13, 18, *19*, ***36***, 40, 45
jaws 17
jumping **8–9**, 32, 37
leopards 4, *5*, *6–7*, *9*, *11*, *12*, *13*, *17*, 18, *20*, *22*, ***30–31***, 34, 35, 36, 37, *42*
Amur/Korean *31*
skins *45*
lions *4*, 5, 12, *14–15*, *16*, *18*, *19*, *20*, *21*, *22*, 23, *24–25*, ***28–29***, 33, 34, 35, 45
Asian 29
prides 28
lynxes *39*
mammals **4**, 6
mane 28, ***29***
margays *39*
mating **20–21**, 33
miacids 4
mountain lions *see* pumas
muzzle 6
nose 6, 11
nostrils 8
Olmecs *45*
panther group 4
panthers *see* pumas
paws **7**, 8, *13*, *32*, *37*, 39
pads **7**, 8, *13*
play-fighting 23
Project Tiger 43
pumas 4, *5*, *9*, 36, ***37***, *40*
Florida panther *40*
radio collar *42*
running **8**, 34
rusty-spotted cats 38
safaris *43*
senses 10–11
hearing **10**, 38
sight 10, 11
smell 10, **11**, 20, 39
touch 10, **11**
servals *38*
snow leopards 4, 9, *13*, ***32–33***, 39
Sphinx *44*
swimming 27, 36, *41*
tail 7, 8, 9, 13, 19, 39
tapetum lucidum *11*
teeth 4, **16–17**, 22, 30, 33
territories 5, 18, 19, **25**
tigers 4, 5, 6, *12*, 13, 15, 17, 18, *23*, *25*, ***26–27***, 30, *41*, *43*
Amur/Siberian 13, *26*, 43
Bali 26
Bengal *27*, *41*, 43
Caspian 26
Javan 26
South China 43
white *27*
tongues *25*
tracking 42
whiskers 6, ***11***
zoos 43
Zulu people *45*

# Acknowledgements

Every effort has been made to trace the copyright holders of the material in this book. If any rights have been omitted, the publishers offer to rectify this in any subsequent editions following notification. The publishers are grateful to the following organizations and individuals for their permission to reproduce material (t=top, m=middle, b=bottom, l=left, r=right):

**Cover** © Digital Vision; **P1** © Digital Vision; **P2** © Bruce Coleman Inc.; **P3** © Darrell Gulin/CORBIS; **P4** © Digital Vision; **P5** (mr) © Joe McDonald/CORBIS, (br) © David A. Northcott/CORBIS; **P6-7** © Alain Compost/Bruce Coleman; **P8** © Gallo Images/CORBIS; **P9** © Digital Vision; **P10** © Digital Vision; **P11** © Digital Vision; **P12** (tm) © Anup Shah/Nature Picture Library, (tr) © Torsten Brehm/Nature Picture Library, (b) © W. Perry Conway/CORBIS; **P13** (t) © Lee Green/CORBIS, (b) © Tom Brakefield/CORBIS; **P14-15** © Peter Blackwell/ Nature Picture Library; **P15** © Tom Brakefield/CORBIS; **P16** © Norman Tomalin/Bruce Coleman; **P17** © Bruce Coleman Inc.; **P18** © Lynda Richardson/CORBIS; **P19** (t) Luiz Marigo/Still Pictures, (b) © Alissa Crandall/CORBIS; **P20** © Joe McDonald/CORBIS; **P21** © Mary Ann McDonald/CORBIS; **P22** (l) © Richard Du Toit/Nature Picture Library, (r) © Tom Brakefield/CORBIS; **P23** (t) George D. Lepp/Science Photo Library, (b) © Peter Johnson/CORBIS; **P24-25** © Peter Blackwell/Nature Picture Library; **P25** © Gallo Images/CORBIS; **P26** © Tom Brakefield/CORBIS; **P27** (t) © Associated Press/John Moore, (b) © Kevin Fleming/CORBIS; **P28** © Yann Arthus-Bertrand/CORBIS; **P28-29** © Pictor International/Pictor International, Ltd./PictureQuest; **P30** (t) © Digital Vision, (b) © Digital Vision; **P31** © Tom Brakefield/CORBIS; **P32** © Stuart Westmorland/CORBIS; **P33** (m) © Terry Whittaker/CORBIS, (b) © Alain Compost/Bruce Coleman; **P34** © Simon King/Nature Picture Library; **P35** (l) © Gallo Images/CORBIS, (r) © Pete Oxford/Nature Picture Library; **P36** © Lynn M. Stone/Nature Picture Library; **P37** (t) © D. Robert & Lorri Franz/CORBIS, (b) © John Conrad/CORBIS; **P38** © Torsten Brehm/Nature Picture Library; **P39** (t) © D. Robert Franz/CORBIS, (b) © Kevin Schafer/CORBIS; **P40** © Lynn M. Stone/Nature Picture Library; **P41** (t) © Yogi, Inc./CORBIS, (b) Andy Rouse/NHPA; **P42** © Gallo Images/CORBIS; **P43** (t) © Reuters/John Sommers, (b) Daryl Balfour/NHPA; **P44** © Wolfgang Kaehler/CORBIS; **P45** (t) © The British Museum, (ml) © AKG London/Erich Lessing, (r) © Gallo Images/CORBIS

Photographic manipulation by John Russell.

 First published in Great Britain in 2002 by Usborne Publishing Ltd.

ISBN 0-439-70953-9

 Published by Scholastic Inc., 557 Broadway, New York, NY 10012, by arrangement with Usborne Publishing Ltd. The name Usborne and the devices are trademarks of Usborne Publishing Ltd. SCHOLASTIC and associated logos are trademarks and/or registered trademarks of Scholastic Inc.

12 11 10 9 8 7 6 5 4 3 2 4 5 6 7 8 9/0

Printed in the U.S.A. 40

First Scholastic printing, October 2004